MYTH AND SCRIPTURE

Society of Biblical Literature

Resources for Biblical Study

Susan Ackerman, Old Testament/Hebrew Bible Editor

Number 78

MYTH AND SCRIPTURE

CONTEMPORARY PERSPECTIVES ON RELIGION, LANGUAGE, AND IMAGINATION

Edited by
Dexter E. Callender Jr.

SBL Press
Atlanta

Copyright © 2014 by SBL Press

All rights reserved. No part of this work may be reproduced or transmitted in any form or by any means, electronic or mechanical, including photocopying and recording, or by means of any information storage or retrieval system, except as may be expressly permitted by the 1976 Copyright Act or in writing from the publisher. Requests for permission should be addressed in writing to the Rights and Permissions Office, Society of Biblical Literature, 825 Houston Mill Road, Atlanta, GA 30329 USA.

Library of Congress Cataloging-in-Publication Data

Myth and scripture : contemporary perspectives on religion, language, and imagination / Dexter E. Callender, Jr., editor.
     p. cm. — (Society of Biblical Literature resources for biblical study ; Number 78)
Includes bibliographical references and index.
ISBN 978-1-58983-961-8 (paper binding : alk. paper) — ISBN 978-1-58983-962-5 (electronic format) — ISBN 978-1-58983-963-2 (hardcover binding : alk. paper)
    1. Myth in the Bible. 2. Bible. Old Testament—Criticism, interpretation, etc. I. Callender, Dexter E., 1962- editor of compilation. II. Callender, Dexter E., 1962- author. Myth and Scripture : dissonance and convergence..
    BS520.5.M98 2014
    220.6'8—dc23   2014002897

Printed on acid-free, recycled paper conforming to
ANSI/NISO Z39.48-1992 (R1997) and ISO 9706:1994
standards for paper permanence.

Contents

Acknowledgments vii
Abbreviations ix

Introduction: Scholarship between Myth and Scripture
    Dexter E. Callender Jr. and William Scott Green 1

Part 1: Myth in the Hebrew Bible and the Ancient Near East

"Myth" in the Old Testament
    J. W. Rogerson 15

Myth and Scripture: Dissonance and Convergence
    Dexter E. Callender Jr. 27

Covenant and Contingence: The Historical Encounter between
    God and Israel
    Robert S. Kawashima 51

Is Genesis 1 a Creation Myth? Yes and No
    Mark S. Smith 71

Moses' Death
    Susan Ackerman 103

Myth and Social Realia in Ancient Israel: Early Hebrew Poems
    as Folkloric Assemblage
    Hugh R. Page Jr. 119

Myth and History in Ezekiel's Oracle Concerning Tyre
    (Ezekiel 26–28)
    Marvin A. Sweeney 129

Myth and History in Daniel 8: The Apocalyptic Negotiation
of Power
    Amy C. Merrill Willis 149

Part 2: Myth in the New Testament and the Greco-Roman World

Recast, Reclaim, Reject: Myth and Validity
    Steven J. Kraftchick 179

"God Was in Christ": 2 Corinthians 5:19 and Mythic Language
    Luke Timothy Johnson 201

Ancient Greek Demythologizing
    James E. Miller 213

Myth, Allegory, and the Derveni Papyrus
    John T. Fitzgerald 229

Part 3: Myth Theorizing and the Bible: A Conversation

The Life of King Saul as Myth
    Robert A. Segal 245

Response to Robert A. Segal, "The Life of King Saul as Myth"
    Adela Yarbro Collins 275

Theory of Myth and the Minimal Saul
    Ivan Strenski 279

The Indispensability of Theories of Myth for Biblical Studies:
A Response to Robert Segal
    David L. Miller 285

Replies to Ivan Strenski, Adela Yarbro Collins, and David Miller
    Robert A. Segal 291

Contributors 297
Index of Primary Sources 301
Index of Authors 310

Acknowledgments

Of the many expressions of gratitude that one might reasonably voice here, I would be remiss not to acknowledge the efforts and influence of Neal Walls, my original co-editor of this volume, who was called to administrative responsibilities that made it impossible for him to continue with the project. Such are the vicissitudes of academic life. Neal's own seminal writings on ancient Near Eastern myth, particularly in *Desire, Discord, and Death*, exemplify the kind of breadth of knowledge, depth of analysis, creativity, and interdisciplinary resourcefulness increasingly needed in biblical studies. Our discussions over the years led to the Society of Biblical Literature's Bible, Myth, and Myth Theory program unit (a reincarnation of sorts of earlier efforts under the auspices of the American Academy of Religion in the 1970s and again in the 1990s, whose fruits include the now classic *Myth and Method*, edited by Laurie Patton and Wendy Doniger), which Neal and I co-chaired for several years and which continues to thrive today under the leadership of Robert Kawashima (another contributor to this volume) and Stephen Russell.

This volume is the culmination of a collaborative research project between members of the Society of Biblical Literature and the American Academy of Religion and owes much to the participation of AAR stalwarts Robert A. Segal, Ivan Strenski, David L. Miller, and William Scott Green, who have joined together with members of the SBL, many of whose names are instantly recognizable and all of whom are to be thanked for their efforts. For editorial advice and assistance in preparing this volume for publication, I wish to thank John T. Fitzgerald, my former colleague at the University of Miami. Finally, thanks are in order to North-West University in Potchefstroom, South Africa, whose research assistance helped make the completion of this volume possible.

Abbreviations

AB	Anchor Bible
ABD	*Anchor Bible Dictionary.* Edited by D. N. Freedman. 6 vols. New York: Doubleday, 1992.
AJP	*American Journal of Philology*
AnBib	Analecta biblica
ANET	*Ancient Near Eastern Texts Relating to the Old Testament.* Edited by J. B. Pritchard. 3rd ed. Princeton: Princeton University Press, 1969.
AOAT	Alter Orient und Altes Testament
ATD	Das Alte Testament Deutsch
BA	*Biblical Archaeologist*
BASOR	*Bulletin of the American Schools of Oriental Research*
BDAG	W. Bauer, F. W. Danker, W. F. Arndt, and F. W. Gingrich. *Greek-English Lexicon of the New Testament and Other Early Christian Literature.* 3rd ed. Chicago: University of Chicago Press, 2000.
BRev	*Bible Review*
BZAW	Beihefte zur Zeitschrift für die alttestamentliche Wissenschaft
CANE	*Civilizations of the Ancient Near East.* Edited by J. Sasson. 4 vols. New York: Scribner, 1995.
CBET	Contributions to Biblical Exegesis and Theology
CBQ	*Catholic Biblical Quarterly*
CBQMS	Catholic Biblical Quarterly Monograph Series
CC	Continental Commentaries
COS	*The Context of Scripture.* Edited by W. W. Hallo. 3 vols. Leiden: Brill, 1997–2002.
CP	*Classical Philology*

DK	Hermann Diels and Walther Krantz, eds. and trans. *Die Fragmente der Vorsokratiker: Griechisch und Deutsch.* 7th ed. 3 vols. Berlin: Weidmann, 1954.
ER	*Encyclopedia of Religion.* Edited by Mircea Eliade. 16 vols. New York: Macmillan, 1987.
FAT	Forschungen zum Alten Testament
FGrHist	*Die Fragmente der griechischen Historiker.* Edited by Felix Jacoby. Leiden: Brill, 1954–1964.
FOTL	Forms of the Old Testament Literature
HALOT	L. Koehler, W. Baumgartner, and J. J. Stamm, *Hebrew and Aramaic Lexicon of the Old Testament.* Translated and edited by M. E. J. Richardson. 5 vols. Leiden: Brill, 1994–2000.
HSM	Harvard Semitic Monographs
HTR	*Harvard Theological Review*
HUCA	*Hebrew Union College Annual*
IBC	Interpretation: A Bible Commentary for Teaching and Preaching
ICC	International Critical Commentary
Int	*Interpretation*
IOS	*Israel Oriental Studies*
JAOS	*Journal of the American Oriental Society*
JBL	*Journal of Biblical Literature*
JNES	*Journal of Near Eastern Studies*
JQR	*Jewish Quarterly Review*
JR	*Journal of Religion*
JSOT	*Journal for the Study of the Old Testament*
JSOTSup	Journal for the Study of the Old Testament Supplement Series
JSPSup	Journal for the Study of the Pseudepigrapha Supplement Series
JTS	*Journal of Theological Studies*
KTU	*Die keilalphabetischen Texte aus Ugarit.* Edited by M. Dietrich, O. Loretz, and J. Sanmartín. AOAT 24/1. Neukirchen-Vluyn: Neukirchener, 1976.
LCL	Loeb Classical Library
LHBOTS	Library of Hebrew Bible/Old Testament Studies
MARI	*Mari: Annales de recherches interdisciplinaires*
NCBC	New Century Bible Commentary

NICOT	New International Commentary on the Old Testament
OTL	Old Testament Library
RB	*Revue biblique*
RIH	Ras Ibn Hani (excavation number)
RSV	Revised Standard Version
SBL	Society of Biblical Literature
SBLDS	SBL Dissertation Series
SBLWAW	SBL Writings from the Ancient World
SBT	Studies in Biblical Theology
SHCANE	Studies in the History and Culture of the Ancient Near East
SJLA	Studies in Judaism in Late Antiquity
SJOT	*Scandinavian Journal of the Old Testament*
VT	*Vetus Testamentum*
VTSup	Vetus Testamentum Supplements
WBC	Word Biblical Commentary
ZAW	*Zeitschrift für die alttestamentliche Wissenschaft*
ZPE	*Zeitschrift für Papyrologie und Epigraphik*

Introduction:
Scholarship between Myth and Scripture

Dexter E. Callender Jr. and William Scott Green

Introduction

This is a book about how scholars make sense of what we study.[1] As a field of research whose primary focus is a fixed and finite set of data, biblical studies innovates less by discovering new objects of study than by finding fresh ways—or refining old ways—to examine its basic subject matter. Scholars investigate by designing categories of analysis and interpretation to achieve understanding. Regular assessment of the value of these categories—however recondite it may appear to a field's outsiders—provokes scholarly self-consciousness and thereby strengthens the quality of research and advances knowledge.

"Myth" and "scripture" are two established categories used to describe and analyze the Hebrew Bible and the New Testament. Each has figured prominently as a way of rendering the meaning or "truth" of human experience. *Myth* is an established category in the academic humanities and social sciences, particularly in classics, literature, anthropology, and religion. For the purposes of this volume, *scripture* is a generic native category that biblically based religions use to depict themselves, though some scholars apply it to other religions as well.[2]

Religions typically claim that there is an order to existence—usually the work of deities or other superhuman beings—that humans did not make and in principle cannot change. For instance, the creation accounts

---

1. This volume was completed with generous research assistance from North-West University, Potchefstroom, South Africa.
2. For a concise comprehensive overview of the category, see Graham 1987; for Judaism and Christianity, see esp. pp. 135–36.

of the Hebrew Bible and New Testament do not suggest that humans played any role in shaping the structure of reality, creating light and darkness, time and space, day and night, or in making the "Word" become flesh. For its adherents, a religion's cosmic order establishes the givens of existence and constitutes the prerequisites of human experience.

In religion, the cosmic structure is objective, factual, true, and—most important—normative. Religion assumes that humans on their own are, can be, or will be out of sync with the normative cosmic order and the superhuman beings who generated it. Religion further claims to know how to correct and prevent this inconsonance. Full and proper knowledge and understanding of this dynamic is highly specific, if not exclusive, to a religion itself. Religions aver that only by adhering to their own specific and distinctive teachings, which entail proper interactions with its deities or other superhuman beings, can humans either prevent or repair a breach with the created order. Religions teach their adherents why and how the world should work as it does, what humans should do to live in accord with that normative structure, and what will happen to them if they do or do not do so. The validity of a religion's specialized claims about the cosmos comes from the experience of living them.

Each religion has its own particular sources of authority—texts, canons of scripture, revelations, sages, enlightened ones, prophets, chains of tradition, and so on—that reveal, transmit, and certify its privileged knowledge of the cosmic order.[3] In the biblically based religions, the writings generically designated as "scripture" (Torah, Tanak, Testament, Gospel, Word of God, the Bible, etc.) constitute one—perhaps the preeminent—source of authority.[4] "Scripture" thus constitutes the religious community's charter account of the cosmic order and provides guidance on how to conform to it.

It is a scholarly commonplace that a "scripture" has authority because a community grants it. There are no inherent or required literary traits or genres that define or constitute "scripture." Biblical texts include narrative, law, poetry, oracles, genealogies, letters, among other forms. Religions mark the distinctiveness of "scripture" both in their claims about and in their use of such texts. In biblically based religions, for instance,

---

3. This and the preceding two paragraphs are drawn from Green 2010.

4. As Dexter Callender points out, at Sinai, the deity—the God of Israel—transforms divine speech into writing, and the writing becomes both the emblem and repository of the deity's power and wisdom.

"scripture" is not only a source of instruction and inspiration but also a routine component of prayer and liturgy. It can serve as a sacred artifact that evokes special behavior. In Judaism, the Torah Scroll is an object of veneration. Roman Catholic priests remove their skullcaps in the presence of the Gospel, and Lutherans rise when the Gospel is read during worship. Secular legal or political documents elicit no comparable response or action because they are both devised and alterable by human beings alone. "The Word of God" makes a broader claim to legitimacy than does "the consent of the governed." The President of the United States swears loyalty to the Constitution on the Bible. Our society would regard the reverse as ludicrous.

If "scripture" is a relatively settled native category of religion, "myth"—as the essays gathered here suggest—is somewhat less stable.[5] Although it ordinarily and historically is associated with narratives about deities and other superhuman beings, "myth" has markedly divergent connotations. It denotes both a narrative that is insusceptible of proof—which connotes fiction, if not falsehood—and a narrative that expresses a religious community's deepest convictions and assumptions—which connotes gravitas and value, if not a kind of truth. Both understandings are evident in contemporary biblical studies. For example, a section in chapter 1 of Christine Hayes's *Introduction to the Bible*, entitled "Myths and Facts about the Bible," clearly uses the term in the sense of error or falsehood (2012, 5–9). Douglas Knight and Amy-Jill Levine, on the other hand, adhere to the second understanding when they write:

> "Myth" … means a story, usually set in the distant past when the normal rules of physics do not apply (i.e., that world is not our world), that offers a summary of a cultural worldview; it explains how life as we know it came to be; it expresses our hopes and fears. It is true, in the same way that a parable is true. (Knight and Levine 2011, 66–67)

These disparate connotations yield contrary utilities for "myth" in the study of biblical literature.[6] On the one side, understood as falsehood, "myth" has little analytical payoff when applied to "scripture." It hardly

---

5. For a useful and insightful survey of the varied definitions of myth in the context of biblical studies and the Greco-Roman world, see Oden 1992a and 1992b and Graf 1992. See, more recently, Callender 2013.

6. To be sure, these different connotations are not necessarily mutually exclusive.

can explain a phenomenon it dismisses. This conception of "myth" can lead to the position that "scripture" is devoid of "myth" and that the category "myth" is misapplied in the study of biblical writings. On the other side, understood as the expression of a religion's fundamental convictions, "myth" can create fresh contexts for understanding biblical texts.

Description

"Myth" and "scripture" intrude on one another most intensely and are particularly—perhaps only—pertinent to one another when scholars study biblical texts as religious writing. The present volume brings together specialists in the Hebrew Bible and ancient Near East, the New Testament and the Greco-Roman world, along with theorists of religion and myth, illustrating a range of ways each category can affect the other.

Part 1 of the volume addresses myth in the Hebrew Bible and the ancient Near East. John Rogerson, whose *Myth in Old Testament Interpretation* (1974) remains a standard in the field, revisits the topic of myth in the Old Testament, specifically taking on the matter of definitions and their consequences. Rogerson begins by distinguishing "myths" as particularly literary phenomena and "mythological elements" as the themes, motifs, or personalities within myths from "myth" proper. Rogerson's conception of myth is grounded in the idea of a common possession held by ancient and modern humans alike—a conception he works out through a consideration of charter myths, the mythicizing of history, the origin of myth itself, and the truth of myth. What emerges stems from the impulse to give account of the hows and whys of the world as we experience it. Myth frames our empirical encounter with the "facts" of the world. It takes shape in traditional accounts drawn from a broader cultural repository and, in the case of the Bible, often features images that point ambiguously to life and death. Although assessments of its "truth" are governed by the particular epistemological commitments of the interpreter, literary context provides clues to the nature of the truth conveyed by the biblical tradents.

Dexter Callender considers the terms *myth* and *scripture*, specifically as emotionally charged categories tied to institutional structures. He gives

---

A religious community's charter account of cosmic structure can reflect a cultural worldview that is erroneous or false.

attention to the role conceptions of speech and writing play in the exploration of experience (particularly religious experience) and reflects upon how these come together in the notion of Torah, which itself is presented in a manner that betrays serious concern with how language embodies and relates to experience.

Robert Kawashima, analyzing the narrative traditions of the Hebrew Bible through the lens of Foucault's "archaeology of knowledge," argues that myth and history constitute two distinct discourse configurations or epistemes. If mythic thought conceives of the cosmos as an eternal and necessary structure, historical thought conceives of the world as a realm governed rather by contingence and time. Consider, for example, the concept of the human condition. According to various myths, humans and gods are joined in an unalterable "natural unity" established in the time of creation. According to biblical prose narrative, however, humankind and God are alienated from each other. Yahweh solves the problem of alienation by placing his "call" upon Israel in an historical encounter that Althusser referred to as "interpellation." The "human unity" established in this contingent encounter is the covenant.

Mark S. Smith pursues an inductive approach to myth, inquiring into the nature of Gen 1 in light of features present in ancient Near Eastern texts generally taken as myth. For Smith, features within these texts and the ways scribes presented the texts (as narrative songs whose performance invokes gods and their world) indicate conscious interest in ritual access to the divine world. Observing how scribes combined mythic narratives with a wide variety of other literary forms (including older mythic narratives) and following Jonathan Z. Smith's insight likening traditional narrative structures to the objects manipulated by the diviner, he demonstrates how the nature of myth's identity is contingent on the particular situation of its use. The identity of myth is thus contextual and complex. The truth of Gen 1 as myth is nuanced by both its literary contextualization among variant creation traditions and its incorporation into the canonical expression of the Bible by which it becomes scripture. Smith's response to the question of whether Gen 1 is myth points to fundamental issues common to antiquity and modernity regarding the religious and epistemological aims and sensibilities of the interpreter.

Susan Ackerman applies the idea of the tragic hero to uncover the problems of Moses' death in Transjordan and in the process takes up consideration of the hagiographic accounts of religious heroes. This move reflects a conscious turn from older models of reconstructing Israel's history. Ackerman grounds her approach in the rites-of-passage pattern observed by Arnold van Gennep, which later scholars extended beyond the sphere of life-cycle rituals to include heroic narratives (and all phenomena that mark journeys from the profane to the sacred). Continuing a line of investigation begun by biblical scholars who find in these insights a potentially fruitful approach not only to the narratives of individual biblical heroic figures but also to those of collective Israel, Ackerman reflects upon Moses' identity as intermediary to explain his death within the structure of the exodus narrative.

Hugh Rowland Page pursues a folkloric approach, offering a reading of "archaic poetry" as an assemblage whose data can shed light on "human" and "divine" as categories, clarify conceptions of personhood, and reveal strategies of engendering implicit and explicit spiritualities. The questions Page puts to the texts are similar to those posed by Mark Smith (and Amy Merrill Willis) regarding scribal attitudes toward the materials, their effect, and their relation to present reality. Page considers the process of scripturalization and cross-cultural social scientific research into the behavior of gathering and preserving and exchange, known in some quarters as the "anthropology of collecting." Building on the work of Susan Pearce, who linked collecting to social praxis involving the construction of identity and establishing of social roles, Page suggests the same for the scholarly collection of literary artifacts and discerns other areas of social control at work.

The approach taken by Marvin Sweeney considers mythological motifs from around the ancient Near East as more than mere evidence of Ezekiel's literacy. These, in conjunction with similar oracles concerning Sidon and the restoration of Israel in Ezek 28, function within the structure of the book to prefigure the rebuilding of the temple at the center of creation. Sweeney understands Ezekiel's creation-oriented mythopoeic imagery as part of his Zadokite priestly heritage, and sees its objective as making sense of the prophet's own earthly circumstances in terms of divine involvement both in accomplished events and in events set in a future that provides the framework for hope.

Amy Merrill Willis takes a decidedly Ricoeurian approach to address the myth and history dichotomy in the context of apocalyptic literature. Drawing attention to the narrative property that connects the two, she argues that their relationship is symbiotic through the shared property of narrative. Building upon John Collins's recognition in Dan 8 of the same mythic pattern seen in Isa 14, Merrill Willis argues that this "rebellious subordinate" pattern is appropriated historiographically within the four-kingdoms narrative and constitutes an example of a Ricoeurian configuration of events—a *refiguration* that establishes a temporal unity, thereby producing meaning. Historical details are taken up into mythic narrative patterns, contextualizing them within the ultimate cosmic whole, providing a means of attaining cognitive coherence (cf. Festinger 1962 and Carroll 1979).

Part 2 of the volume includes papers that focus on writings from the Greco-Roman world and the New Testament. Steve Kraftchick addresses how the ways scholars construct myth, its definitions and valuations, affect our analyses of it. He offers a comparison of the work of four theorists whose work engages myth and biblical studies, particularly in view of notions of truth and meaning. These four, Rudolf Bultmann, Thomas Altizer, Craig Evans, and Gerd Theissen, he characterizes as recasting, refashioning, rejecting, and reclaiming myth, respectively. Kraftchick's survey points to four areas of concern that he raises as important in moving forward: the opposition of myth to categories such as history, logos, and truth variously across disciplines; attention to antiquity and modernity; the usefulness of considering nonrational truth, entertainment, and imagination; and the ethical implications of studying myth with respect to the Bible.

Luke Timothy Johnson considers the difficult language of 2 Corinthians to discuss myth as language tied to the experience of reversing human alienation. A mythic use of language, Johnson asserts, is evident in Paul's interweaving of statements concerning himself and his readers with statements concerning God and Christ. Myth, by Johnson's definition, lies in first-order statements that feature human and divine persons in situations of mutual agency. These statements invoke the empirical yet remain beyond the limits of empirical investigation. Still, as Johnson argues, mythic language is essential to the communication of religious experience and hence its truth claims are subject to verification on the basis of experience itself and the symbolic world within which such statements make sense. The logic of mythic language lies in shared convictions regarding the empirical world.

James E. Miller takes a traditional approach to what myth is in his consideration of demythologizing in Greek literature to caution against confusing the ancient polemic with the concerns of the modern interpreter, and in the process examines standards of rationality, truth, and belief. Miller observes differences in demythologizing associated with a variety of different contexts and aims (e.g., ancient classical, Homeric criticism; criticism of the Hebrew Bible; criticism of the New Testament) and tied, in part, to different understandings of myth.

John T. Fitzgerald's examination of the Derveni papyrus considers traditional views of the gods inspired by Homer and Hesiod and those of the pre-Socratics that lead to what is now commonly referred to as pagan monotheism. A central concern for Fitzgerald's inquiry is the practice of allegory, which he asserts reconciled "human uncertainty about the divine." In the papyrus, a treatise on an Orphic mythological poem that declares the poem's true meaning as allegorical and consonant with empirical reality, Fitzgerald discerns a perspective in which allegory itself emerges as religious practice—not only rescuing Orphic theological language, but creating the conditions for the experience of a *hieros logos*.

Part three of the volume is devoted to an essay by Robert A. Segal, in which he considers patterns in myth and the category of the hero myth as part of a broader inquiry into the place of theories of myth in biblical studies. Segal's treatment goes beyond the mere recognition of a pattern to pursue theoretical questions regarding origin, function, and subject matter. To this end, he applies the psychoanalytic theorizing of Otto Rank and the theorizing of folklorist Lord Raglan to the life of King Saul. Segal's essay is an abridged version of a longer paper delivered at the 2007 Society of Biblical Literature annual meeting in San Diego, California, in a special joint session of the SBL's Bible, Myth, and Myth Theory consultation and the Religion and Social Sciences section of the American Academy of Religion under the theme "The Place of Theories of Myth in Biblical Studies." Responses presented in that session by New Testament scholar Adela Yarbro Collins, Jungian analyst David Miller, and social scientific theorist of religion Ivan Strenski follow Segal's paper in this volume, along with Segal's reply to each.

Preliminary Reflections

The papers gathered here suggest that the interaction of "myth" and "scripture" can enrich our understanding of biblical writings. Even the most elementary understanding of "myth" as a story about gods or heroes creates a framework within which to set biblical writings in both cultural and literary comparative contexts. In the realm of culture, the category has enabled biblical scholars to read biblical accounts alongside religious charter narratives from other ancient Near Eastern cultures and better understand what is commonplace and shared among them. From these studies, new knowledge of ancient Near Eastern multiculturalism or "interculturalism" has emerged. In the area of literature, the category of "myth" has helped biblical scholars identify broad literary traits—motifs and plot lines, for instance—that transcend discrete cultures and demarcate narratives about gods and heroes.[7] In different ways, this use of "myth" has widened and enriched our understanding of the nature and character of biblical texts.[8]

By the same token, that contextualization provides fresh, empirical evidence for how biblical writings, distinctively, became "scripture." Mark Smith astutely observes that the diverse texts contained in the Hebrew Bible ultimately became part of a collection that was read and understood as a unity. In this respect, biblical creation texts, at least, differed from those of surrounding ancient Near Eastern nations, and, it might be added, of Greece and Rome as well. He explains that in ancient Israel:

> texts regarded as holy or inspired were coming to be read and interpreted together; … words or complexes of terms shared by different religious texts not only could be read in tandem but should be read together across the boundaries of their original contexts, beyond the limits of any individual passage or document. It is this process of scriptural reading, linking passages across their former textual boundaries, that eventually distinguishes works that belong to the Bible.[9]

Critical scholarship has persistently shown that the books and fragments of books collected in the canons of the Hebrew Bible and the New Testament have distinctive and even divergent perspectives and positions. That is what a secular analytical reading should demonstrate. But insofar as religious communities regard these collections as providing a divinely sanctioned charter account, as expressing an authoritative—and thus necessarily unified—depiction of the nature of the cosmos and humanity's place in it, they constitute "scripture." In establishing its writings as "scripture," *how* a community reads may be as important as *what* it reads.

Finally, it is possible to understand "scripture" itself as "myth." For example, Robert Kawashima elegantly defines "myth" by distinguishing it from "history." He suggests that "mythical thought conceives of the

---

7. Susan Ackerman's contribution to this volume provides lucid illustration of this point.

8. See, e.g., the contribution by Marvin Sweeney.

9. Mark Smith, 96 below.

cosmos as a static system, composed of various elements and relations that are eternal, necessary, and essential." By contrast, "Historical thought ... apprehends the world as a realm of accidence, contingence, and time. This properly empirical reality is thinkable as such only in opposition to some strictly utopian ideal beyond the empirical." These two categories create an "epistemic rupture" across the Israelite biblical tradition and yield "two versions of the human condition." The version of myth holds that Israel and God have a natural, essential connection and unity. By contrast, the version of history avers that "were it not for key human decisions"—largely "formalized" in the institution of covenant—Israel could have been other than it came to be.

This is a cogent and defensible analytical distinction. An "unscriptural" reading of these "two modes of narrative" about the human condition treats them as discrete and yields the "epistemic rupture" that Kawashima identifies. Alternatively, reading both modes of narrative as "scripture"—as authoritative and, in Mark Smith's words, "across the boundaries of their original contexts"—gives the historical mode of narrative a mythic character. Read as "scripture," the "human decisions" that connect Israel to God become paradigmatic and normative and set the conditions for all future covenantal "human decisions." This approach adds a mythic dimension to scripture. From the perspective of "scripture" as "myth," human beings may well be free to make their own decisions (perhaps because they are themselves created in the mythical "image of God"?), but the results of those decisions are clear and immutable. A text such as, "I offer you the choice of life or death, blessing or curse. Choose life, and you and your descendants will live; love the LORD your God, obey him and hold fast to him: that is life for you and length of days, on the soil which the LORD swore to give to your forefathers, Abraham, Isaac, and Jacob" (Deut 30:19–20), precludes death as a consequence of choosing to love God. Thus "scripture" transforms the "contingency" of history into the "necessity" of myth.

If this volume prompts fresh assessment of some basic categories for the analysis and understanding of biblical writings, the collective work represented here will have served a constructive purpose.

Works Cited

Callender, Dexter E., Jr. 2013. Mythology and Biblical Interpretation. Pages 26–35 in vol. 2 of *The Oxford Encyclopedia of Biblical Interpreta-*

tion. Edited by Steven L. McKenzie. 2 vols. Oxford: Oxford University Press.

Carroll, Robert. 1979. *When Prophecy Failed: Reactions and Responses to Failure in the Old Testament Prophetic Traditions.* London: SCM.

Festinger, Leon. 1962. *A Theory of Cognitive Dissonance.* Repr., Stanford: Stanford University Press.

Graf, Fritz. 1992. Myth and Mythology: Myth in the Greco-Roman World. *ABD* 4:961–65.

Graham, William A. 1987. Scripture. *ER* 13:133–45.

Green, William Scott. 2010. A "Humanly Relevant Cosmos": What We Study When We Study Religion. Pages vii–xxiii in *Introduction to World Religions: Communities and Cultures.* Edited by Jacob Neusner. Nashville: Abingdon.

Hayes, Christine. 2012. *Introduction to the Bible.* New Haven: Yale University Press.

Knight, Douglas A., and Amy-Jill Levine. 2011. *The Meaning of the Bible: What the Jewish Scriptures and Christian Old Testament Can Teach Us.* New York: HarperCollins.

Lincoln, Bruce. 2009. *Theorizing Myth: Narrative, Ideology, and Scholarship.* Chicago: University of Chicago Press.

Oden, Robert. 1992a. Myth and Mythology: Mythology. *ABD* 4:946–56.

———. 1992b. Myth and Mythology: Myth in the OT. *ABD* 4:956–60.

Rogerson, John. 1984. Slippery Words: Myth. Pages 62–71 in *Sacred Narrative: Readings in the Theory of Myth.* Edited by Alan Dundes. Berkeley: University of California Press.

Suggs, M. Jack, et al., eds. 1992. *The Oxford Study Bible.* Oxford: Oxford University Press.

Part 1
Myth in the Hebrew Bible and the Ancient Near East

"Myth" in the Old Testament*

J. W. Rogerson

For the sake of clarity, I begin with an attempt to define the main terms that I shall use in this lecture. I wish to distinguish between the terms *myths*, *mythological elements*, and *myth*. The easiest term to define is *myths*. Myths are literary phenomena. They can be transmitted either orally or in writing, and can be recognized as myths on account of their content. They are often stories about gods or narratives about the origin of the world and the human race, or attempts to explain the fate of humanity, attempts that are placed in the context either of a primal world or a primal condition of the human race. *Mythological elements* are the themes or motifs or personalities that are found in myths and that are taken over into literature or art or drama.

The most difficult term to define is *myth*, and I have considerable sympathy for the thesis in the book by Ivan Strenski, *Four Theories of Myth in Twentieth-Century History*, that there is no such thing as "myth" and that the word *myth* is the name for many, and often contradictory, subjects of research (Strenski 1987, 1–2).[1] It would, indeed, be possible to say against me that the title of this lecture ought to be "Myths" rather than "Myth" in the Old Testament. However, I have deliberately chosen the word *myth* in order to give warnings about the unclarity of this term, and I shall give reasons for this point.

---

* This essay is an English translation by the author of a lecture delivered in German on 17 June 2003, in the Theological Faculty of the Ludwig-Alberts-Universität, Freiburg-im-Breisgau. I am grateful to Professor Dr. H. Irsigler for the invitation to deliver this lecture and for the hospitality given on that occasion. The lecture was an orientation for subsequent specialized lectures published in Irsigler 2004.

1. See also the conclusion to Rogerson 1974, 174.

In everyday English, and perhaps also in everyday German, the word *myth* has acquired the meaning of something that is a lie or something that is false. If one uses the word *myth* in connection with the church, the Bible, or theology, there is the danger that one will be accused of lack of faith or charged with saying that the Bible is untrue. Behind these popular meanings are theories of myth that were widespread in the nineteenth and twentieth centuries. According to these theories, myth was a kind of prescientific way of understanding the world that had no knowledge of scientific causes of occurrences in nature and that attempted to find supernatural explanations for these events. An eclipse of the moon, for example, was understood as the attempt of a cosmic dragon to eat the moon. A consequence of this view was that myth was held to belong to a prescientific age of the human race, and that the more the true scientific causes of events in nature were discovered, the less necessary it was to use the term *myth*.

According to another theory of myth, myths were originally magical stories or sayings that had the purpose of preventing catastrophes or ensuring good fortune in life. Such myths were later connected with rituals, which were regularly performed. In the twentieth century this theory had particular influence upon Old Testament scholarship, especially in England and Scandinavia (see Rogerson 1974, 66–84; Segal 1998). The discovery of texts from Babylon that dealt with the New Year festival, in which an account of creation was recited, led some scholars to conclude that in ancient Israel there was also a New Year festival, in which the biblical account of the creation of the world was recited. That meant that the biblical account of creation was a myth in the sense that it functioned as a magical text in the context of a ritual, whose aim was to ensure the good fortune of the community in the coming year.

The first theory, which understood myths as prescientific accounts to understand events of nature, contained more than an element of the truth. Not all of the conclusions that were drawn from this view, however, can be accepted. The terms *scientific* and *prescientific* are relative. We should not believe that everything that can be proved in the natural sciences today will remain unchallenged. In fifty years scientists may well have quite different views of causes and workings of things in the world compared with today. Fifty years from now, some of our present scientific theories may appear to be prescientific. In addition, the view that modern humans have no myths or do not need them is highly contentious (see Toulmin 1957), and it must be added that if "prescientific" humans tried to explain happenings in nature by means of supernatural agencies, we cannot be sure that their explanation did not contain genuine insights into the nature of reality. This whole discussion supports what I have quoted earlier from Strenski, that *myth* is mainly a word that stands for many and sometimes contradictory elements in research. If one insists that myth is always "prescientific," then one must conclude that modern humans do not need or have myths. If one defines the term differently, one can maintain that there are modern myths that enable people to express their hopes and fears in today's world and to understand their place in that world. In other words, the stress is put much more upon the existential function than the explanatory scientific potential of narratives that are defined as myths.

The other theory, that myths were originally magical narratives or sayings, can be quickly dealt with. It implies a view of magic that modern anthropologists would hardly recognize. It is connected with the theories of the English anthropologist James Frazer, who believed that magic was a form of primitive science, as well as an early stage of religion that, in its turn, was an early stage of modern natural science. In modern anthropological research the stress is put upon the social and existential functions of symbolic actions (which is how magic is understood) and not upon their allegedly scientific characteristics (see Rogerson 1978).

Are there myths in the Old Testament? In the history of Old Testament research this question has been answered both positively and negatively. On the one hand, some have asserted that there are no myths in the Old Testament. Myths are stories about gods, and since the Old Testament assumes belief in one true God, there can be no myths in the Old Testament (so Gunkel 1997, xiii). Further, if the Old Testament is inspired by God, it cannot be mythical. According to this point of view, only one concession can be made regarding the possibility of there being anything mythical in the Old Testament, and that is the recognition that at the most there are mythical elements in the Old Testament. An example of this would be Gen 6:1–4 (RSV):

> When men began to multiply on the face of the ground, and daughters were born to them, the sons of God saw that the daughters of men were fair; and they took to wife such of them as they chose. Then the LORD said, "My spirit shall not abide in man for ever, for he is flesh, but his days shall be one hundred and twenty years." The Nephilim were on the earth in those days, and also afterward, when the sons of God came in to the daughters of men, and they bore children to them. These were the mighty men that were of old, the men of renown.

The occurrence of "sons of God" in this passage as active beings independent of God is unique in the Old Testament, and the only place in it where one can find anything similar to the stories of the gods among the Greeks. Even those who deny the existence of myths in the Old Testament will accept that in Gen 6:1–4 a fragment of mythology has somehow entered into the text; indeed, it is the uniqueness of this passage that supports their view that there are no myths in the Old Testament. A presupposition of this view is, of course, that myths are stories about gods (Gunkel 1997, 56–60).

On the other side is the view that a cultural pattern in the ancient Near East was widespread in which myths and rituals were regularly performed in order to assure the good fortune of the people and the land. According to this view, ancient Israel shared this outlook. Not only the biblical story of creation, but also several psalms were thought to be liturgies, which accompanied the performance of rituals in which the king played a central role. On the ground of comparisons with the supposed observances of the Babylonian New Year festival, researchers such as the British Old Testament scholar Aubrey Johnson reconstructed festivals in ancient Israel in which the king was ritually humiliated, beaten, and killed in order to rise again ritually and to consummate a symbolic marriage with a temple prostitute. Johnson based his interpretation partly on the following verses from Ps 118:7–14 (in Johnson's translation [1967, 125]):

> With Yahweh on my side I do not fear
> What man may do to me.
> With Yahweh on my side to give me aid,
> I gaze in triumph on them that hate me.
> It is better to seek refuge in Yahweh
> Than to trust in man.
> It is better to seek refuge in Yahweh
> Than to trust in princes.
> All nations surrounded me;
> Through the Name of Yahweh I cut them off.
> They surrounded me, yea, they surrounded me;
> Through the Name of Yahweh I cut them off.
> They surrounded me like bees;
> They died away like a fire of thistles;
> Through the Name of Yahweh I cut them off.
> Thou didst press me sore that I might fall,
> But Yahweh came to mine aid.
> Yah, who is my strength and song,
> Hath become my salvation.

Johnson wrote:

> The Messiah has been made to suffer humiliation; he has been "chastened sore" and thereby brought close to the gates of the Underworld. Nevertheless through Yahweh's devotion (חֶסֶד) and righteousness (צֶדֶק) his faith has been justified and he has been delivered from the power of "Death" and thereby proved righteous (צַדִּיק); but *ipso facto* the people themselves, as forming a psychical whole with its focus in the king … have also been delivered from "Death" and proved righteous (צַדִּיק). (1967, 126)

This is admittedly a somewhat extreme position. However, one of the results of the position taken by scholars such as Johnson was that the assumption became widespread in Old Testament scholarship that it was possible to find in the Old Testament traces of ancient Near Eastern myths in which there was a battle between the gods and the powers of chaos, the latter being represented by the sea. An example often quoted comes from Ps 74:12–14 (RSV):

> Yet God my King is from of old,
> working salvation in the midst of the earth.
> Thou didst divide the sea by thy might;
> Thou didst break the heads of the dragons on the waters.
> Thou didst crush the heads of Leviathan,
> Thou didst give him as food for the creatures of the wilderness.[2]

Attempts have further been made to connect the Hebrew word *tĕhôm* (deep) in Gen 1:2 with the goddess Tiamat in the Babyonian epic *Enuma Elish*. Tiamat is slain by the god Marduk and her carcass used in order to create the world. Even if one is not convinced by this argument, it is undeniable that the motif of the sea as a symbol of chaos is found in Dan 7: "I saw in my vision by night, and behold, the four winds of heaven were stirring up the great sea. And four great beasts came up out of the sea" (Dan 7:2–3 RSV).

What theories of myth are presupposed in these examples? In the case of belief in the existence of a "myth and ritual" cultural pattern in

---

2. See Kraus 1989, 100. Kraus draws attention to the section "The Traditions of a Primeval Sea" in Gunkel's *Schöpfung und Chaos* (original 1894; now translated in Gunkel 2006, 61–75). Gunkel was the first to make this connection. See also Day 1985.

the ancient Near East, an important element was that "myth" was a way of viewing the world that was quite different from the way the world is viewed today in Western societies, including the belief that it was possible to influence and control the world by means of magical practices. Hermeneutically, it was necessary to reconstruct the cultural and ritual background of the ancient Near East if Old Testament texts were to be understood correctly. For example, it is not obvious that Ps 118 was a liturgy accompanying an annual sacred drama in which the king suffered ritual death and resurrection. This only became credible if the "myth and ritual" theory was accepted, together with the view that the Old Testament texts preserved what had once been a widespread pattern of culture in the ancient Near East.

The aim of this paper so far has been to show that the question of whether there are myths in the Old Testament is entirely dependent on how one defines the term *myth*. In what follows, I discuss four themes in the light of an attempted definition of myth. They are (1) charter myths, (2) the mythologizing of history, (3) the origin of myths, and (4) the "truth" of myths. The view of myth that I presuppose is as follows: all people, modern as well as ancient, possess charter myths, that is, narratives that attempt to account for the creation of the world, or of a nation, or other features of daily life. In today's world, scientific explanations of the origin of the world have made charter myths dealing with creation redundant, so that modern charter myths are more concerned with social conditions. I must add, however, that ancient myths about the creation are as much concerned to answer the question *why* as the question *how*. That scientific theories are not concerned with the question *why* has spawned in today's world grotesque mythical narratives that feature aliens or other otherworldly beings. The mythical imagination is not dead!

Moreover, modern as well as ancient societies mythicize their history and in so doing produce narratives that look for meaning in events and that express universal values. A good example is the English popular version of what happened in 1588 when the Spanish Armada sailed against Britain. The popular story relates how, when the commander of the English fleet, Sir Francis Drake, heard the news that the Spanish Armada was on its way, he finished the game of bowls that he was playing, and then set out to destroy the Spanish fleet with far fewer ships than the Spaniards had at their disposal. This account, which does not correspond with the facts, expresses the opinion that English fighters are better than Spanish ones, that good (i.e., England) triumphs over bad (i.e., Spain), and that an

English characteristic is that of being unperturbed in the face of imminent danger. An example from the Old Testament would be the story of David and Goliath.

Charter Myths in the Old Testament

In the first eleven chapters of Genesis there are short formulae that show that the narratives are set in a primal time that is different from that of the time of the biblical writers but that is in continuity with that time (see Rogerson 1991, 53–55). For example: "In those days there were giants upon the earth" (Gen 6:4); "Now the whole earth had one language and few words" (11:1). In addition, events occur in these chapters that would be outside the normal experience of biblical writers and their presumed hearers or readers. A serpent converses with a woman, presumably in Hebrew, and moves other than on its belly. The patriarchs enjoy lives that last, in some cases, over nine hundred years. After the flood the entire human population of the world numbers only eight. These are charter myths set in primal time. Their aim is to describe where the world and its inhabitants came from. Various features of daily life are explained: why people wear clothes, why childbirth is painful, why agriculture is such hard work, where the rainbow came from, why people speak different languages.

The Mythicizing of history

An excellent example of this is the account of the wilderness wanderings in the books of Exodus and Numbers, and the beginning of Deuteronomy. It describes the ungratefulness of the generation that was delivered from slavery in Egypt. Repeatedly, the people complain about conditions in the wilderness and about the leadership of Moses. They regret having left Egypt and charge God with having delivered them because he hated them (Deut 1:27). When the opportunity presents itself, they make a golden calf, and worship that instead of God (Exod 32).

The reason for describing this as the mythicizing of history is that the narrative does not correspond with the facts. While, indeed, the historical facts behind the accounts of the exodus from Egypt and the passage to the land of Canaan are beyond recovery, the study of the growth of the literary traditions of the Old Testament has made clear that Israel as a twelve-tribe political entity is a literary rather than an historical construct, and that it is impossible that Israel in this form can have taken part in the exodus and wilderness wanderings (see Achenbach 2005, 1746–47). Yet the narratives about the exodus and passage through the wilderness are some of the most profound stories in the Old Testament. They explore the dynamics of the problematic relationship between divine power and human weakness, and make all too clear the heavy price paid by any leader who is called by God to be an intermediary between God and the people. Moses is repeatedly criticized and rejected by the people, and even has to share the same fate as the generation that is not allowed to enter the promised land.

The Origins of Myths

Where do myths in the Old Testament come from? The first answer is simple. The myths that are found in the first eleven chapters of Genesis belong to the common cultural tradition of the peoples of the ancient Near East. This became clear when George Smith delivered a lecture in London in 1872 in which he gave the news that he had discovered a Babylonian version of the story of the flood (Smith 1873). Several years later Smith informed the learned world that he had discovered a Babylonian account of the creation of the world (Smith 1876). Although not all the narratives in Gen 1–11 can be paralleled by texts from the ancient Near East, there is sufficient evidence that the narratives in this part of the Bible are not unique.

A second answer to the question deals with the mythological motifs or symbols that occur in biblical narratives. They are mostly things that stand on the boundary between life and death. For example, the serpent, which plays an important role in Gen 3, can denote either life or death (see Handy 1992). In the narrative of the serpent of brass in Num 21:4–9, the Israelites are plagued by deadly snakes. However, an image of a snake set up on a pole by Moses enables those smitten to be healed. Another example is water. It is necessary for life, but it can form floods that are destructive of life. Similarly, cities lie on the boundary between life and death. Cain, described in Gen 4:17 as the founder of the first city, is a murderer. As centers of resources for human life, cities become necessary for the development of communal life; but they can and do become centers of corruption and the abuse of power.

Myths, as found in the Bible and in texts from the ancient Near East, are narratives that contain ambiguous symbols in order to explore the ambiguities of human life—and human fate. Where they are instances of mythologized history the events they describe happened, or could have happened. Their importance lies, however, not in the sphere of history, but as evidence for attempts to explore the profundities of human existence so as to be able to cope with life's ambiguities. Many of the incidents in the narratives of the wilderness wanderings, such as the provision of manna or the descent of the quails, can be given natural explanations in terms of features of life in the Sinai wilderness.[3] To explain them in naturalistic terms, however, is to miss their point, which is to explore the paradoxes of freedom and of what it means to be commissioned to be the people and servants of God.

The Truth of Myths

For those who maintain that myths are expression of a prescientific mentality, or texts designed to accompany magical practices, myths can have no truth in an objective (i.e., potentially falsifiable) sense. An alternative view would be that myths can express intuitions of eternal truths or values, depending, of course, that one accepts that there are such things as eternal truths or values. The view that is taken of this matter will almost certainly be determined by the beliefs and understanding of the nature of reality on the part of the particular theorist.

If the first eleven chapters of Genesis are compared with the texts from the ancient Near East, the differences between them are striking (see Rogerson and Davies 2005, 111–23). In the Babylonian myths the human race is created in order to do the menial tasks for the gods that the gods do not wish to do themselves. In Genesis the human race is created in order to exercise a responsible stewardship over the world on behalf of God. In one version of the Babylonian story of the flood, the flood is brought upon the earth because the humans have been making too much noise and the gods can get no rest (Lambert and Millard 1969, 73). In Genesis the earth is destroyed as divine judgment upon the wickedness of the human race.

It must be added that the story of the flood in Gen 6–8 is an important part of the narrative structure of Gen 1–9, which expresses a remarkable theology. The world described in Gen 1 is a vegetarian world, vegetarian for animals as well as humans (Rogerson 1991, 21–24; Barr 1992, 76). In other words, the world described in Gen 1 is not the world of our experience, but one in which there is harmony and peace between humans and

---

3. For details, see Noth 1962, 132.

animals. The world of our experience, in which there is enmity between humans and animals and in which humans are not vegetarian, does not come into existence until after the flood. With the help of mythical motifs, Gen 1–9 expresses the astonishing view that the world has been created by God but that it is not the world as God intends it to be, on account of the wickedness of the human race. As far as the theme of this section is concerned, the truth of myths in the Old Testament is connected closely with their *Sitz in der Literatur* (setting in literature), which enables them to express insights into Old Testament belief in God.

Although this paper has dealt with the subject of myth only superficially, I hope that it has provided the basis for further thought and reflection on the subject.

Works Cited

Achenbach, Reinhard. 2005. Wüstenwanderung/Wüstenwanderungsüberlieferung. Pages 1746–47 in vol. 8 of *Religion in Geschichte und Gegenwart*. Edited by Hans Dieter Betz et al. 4th ed. Tübingen: Mohr Siebeck.

Barr, James. 1992. *The Garden of Eden and the Hope of Immortality*. London: SCM.

Davies, Philip R., and John Rogerson. 2005. *The Old Testament World*. 2nd ed. Louisville: Westminster John Knox.

Day, John. 1985. *God's Conflict with the Dragon and the Sea: Echoes of a Canaanite Myth in the Old Testament*. Cambridge: Cambridge University Press.

Gunkel, Hermann. 2006. *Creation and Chaos in the Primveval Era and the Eschaton*. Translated by K. William Whitney Jr. Grand Rapids: Eerdmans.

———. 1997. *Genesis*. Translated by Mark E. Biddle. Macon, Ga.: Mercer University Press.

Handy, Lowell K. 1992. Serpent (Religious Symbol). *ABD* 5:1113–16.

Irsigler, Hubert, ed. 2004. *Mythisches in biblischer Bildsprache: Gestalt und Verwandlung in Prophetie und Psalmen*. Quaestiones disputatae 209. Freiburg: Herder.

Johnson, Aubrey R. 1967. *Sacral Kingship in Ancient Israel*. Cardiff: University of Wales Press.

Kraus, Hans-Joachim. 1989. *Psalms 60–150*. Translated by Hilton C. Oswald. CC. Minneapolis: Augsburg.

Lambert, W. G., and A. R. Millard. 1969. *Atra-ḫasīs: The Babylonian Story of the Flood.* Oxford: Clarendon.

Noth, Martin. *Exodus.* 1962. Translated by J. S. Bowden. OTL. London: SCM.

Rogerson, J. W. 1974. *Myth in Old Testament Interpretation.* BZAW 134. Berlin: de Gruyter.

———. 1978. *Anthropology and the Old Testament.* Oxford: Blackwell.

———. 1991. *Genesis 1–11.* Sheffield: Sheffield Academic Press.

Segal, Robert A., ed. 1998. *The Myth and Ritual Theory: An Anthology.* Oxford: Blackwell.

Smith, George. 1873. The Chaldean Account of the Deluge. *Transactions of the Society of Biblical Archaeology* 2:213–34.

———. 1876. *The Chaldean Account of Genesis.* London: Sampson Low, Marston, Searle and Rivington.

Toulmin, Stephen. 1957. Contemporary Scientific Mythology. Pages 13–81 in *Metaphysical Beliefs: Three Essays.* Edited by Stephen Toulmin, Ronald W. Hepburn, and Alasdaire MacIntyre. London: SCM.

Myth and Scripture: Dissonance and Convergence

Dexter E. Callender Jr.

The terms *myth* and *Scripture* have often been galvanizing terms when applied to the Bible. In biblical studies, serious interest in myth typically falls under the domain of the secular academy, whereas serious interest in "Scripture" has typically been the concern for communities of faith and the academic institutions they support. This has been most clearly articulated in Robert Oden's *The Bible without Theology*, subtitled *The Theological Tradition and Alternatives to It*, in which Oden eschews questions of theology in his treatment of myth, in support of what he refers to as "the process by which biblical study is moving to the center of the modern university"—a process that almost by necessity has included the "jettisoning of much of the theological tradition." The relationship between myth and Scripture might be modeled as one of dissonance, whereby the two are rarely, if ever, placed alongside one another and seem in many respects at odds with one another. The objective of this paper is to consider how the two terms can fruitfully be brought together.

I do understand that the opposition of "dissonance" and "convergence" in the same title is itself dissonant, but I have done so to make a point. Insofar as convergence reflects movement, a "coming together," my aim is to argue here for common ground that calls for and allows the two to move together, maintaining their distinct aims, interests, worldviews—*cultures*—to challenge, sharpen, and enlighten one another. The usefulness of myth as a concept lies in the attention it draws to language use. It naturally involves a hermeneutic of suspicion. Scripture as a concept is useful to point out conventionality. Like "literature," it is the inscribing of a canon—a fixed set of symbols that in some way lays claim to its own inherent importance. But its claim to importance comes from its images and how they are used.

Myth as a Concept

To speak of myth (*mythos*) is to invoke a Greek emic category. For our purposes here, to speak of myth as a concept, it is useful to give attention to the word in its native Greek context. We can then use the semantic range of the term as a heuristic framework to consider similar phenomena in ancient Israel.

In the early history of the term, *mythos* was interchangeable with *logos*, indicating simply word or speech—even an unspoken thought. It is used as speech in contrast to *ergon* or action. It signifies a story, tale, or an account. In prose sources, it was increasingly contrasted with *logos* and came to be identified with traditional stories of gods and humans. Luc Brisson observes, "Myth was given a name when its status came to be contested and its function questioned" (2004, 29). Of course, the Greek historiographical tradition played a significant role in defining the nature of myth. Herodotus worked by relying first upon what he was able to witness or by questioning other eyewitnesses. Thucydides distinguished myth from history by emphasizing the goal in history of finding use in knowing exactly what happened, although it may be less attractive or entertaining than what myths present. When historical writers such as Theopompus included myths in their works, they did so as an amusing digression to give the reader a rest (see Wardman 1996).

Scholarly consensus establishes Plato as the beginning of systematic reflection on myth (see Von Hendy 2002). For Plato, myth is an unverifiable discourse and a nonargumentative discourse. It is unverifiable by virtue of its referent being, as Brisson summarizes, "at a level of reality inaccessible both to the intellect and to the senses, or at the level of sensible things, but in a past of which the speaker of the discourse can have no direct or indirect experience" (2004, 23). It is nonargumentative by virtue of being narrative—that is, relating events as they are supposed to have happened, without explanation, and whose parts are linked in a contingent chain. Plato's ambivalence to myth is apparent in his presentation of myth on some occasions as false discourse and on other occasions as true, the truth lying in the extent to which it *conforms* to *philosophical* discourse. The usefulness of myth for Plato is found especially in the areas of ethics and politics, insofar as it leads individuals through its persuasive power *to model behavior* according to its paradigms (Brisson 2004, 24–27). Plato understands myth as having an effect on the soul—an ability to give pleasure to the *epithymia*, the seat of our most primal cravings (and feelings). He presents this effect, this power, in terms of an incantation, a drug, a charm, or more simply as persuasion. The pleasure involved makes myth a game, but one of consequence, given its powerful effect on the soul of the addressee (Brisson 1998, 83).[1] Myth here has an affective dimension that predisposes one to action or to a shift in disposition.

What is more, there is a rhetorical dimension that makes appeal to myth appropriate in certain contexts, where *mythos* and *logos* are two strategies of persuasion. In *Protagoras*, when Socrates expresses skepticism regarding whether virtue can be taught and asks Protagoras to show him clearly otherwise, Protagoras responds:

> Shall I, as an elder, speak to you as younger men in an apologue or myth, or shall I argue out the question [go through a *logos*]?
>
> To this several of the company answered that he should choose for himself.
>
> Well, then, he said, I think that the myth will be more interesting. (*Protagoras* 320c, trans. Jowett)

The *mythos* he proceeds to recount is a story of gods and humans. Following the creation and endowing of animals, Prometheus endows humans with a share of the divine attributes: practical wisdom and fire, allowing a measure of survival for individuals. Zeus then sends Hermes to humans bearing respect and justice—to be distributed and ultimately imposed upon all under pain of death—to ensure survival through community. A similar example appears at the end of the *Phaedo*, where *timeliness* is a stated factor in Socrates's decision whether to engage the discourse of myth:

> SOCRATES If this is the right moment (*kalon*) to tell a myth (*muthon*) Simmias, it will be worth your while to hear what it is really like upon the earth which lies beneath the heavens.

---

1. See also Brisson 2004, 19. Brisson also notes Plato's occasional derivative or figurative use of the term "to evoke types of discourse other than the one usually called 'myth.' Two of these instances refer to rhetorical discourse. ... Five of these derivative occurrences refer to philosophical doctrines Plato criticizes. ... In eleven other cases, *he uses this same term to characterize his own discourse*" (2004, 27).

SIMMIAS Yes, indeed, Socrates, it would be with pleasure (*hēdeōs*) to us, at any rate to hear this myth (*tou muthou*).[2]

In these examples we also witness the idea that the appropriateness or timeliness of deploying the discourse of myth is contingent on the *disposition of the hearer*.

Whereas for Plato, philosophy implies a radical departure from traditional discourse, Aristotle finds a closer relationship between myth and philosophy and adopts the stance of those who wished to preserve myth in tragedy or in allegory. The poets of tragedy recast the myths of Homer, Hesiod and others as expressions of the new values of the city (Brisson 2004, 29–30). Others took myths as repositories of deep truths that were harmonious with new ideas, truths to be recovered through allegorical exegesis.[3] Following in this tradition, myths were interpreted in many ways, in response to patent falseness, measured by commonsense empiricism, or better, determining the manner of truth it expresses in view of a rejection of the plain sense and "scandalous content."[4]

Viewed along these lines, a concept of myth embodies a type of speech that is incongruent with commonsense empiricism and discordant with historiography's principles of verifiability.[5] It provokes an evaluation in terms of truth or falsity and it invites a hermeneutic of suspicion. These traditional tales come to reflect a different type of speech act with different goals. When Aristotle distinguishes poetry from history in the *Poetics* and writes of *katharsis*, he speaks directly of tragedy, where the stock of traditional stories and motifs found expression (Dörrie 1996, 105). The myths of Homer and others (in the popular sense) provided the Greek tragedian poets with material to formulate "truths" not necessarily or best

---

2. As quoted in Brisson 1998, 83.

3. The fourth-century C.E. writer Sallustius, whose *On the Gods and the Universe* gave a systematic analysis of myth, echoed the ideas of earlier writers and saw different types of myth according to what they intend to express—be it theological, physical, psychical, material, or some blend of these. See Barrett 1996, 346.

4. Kronos (or Cronus) swallowing his children, as Francis Bacon observed in *Wisdom of the Ancients,* exemplifies both concerns. Although Bacon's criteria for seeing value in fables were written at the dawn of the scientific revolution, they were nonetheless informed by sensibilities that had operated since the beginnings of critical discursive reflection in the fifth century B.C.E.

5. The events it admits are verifiable, either witnessed by others or given to common experience, and the language is deemed appropriate to express it.

conveyed in terms of other forms of discourse. Myth serves the aims of rhetoric, moving the audience—the community—to a particular frame of mind, much in the same sense that metaphor does, but also to action. The appropriateness of its use was contingent upon the context in which it found expression. Appropriateness is critical.

Among the biblical writers, we encounter a similar conception myth in Sir 20:18–20. In three successive verses, three types of speech act are compared—parapraxis, myth, and proverb:

> [18] A slip on the pavement is better than *a slip of the tongue*; so the downfall of the wicked will occur speedily.
>
> [19] An ungracious man is like *a story* [*mythos*] told at the wrong time, which is continually on the lips of the ignorant.
>
> [20] A *proverb* from a fool's lips will be rejected, for he does not tell it at its proper time.

The first, parapraxis, is untimely by definition, whereas a myth and a proverb have their own respective contexts in which they are appropriate and effective or useful speech acts. The affective dimension is evident in the Syriac variant, "as the fat tail of a sheep, eaten without salt, so is a word spoken out of season."

To summarize, we may characterize myth as drawing special attention to language *use*. Inasmuch as myth's identity was forged by the very questioning that sought to undermine it, it emphasizes language in the service of a goal, as a specific discrete speech act. But its reception is predicated on *timeliness*, that is, on *context*. In this, myth's success requires interlocution.

Scripture as a Concept

Scripture may be considered in two ways. From a formal standpoint, it is the result of the development of a literary canon that is considered sacred. In the case of ancient Israel and Judah, this process of "scripturalization" generally regards the production and incorporation of literary texts into what became the Hebrew Bible, beginning with the Torah, most notably in its manifestation as the Pentateuch. As a concept, Scripture conveys the idea of a fixed corpus of material with special status, a "bilateral term," as Wilfred Cantwell Smith puts it, that inherently implies a relationship with a community (1993, 4; see also Barton 2007). Scripture in this sense is a matter of communal acceptance regarding what to copy and preserve (van der Toorn 2007). It involves what recognized authorities read and taught publicly as well as what was read and taught in the home (Heaton 1994; Davies 2007). It further involves the conferring of official status.

In considering the emergence of Scripture we must distinguish the canonical process from the literary development of its materials, although the two are closely related (Childs 1979, 62; Smith 1993, 4; see also Barton 2007). Further, inasmuch as language is convention, the writings of ancient Israel and Judah incorporate imagery shared with the broader cultural environment of the ancient Near East—imagery generally denoted "myth," "mythic," or "mythopoeic," and which raises issues of language use.[6] Here the writers selected the core images and language that would anchor public discourse. These images were not cut from whole cloth, but chosen from the stock of the most effective expressions of salient experience, and then pressed into the service of any number of socioeconomic, -political, and -cultural programs. Thus, in examining materials *as Scripture* we must consider the nature of the special status, how the community engages the text, but also how the individual engages the text.[7] The religious specialists featured as creators and custodians of Scripture conferred its special status by way of proclaiming its inherent importance in metaphors associated with prophecy and wisdom, but also cult. The idea of divine origin that informed canonical decisions at the "book" level for the community as a whole also informed personal experience.

Thus alternatively we can view Scripture conceptually in terms of the metaphors and images that ground it, regarding these as expressions of experience. In the case of the Hebrew Bible, torah constitutes the Israelite and Judahite emic expression of the concept of Scripture, specifically in the idea of *inscribed divine speech*. It is in this sense that torah also provides a depth of expression that is useful when viewed alongside myth as we have discussed it. We encounter this constitutive expression of torah in the imagery of the tablets.

---

6. See the essay of Mark Smith in this volume.

7. Note Childs's caution against "hypothesiz[ing] the history of the literature's growth in such a way as to eliminate *a priori* the religious dimensions associated with the function of the canon."

Torah: The Essence of Scripture

The root metaphor of torah is *instruction*, which emerges in the form of *inscribed divine speech* and lays a foundation for Scripture. Torah as a concept is preeminent in Deuteronomy. The writers present torah as beginning in experience, a confrontation that is communicative and thus expressed in the metaphor of interlocution. Torah is then inscribed on stone tablets and as such is fixed, torn from its original experiential context in the moment. As inscribed in the Decalogue, torah is rendered emblematic (see van der Toorn 1996, 360; 1997). The final edition of the book of Deuteronomy presents the book as an exposition of "this Torah."[8] The Deuteronomic writer relates the speech event that lies at the heart of torah in Deut 4:10–14:

> how you once stood before the Lord your God at Horeb, when the Lord said to me, "Assemble the people for me, and *I will let them hear my words, so that they may learn to fear me* as long as they live on the earth, and may teach their children so"; you approached and stood at the foot of the mountain while the mountain was blazing up to the very heavens, shrouded in dark clouds. Then *the Lord spoke to you out of the fire. You were hearing the sound of words but seeing no form; there was only a voice.* He declared to you his covenant, which he charged you to observe, that is, the ten commandments; and he wrote them on two stone tablets. And the Lord charged me at that time to teach you statutes and ordinances for you to observe in the land that you are about to cross into and occupy.

Torah foremost is *speech*, "words" (דברים), and it begins with a speech *event*. Here the root metaphor is laid bare in exposition as a confrontation, a face-to-face encounter, in the phrase "standing before the Lord" at Horeb.[9] As a communicative confrontation, the speaker is God, who as mystery speaks mysteriously, given here as "out of the fire" (מתוך האש, v. 12).[10] In this, the giving of torah is typologically likened to Moses' first experience on Sinai in Exod 3, where Yahweh called to Moses "out of the bush" (מתוך הסנה) described as "burning with fire" (בער באש). The ambiguity of the word קול "sound" or "voice" and its expression apart from the

---

8. Deut 1:5. The term באר indicates making plain or clear.
9. The idiom "face to face" is used explicitly in Deut 5:4.
10. Note also Deut 5:4: "The Lord spoke with you face to face at the mountain, out of the fire" (cf. 5:22; 4:33).

words themselves convey the divine linguistic nature of the speech: "You were hearing the sound of words [קול דברים] but were seeing no form; there was only a voice [קול]."[11]

The original experience is instructive and points back to itself: "I will let them hear my words, *so that they may learn to fear me ... and teach their children* so" (4:10).[12] The experience of hearing divine speech is a teaching. The original experience of hearing instills an immediate affective response to the direct confrontation with God, expressed as "fear." The *direct* nature of the encounter as the source of this fear is clear in Moses' words: "Has any people ever heard the voice of a god speaking out of a fire, as you have heard, and lived?" (4:33).[13] This experience, already presented as divinely linguistic through ambiguity, is rendered more *humanly* linguistic when the "words" that Yahweh "lets them hear" mentioned in 4:10 and reiterated in the phrase *"sound of words"* (v. 12) are clarified as a speech act—*a declaration*. "He declared [ויגד] to you his covenant" (v. 13). Here the covenant is proclaimed, fixing the experience of speech under a legal metaphor—expounded in the *ten words* to observe, which render a schematic presentation of the statements on the tablets, and further expounded in the statutes and ordinances (חקים ומשפטים) to observe.[14] The statutes and ordinances exemplify "this entire torah" (v. 8). Covenant, Decalogue, and "statutes and ordinances" are emblematic of the original salient experience of hearing the voice of God. Thus, as instructive, *fear* attending the experience of the sound assumes a distinctive form of covenant loyalty, which is given further linguistic shape and fixed, assuming as a medium of instruction the propositional knowledge of the Decalogue and the statutes and ordinances.[15]

The tablets of the Decalogue essentialize the imagery of *inscribing*. Further, the divine nature of the inscribed speech is equally central. The inherent importance of the inscribed words is expressed in the imagery of

---

11. Cf. Exod 19:19, where the ambiguity of קול is related to the sound of the ram's horn.

12. Cf. Deut 4:9. The didacticism is evident also in 4:36 in the experience of the fire as "discipline."

13. Cf. Deut 5:5, "you were afraid before the fire [יראתם מפני האש]," and 5:24–25.

14. On the relation of the statutes and ordinances to the Decalogue, see McConville and Millar 1994, 54; Miller 1990, 66–69.

15. On fear as covenant loyalty and wisdom, see Weinfeld 1972, 274–81.

God himself inscribing the speech on the two tablets he makes himself.[16] In this expression of inherent importance torah emerges as Scripture. The use of stone tablets as the medium as opposed to a scroll is especially significant, given the relative paucity of lapidary inscriptions in the land.[17] In Deuteronomy Moses himself constructs the ark as a repository for the tablets, underscoring their nature as fixed and to be preserved (Deut 10:1–5). But the fixed forms of language are emblematic of the original mysterious experience and must in some way return to it. This return is accomplished through meditation and exposition. The address of Moses in Deut 4 closes by reiterating the experience as instructive:

> [35] To you it was shown so that you would acknowledge that the LORD is God; there is no other besides him. [36] From heaven he made you hear his voice to discipline you. On earth he showed you his great fire, while you heard his words coming out of the fire. [37] And because he loved your ancestors, he chose their descendants after them. He brought you out of Egypt with his own presence, by his great power, [38] driving out before you nations greater and mightier than yourselves, to bring you in, giving you their land for a possession, as it is still today. [39] So acknowledge today and take to heart [והשבת אל-לבבך] that the LORD is God in heaven above and on the earth beneath; there is no other. [40] Keep his statutes and his commandments, which I am commanding you today so it goes well for you [ייטב לך] and for your children after you, so that you may long remain in the land that the LORD your God is giving you for all time.

In verses 35–40 Moses summarizes the Sinai experience under the teaching metaphor of discipline: "From heaven he made you hear his voice *to discipline you*. On earth he showed you his great fire, while you heard his words coming out of the fire."[18] This with the experience of deliverance from Egypt (vv. 37–38) discloses "that Yahweh is God" and "no other" (vv. 35, 39)—which is to be a matter of knowledge (or recognition) and reflection, "acknowledge [וידעת] today and take to heart [והשבת אל-לבבך] that

---

16. Deut 9:10; cf. Exod 31:18; 32:15–16.
17. On the tablets as expressions of suzerain-vassal treaties, see Kline 1963.
18. Deut 4:36; cf. v. 33; Exod 20:22. On discipline in Deuteronomy and in Wisdom literature see Weinfeld 1972, 303. Heaven and earth here are undermined in their semantic associations with "sky" above and "earth" below and clearly suggest mystery behind and manifestation in front, consistent with the expression "out of the fire" (מתוך האש).

the Lord is God in heaven above and on the earth beneath; there is no other [אֵין עוֹד]" (v. 39).¹⁹ The phrase "take to heart," literally "make return to your heart," indicates a deliberately repetitive action, hence signifying meditation or reflection on the covenant metaphor. As in 4:13–14, the covenant includes additional legal prescriptions, which appear in verse 40 as "his statutes and commandments" (חֻקָּיו וְאֶת־מִצְוֹתָיו). These are to be observed for the well-being of present and future generations, "you and your children after you," a phrase that returns us to Yahweh's initial statement of instructive intent revealed to Moses (4:10).

In Deut 6:6–9 and 11:18–20, torah in its propositional dimension is to be studied, taught, and practiced (6:4–9). The covenant metaphor in the Shema (6:4–5; cf. 4:35, 39) is to be taken to heart: "Keep these words that I am commanding you today in your heart" (v. 6), and is further emblematized *physically* (6:8) as a starting point for meditative reflective activity. In 6:7 recitation (שִׁנַּנְתָּם לְבָנֶיךָ) of the fixed propositional form is combined with discursive engagement, "talk about them" (דִבַּרְתָּ בָּם). Torah is given further verbal explication interpreted by individuals as teaching to children (6:7, 20–25; 11:19), returning torah to interlocution proper. In 6:20–25 teaching the children about the statutes and ordinances is given in the language of the covenant loyalty metaphor as the divine utterances are associated with the fear of the Lord, with good, and with life: "Then the Lord commanded us *to observe* all these statutes, *to fear* the Lord our God, for our lasting good, so as *to keep us alive*, as is now the case" (6:24).

Ezra's public reading in Neh 8:1–12 provides a witness to the literary development and canonical process, the scripturalization of torah. It presents a view of its role in the community.²⁰ As the "book of the torah of Moses, which the Lord had given to Israel" (8:1), the torah in Nehemiah is most directly associated with the book of Deuteronomy.²¹ Here too we find emphasis on explication and the torah as a thing taught: not self-evident but appropriated through a process of rendering it in other terms. Over two dozen named officials, including the Levites, participate

---

19. Deut 4:39. Verse 35 adds מִלְבַדּוֹ "besides him."
20. On the setting see Deut 31:9–13. For discussion see Kugel and Greer 1986, 20–22.
21. On the associations between Deuteronomy and Nehemiah, see Blenkinsopp 1989, 153–55; Pakkala 2004, 285.

in the reading and giving of interpretation.[22] The participation of the Levites accords with Deut 33:8–10, which presents them as torah teachers. According to the writer, "They read from the book, from the torah of God, with interpretation [מפרש]. They gave the sense [וְשׂוֹם שֶׂכֶל], so that the people might understand the reading [וַיָּבִינוּ בַּמִּקְרָא]" (Neh 8:8). Although the reading of the Hebrew torah would likely have been an issue to what was becoming an aramaized audience, that we are told in verse 2, "Ezra brought the torah before the assembly, both men and women *and all who could hear with understanding* [כֹּל מֵבִין לִשְׁמֹעַ]" (cf. 8:3), suggests more than a simple matter of translation.[23] At the end of the first day we read of the people rejoicing "because they had understood the words that were declared to them" (כִּי הֵבִינוּ בַּדְּבָרִים אֲשֶׁר הוֹדִיעוּ לָהֶם; v. 12).

The experience of divine speech is conveyed in other terms, among which is the idea of *wisdom*. Divine speech was not restricted to prophets but was mediated in various ways by a variety of human beings—sages and elders, priests and temple personnel, judges and wise men; it fell increasingly under the purview of scribes and sages (see Kugel and Greer 1986, 15). In Deuteronomy observance of the "statutes and ordinances" is itself a display of wisdom (חכמה) and understanding (בינה).[24] Deuteronomy gives Joshua's credentials as Moses' successor in terms that approach possession language, describing him as "full of the spirit of wisdom" (מלא רוח חכמה).[25]

The expansion of the canon (which had come to be embodied in the Pentateuch) appears to have been influenced by a variety of factors. These include the increasing age of texts and the influence of Greek culture. The conception of the Greek poet-prophet provided a relatively easy comparison with the tradition of the Israelite prophet, and contributed a model

---

22. The two lists of thirteen names each may be corrupt. The second group of thirteen are called "the Levites," whereas the first group is not identified, but may correspond to the elders (cf. Deut 27:1 as opposed to 27:8). Cf. Deut 17:18; 31:9, 26.

23. For discussion on whether the activity was translation or interpretation, see Fensham 1982, 216–18; Blenkinsopp 1989, 288.

24. Deut 4:6. See also Ps 37:30–31; 119.

25. Deut 34:9. Note the parallel passage in Num 27:18–23: "The LORD said to Moses, "Take Joshua son of Nun, a man in whom is the spirit, and lay your hand upon him. ... You shall give him some of your authority, so that all the congregation of the Israelites may obey." Cf. Num 11:16–17, 29. On the spirit of wisdom, and on the idiom "rest upon" (נוח), see Isa 11:2.

for inspired literature, more broadly construed. Such is evident when Socrates observes:

> All good poets, epic as well as lyric, compose their beautiful poems not by art, but because they are inspired and possessed. ... For the poet is a light and winged and holy thing, and there is no invention in him until he has been inspired and is out of his senses, and the mind is no more in him. When he has not attained to this state he is powerless and unable to utter his oracles. ... And therefore God takes away the minds of the poets, and uses them as his ministers, as he also uses diviners and holy prophets. ... For in this way the God would seem to indicate to us and not allow us to doubt that these beautiful poems are not human or the work of man, but divine and the work of God; and that the poets are only the intermediaries of the gods by whom they were severally possessed.[26]

James Kugel draws attention to its context in Plato's *Ion*, "in which poetic inspiration is compared to the force of a great magnetic stone, which can then be transferred from the stone itself (that is, the inspiring deity) to a series of magnetized rings: the poet, the reciter of his poems, and the audience all receive and emit the inspiring power" (1990, 15–16). The comparison is interesting by virtue of the invisibility and intangible character of the force. What is transmitted is perceived not as the symbols of language, but as an aesthetic or affective force that attends the language. The human is a medium who then uses the medium of language to transmit to another that which has seized her or him. And what is transmitted is received as "beauty."

It is the oracular writings of the Sibyl that for Kugel mark "the exact point of confluence" of Greek and Jewish traditions. These "prophet-like utterances" show formal influence of biblical prophetic and Jewish apocalyptic writings but were "spoken in verse by an ecstatic pagan poet, one nonetheless inspired by the true God" (17). Her claim to ecstatic speech is relevant: "I will speak the following with my whole person in ecstasy / For I do not know what I say, but God bids me utter each thing" (17). Her subject matter included not only foretelling the future, but recounting the history of the world (18). Although material in Judges, Samuel, and Kings does not purport to be given by an inspired teller, in the postexilic period Chronicles identifies prophets as the writers of histories (e.g., 2 Chr 26:22;

---

26. As quoted by Kugel 1990, 16.

33:19). William Schniedewind has demonstrated the rise of the prophet as historian and as inspired messenger, who both receives *and interprets* the "word of God" (1995). Also notable among the many miscellaneous types of documents that became Scripture were psalms and songs. Here the experience of the individual comes increasingly to the fore.

PSALM 119

Psalm 119 provides another window into the nature of torah as Scripture, particularly in the way it dislodges torah from its fixed linguistic state. It treats the concept with respect to its power. Here torah is expressed in terms of experience, portrayed as an intangible, invisible force of change. Psalm 119 is anthological in style in its allusions to other biblical texts, with affinities to Deuteronomic literature.[27] This represents another gesture toward scripturalization, a broadening core of material that is fixed and increasingly drawn upon. Despite the centrality of torah in the psalm, commentators have noted that its contents are not disclosed. Torah is an entity independent of the text, the linguistic form it took in the Pentateuch (Levenson 1987, 561; Reynolds 2010).

In Ps 119 the model for inspiration is given in terms of wisdom, and torah is equated with wisdom (Hurvitz 1988; Reynolds 2010). The commandments referenced in the psalm reflect the language of wisdom circles, where the commandment suggests the advice of a sage, but is tantamount to the revelation of God's will (Levenson 1987, 566–67). The dimension of individual experience is emphasized in Ps 119. The psalmist's experience, characterized as possessing wisdom, insight, and understanding, comes by way of reflection on decrees, precepts, and commands, recalling the personal reflection in Deut 6 and 11:

> 99 I have more insight [השכלתי] than all my teachers,
> for your decrees are my meditation.
> 100 I understand [אתבונן] more than the aged,
> for I keep your precepts

Further, the psalmist's claim to exceed his teachers and the elders in insight and understanding uses the roots שכל and בין, recalling Neh 8:8, where

---

27. The anthological style was first recognized by Deissler 1955. Cf. Miller 1999; Freedman 1999, 90.

the Levites and other officials explain the torah to the people, the idiom of giving "sense" (שׂכל) results in the people understanding (בין).28

Further, references to observing the torah with the whole heart (שמר בכל לב), and delighting (חפץ) in the commandments (vv. 34–35) reveal the intensity of such experience (cf. Neh 8:17). Possessing the commandment becomes an endowment in an even deeper sense in that the word itself becomes a dispensation of charisma. In verse 43 we read:

> Do not take away [אל־תצל] from my mouth
> your word of truth [דבר־אמת],
> For I have put my hope in your laws [משפטיך]

The imagery of "taking away" God's word of truth from the psalmist here recalls Num 11:17, 25 (the only other occurrence of this sense of the verb אצל), where God "strips away" the spirit from Moses, sharing it with the seventy elders, who prophesy, validating their office (Levenson 1987, 565).

As for the psalm's own linguistic dimension, Levenson suggests that the very structure and length of the psalm have an affective aim, "[i]f the goal of the author was to create the *psychic conditions* conducive to the *spiritual experience* he seeks"; more specifically, "the state of mind that comes from reading it in a deliberate and reflective fashion."29 All of this lies beyond what he refers to as "merely *knowing* the theology" (1987, 566, emphasis added).

The mystery of the special experience of the individual is established through the equation of torah with wisdom. Here we may also note that the presentation of torah in Ps 119 leads D. N. Freedman to conclude that

---

28. The same two roots appear in Ezra referring to Levites who possess a special dispensation of wisdom of such quality to procure the protection of God against the enemies of the returnees (8:16, 18; cf. Deut 4:1–4; 6:17). Thus it is not surprising that the psalmist states, "your commandment makes me wiser than my enemies" (Ps 119:98).

29. "It seems likely that the psalm was written to serve as an inducement for the kind of revelation and illumination for which it petitions. Its high degree of regularity and repetition can have a mesmerizing effect upon those who recite it, with the octad of synonyms functioning like a mantra and providing a relaxing predictability while banishing thoughts that distract from the object of contemplation" (Levenson 1987, 566).

the psalm grants torah "virtually the status of a divine hypostasis," which leads us to the presentation of Wisdom in Prov 8 (Freedman 1999, 89–90).³⁰

Proverbs 8:22–31

The presentation of חכמה (ḥokmâ) "Wisdom" in Prov 8:22–31 provides an especially useful example to consider the intersection of myth and Scripture. It is part of a larger poem that extols the virtues of wisdom and it presents wisdom in personal terms—important to discussions of myth in ancient Israel, which often dichotomize monotheism/polytheism and the stance toward the existence of other "gods" (see esp. Kaufmann 1960). Wisdom proclaims her preexistent status, "created at the beginning [ראשית] of [God's] work," (v. 22), "before the beginning of the earth," before the mountains, the hills (v. 25). She was present when the heavens were established (v. 27), when the skies and great deep (תהום) were circumscribed (v. 28), when the sea was given its bounds and the foundations of the earth marked out (v. 29). In verse 30 she was present either as a "craftsman" or perhaps as a "child" of the deity.³¹

The nature of the imagery has been the matter of considerable discussion. Does the text portray an independent mythological figure or is it merely a trope, a metaphor in the simple sense? R. N. Whybray understands it as the hypostasis of a divine attribute, metaphorical and not mythological (1965, 101). Helmer Ringgren seeks a middle ground in seeing the personification of a divine attribute to which mythological characteristics taken from other traditions were added to enhance the vividness of wisdom's portrayal (1947, 132–48). Gerhard von Rad sees a personification of the "primeval order" of the universe,

> neither a mythological residue which unconsciously accompanied the idea, nor … a free, poetic and didactic use of imagery. The personified image was the most precise expression available for the subject matter to be explained. It was much more than simply the objective realization of such a primeval order; *it was, rather, a question of crystallizing specific*

---

30. Freedman makes an explicit connection with Prov 8, citing common vocabulary and theology.

31. The reading (אָמוֹן) "master worker" reflects LXX ἁρμόζουσα and the Akkadian *ummanu* tradition, whereas the reading "child" (אָמֻן) reflects τιθηνουμένη, preserved in Aquila.

experiences which man had had in his encounter with it. He had experienced it not only as a static organism of order, he felt himself assailed by it ... he experienced it as a bestower of gifts. He saw himself led by her into a confessional state. (1972, 174, emphasis added)

Von Rad's conception of the self-revelation of creation, distinctively Israelite in its address to humans, does not lie far from what one senses in Yahweh's self-revelation. Peter Schäfer, recognizing the affinity with Maat/Isis imagery, sees in Prov 8 no less than an image of God, in an attempt to materialize *revelation itself*. Wisdom here is "God's voice on earth, and more than that, as his daughter, she is God's embodiment on earth"—imagery that he suggests the Israelites quickly abandoned (2002, 29).[32] The difficulties of separating image, linguistic construct, and experience become apparent in these suggestions—such also are the difficulties that attend the apologetically motivated scholarly construct known as Israelite "demythologizing."

Here, along with questions of myth, we may also observe that the passage cuts a path that returns us to Scripture—and does so by way of torah. As Yahweh spoke from heaven *for discipline* in Deuteronomy (4:36; cf. 4:10; 11:2; 8:5–6), Wisdom *continues speaking* to the same end. The entire poem presents her as speaking iteratively, and in Prov 8:33–34 she calls out:

> Hear discipline and be wise [שמעו מוסר וחכמו]
> And do not neglect it.[33]
> She requires attentiveness on the part of the hearer:
> Happy is the one who listens to me [אשרי אדם שמע לי],
> Watching [לשקד] daily at my gates,
> Waiting [לשמר] beside my doors [מזוזת פתחי].

Attending to gates and doors recalls the doorposts and gates of Deut 6:9 (Cross and Saley 1970; see also van der Toorn 1997, 241). Those who are attentive are rewarded with life and favor, recalling what we have seen

---

32. Schäfer 2002, 29. Note also the proposal of Judith Hadley that "Lady Wisdom" is "literary compensation" for the eradication of the worship of goddesses like Asherah (Hadley 1997). See also my discussion in Callender 2000.

33. Cf. Prov 8:10. For the root פרע "neglect" applied to discipline see also 1:25; 13:18; 15:32. On the iterative nature see esp. 8:1–10.

emphasized in Deuteronomy as the blessing of the covenant metaphor (Prov 8:35–36):

> For whoever finds me finds life
> and obtains favor [רצון] from the LORD;
> but those who miss me [וחטאי] injure themselves;
> all who hate me love death.

The writer of Ben Sira renders the identification of personified wisdom and torah explicit.[34] In chapter 24 Wisdom is a being in the divine assembly (v. 2), making statements akin to the Egyptian Isis (vv. 6, 7). Moreover, she is equated with a divine speech act, coming forth from the mouth of the Most High (v. 3).[35] Her throne is "in a pillar of cloud," identifying her with experience of the wilderness theophany (v. 4). She is identified with the cult in two senses, both as the divine presence "dwelling" among the Israelites and as a priest "ministering" in the holy tent (vv. 8, 10). The writer himself states, "All this is the book of the covenant of the Most High God, the law that Moses commanded us" (v. 23). He then likens the book to the source of the primordial rivers of Eden, with wisdom, understanding, and instruction flowing forth from it (vv. 25–27).[36]

Equally important is the writer's own *inspired exposition*, which he goes on to express as a reinstantiation of the original dispensation. After likening himself to a watercourse feeding a garden (vv. 30–31), he states, "I will *again* make instruction shine forth like the dawn and I will make it clear from far away. I will again pour out teaching *like prophecy*, and leave it to all future generations" (vv. 32–33). In this his speech approaches possession as he himself speaks the words. Here he likens himself to a canal, channeling wisdom, which waters the garden (cf. Gen 2:10) and increases in power, becoming a river, then a sea (vv. 30–31). This recalls the prophetic imagery of the water flowing (יצא) from the temple in Ezek 47, about which we read, "everything will live where the river goes."[37] In Isa 2:2–3 and Mic 4:1–3 the nations will "stream" (נהר) up the "mountain

---

34. Cf. Bar 3. See Blenkinsopp 1983, 162–67.
35. Cf. Prov 2:6: "The LORD gives wisdom; from his mouth come knowledge and understanding."
36. Sir 24:25–27; v. 27 follows the Syriac.
37. Ezek 47:9. Seen elsewhere in the "living waters" that flow (יצא) from Jerusalem (Zech 14:8). In Zech 13 the cleansing spring that removes sin and impurity is associated with prophecy, true also in Ps 46:4–6 (cf. Amos 1:2; Joel 3:16).

of Yahweh's abode" to receive instruction: "That he may teach us [ירה] his ways ... for torah will flow from Zion and the word of Yahweh from Jerusalem."[38] The prophetic image of Yahweh teaching at the divine abode marks a return by way of torah to the instructive experience of a "face-to-face" encounter at Sinai.

Conclusion

In the metaphor of divine speech inscribed on tablets by God's own finger, torah in its inception does not lie far from myth. It sets in motion a process that follows the mystery of linguistic communication as a means of effecting the experience of direct confrontation. Scripture begins as "event" in confrontation, given as interlocution, a "being spoken to." It is inscribed in writing that tears it from its original context as lived event and requires a return to it, effected by "inspired" expositors who interpret the oracle and transmit the experience. Its fixed nature in the inscribed tablets is but one emblematic stop through a variety of forms of expression, forms that become even more numerous in the requirement to teach. Ultimately, the experience is mimetically reproduced *linguistically* in teaching and recitation and mimetically reproduced *ritually* in prescribed patterns of behavior and appropriate conduct (cf. Ps 111:10). The diviner-specialist possesses and is possessed of wisdom, an endowment that is available to anyone—to all who belong to the community that calls itself into existence.

If with Brisson we see myth emerge as myth from questioning regarding its status and function, we might then also assert that myth lies close to a kind of hermeneutic of suspicion—not in the narrow sense in which the term is commonly used (revealing false consciousness) but more broadly construed.[39] Such a disposition to the materials of myth,

---

38. Cf. Prov 13:13–15. In Tg. Zech. 13:1 the teaching of the law is likened to a spring. Further examples of torah conceptualized both in and beyond the written word can be multiplied in rabbinic literature. On the ontology of torah as living and organic, see Holdrege 1989, esp. 184–85.

39. Arvind Sharma, who provides a discussion of the reception of Ricoeur's term and recasts it within the context of the materials of Hinduism, asserts "the assumption of negativity, which might be implied in the word 'suspicion' in the expression 'hermeneutics of suspicion,' prevents the full potential of this hermeneutical concept from being realized" (2002, 356).

regardless of their particular narrative form,[40] views their relation to reality (positively or negatively) as contextually dependent. It embodies and calls attention to the existence of language systems at work in the procuring of reality that are not fixed to content but manifested in use.[41] Scripture, on the other hand—as seen in the ancient Israelite/Judahite conception, grounded in its image of inscribed divine speech—lies closer to what we might alternatively call a hermeneutic of faith or acceptance. Fixed in stone, its propositions are raised to the highest order as the threshold to the insider experience of Sinai, a threshold crossable by a Kierkegaardian leap.[42] Yet the claim that Scripture's propositions lay to ultimate significance for the individual requires that it participate in myth, both with respect to traditional content and in adverting to language systems. Myth directs attention to a general exploration of language and the symbolic order while Scripture provides an avenue to an assessment of religious phenomena per se, particularly in the context of "postsecular" society. Approaching myth and Scripture in this way reveals how the two can in fact be fruitfully brought together, laying a foundation for further work in the humanities and in the sciences.

Still, in the end Scripture must remain Scripture and myth must remain myth, and we lose something if we seek to collapse the two. Their meeting can bear fruit only under the appropriate conditions, in the proper contexts, where the forms of discourse and imagination that call them into being can be mutually illuminated. Scripture must remain the word

---

40. On myth in relation to narrative, see Cohen 1969; Ricoeur 1984; Segal 2004, 4–5. Note also Bruce Lincoln's definition of myth as "ideology in narrative form" (1999, 147).

41. See also in this regard Barthes's account of the reception of myth in terms of how one approaches the relationship between meaning and form ("the duplicity of the signifier") by focusing on meaning, on form, or on both at the same time: "The first two types of focusing are static, analytical; they destroy the myth, either by making its intention obvious, or by unmasking it: the former is cynical, the latter demystifying. The third type of focusing is dynamic, it consumes the myth according to the very ends built in to its structure: the reader lives the myth as a story at once true and unreal" (1972, 128).

42. Here we may consider both the "precritical immediate belief" that Ricoeur refers to as the naïve "first faith of the simple soul," and what he describes as "the second naiveté," in "postcritical faith," writing of the hermeneutical circle, "you must believe in order to understand, you must understand in order to believe" (1970, 28; 1974, 298).

of God, the possession of a community it calls forth and its grounds for communication. Myth, for its slipperiness with respect to definition, likewise must continue to fill its role as a mediating concept—a touchstone for examining language use as it engages truth, imagination, imagery, play—and as part of the genetic code of Scripture that allows it to reflect upon itself *as language*.

Works Cited

Barrett, C. K. 1996. Myth and the New Testament: The Greek Word *mythos*. Pages 25–28 in *Philosophy, Religious Studies, and Myth*. Edited by Robert A. Segal. New York: Garland.

Barthes, Roland. 1972. *Mythologies*. Translated by Annette Lavers. New York: Hill and Wang.

Barton, John. 2007. *The Old Testament: Canon, Literature and Theology: Collected Essays of John Barton*. Aldershot: Ashgate.

Blenkinsopp, Joseph. 1983. *Wisdom and Law in the Old Testament: The Ordering of Life in Israel and Early Judaism*. Oxford: Oxford University Press.

———. 1989. *Ezra-Nehemiah: A Commentary*. OTL. London: SCM.

Brisson, Luc. 1998. *Plato the Myth Maker*. Translated and edited by Gerard Naddaf. Chicago: University of Chicago Press.

———. 2004. *How Philosophers Saved Myths: Allegorical Interpretation and Classical Mythology*. Translated by Catherine Tihanyi. Chicago: University of Chicago Press.

Callender, Dexter E., Jr.. 2000. *Adam in Myth and History: Ancient Israelite Perspectives on the Primal Human*. Winona Lake, Ind: Eisenbrauns.

Childs, Brevard S. 1979. *Introduction to the Old Testament as Scripture*. Philadelphia: Fortress.

Cohen, Percy S. 1969. Theories of Myth. *Man* NS 43:337–53.

Cross, Frank Moore, Jr., and Richard J. Saley. 1970. Phoenician Incantations on a Plaque of the Seventh Century B.C. from Arslan Tash in Upper Syria. *BASOR* 197:42–49.

Davies, Philip R. 1998. *Scribes and Schools: The Canonization of the Hebrew Scriptures*. Louisville: Westminster John Knox.

Deissler, Alfons. 1955. *Psalm 119 (118) und seine Theologie: ein Beitrag zur Erforschung der anthologischen Stilgattung im Alten Testament*. Munich: Zink.

Dörrie, Heinrich. 1996. The Meaning and Function of Myth in Greek and

Roman Literature. Pages 105–27 in *Philosophy, Religious Studies, and Myth*. Edited by Robert A. Segal. New York: Garland.

Fensham, F. C. 1982. *The Books of Ezra and Nehemiah*. NICOT. Grand Rapids: Eerdmans.

Freedman, David Noel. 1999. *Psalm 119: The Exaltation of Torah*. Winona Lake, Ind.: Eisenbrauns.

Hadley, Judith M. 1997. From Goddess to Literary Construct: The Transformation of Asherah into Ḥokmah. Pages 360–99 in *A Feminist Companion to Reading the Bible: Approaches, Methods and Strategies*. Edited by Athalya Brenner and Carole Fontaine. Sheffield: Sheffield Academic Press.

Heaton, E. W. 1994. *The School Tradition of the Old Testament*. Oxford: Oxford University Press.

Holdrege, Barbara A. 1989. The Bride of Israel: The Ontological Status of Scripture in the Rabbinic and Kabbalistic Traditions. Pages 180–261 in *Rethinking Scripture: Essays from a Comparative Perspective*. Edited by Miriam Levering. Albany: State University of New York Press.

Hurvitz, Avi. 1988. Wisdom Vocabulary in the Hebrew Psalter: A Contribution to the Study of "Wisdom Psalms." *VT* 38:41–51.

Kaufmann, Yehezkel. 1960. *The Religion of Israel: From Its Beginnings to the Babylonian Exile*. Translated and abridged by Moshe Greenberg. Chicago: University of Chicago Press.

Kline, Meredith G. 1963. *Treaty of the Great King: The Covenant Structure of Deuteronomy*. Grand Rapids: Eerdmans.

Kugel, James L. 1990. Poets and Prophets: An Overview. Pages 1–25 in *Poetry and Prophecy: The Beginnings of a Literary Tradition*. Edited by James L. Kugel. Ithaca, N.Y.: Cornell University Press.

Kugel, James L., and Rowan A. Greer. 1986. *Early Biblical Interpretation*. Philadelphia: Westminster.

Levenson, Jon D. 1987. The Sources of Torah: Psalm 119 and the Modes of Revelation in Second Temple Judaism. Pages 559–74 in *Ancient Israelite Religion: Essays in Honor of Frank Moore Cross*. Edited by Patrick D. Miller Jr., Paul D. Hanson, and S. Dean McBride. Philadelphia: Fortress.

Lincoln, Bruce. 1999. *Theorizing Myth: Narrative, Ideology, and Scholarship*. Chicago: University of Chicago Press.

McConville, James Gordon, and J. G. Millar. 1994. *Time and Place in Deuteronomy*. LHBOTS 179. Sheffield: Sheffield Academic Press.

Miller, Patrick D. 1990. *Deuteronomy*. IBC. Louisville: John Knox.

———. 1999. Deuteronomy and Psalms: Evoking a Biblical Conversation. *JBL* 118:3–18.

Oden, Robert. 1987. *The Bible without Theology: The Theological Tradition and Alternatives to It*. San Francisco: Harper & Row.

Pakkala, Juha. 2004. *Ezra the Scribe: The Development of Ezra 7–10 and Nehemiah 8*. BZAW 347. Berlin: de Gruyter.

Rad, Gerhard von. 1972. *Wisdom in Israel*. Translated by James D. Martin. London: SCM.

Reynolds, Kent Aaron. 2010. *Torah as Teacher: The Exemplary Torah Student in Psalm 119*. VTSup 137. Leiden: Brill.

Ricoeur, Paul. 1970. *Freud and Philosophy: An Essay on Interpretation*. Translated by Denis Savage. New Haven: Yale University Press.

———. 1974. *The Conflict of Interpretations: Essays in Hermeneutics*. Evanston, Ill.: Northwestern University Press.

———. 1984. *Time and Narrative*. Translated by Kathleen McLaughlin and David Pellauer. 3 vols. Chicago: University of Chicago Press.

Ringgren, Helmer. 1947. *Word and Wisdom: Studies in the Hypostatization of Divine Qualities and Functions in the Ancient Near East*. Lund: Ohlssons.

Schäfer, Peter. 2002. *Mirror of His Beauty: Feminine Images of God from the Bible to the Early Kabbalah*. Princeton: Princeton University Press.

Schniedewind, William M. 1995. *The Word of God in Transition: From Prophet to Exegete in the Second Temple Period*. JSOTSup 197. Sheffield: JSOT Press.

Segal, Robert A. 2004. *Myth: A Very Short Introduction*. Oxford: Oxford University Press.

Sharma, Arvind. 2002. The Hermeneutics of Suspicion: A Case Study from Hinduism. *HTR* 94:353–68.

Smith, Wilfred Cantwell. 1993. *What Is Scripture? A Comparative Approach*. Minneapolis: Fortress.

Toorn, Karel van der. 1996. *Family Religion in Babylonia, Syria, and Israel: Continuity and Changes in the Forms of Religious Life*. Leiden: Brill.

———. 1997. The Iconic Book: Analogies between the Babylonian Cult of Images and the Veneration of the Torah. Pages 229–48 in *The Image and the Book: Iconic Cults, Aniconism, and the Rise of Book Religion in Israel and the Ancient Near East*. Edited by Karel van der Toorn. CBET 21. Louvain: Peeters.

———. 2007. *Scribal Culture and the Making of the Hebrew Bible*. Cambridge: Harvard University Press.

Von Hendy, Andrew. 2002. *The Modern Construction of Myth*. Bloomington: Indiana University Press.
Wardman, A. E. 1996. Myth in Greek Historiography. Pages 357–67 in *Philosophy, Religious Studies, and Myth*. Edited by Robert A. Segal. New York: Garland.
Weinfeld, Moshe. 1972. *Deuteronomy and the Deuteronomic School*. Oxford: Clarendon.
Whybray, R. N. 1965. *Wisdom in Proverbs: The Concept of Wisdom in Proverbs 1–9*. SBT 1/45. London: SCM.

Covenant and Contingence: The Historical Encounter between God and Israel

Robert S. Kawashima

However one chooses to define myth—and as this volume demonstrates, there exists more than one viable option—it is an intrinsically comparative concept, designating as it does a broad class of cross-cultural phenomena. Consider, for example, Georges Dumézil, that great Indo-European mythologist, who made of comparison a type of fundamental intellectual principle: "On ne définit très bien les choses que par comparaison avec autre chose."[1] To employ the concept of myth in biblical studies, then, is to situate some aspect of biblical literature in relation to "the mythical." These comparisons may be conceptualized concretely in terms of more or less direct historical relations—for example, the relation of Gen 1 to ancient Near Eastern creation myths—or abstractly in terms of formal or structural resemblances—the approach taken here.[2] Comparison, furthermore, can be negative (contrastive) as well as positive. Indeed, in the present study, as its title implies, I make just such a negative comparison, arguing as I do for the historical, as opposed to mythical, nature of the "encounter" between Israel and its God, at least according to certain traditions. I do not question the importance of myth as a critical lens for studying the Hebrew Bible. I merely propose (as a particular application

---

1. "One does not define things well except by comparison with something else" (televised interview with Bernard Pivot, *Apostrophes*, 18 July 1986). On Dumézil's comparative work as a structuralist, see Milner 2008, 45–63.

2. For a more detailed discussion of comparison, specifically with respect to biblical studies, see Kawashima 2007.

of Dumézil's dictum) that in order to define myth, one must compare it to what it is not, namely, history.

In this chapter, I adopt Mircea Eliade's structural-symbolic definition of myth.[3] Properly mythical events, in his view, take place in a qualitatively distinct past he refers to as *illud tempus*, "that time": "This primordial situation is not historical, it is not calculable chronologically; what is involved is a mythical anteriority, the time of origin, what took place 'in the beginning,' *in principio*" (1959, 92). In other words, it does not precede reality in chronological fashion, but underlies it as its paradigm. What this means, as I have argued elsewhere at greater length, is that mythical thought conceives of the cosmos as a static system, composed of various elements and relations that are eternal, necessary, and essential (Kawashima 2006; see also Levenson 1987, 102–3). For if Louis Althusser—to anticipate subsequent discussion—would have the "aleatory materialist" philosopher reason "not in terms of the Necessity of the accomplished fact, but in terms of the contingency of the fact to be accomplished" (2006, 174), the symbolic significance of "that time" (the mythic past) is precisely to be always-already accomplished, that is, necessary.

History, in contrast, belongs to what I call "this time"—a concept implied but apparently not explicitly developed by Eliade. The historical past, too, may be irreversible and therefore necessary, but the properly historical event was not always already a fait accompli. Rather, by virtue of the fact that it takes place within "this time," it had to emerge at a certain "measurable" moment (the date of the event) out of the contingency of an unknown future. Historical thought thus apprehends the world as a realm of accidence, contingence, and time. This properly empirical reality is thinkable as such only in opposition to some strictly utopian ideal beyond the empirical—Israel's God, Plato's forms. Historical thought, in other words, constitutes a dualism. Alexandre Kojève touches on this point: "For it is quite obvious that Realism is necessarily dualist, and that an ontological dualism is always 'realist'" (1969, 154). In stark contrast, the cosmos of myth, which precedes dualist thought—both logically and historically—is a monism, a single metaphysical system comprising humanity, divinity,

---

3. Eliade's theories have come under a great deal of criticism, perhaps most notably those of Jonathan Z. Smith: see esp. 1978, 88–103, 289–309; and 1987, 1–23. While I cannot engage in these controversies here, I do maintain that Eliade's definition of myth holds up under scrutiny; see Kawashima 2006, 228 n. 7.

and nature. For the immanent gods of myth ultimately represent the forces and principles of the cosmos itself.

Myth and history thus designate two modes of narrative, each corresponding to a distinct conception of the past. Myth, by projecting the cosmos into "that time," represents it as a system of relations that is, as R. G. Collingwood observes, "quasi-temporal": "the narrator is using the language of time-succession as a metaphor in which to express relations which he does not conceive as really temporal [namely,] ... the relations between various gods or various elements of the divine nature" (1946, 15). History purports rather to recount the empirical past, a set of contingent temporal events transpiring within "this time." Following Eliade, then, I do not define myth in terms of the actors involved (gods and heroes); thus not every narrative involving divine agency (e.g., the Deuteronomistic History) is a myth. Nor do I define it in terms of the theme of origins; thus not all etiological tales (e.g., J's Primeval History) are myths. Least of all do I define it in terms of its truth value (fiction vs. fact), for myth no less than history concerns itself with truth, but truth conceived of as timeless. Conversely, a history can be false—one denying the Holocaust, for example—just as the modern novel, although a fabrication, is an historical narrative form—"history-like," to borrow Hans Frei's (1974, 10–16) famous term.

Myth, History, and the Archaeology of Knowledge

Ultimately, one should analyze myth and history in terms of that larger historical-epistemological project Michel Foucault called the "archaeology of knowledge."[4] They constitute two discrete modes of thought, two epistemes or discourse configurations, separated as such by a "rupture" or "break." The long-standing thesis in biblical studies positing a "Mosaic" or "monotheistic" revolution in Israelite religion is a partial recognition of this underlying mutation in thought.[5]

---

4. See, e.g., Foucault 1972. For an overall survey of Foucault's work, see Gutting 1989; for an extremely succinct yet incisive discussion of Foucault's major theses, see Milner 1991, 27–31.

5. For a fuller discussion of the "archaeology" of biblical religion, see Kawashima 2004a, 190–214; and 2006. For an informative but radically different (negative) account of the "distinctiveness" hypothesis, see Machinist 1991. For a general survey of the field, see Miller 1985.

Three caveats are in order, however, with respect to this traditional hypothesis. First, it is imprecise, because the distinction between polytheism and monotheism is too superficial to capture the profound metaphysical divide separating myth from history. Second, it is a mistake to speak of the "uniqueness" of Israelite religion, whether this is thought to bear witness to a putative revelation—so G. Ernest Wright (1950)— or to the singular genius of a particular people—so, at least arguably, Yehezkel Kaufmann (1972).[6] In contrast, my thesis merely but precisely states that an epistemic rupture has taken place. By an accident of history this break happens to cut through biblical traditions, but it is in no way peculiar to them. Inasmuch as this cut traverses other traditions in the ancient world, the concept of history, not unlike that of myth, is inherently comparative. In this regard, I have already referred to (and will return to) ancient Greek thought. I suspect that this epistemic event is ultimately related to the so-called Axial Age, but this larger hypothesis must wait for another day.[7] As a corollary, one should note that inasmuch as this cut traverses biblical traditions, it distinguishes between mythical (i.e., "pagan") and historical elements within the biblical corpus itself.[8] In other words, my archaeological analysis is not yet another instance of ancient Israelite "exceptionalism." Finally, my thesis does not address the ostensible superiority of one or another religious tradition. As a purely agnostic project, it examines the discursive break separating various theological statements, without addressing the truth values, relative or absolute, of those statements.

---

6. Wright's theological bias is undeniable. Whether and to what extent Kaufmann's magnum opus is apologetic is open to debate. Kaufmann himself explicitly denies this allegation: "It is not undertaken in an apologetic spirit and in the hope of restoring tradition to its lost eminence" (1972, 1). But inasmuch as he traces everything nonpagan in the world back to Moses and his revelatory experience, his argument seems irreducibly theological and apologetic: "As Moses must be considered the initiator of a religious revolution, so he must be considered the creator of an original idea" (227); "The beginning of his work was a prophetic experience. He did not learn a priestly doctrine in Egypt, Midian, or elsewhere" (228). See Levenson's critical remarks on Kaufmann (1988, 3–13).

7. See Halpern's related remarks (1987, 88).

8. My archaeological analysis of myth and history thus does not preclude the discovery of mythic elements within the collection of texts now known as the Hebrew Bible; see, e.g., Childs 1960; Levenson 1987, 102–11.

If I do not claim that historical thought is inherently superior (or inferior) to mythical thought, I do maintain that it is necessarily secondary. Before human knowledge conceived of the finitude of historical existence, it possessed the more intuitive or natural concept of nonfinite being, namely, the cyclical time of myth, what Eliade called the "eternal return." I propose this as a revision of Descartes's position: "I must not think that my conception of the infinite has come about, not through a proper idea, but by a denial of the finite. ... [M]y primary concept is rather of the infinite than of the finite" (1971, 85). The relatively artificial, derived nature of historical thought can also arguably be inferred from Foucault's archaeology of the human sciences. For in *The Order of Things* he contends that knowledge throughout the "classical age"—that is, the mid-seventeenth through eighteenth centuries—is based on a "coherence ... between the theory of representation and the theories of language, of the natural orders, and of wealth and value" (1973, xxiii), so that the "natural history" of Linnaeus, for example, in fact classifies nature, maps it onto a two-dimensional surface, a "general grid of differences" (145). Within the classical episteme, then, "time is never conceived as a principle of development for living beings in their internal organization" (150); and as a result, it is "impossible for *natural history* to conceive of *the history of nature*" (157). It is only in the "modern episteme," analyzed in part 2 of *The Order of Things* (217–387), that "labour, life, [and] language" (250) become objects of a form of knowledge in which "a profound historicity penetrates into the heart of things" (xxiii).

One of the burdens of theistic religions is defining the relationship between the human and the divine. What institutions and obligations bind these two parties, and how were they established? What, in other words, is the "human condition"? In what follows, I will argue for the existence of two versions of the human condition, two concepts, one mythical, the other historical. In spite of their surface similarities and the analogous religious-symbolic functions they perform, I will argue that they are homonyms, not synonyms—terms developed especially by Lacan and his followers to distinguish between the superficial meaning of words and their underlying significance as concepts. As Georges Canguilhem relatedly observed of the life sciences: "the historian should not make the error of thinking that persistent use of a particular term indicates an invariant underlying concept or that persistent allusion to similar experimental observations connotes affinities of method or approach" (1988, 11). In the present case, one should not be misled by the similarities of various "cognates," "parallels," and so forth, into precipitously treating them as synonyms. They may be homonyms, that is, they may belong to different epistemes.

The early Althusser's concept of alienation provides an elegant account of the distinction between these two homonyms:

> In short, the final historical totality, which marks the end of alienation, is nothing but the reconquered unity of the labourer and his product. This end is simply the restoration of the origin, the reconquest of the original harmony after a tragic adventure. ... Yet it is only in a formal sense that the final unity is the restoration of the original unity. The worker who reappropriates what he himself produces is no longer the primitive worker, and the product he reappropriates is no longer the primitive product. Men do not return to the solitude of the domestic economy, and what they produce does not revert to being what it once was, the simple object of their needs. This *natural* unity is destroyed; the unity that replaces it is *human*. (1997, 137; written in 1947)

His clear distinction between "natural" and "human" unity is analogous to what I am calling, respectively, myth and history. The later Althusser, while placing greater emphasis on the "encounter," would similarly speak of the "void"—the contingent space of history—in which, taking his cue from Epicurus and Lucretius, the *clinamen* "causes an atom to 'swerve' from its vertical fall in the void, and, breaking the parallelism in an almost negligible way at one point, induce *an encounter* with the atom next to it" (2006, 169). Lacan's well-known interest in the "encounter," which no doubt influenced Althusser in this regard, is also relevant:

> Where do we meet this real? ... First, the *tuché*, which we have borrowed ... from Aristotle, who uses it in his search for cause. We have translated it as *the encounter with the real*. The real is beyond the *automaton*, the return, the coming-back, the insistence of the signs, by which we see ourselves governed by the pleasure principle. ... What is repeated, in fact, is always something that occurs—the expression tells us quite a lot about its relation to the *tuché*—as if by chance. (1978, 53–54)[9]

---

9. For trenchant and lucid explications of these epistemological issues in Lacan's thought, see Milner 1991 and 2003.

The natural unity of myth is necessary and therefore timeless, given as such without need of becoming. In the absence of a natural unity—alienation, the void—human unity can only come about through a contingent historical event, an "encounter with the real" that occurs "as if by chance." Alienation, contingency, encounter—these concepts will trace the outline of the Bible's historical thought.

The Human Condition

According to various myths, the human condition is established in the time of creation as part of the cosmic order. That is, it is conceived of as an eternal, necessary, essential relation defining the place of humans vis-à-vis the gods—a natural unity. Consider the primary institutions joining heaven and earth. The city, comprising both temple and palace, is timeless and of divine origin (see Kawashima 2004b, 491–92). Thus, in *Enuma Elish*, for example, Marduk, after vanquishing Tiamat, establishes his cosmic rule by founding his temple Esagila in Babylon, which city he designates the "centre of religion" (V.130; in Dalley 2000, 259). Similarly, in the prologue to the Laws of Hammurabi, the king locates his divine calling in the mythic past, when Anu and Enlil "allotted supreme power over all peoples to the god Marduk" (i.1–26; in Roth 1995), namely, the time of creation. In effect, his rule is, to borrow Eliade's phrase, "homologizable to a founding of the world" (1959, 21). As the Sumerian King List relatedly informs us, "kingship was lowered from heaven" (*ANET*, 265). To modern ears, these fantastic claims made on behalf of earthly realities—Babylon, Hammurabi—sound like boasts of hubris and/or madness. What they mean to say, however, is that civilization is neither human nor historical, but rather mythical and divine.

Within these institutions, the essence of human life is likewise determined. *Enuma Elish*, by establishing a natural unity between Babylon and Marduk, simultaneously creates by extension an eternal relation between Marduk and the Babylonians. According to Marduk's decree, the basic function of humankind is to serve the gods: "Let me create a primeval man. / The work of the gods shall be imposed (on him), and so they shall be at leisure" (VI.7–8). Ea, in the Atrahasis Epic, similarly declares: "Create primeval man, that he may bear the yoke! / Let him bear the yoke, the work of Ellil, / Let man bear the load of the gods!" (I.195–197; in Dalley 2000). The burden of humankind is precisely the work of culture, in particular, agriculture and sacrifice: "They took hold of … / Made new picks and spades, / Made big canals / To feed people and sustain the gods" (I.336–339).[10] In other words, work, like the city, is eternal.

The rule of law finds its place within the same configuration. According to the Mesopotamian concept of kingship, Wolfram von Soden notes, the kings were to be "representatives of the gods, or of the high god," and were, more generally, to oversee "service to the gods" and "provision for the poor and the weak" (1994, 63). The Laws of Hammurabi, spelling out the principles of justice enjoined upon the king and his subjects, were presumably bequeathed to this "pious prince, who venerates the gods, to make justice prevail in the land" (i 27–49) at the moment of his divine appointment—as suggested by the stela's depiction of Hammurabi and Shamash, the god of justice.

The human condition, then, consists of two unchanging obligations: "veneration" of the gods through just behavior, and "service" of the gods through sacrificial observance. Establishing the relation of humans to the divine world at the moment of their creation makes it internal to human nature, indeed, internal to the cosmic order. Thus, if this view of human existence seems tragically deterministic, it is also, as the Atrahasis Epic demonstrates, absolutely necessary and essential to the cosmos as a whole. For without humans to serve them, the gods would turn on one another, as the Igigi did against the Anunnaki, in revolt against their all-too-human existence (Kawashima 2006, 249–50).

The flood, in Mesopotamian tradition, constitutes a distinct boundary in time—a vivid illustration of Eliade's concept of *illud tempus*. That kingship, according to the Sumerian King List, must be lowered from heaven a second time after the flood, indicates that the latter completely disrupts human existence. One might be tempted to interpret the figure of Atrahasis (the flood's sole survivor) as the embodiment or guarantor of the continuity of humanity, but this shift in cosmic time coincides with a transformation of the human species itself—from "primitive" to "modern"—that effectively cuts him off from his ostensible progeny. The version of the flood myth embedded in tablet 11 of the Epic of Gilgamesh further develops this notion in Utnapishtim's apotheosis and his spatial-symbolic relocation to the mouth of the rivers—"that place" as the correlative of "that time." In this way, the mythic past is hermetically sealed, even

---

10. The eventual transformation of "primeval man" (*lullû*) into "mortal man" (*awīlu*) in no way affects this primary condition.

from the immediately succeeding age of epic heroes. Gilgamesh, himself two-thirds divine, may bring back the rumor of the time before the flood, but the singular nature of his achievement—the proverbial exception that proves the rule—only underscores the inaccessibility of the antediluvian era. One should recall here Hesiod's myth of the five ages, each of which corresponds to a different race of men, comparable to the mutation that takes place in the Atrahasis Epic. As Jean-Pierre Vernant has observed of its apparently linear dimension: "If the race of gold is called 'the first,' it is not because it arose one fine day, before the others, in the course of linear and irreversible time. ... [I]t embodies virtues—symbolized by gold—which are at the top of a scale of nontemporal values. The succession of the races in time reflects a permanent, hierarchical order in the universe" (1983, 6). To return to the king list, then, its emphatically linear form does not give literary expression to a genuinely historical mode of thought, but rather to a one-dimensional "science of order" (von Soden 1994, 145–48).

Finally, it is worth noting that Israel, too, possessed a mythic tradition touching upon the human condition. The Song of Moses (Deut 32) preserves what appears to be a fragment of a Yahwistic myth of Israel's national-ethnic identity:

> When Elyon bequeathed [*hanḥēl*] the nations [*gôyim*],
> When he divided up humankind,
> He set the boundaries [*gĕbūlōt*] of the peoples [*'ammîm*],
> By the number of the sons of God.
> Thus Yahweh's portion is his people,
> Jacob his allotted estate [*naḥălātô*]. (Deut 32:8–9)

According to the well-known variant reading attested to in both the Dead Sea Scrolls (4QDeut^j) and the Septuagint,[11] Elyon, as head of the pantheon, created the "nations"—that is, the "peoples" along with their "boundaries"—as private "estates" for each of his "sons."[12] Each nation, then, constitutes the correlation of a particular people, land, and god. This myth, by projecting Israel's origin into "that time," much as Hammurabi did his divine mandate, establishes a natural unity between each national-ethnic group and its respective god. The exclusivity of this mythic relationship,

---

11. For a general discussion, see Knohl 2003, 52–53, and references.
12. On the "olden gods," see Cross 1998, 73–83.

one should further note, already conforms to the concept of proto-monotheism that Baruch Halpern discerns in Israel as well as its neighbors:

> [T]he "Hebrew" successor-states to the Egyptian empire in Asia, all of which crystallized at the close of the Bronze Age along the major trade routes from Mesopotamia to Egypt ... appear uniformly to have devoted themselves to the worship of the national god. ... On the Mediterranean littoral, adherence to the cult of a single high god seems to have been taken early as the natural way of things. (1987, 84; see also Wellhausen 1957, 440)

In other words, the transformation of myth into history does not coincide with the evolution of polytheism into monotheism.

The Encounter

According to the prose sources of the Bible, the God of Israel is transcendent, not immanent as are the gods of myth. As a corollary, the institutions joining God to humanity—city, temple, palace—do not exist from the beginning of time; they must come into being. The human condition is thus defined not as a natural unity but as a state of alienation. An echo of the idea of "natural unity" is to be found in the garden of Eden, which, it is understood, is attached to God's home—apparently eternal, not unlike Marduk's. The function of this prelapsarian unity, however, is precisely to be lost (Kawashima 2004b). J's Primeval History thus goes on to trace how humans are progressively alienated from Yahweh, from Adam and Eve's expulsion from the divine estate (Gen 3:22–24), to Cain's banishment from God's presence or "face" (4:14), to humankind's dispersal from Babel "over the face of all the earth" (11:8). P's concept of alienation is more radical (Knohl 1995, 124–64). According to Gen 1, there is no original unity, only the metaphysical dualism of spirit and matter, hypostasized in the description of "the wind of God ... sweeping over the face of the waters" (v. 2). God, in other words, is wholly alien to the physical world, not to mention the human species inhabiting that world (Kawashima 2006). Indeed, it is only in Egypt under Moses' tutelage that Israel (and only Israel) comes to know the Tetragrammaton (Exod 6:2–3). While E's account of creation is lost to us—if it ever existed—one can still infer the same structure of alienation. For, again, Israel does not learn Elohim's proper name until the time of the exodus from Egypt (Exod 3:14–15). According to both E and P, then, and in striking contrast even to J, none of the ancestors from Abraham to Moses knows the true identity of "the god of the fathers."[13] In order to put the biblical concept of alienation into proper perspective, one need only recall Bruno Snell's observation of the Greeks' relation to their gods: "they looked upon their gods as so natural and self-evident that they could not even conceive of other nations acknowledging a different faith or other gods" (1982, 24).

These writers thus conceive of the human condition as a problem to be solved in and through history. The solution they provide is the concept of the encounter between Israel and Yahweh, that is, the call. It is closely related to Althusser's theory of the constitution of the subject in ideology, namely, interpellation. He provides a genuine insight into the biblical text itself when he offers in illustration of his theory the example of Moses at Sinai:

> God thus defines himself as the Subject *par excellence*, he who is through himself and for himself ("I am that I am"), and he who interpellates his subject, the individual subjected to him by his very interpellation, i.e. the individual named Moses. And Moses, interpellated-called by his Name, having recognized that it "really" was he who was called by God, recognizes that he is a subject, a subject *of* God, a subject subjected to God, *a subject through the Subject and subjected to the Subject*. The proof: he obeys him, and makes his people obey God's Commandments. (2008, 53)

---

13. The initial alienation of this divine kinsman stands in stark contrast to the general system of family religion in the ancient Near East. As van der Toorn rightly observes: "Though for most generations the family god was simply the 'god of their father,' whom they had inherited rather than chosen, the devotion of the family to a particular deity must have had a beginning. What was the motive of their distant ancestor who decided that this deity and not another one would be his god and the god of his children?" (1996, 78–79). The motives he provisionally reconstructs all presuppose a natural unity between ancestor and deity: a "link between profession and devotion," i.e., scribes (81), and "topographical proximity" (82), i.e., natives. Even in the case of Amorite family religion, which was "rooted in a tradition of pastoral nomadism," the family deities were related to "the traditional land of their ancestors" (88)—native, again. Abraham's nomadic relation to God is altogether different. Yahweh, by all accounts, comes from neither Ur of the Chaldeans nor Haran nor, for that matter, Canaan.

If Althusser thus explicitly bases interpellation on an encounter—here God and Moses, earlier a policeman and a civilian (48)—our analysis of biblical narratives on this point reveals that the encounter is meaningless in the presence of a natural unity. No call without prior alienation. Not coincidentally, J's Primeval History functions as an exposition to the calling of Abraham, that turning point in human history: "Go from your land and from your kin and from your father's house to the land that I will show you, and I will make you a great nation and bless you and make your name great, so that you will be a blessing" (Gen 12:2). Abraham is, in effect, commissioned to reunite his descendants with Yahweh: "For I have singled him out, so that he might command his sons and his house after him to keep the way of Yahweh by doing righteousness and justice, so that Yahweh might bring forth for Abraham what he promised him" (Gen 18:19). J's history thus has the structure of a "tragic adventure": humans were never meant to remain in the garden (Kawashima 2004b); on the contrary, their expulsion, although an apparent setback, plays a crucial positive role in history. Abraham's historical role, deriving from his human unity with Yahweh, presupposes the dissolution of that natural unity associated with Eden.

According to E as well, Abraham must be singled out and commissioned by God, an event we hear about thanks only to a tangential remark he makes to Abimelech: "God made me wander from my father's house" (20:13). One should also recall in this regard E's famous account of the Binding of Isaac, in which Elohim's call of Abraham is put to the "test" (Gen 22).

For P, alienation takes the spatial form of the dualism established in Gen 1. P's history thus comprises a series of dispensations that progressively introduce God into empirical reality under the aegis of a sequence of divine names: the Noahic covenant as Elohim, the Abrahamic covenant as El Shadday, and the Mosaic covenant as Yahweh. In this way, God is finally united with Israel when he takes up residence in the "tent of meeting," the telos of P's history: "And they will know that I am Yahweh their God who brought them out of the land of Egypt so that I might dwell among them" (Exod 29:46). The future-contingent tense indicates that previously Israel had not known their God, and their God had not dwelt among them. If P's God does not precisely "call" his chosen ones, he does address them in a series of second-person imperatives: you will not consume blood (Gen 9:1–17); you will circumcise your sons (17:1–14); you will observe the Sabbath (Exod 31:12–17; 35:1–3).

The call makes possible a relationship between previously alien parties—a human unity. It is formalized in the biblical concept of the covenant. The historical (rather than mythical) discourse surrounding alienation and the call explains the noteworthy extension of ancient Near Eastern political forms to the relation—whether *bĕrît* or *'ēdût*—joining the human community to the divine realm.[14] Out of the political "covenant," a theological homonym was forged, necessitated by a gap or lacuna in mythic thought.[15] It matters little whether it was an Israelite invention, and thus more or less peculiar to biblical tradition.[16] Wherever it is found, rather, it provides evidence of the appearance of historical thought. Conversely, one should consider its uneven distribution within the biblical corpus. It is no coincidence that the mythic fragment in Deut 32 discussed above fails to mention such a covenant.[17] For here Israel belongs to Yahweh by eternal birthright, rendering superfluous in advance any subsequent pact. Nor does it appear in those poems generally identified as "archaic," and for the same reason: Gen 49, Exod 15, Judg 5, Hab 3, and so on.[18] The cut between history and myth does not coincide with that between the biblical and the nonbiblical, but traverses these categories.

In a telling contrast, the prose sources emphasize the centrality of the covenant, which is premised in turn on the encounter between God and Israel. In J it begins with Abraham's divine call in Gen 12:1–3, and it culminates in the covenant Yahweh establishes with Abraham in Gen 15. The

---

14. For a discussion of the covenant and its relationship to the language of kinship, see Cross 1998, 3–21.

15. In fact, every revolution in thought produces a revolution in terminology, viz., a set of crucial homonyms; see, e.g., the theses on "terminology" Althusser proposes in relation to Marx vis-à-vis "classical political economy" (1970, 148).

16. See, e.g., McCarthy 1963, 168–77; and Sarna 1986, 140.

17. If one insists that this passage establishes a covenant relationship, it is a mythical (for the reasons stated above) homonym of the historical version to be found in the prose narratives.

18. The tangential reference to a "covenant" in Deut 33:9 is a possible exception. Related to this general absence, various "archaic" poems refer to Yahweh's battle march from what appears to be his strictly earthly abode: Deut 33:2; Judg 5:4–5; Ps 68:8–9, 18; Hab 3:3, 7 (see McCarter 1992, 124–29). If Yahweh is immanent, then these poems (or at least fragments therein) are arguably mythical (pagan), comparable to the Baal Cycle and *Enuma Elish*. Cross (1998, 19–21) seems to trace the covenant all the way back to the traditions and institutions underlying archaic poetry. How to map the cut between myth and history onto his reconstruction of early Israelite religion is an interesting and important question, which I cannot address here.

encounter at Sinai does not so much establish the covenant as fulfill it. The tokens of the divine presence—"smoke" (*'āšān*) and "fire" (*'ēš*) (Gen 15:17 and Exod 19:18), not cloud and lightning as in E—serve to link the Abrahamic covenant to its completion at Sinai. According to E, the children of Israel are reunited with their newly acquainted God, Yahweh, in the covenant ceremony at Horeb. The covenantal obligations in this tradition are contained in the Book of the Covenant, E's collection of ethical, civic, and cultic laws. The importance of this encounter is emphasized by the meal concluding the proceedings, as Israel's representatives, Moses, Aaron, his sons, and the seventy elders, ascend the mountain and have a "visionary experience" (*wayyeḥĕzû*) of God (24:11). Finally, P, in order to overcome the problem of divine transcendence or alienation (Kawashima 2006), actually constructs a series of covenants in a series of encounters: Elohim and Noah, El Shadday and Abraham, and Yahweh and Moses along with the Israelites (Cross 1973, 295–300; Kawashima 2010, 56–58). Each encounter, sealed with a covenant, brings Yahweh closer to unification with Israel. P's periodization of history may resemble Eliade's notion of mythic time—recall, for example, Hesiod's myth of the Five Ages. But whereas Hesiod's ages are nonlinear and discrete (see above), P's four ages take place in a linear and continuous time line. Unlike Hammurabi's law code, this law is given in human time, albeit an abnormal time—the so-called wilderness period.

What separates the concept of the covenant as a "human unity" from the "natural unity" of myth is not merely the structure (dialectical or not) of "alienation," but also the logic of contingence. For the encounter underlying the covenant could fail to take place. It only comes about through what Althusser calls the "swerve" or "clinamen," which he identifies as the figure of an "underground history" of the "materialism … of the aleatory and of contingency" (2006, 167). What is more, the encounter could fail to take hold. Interpellation must hit its mark; the call must elicit the proper response; and so on. As late as 1970, Althusser more or less took for granted its success: "verbal call or whistle, the one being hailed always recognizes that it is really him who is being hailed" (repr., 2008, 48). This confidence seems to derive from his belief that ideology is "eternal": "ideology has always-already interpellated individuals as subjects" (49). But as he would later—no doubt chastened by the disappointments of history—acknowledge in a patent revision of his earlier position: "everything in [history] could have swung the other way, depending on the encounter or non-encounter of Moses and God, or the encounter of the comprehension or non-comprehension of the prophets. The proof is that it was necessary to explain to the prophets the meaning of what they reported of their conversations with God!" (2006, 179). Althusser once again perceives something crucial in biblical tradition. Yahweh becomes the God of Israel, and Israel the "chosen" people, within a history that could have, and nearly did, turn out otherwise.[19] Biblical narrative repeatedly emphasizes the precariousness of Yahweh's nationalist project. Israel would not exist were it not for certain key human decisions: "And [Abram] believed Yahweh, and Yahweh reckoned it to him as righteousness" (Gen 15:6; J); "Everything that Yahweh has spoken we will do and obey" (Exod 24:7; E). Conversely, certain critical errors threaten this enterprise: "I have seen this people, and look, it is a stiff-necked people. And now, let me alone, so that my anger may burn against them, and I may finish them off, and I will make you into a great nation" (Exod 32:9–10; E); "I will strike them with a pestilence and disown them, and I will make you into a great nation, mightier than them" (Num 14:12; J).

The very idea of the so-called wilderness generation—an entire generation (save for a few exceptional souls) sentenced to die on the way to Canaan—has, among other symbolic functions, that of indicating that the nation would never have come into existence but for the unexpected amnesty God grants to their offspring. Even P, who arguably makes the fewest concessions to human freedom, teaches this lesson. For the deaths of Nadab and Abihu (Lev 10) demonstrate that God's very presence, belatedly established in the tent of meeting, is volatile, the result of a delicate balance that can easily be lost, as Ezekiel would later testify. It is remarkable that a culture should imagine so vividly its own aborted birth—the collective equivalent of an individual's awareness of mortality. But the nation's existence must be fragile, when it is in principle contingent upon each and every Israelite's covenant loyalty (ḥesed), an idea expressed most fully by the Deuteronomistic editor: "And I am making this covenant and this oath, not only with you, but both with those who are here with us today standing before Yahweh our God, and with those who are not here with us today" (Deut 29:14–15).

One might be tempted to discern the concept of alienation in Hesiod's myths of Prometheus and Pandora, and of the Five Ages. From the age

---

19. This sense of contingence is related to what Amos Funkenstein refers to as ancient Israel's "historical consciousness" (1993, 52).

of gold to iron, humans grow increasingly distant from the gods, just as they are fated, thanks to Prometheus's trickery, to live a life of pain, toil, and privation, culminating in death. In this tradition, however, the distance that opens up between heaven and earth is not a problem to be overcome. Rather, it is precisely that which separates careworn mortals from blessed immortals that joins them in a natural unity, an eternal relation willed by Zeus, whose designs do not fail. There is no question of overcoming this divide in and through history—that would be hubris. Rather, it is precisely by cooking that part of the animal designated for human consumption while burning the rest for the Olympians, by working the soil in order to extract the grain that Zeus has hidden away, and by marrying that treacherous "gift" bestowed by the gods upon men, that humankind assumes its proper place within the cosmos (Vernant 1981a and 1981b). In this light, the biblical idea that a people must be "redeemed," "ransomed," or "rescued" from their state of alienation in order to enter into a collective relationship with the national deity takes on its proper significance as a radical development in religious thought. The Greek tradition, too, would eventually conceive of the human condition as a problem. Most notably, alienation will be defined in relation to Truth, specifically as ignorance, whether due to some primary lack or secondary loss. The solution to this newly conceptualized problem, from Parmenides's chariot ride to Plato's ascent of the soul, is philosophy.

Conclusion

The radical distinction between myth and history is arguably a major break, that is, it cuts through all subsystems of thought, producing homonyms out of the concepts dealing with the gods, humans, the world, and so on. The human condition is one such set of homonyms. In the analysis offered here, interpellation serves as the governing heuristic concept: a contingent encounter between alienated parties. One should keep in mind, however, that interpellation's original function was to account for the constitution of subjects, subjects of ideology. It is premised specifically on a speech act between a first ("I") and second ("you") person: the "hail." Indeed, the biblical traditions I examined above reflect this speech act in the call an alienated God places upon his historically chosen people, in particular, in apodictic law, which scholars have noted is a distinctive, if not unique, feature of biblical law (see Mendenhall 1954; Sarna 1986, 142). My archaeological analysis thus raises a final point calling for further investigation: that the epistemic rupture contained in certain biblical traditions gave rise to a new concept of the human subject, a contingent, historical subject not determined by the "natural" unities of the mythic cosmos. The very idea of the subject, in other words, actually comprises a series of homonyms. One will thus need to write, with respect to biblical traditions, a history of the self and its related "technologies."

WORKS CITED

Althusser, Louis. 1970. Pages 11–198 in Louis Althusser and Étienne Balibar, *Reading Capital*. London: New Left Books.

———. 1997. *The Spectre of Hegel: Early Writings*. London: Verso.

———. 2006. *Philosophy of the Encounter: Later Writings, 1978–1987*. London: Verso.

———. 2008. *On Ideology*. London: Verso.

Canguilhem, Georges. 1988. *Ideology and Rationality in the History of the Life Sciences*. Cambridge: MIT Press.

Childs, Brevard S. 1960. *Myth and Reality in the Old Testament*. SBT 1/27. London: SCM.

Collingwood, R. G. 1946. *The Idea of History*. Oxford: Oxford University Press.

Cross, Frank Moore. 1973. *Canaanite Myth and Hebrew Epic*. Cambridge: Harvard University Press.

———. 1998. *From Epic to Canon: History and Literature in Ancient Israel*. Baltimore: Johns Hopkins University Press.

Dalley, Stephanie, ed. and trans. 2000. *Myths from Mesopotamia: Creation, the Flood, Gilgamesh, and Others*. Rev. ed. Oxford: Oxford University Press.

Descartes, René. 1971. *Philosophical Writings*. Trans. E. Anscombe and T. Geach. New York: Macmillan.

Eliade, Mircea. 1959. *The Sacred and the Profane: The Nature of Religion*. New York: Harcourt Brace & World.

Foucault, Michel. 1972. *The Archaeology of Knowledge*. Translated by A. M. Sheridan Smith. New York: Pantheon.

———. 1973. *The Order of Things: An Archaeology of the Human Sciences*. New York: Vintage.

Frei, Hans. 1974. *The Eclipse of Biblical Narrative*. New Haven: Yale University Press.

Funkenstein, Amos. 1993. *Perceptions of Jewish History*. Berkeley: University of California Press.

Gutting, Gary. 1989. *Michel Foucault's Archaeology of Scientific Reason.* Cambridge: Cambridge University Press.

Halpern, Baruch. 1987. "Brisker Pipes than Poetry": The Development of Israelite Monotheism. Pages 77–115 in *Judaic Perspectives on Ancient Israel.* Edited by Jacob Neusner, Baruch A. Levine, and Ernest S. Frerichs. Philadelphia: Fortress.

Kaufmann, Yehezkel. 1972. *The Religion of Israel: From Its Beginnings to the Babylonian Exile.* Translated and abridged by Moshe Greenberg. New York: Schocken.

Kawashima, Robert S. 2004a. *Biblical Narrative and the Death of the Rhapsode.* Indiana Studies in Biblical Literature. Bloomington: Indiana University Press.

———. 2004b. *Homo Faber* in J's Primeval History. *ZAW* 116:483–501.

———. 2006. The Priestly Tent of Meeting and the Problem of Divine Transcendence: An "Archaeology" of the Sacred. *JR* 86:226–57.

———. 2007. Comparative Literature and Biblical Studies: The Case of Allusion. *Prooftexts* 27:324–44.

———. 2010. Sources and Redaction. Pages 47–70 in *Reading Genesis: Ten Methods.* Edited by Ronald Hendel. Cambridge: Cambridge University Press.

Knohl, Israel. 1995. *The Sanctuary of Silence.* Minneapolis: Fortress.

———. 2003. *The Divine Symphony.* Philadelphia: Jewish Publication Society.

Kojève, Alexandre. 1969. *Introduction to the Reading of Hegel.* New York: Basic Books.

Lacan, Jacques. 1978. *The Four Fundamental Concepts of Psycho-Analysis.* Translated by Alan Sheridan. New York: Norton.

Levenson, Jon D. 1987. *Sinai and Zion: An Entry into the Jewish Bible.* Repr., San Francisco: HarperSanFrancisco.

———. 1988. *Creation and the Persistence of Evil.* Princeton: Princeton University Press.

Machinist, Peter. 1991. The Question of Distinctiveness in Ancient Israel: An Essay. Pages 196–212 in *Ah, Assyria …: Studies in Assyrian History and Ancient Near Eastern Historiography Presented to Hayim Tadmor.* Edited by Mordechai Cogan and Israel Ephʻal. Jerusalem: Magnes.

McCarter, P. Kyle, Jr. 1992. The Origins of Israelite Religion. Pages 119–36 in Hershel Shanks et al., *The Rise of Ancient Israel.* Washington, D.C.: Biblical Archaeology Society.

McCarthy, Dennis J., S.J. 1963. *Treaty and Covenant: A Study in Form in the Ancient Oriental Documents and in the Old Testament*. AnBib 21. Rome: Pontifical Biblical Institute.
Mendenhall, George E. 1954. Ancient Oriental and Biblical Law. *BA* 17:26–46, 50–76.
Miller, Patrick D. 1985. Israelite Religion. Pages 201–37 in *The Hebrew Bible and Its Modern Interpreters*. Edited by Douglas A. Knight and Gene M. Tucker. Philadelphia: Fortress.
Milner, Jean-Claude. 1991. Lacan and the Ideal of Science. Pages 27–42 in *Lacan and the Human Sciences*. Edited by Alexandre Leupin. Lincoln: University of Nebraska Press, 1991.
———. 2003. The Doctrine of Science. Pages 264–94 in vol. 1 of *Jacques Lacan: Critical Evaluations in Cultural Theory*. Edited by Slavoj Žižek. London: Routledge, 2003.
———. 2008. *Le périple structural: Figures et paradigme*. Paris: Verdier.
Roth, Martha T. 1995. *Law Collections from Mesopotamia and Asia Minor*. SBLWAW 6. Atlanta: Scholars Press.
Sarna, Nahum. 1986. *Exploring Exodus*. New York: Schocken.
Smith, Jonathan Z. 1978. *Map Is Not Territory: Studies in the History of Religions*. SJLA 23. Leiden: Brill.
———. 1987. *To Take Place: Toward Theory in Ritual*. Chicago: University of Chicago Press.
Snell, Bruno. 1982. *The Discovery of the Mind*. Mineola, N.Y.: Dover.
Soden, Wolfram von. 1994. *The Ancient Orient: An Introduction to the Study of the Ancient Near East*. Translated by Donald G. Schley. Grand Rapids: Eerdmans.
Toorn, Karel van der. 1996. *Family Religion in Babylonia, Syria, and Israel*. SHCANE 7. Leiden: Brill.
Vernant, Jean-Pierre. 1981a. The Myth of Prometheus in Hesiod. Translated by Janet Lloyd. Pages 43–56 in *Myth, Religion and Society: Structuralist Essays*. Edited by R. L. Gordon. Cambridge: Cambridge University Press.
———. 1981b. Sacrificial and Alimentary Codes in Hesiod's Myth of Prometheus. Translated by Janet Lloyd. Pages 57–79 in *Myth, Religion and Society: Structuralist Essays*. Edited by R. L. Gordon. Cambridge: Cambridge University Press.
———. 1983. *Myth and Thought among the Greeks*. London: Routledge & Kegan Paul.

Wellhausen, Julius. 1957. *Prolegomena to the History of Israel*. New York: Meridian.
Wright, G. Ernest. 1950. *The Old Testament against Its Environment*. SBT 1/2. London: SCM.

Is Genesis 1 a Creation Myth? Yes and No

Mark S. Smith

Myth and Its Modern Definers

Is Gen 1 a myth? The answer to this question depends on what one thinks a myth is and also on what one think about Gen 1. For believers in the Bible, the answer is, of course not. For many readers of the Bible, the idea of biblical stories as myths became a critical issue because of the discovery of tablets with stories from ancient Mesopotamia. For centuries, the Bible was considered the word of God, but texts emerging from excavations in Mesopotamia challenged the idea of the Bible as unique. When the Bible was studied in the context of ancient Near Eastern literature during the nineteenth and twentieth centuries, it no longer seemed to be so divine in its origins. Scholarly study of the Bible led to a reevaluation of the relationship of biblical literature to literature outside the Bible. Ancient Near Eastern literature was obviously not divine revelation for Jewish or Christian traditions, yet if extrabiblical literature showed stories or traditions that appear also in the Bible, then perhaps the Bible was not so divine either. Because of this, modern biblical study provoked a crisis of traditional faith. Perhaps the most dramatic example of biblical traditions found outside the Bible involved Mesopotamian tablets with the story of the flood as known from Gen 6–9.[1] The flood story was evident from a number of Mesopotamian stories (e.g., Atrahasis and Gilgamesh, tablet XII).[2] Sometimes the texts in the Bible and their Mesopotamian parallels

---

1. For the religious views of the sources of the biblical flood story as well as their resultant redaction together, see Harland 1996.
2. For convenient reference, see Dalley 2000. For a survey of ancient Near Eastern traditions about the flood, see Schmidt 1995. Atrahasis is discussed further below. Regarding the combination of Inanna's divine roles, note the comment of Harris

appeared to be so close that they seem to suggest a shared worldview or tradition. (To be sure, scholars also noted important differences between the Bible and these Mesopotamian stories.)

Modern discoveries have affected the understanding of Gen 1 in particular. Genesis 1 has often been compared with ancient Near Eastern texts, in particular with *Enuma Elish*. This narrative poem exalts the central figure, the god Marduk, who creates the universe in the wake of his victory over Tiamat, the cosmic Sea personified. While scholars generally view *Enuma Elish* as a myth, sometimes they have been reluctant to do the same with Gen 1. Yet, on the face of it, the biblical chapter resembles *Enuma Elish* in many respects, and it satisfies the common definition of myth as a story centered on divine figures or with any number of divine figures featuring prominently.[3] So for many readers of these texts, Gen 1 would certainly seem to be a myth.

Yet many other readers, professionals and nonprofessionals alike, have rejected the significance of the similarities, in part motivated by their religious attitudes toward the Bible. They champion the Bible's inerrancy and view extra-Israelite literature as pagan and untrue. Some scholars reject the comparisons on more formal grounds, that Gen 1 did not present the sorts of divine world and beings found in so many ancient Near Eastern myths.[4] Another way that some authors have tried to get around this problem has been to distinguish stories involving multiple deities in ancient Near Eastern literature from stories involving only one deity. In this approach, the Bible is monotheistic and not polytheistic, and therefore its texts are not myth.[5] That way, some scholars could regard the ancient Near Eastern texts as myths, but Gen 1 would not be a myth, and so its

---

(1991, 264): "The composer of the so-called standard version of the Gilgamesh Epic incorporated the original separate flood story into his version, surely aware of the contradictory depictions of the goddess."

3. This is a fairly typical approach to myth. Among more general treatments, see Segal 2004, 4–5; Kirk 1974, 23, 28–29; Oden 1987, 56; Mettinger 2007, 68–69.

4. Here note the comments of Coats 1983, 47: "If ancient Near Eastern myths lie behind this unit, it is nonetheless clear that the unit is no longer myth. The generic character of parallel mythology is not reproduced in the narrative itself." Coats concludes that Gen 1 is to be classified as a "report."

5. For example, Graf (2004, 53) writes, "In monotheistic Israel, every intervention of God in the visible world—from the creation to the ongoing protection of God's people—is understood as history: where God reveals the past, there is no place for myth."

divine revelation about creation could be maintained. As it turns out on further reflection, the logic behind this distinction does not seem particularly strong: why should the form of divinity serve as the criterion for the genre of myth? Indeed, many scholars see little logic in using theism as a criterion of genre, and so they do not draw this distinction. If we use the simple definition of myth as a story about the gods or divinity, then Gen 1 is a myth.

Still, the matter is not this simple. The difficulty goes back to ancient Greece, where the word *myth* originated. The English word *myth* derives from the Greek word *mythos*. If you look the word up in a dictionary of Classical Greek (e.g., Liddell and Scott 1996, 1151), you will find the meanings, "word, speech," as in public speech, conversation, a saying, or a command. It can also refer to a thing thought or an unspoken word. It also applies to a tale, a narrative, or a story, and it was used initially without any distinction between true or false stories. Over time the word came to refer to a fiction, fable, or children's story. The Harvard classicist Gregory Nagy attributes the lack of modern consensus about myth in part to the semantic shift of the word in antiquity to meaning something untrue, as opposed to "true things" (*alētheia*).[6]

The word *myth* has also had a complicated modern history. Some more recent studies, such as that of Andrew Von Hendy (2002), have shown how the word has had a long career, often reflecting modern attempts to define and understand religion and science and their proper relationship. The modern history of definitions of myth reads more like the story of trying to come to grips with the emergence of science within Europe and the discovery of other cultures outside Europe and the resulting efforts at finding a place for religion in light of these modern developments. Von Hendy correlates the rise of myth as a term in the second half of the eighteenth century to "epidemic defections from institutional Christianity and remarkable intellectual turmoil about the nature both of religion and of belief" (3). The word *religion* is a way to speak about the phenomena associated with religious practices across cultures (see J. Smith 1998), and *myths* serve as a term for the sacred stories of various cultures. *Myths*

---

6. For an explicit expression of this contrast, Nagy cites Pindar, *Olympian*, 1.27-29 (see Nagy 2002, esp. 241). Nagy attributes the change in the meaning of myth to the breakdown of the symbiosis between myth and ritual in the archaic and classical periods of ancient Greece. Prior to this breakdown, myth was at home, according to Nagy, in contexts of ritual performance.

could thus refer to religious stories both within Christianity and outside it. In the end, *myth* is an extremely problematic term because it developed to handle modern Western concerns about religion and science in relation to each other and in relation to non-Western cultures. Von Hendy considers *myth* in the modern context "a concept whose two and a half centuries under construction constitutes one the significant attempts at what the German philosopher of culture Hans Blumenberg calls the legitimation of modernity" (xviii). The history of the definitions for the word *myth* in modern usage does not resolve the problem of understanding myth; this history reflects the modern problem itself. For this reason alone, we should be skeptical about discovering some relatively neutral definition of myth beyond the basic (and arguably banal) definition of myth as religious stories.

Von Hendy's book also shows another problem with defining myth: its definitions often reflect the concerns of the fields of the scholars offering the definitions. It is not uncommon that scholars define myth in the image and likeness of their own disciplines.[7] It is unsurprising that theologians, depth psychologists, anthropologists, Marxists, or literary critics tend to see the concerns of their own fields in myths. At the same time, the different perceptions of myths by different disciplines are hardly without basis. As various approaches have suggested, myths do refer to political phenomena (e.g., in *Enuma Elish* and the Ugaritic story known as the Baal Cycle). Other myths do mention social groups (e.g., priestesses, at the end of Atrahasis). Religious institutions are referenced (*Enuma Elish*'s description of the temple Esagila and its mention of "Babylon, home of the great gods. We shall make it the centre of religion" [Dalley 2000, 259]).[8] Myths do evoke natural phenomena (e.g., the weather in the Baal Cycle, and the Tigris and Euphrates in *Enuma Elish* [Dalley 2000, 257; note also the discussion of the flood stories in Dalley 2000, 7)]). Myths also commemorate the past (e.g., Nintu's necklace of flies in Atrahasis [Lambert and Millard 1969, 163; Dalley 2000, 38 n. 42]). Myths draw widely on what scribes knew of their world, and they included all the various aspects of life and reality that different modern fields have seen in them. Out of the experience of the ancients came their literature, and out of their religious experience came their religious literature. It is valuable to see these different

---

7. See also Kirk 1974, 13–19. Note also critique of the recent tendency to privilege the political in myths by Sourvinou-Inwood 1997, 143; see also Clark 2004, 175–76.

8. See also Glassner 1995, 1815.

aspects of myth. These fields have made important contributions toward understanding the different dimensions of myth.[9]

At the same time, with all these particular modern fields weighing in on a definition or approach to myth, we do not arrive at a basic definition or idea of myth. Robert A. Segal provides a reason for this situation:

> Each discipline harbours multiple theories of myth. Strictly, theories of myths are theories of some much larger domain, with a myth a mere subset. For example, anthropological theories of myth are theories of myth *applied* to the case of myth. Psychological theories of myth are theories of the mind. Sociological theories of myth are theories of society. There are no theories of myth itself, for there is no discipline of myth in itself. Myth is not like literature, which, so it has or had traditionally been claimed, must be studied as *literature* rather than as history, sociology, or something else nonliterary. There is no study of myth as myth (2004, 2; Segal's italics).[10]

---

[9]. Let me add a qualification to this point: we should not dismiss the potential contributions of these approaches out of hand. They all have important perspectives to contribute to our understanding of the texts that we tend to regard as myths. For example, a book formative in my education was Erich Neumann's captivating work, *The Origins and History of Consciousness* (the foreword to the book was penned by Carl Jung; see Neumann 1954). This book offered a systematic presentation of Jung's thought as it applied to myth, to show how myths from across the globe captured different points in human psychological development. This is a contribution, and it is one that is perhaps being extended by those who attempt to include potential insights from neural science. See, for example, the essays in Hassin et al. 2005. One wonders what interesting sort of theorizing of myth may develop out of these sorts of studies.

Perhaps each person has what Wyatt (2005) calls "the mythic mind." Still the differences among myths are at least as interesting as those that are shared. Note the critique of Dundes (1996, 150–51) for the variety of myths in the world, which arguably undermines the notion of universal archetypes. One might be inclined to reformulate the contribution coming from such quarters, namely that different cultures generate myths that draw on their different cultural perceptions of human development. For a productive use of such theory, see Walls 2001.

[10]. This point is generally born out by Segal's (2004) short survey of nineteenth- and twentieth-century theories of myth and by the probing survey of this territory from the eighteenth century on produced by Von Hendy (2002). Von Hendy places a particular emphasis on the importance of German Romanticism on later modern theorizing about myth, as he believes this point has been overlooked in several quarters.

In this perspective, the problem with defining myth is not simply an etymological problem involving Greek *mythos*; it is also a modern problem that involves the way knowledge is organized in modern societies. That this may be a modern problem is suggested by the explosion of interest in myth in the twentieth century.[11] In other words, we may ask what drove this interest and correspondingly what impact it had on how moderns have understood myth. I would note one further problem about the modern exploration of myth: modern theorizing about myth has largely revolved around classical mythology, and its efforts to address ancient Near Eastern myths have been rather superficial.[12]

Because of these ancient and modern problems with the word *myth*, scholars have struggled to produce a proper definition. The classicist Fritz Graf could respond to the question of the nomenclature of "myth," "legend," or "epic poems" in this critical manner: "The question is irrelevant at best, misleading at worst: it is a matter of our categories, and there is no scholarly consensus as to what these categories mean" (2004, 54). His fellow classicist, Gregory Nagy, asks in the title of one of his essays, "Can Myth Be Saved?" (2002). The issue has been addressed also by scholars of ancient Mesopotamia, including Thorkild Jacobsen (1987, xiii) and Stephanie Dalley (2000, xvii). In biblical scholarship, Michael Fishbane (2003, 11 n. 46) declines to define myth in terms of a specific genre. Instead, he sees myths as accounts of deeds and personalities of the gods and heroes or their actions. In this approach, myth is as much a matter of content as it is the formal features of a genre. The classicist Geoffrey S. Kirk suggests that progress in understanding myth "is to be made by recognizing myth as a broad category, within which special forms and functions will require different kinds of explanation. The analysis that is to be applied to a myth

---

11. Von Hendy makes the point in the introduction to his fine book: "I was surprised in the course of this project, however, to discover how overwhelmingly the true century of myth is the twentieth" (2002, xiii).

12. On this point, I take Segal 2004 as representative of modern theorizing. Symptomatic of this classical bias in Segal's book is his otherwise engaging use of the Adonis myth to test various theories of myth; neither Segal not the authors whom he discusses ever mention the foreign setting of the story in Cyprus. Some modern theorists, such as Erich Neumann and Joseph Campbell, have ventured into ancient Near Eastern texts, but their efforts tend to conform these texts or their interpretation to the notions that they have derived on the basis of other material and hardly reflect a substantive engagement with them.

must be both flexible and multiform" (1984, 60). In other words, a simple definition of myth is not simple to figure out.

Using a simple definition of myth could also paper over problems. It sometimes lets some dubious assumptions sneak into the discussion. One assumption commonly made is that myths are traditional stories (see Kirk 1974, 23) designed to explain origins and are therefore set in the past. The great twentieth-century scholar of comparative religion Mircea Eliade put quite a good deal of emphasis on the purpose of myth to evoke or to reestablish "the creative era" (Kirk 1974, 63–64). In an address delivered in 1980, the anthropologist Edmund Leach defined a myth as "a sacred tale about past events that justify social action in the present" (1982, 74). Or, compare Alan Dundes's definition of myth as a "sacred narrative of how the world or mankind came to be in their present form" (1996, 148). Now it is true that many stories that are often called myths are set in the past, for example, the Mesopotamian flood narratives. Yet in view of some cases, one may ask how constitutive of myth is a past setting. For example, it is hardly clear that the Ugaritic Baal Cycle is set in a time of primordial origins. This raises the question as to whether other narratives in the more recent past or present and perhaps even in the future may be regarded as equally mythic in character.[13] Biblical and extrabiblical apocalyptic, for example, in Dan 7–12 and in the New Testament book of Revelation, ostensibly predict future events, yet they arguably qualify as myth, especially given their mythic imagery.

A second problem with a simple definition of myth as traditional stories involves the word *traditional*. For many scholars, "traditional" evokes an oral context of storytelling and transmission. Although it is true that many myths may have originated in an oral context, this is not always the case. Some myths probably did not. The Mesopotamian story of Erra and Ishum may be an example of a myth that did not derive from a traditional oral context, but rather may have originated as a written composition, generated within a scribal context. There is a related problem with the idea of "traditional," oral myths. Ancient myths that may have had oral origins survive only in written forms, and we have no access to their oral forms. Among its many accomplishments, Susan Niditch's book *Oral World and Written Word* (1996) has shown that some written works may very well

---

13. Segal 2004, 5: "The story can take place in the past … or in the present or the future."

imitate oral storytelling style. One implication of this fine insight is that we really do not have access to oral literature of the ancient Near East. We probably cannot get at traditional oral literature behind the written record. On this point, we may note Kirk's observation: "The vital fact is that myths in Greek literature exist for the most part only in brief allusions. ... The myths were so well known that formal exposition was unnecessary, and in the high classical period, at least, it was felt to be provincial. This changed in the Hellenistic world after the conquests of the Alexander the Great" (1974, 14). In the case of Mesopotamian myths, this material may stand at quite a distance from a strictly oral environment.

Ancients Signs of What Myths Are

From the discussion up to this point, it is evident it may not be the most productive strategy to deduce a definition of myth and then apply it in order to decide whether Gen 1 is myth, since after centuries of discussion scholars have been unable to arrive at a relatively clear definition of myth (Dundes 1996, 147–59). It seems that we need another strategy to address the question, is Gen 1 a myth? For the purposes of this discussion, I would like to try an inductive approach. It might be more productive to take a look at some of the features involved in the texts generally regarded as myths and then to observe how they compare with material in the Bible, including Gen 1. "Theories of myth may be as old as myth themselves," Segal (2004, 1) suggests, and so we may attempt to intuit from texts generally accepted as ancient Near Eastern myths what they seem to be and do and to see how this sort of information may help to address the question of myth and Gen 1. It will become clear in the discussion that follows that I am drawing on observations made by different scholars working on various ancient Near Eastern texts. I am going to try to synthesize a number of their observations and to use them to help us understand the question of myth and Gen 1.

To begin, we need to decide which texts are going to be considered for our discussion. In other words, which ancient Near Eastern texts should we use as examples of myth? Among scholars, there seems to be a consensus that Akkadian myths include the stories of *Enuma Elish*, Atrahasis, the Descent of Ishtar, Anzu, and Erra and Ishum. We may also add their Sumerian counterparts and antecedents, as well as other Sumerian works such as Enki and the World Order. The vast majority of scholars who use the term *myth* would also include several Hittite narratives, such as Telepinu. They would also include some Ugaritic texts, such the Baal Cycle (*KTU* 1.1–1.6), the Rituals and Myths of the Goodly Gods (*KTU* 1.23), or at least the narrative of lines 30–76, as well as the main part of Nikkal wa-Ib (*KTU* 1.24). These have been called myths in modern collections. James B. Pritchard's *Ancient Near Eastern Texts* (*ANET*) puts them under the rubric of "myths, epics, and legends," and these texts are listed under "canonical texts with a divine focus" in *The Context of Scripture* (*COS*). It also may be noted that the vast majority are narrative poems, a point underscored by the title of the collection *Ugaritic Narrative Poetry* (Parker 1997b), which contains the Ugaritic texts just mentioned. To stay on the safe side, in this discussion I will generally stick to these texts, which seem to fit most people's sense of myth as stories about gods or goddesses.[14]

The problem we are discussing may be seen more clearly for the ancient Near East if we pose the question in this way: how are the texts that modern scholars label as myths represented? In other words, how did the ancient scribes of these texts present them? What did they say these texts were about? To begin, several of these texts explicitly name deities as their subject matter by adding prose labels to the poetic texts. Attached to the only known written forms of the poems, these prose labels represent the earliest known interpretations of the poems. The label for the Ugaritic Baal Cycle is "about [lit. 'to'] Baal," or perhaps more technically speaking, "belonging to [the series of tablets called] Baal" (*lbʻl*, in *KTU* 1.6 I 1). This designation is not a genre marker for myth as such, since Ugaritic shows the same sort of markers for the stories of Kirta and Aqhat, "about Kirta" (*lkrt*, in *KTU* 1.14 I 1; 1.16 I 1) and "[about]"[15] Aqhat (*ʼ[l]aqht*, in *KTU* 1.19 I 1).[16] This sort of label indicates that an individual figure is in some sense the focus of the narrative. For the Baal Cycle, the label is important for showing that its ancient scribes regarded the text as being about the god. The final words of *Enuma Elish* likewise represent the text as "the Song of Marduk, Who defeated Tiamat and took the kingship" (Dalley 2000, 274). This quote suggests that the authors of *Enuma Elish* regarded the god

---

14. This is so even if at the end of the day one might jettison the category of myth altogether or at least avoid the idea of myth as a particular genre. For the latter, see Fishbane 2003, 11 n. 46.

15. The square brackets here are a convention scholars use to mark a letter that is not represented on the tablet where it may be damaged. The letter was probably there in ancient times, but today it cannot be seen.

16. These may all reflect the name or title of the tablet series to which they belong.

Marduk as its central topic. Likewise, the end of Atrahasis tells its audience that it is to extol the greatness of the god Enlil.[17] So in this respect the ancient labeling of these texts fits the modern notion that myths are about gods or goddesses.

Beyond this matter of individual divinities, the texts show a sense of what kind of text they are. Many are not simply narratives but are more specifically identified as songs. This idea is explicitly stated in texts, either in their opening or at their end. For this discussion, I will briefly note a handful of cases (see van der Toorn 2007, 13). The end of *Enuma Elish*, as noted above, refers to the text as "the Song of Marduk" (Lambert and Millard 1969, 7; Dalley 2000, 274). A second example comes from Atrahasis, named after its hero by modern scholars (his name literally means, "exceeding wise"). This text combines creation and flood traditions in a single composition. As the scholars Wilfred G. Lambert and Alan Millard note in their edition of Atrahasis (1969, 7, 104–5), this narrative is called "this song" (*an-ni-a-am za-ma-*[*ra*]), specifically the song sung by the goddess Nintu (in the end of the Old Babylonian version, C = British Museum; see also Dalley 2000, 274). Lambert and Millard comment further: "Thus a deity who confesses to participating in the bringing of the flood at Enlil's command claims to have sung this 'song,' which is equivalent to authorship. The Mother Goddess is a possible candidate" (1969, 165). In this case, the text is not simply about deities or their deeds; it is also a narrative song sung by one deity in praise of another.[18] Like *Enuma Elish*, Atrahasis is labeled this way with the explicit purpose of praising the deity, and also like *Enuma Elish*, its performance is called for in the future as an act of praise.[19]

We have more cases from Akkadian literature. These include the Standard Babylonian version of Anzu, also named for its main divine protagonist. This text opens as song and as praise: "I sing of the superb son

---

17. This is perhaps a bit ironic in view of Enlil's role in the text.

18. This written representation of the narrative as a song serves as a claim for divine authorship. This may be the earliest case of a claim of divine pseudonymous authorship; Atrahasis is "Pseudo-Nintu." Insofar as later readers regard the biblical Pentateuch as ultimately authored by God, it may be considered as "Pseudo-God." The text itself represents some of the laws and not the narratives as actually written by God. See Exod 24:12; 31:18; 32:16; 34:1; Deut 5:22; cf. Exod 24:4 and 34:27 (Moses writing).

19. On Atrahasis and its musical sensibility, see the insightful essay by Kilmer (1996).

of the king of populated lands, Beloved of Mami, the powerful god, Ellil's son; I praise superb Ninurta, beloved of Mami, The powerful god, Ellil's son" (Dalley 2000, 205). Again we see the idea of the text as a song to the god. Another instance is the text called Erra (in the Standard Babylonian version), again named for its main divine character. It closes with the description of "this song" (twice) and it opens: "[I sing of the son of] the king of all populated lands, creator of the world" (translation of Dalley 2000, 285; see Lambert and Millard 1969, 7; Dalley 2000, 38 n. 46).[20] The end of the text says that it was revealed by the god in a dream to the scribe, as van der Toorn (2007, 41, 42) has recently emphasized.[21] Here Erra, like *Enuma Elish* and Atrahasis, is represented as a song to the god sung by a deity. In this sense, the texts are regarded as having divine authorship, not unlike Gen 1.

We should note that the idea of myths as songs appears quite widely in ancient Near Eastern literature. Several Hurrians myths are called "songs," such as "the Song of Ullikumi."[22] Closer to ancient Israel, the Ugaritic text often called Nikkal wa-Ib (*KTU* 1.24) opens as a song: "let me [si]ng of Nikkal wa-Ib."[23] The text then turns to a narrative of the marriage of Nikkal to Yarikh. The last line of the text at line 39 closes with a hymnic note: "O Nikkal wa-Ib, of whom I sing, May Yarikh shine, May Yarikh shine on you!" The text follows with an epilogue (lines 40–50), the first line of which is regularly reconstructed: "[Let me sing of the Katharat ...]." The model for this line may be a wedding song (cf. Ps 45:1–2).[24]

Some of the Mesopotamian examples are songs by deities about deities that their human audience is to imitate. The great scholar of Sumerian, Thorkild Jacobsen, commented: "The strictly literary Sumerian works can

---

20. Stephanie Dalley says that the opening lines to Ishum and Erra "are modelled on the opening of *Anzu*" (2000, 313 n. 1).

21. Van der Toorn attributes this unusual presentation to the text's purpose as prophecy, specifically regarding the "man of Akkad" who will defeat the Suteans (tablet IV, lines 131–136; tablet V, lines 25–38). Functioning as prophecy (or pseudoprophecy), the text, so van der Toorn suggests, "needed the name of the prophet" (2007, 42).

22. For this point, see Hoffner 1990, 38. For a convenient translation of the "songs," see Hoffner 1990, 40–60.

23. For a convenient presentation of the text and translation of this Ugaritic text, see Marcus 1997.

24. Note also the opening of RIH 98/02, lines 1–2, with the first-person invocation preceded by the address for Athtart. See Pardee 2007, 27–39, esp. 30–31.

be defined generally as works of praise. The praise can be for something extant and enjoyed, a temple, a deity, or a human king. It can take narrative form as myth or epic, or descriptive form as hymn" (Jacobsen 1987, xiii). The myths that I have mentioned are, as Jacobsen characterizes them, praise presented largely in narrative form. Some biblical texts might also serve as comparable cases of praise largely in the form of narrative,[25] for example, Exod 15 and even the laments of Pss 74 and 89, which include narrative praise.

For this discussion, it is important to emphasize that the oral representation of these five texts as songs is a scribal idea, aimed at encouraging oral recitation of the written text. In other words, oral singing in these texts is not simply a reflection of their older, traditional origins as oral texts, as presupposed in many discussions of ancient Near Eastern myth.[26] (Of course, they may have drawn on notions of oral performance; see van der Toorn 2007, 12.) Instead, divine orality in these texts is a scribal representation, and it highlights the authority of the scribal production. The presentation of these myths as songs is, in short, a claim to divine performance and revelation of these texts. At the same time, it is very important to observe that many myths do not make any claims about their being songs. The Hittite narrative known as Telepinu is very different in this regard. It incorporates a ritual of appeasement. So this myth may be regarded not so much as a narrative song but as narrative appeasement.

So what is the upshot of this discussion so far for our understanding of myths? Myths are narratives about gods or goddesses, which evoke a world invoked by other means. Myths narrate a world that may be sung about in songs by human devotees of the deity. Or myths may describe appeasement of an angry god or goddess in a manner that corresponds to ritual appeasement of the deity. In other words, in their narrative form, myths evoke deities and their world, which are invoked by songs or incantations or other genres of ritual. This does not mean that myths were necessarily used in rituals (though in some cases, they could have been); what it means is that different sorts of myths and rituals are often concerned with the same divine world as it impinges on human society.

---

25. This point has been emphasized by Fishbane 2003, 37–44, 50–52.

26. Lambert and Millard (1969, 8) mention the conclusion as suggestive of the impression that the poem was intended for public recitation. See also Dalley 2000, xv, xvi, and esp. 38 n. 46.

These sorts of relationships between myths and rituals are evident in some of the cases that I discuss in the next section.

Myths in Relation to Various Genres

How myths are to be understood in their ancient contexts depends further on how they may be connected with other sorts of textual material. Some myths are self-standing, while others are combined with other genres. An example of a self-standing myth would be the Ugaritic Baal Cycle, as far as one can tell from its extent material; apart from its colophon and scribal instruction, it stands alone. Other texts show myth combined with ritual (Dalley 2000, xvi). A fine example of the latter is an Ugaritic text known as the Rituals and Myths of the Goodly Gods (*KTU* 1.23). This is a single text containing a series of rituals in lines 1–29 followed by narrative in lines 30–76.[27]

There are other cases of texts that combine narrative about deities with ritual. In the Sumerian text Enki and the World Order, the narrative shifts to ritual at lines 140–154 and then reverts to narrative (Averbeck 2003).[28] The Hittite narrative of Telepinu includes a ritual designed to appease the god's anger (*COS* 1.152). The Akkadian work often called the Descent of Ishtar, a composition of about 140 lines (cf. the Sumerian Descent of Inanna at some 410 lines), "seems to end with ritual instructions for the *taklimtu*, an annual ritual known from Assyrain texts, which took place in the month of Dumuzi (Tammuz = June/July), and featured the bathing, anointing, and lying-in-state of a statue of Dumuzi" (Dalley 2000, 154). Several Egyptian narratives are prefaced by information that they constitute spells (*COS* 1.32, 33).

Ritual is hardly the only sort of text combined with myth. There is myth with a medicinal recipe, in the prescription of the hangover in one Ugaritic text (*KTU* 1.114.29–31).[29] This prescription is prefaced by and separated with a scribal line from the narrative of El's drunkenness. There may be "prophecy" in myth. On a passage in Erra and Ishum, Stephanie Dalley comments: "This line indicates that there is an important element

---

27. For this text see M. Smith 2006. For a convenient presentation of the Ugaritic text and translation, see Lewis 1997a.

28. I wish to thank Professor Averbeck for bringing this example to my attention.

29. For a convenient presentation of the text and translation of these Ugaritic passages, see Lewis 1997b, esp. 196.

of pseudo-prophecy in the epic" (2000, 315 n. 52). In other words, this myth contains a representation of prophecy. Myth can also be combined with other narrative material. Myths contained within an epic would include tablet XI in Gilgamesh, with its incorporation of the flood myth, or the Descent of Ishtar opening in Gilgamesh tablet VII (Dalley 2000, 130 n. 81; Foster 2001, xxi; 2005, 24).

From these cases, it is clear that narrative myth may be wedded to other forms, including ritual, epic, or even medicinal prescription. To what ends? Jonathan Z. Smith (1975, 37–38) offers an interesting comment that addresses this question: "Myth, as narrative, I would suggest, is the analogue to the limited number of objects manipulated by the diviner. Myth as application represents the complex interaction between diviner, client, and situation." In other words, what myth is depends in part on its context. It is true that some examples involve ritual, and so one might agree with Smith that the world of divination is analogous to the world of narrative. As we have seen, ritual invokes a world that myth evokes. In some cases, such as the Rituals and Myth of the Goodly Gods (*KTU* 1.23), a single text that combines myths and rituals both invokes and evokes the divine world. Yet ritual is only one arena with its "limited number of objects" (to echo Smith's quote). There may be other arenas of human activity with their "number of objects" with correspondences in myth. The sense of myth is potentially as wide as human experience and imagination.

From the combination of myths with other sorts of texts, we see that scribal production is important for understanding myths and what they are. From the examples noted, we can see how complicated mythic narrative may be. In addition, mythic narrative may also borrow from or be modeled on older myths. For example, *Enuma Elish* was a particularly strong textual magnet. Foster (1995, 7, 10) thinks Anzu provided a model for *Enuma Elish* (or at least they share a common stock of material; so Dalley 2000, 230–31; see 240, 277). The creation of humanity in *Enuma Elish* tablet VI perhaps evokes the story of Atrahasis (see Dalley 2000, 261). And the figure of Marduk in battle in *Enuma Elish* recalls the battles of the god Ninurta in Lugal-e (see Jacobsen 1987, 240), while the portrait of Marduk in the same text may also owe something to the West Semitic conflict myth (as represented in the Ugaritic Baal Cycle), as Thorkild Jacobsen (1968, 104–8) suggested decades ago.[30]

---

30. This proposal has gained in plausibility since the publication of an apparent

Other Mesopotamian myths show dependence on yet other myths. Benjamin R. Foster (1995, 9) suggests that the ending of Erra is modeled on the ending of *Enuma Elish*. The relationship may run deeper, with Erra perhaps forming a sort of commentary on the world of *Enuma Elish*.[31] In short, texts may represent narrative agglomerations drawing on other cultural material as well as diverse textual traditions and texts. In this connection, one may note Jonathan Z. Smith's comment:

> There is something funny, there is something crazy about myth. For it shares with the comic and the insane the quality of obsessiveness. Nothing, in principle, is allowed to elude its grasp. The myth, like the diviner's objects, is a code capable in theory of universal application if it would only be properly understood. (1987, 78–79)

Indeed, sometimes agglomeration with various sorts of material even involved translation and migration, whether from Sumerian into Akkadian, or West Semitic into Hurrian-Hittite (Elkunirsa [*COS* 1.149]) and Egyptian (for example, the Legend of Astarte and the Tribute of the Sea [*COS* 1.35]), or Akkadian into Hebrew (Gen 6–8). This textual flexibility may represent one hallmark of ancient Near Eastern myth.[32]

Divine Space in Myth

Up to this point, the discussion has focused on what might be called the external or formal side of myths. It is equally important to note what is

---

"missing link" at the ancient site of Mari located on the great bend of the Euphrates. See Durand 1993, 41–61; and Bordreuil and Pardee 1993, 63–70. For text, translation, and notes, see Nissinen 2003, 22. For further discussion, see Sasson 1994, 299–316, esp. 310–14; see also Sasson 1990, 444 n. 12; and M. Smith 2002, 56–57. By the way, this Mari text goes a considerable way toward confirming the theory of Jacobsen that the description of the conflict between Marduk and Tiamat in *Enuma Elish* was borrowed from West Semitic prototypes (this hardly precludes local Mesopotamian influence as well as various aspects of the description in *Enuma Elish*, as Assyriologists have long noted). Jacobsen had in mind the conflict of Baal and Yamm (Sea) in the Ugaritic Baal Cycle, but the Mari text provides a sort of missing link between them. See Jacobsen 1968, 104–8. See my discussion and further defense of this view in M. Smith 1994b, 108–14.

31. See Jacobsen 1976, 227–28. See also the observations in Machinist 2005.

32. By contrast, ritual perhaps migrates and translates less; in this respect, law seems closer. For discussion, see my essay, M. Smith 2007b.

inside of myths: what do they evoke in their literary presentation of the world? As I mentioned earlier, the discussion of myth has often focused on time, in particular time past. Among scholars, there has been a similar discussion of sacred space in myths; holy mountains, for example, have been prominent in this discussion. Space in myth more generally provides a stage for expressing human perceptions about reality. Two cases illustrate this point. In *Enuma Elish*, one effect is grandeur, with the universe as an object of human contemplation of Marduk's power. It is the universe not only in general, but in its details, at once religious and political, astronomical and divine. Humanity is to see this world that it is theirs and behold its divine realities. These are deserving of human contemplation and praise. In these aspects of myth, Gen 1 likewise evokes this sort of response. It too constructs a divine architecture of grandeur deserving of praise. In these terms, Gen 1 is mythic.

A second example comes from the Ugaritic text known as the Baal Cycle. This narrative presents various gods and goddesses moving through earthly space. In this text deities go to places with names well known in Ugaritic culture, such as Crete and Egypt. The places in this text are sometimes spaces named and inhabited by humans. In this case, deities do not walk in some nonhuman or prehuman "mythic places" of a distant past. They stride the very places known to the ancients who transmitted these texts. Humans barely appear in this text, and so in a literary sense they cede their space to gods and goddesses. Where rituals would invoke divine presence, narrative evokes divine presence in the world. In such a narrative, humans are drawn (or, in a sense, redrawn) into their own worlds that include deities. With deities represented in this literature, they are present in the text, and the world in the text becomes theophanous. This literature allows the human audience to listen in on the deities as they imagine them to be in their world. Myth in such a case is not simply about the narrative as such or about its sequence. Myth provides a literary stage that gives deities a space to reveal who they are in the world of human beings.

For the Baal Cycle, humans visualize and contemplate through the narrative not only who the gods are in general, but also who they are in relation to one another. This includes the intimacy between various deities or groups of deities, and their mysterious bonds with the world of human experience. In the narrative sequence of events, the text sometimes pauses for a moment and allows the audience to overhear a divine conversation. Humans join the deities literarily as they listen in on the words of one deity directed to another, sometimes conveyed with a certain intimacy and sense of affection. For example, the god Baal sends a message to his sister Anat inviting her to come to his mountain to learn the secret word of the universe (*KTU* 1.3 III–IV).[33] Humans learn the content of what Anat learns, as they listen to this intimate communication. In a sense, this sounds more like Gen 2–3 than Gen 1 in providing a stage for the deity on the earthly level.[34] Just as the deities walk through the world in the Baal Cycle, so too God walks through the garden in Gen 3. To be sure, the garden of Eden is no normal space for humans, but the representation of the deity on the earthly level in Gen 3 is not so distant from what we see in the Baal Cycle. By contrast, Gen 1 directs human attention upward from the terrestrial level to the wider universe. In short, myths can be then narratives of revelation. They allow their human audience an opportunity to step into a deeper reality, one underlying its more mundane existence.

Deities themselves captured basic dimensions of reality for the ancients, and the relationships among the deities make certain connections between these aspects of reality. To use an analogy, we may put the point in terms of grammar. Deities are in a sense the grammatical forms or morphology of reality; their relationships are its sentence structure or syntax; and its realities of power, of life and death, of nature and society, stand in coordinate and subordinate clauses. What does this "syntax" express as a whole? Myths can explore reality, they narrate it, but they do not really explain it in the modern sense. They present "causes" (*aetia*, the base for the first part of the word *aetiology* or *etiology* in English), but these are hardly causes or explanations in the modern sense. Instead, they constitute claims that the divinely involved events are connected with conditions in the world known to humans.[35] What myths seem to do is to evoke the basic realities that humans face and present a narration that links these realities to the world of the gods and goddesses.[36]

---

33. For the text and translation of this passage, see M. Smith 1997, 109–10.

34. The mythic dimensions of Gen 2 are discussed in a recent study by Tryggve N. D. Mettinger (2007). See also the earlier studies of Görg 2003; Stordalen 2000; and Wallace 1985.

35. See the theory of myth as *aetia*, in modern times associated with the name of Andrew Lang; for a convenient discussion, see Kirk 1974, 53, 59. More recently, Glassner (1995, 1815) has emphasized the importance of explanation for Mesopotamian myth.

36. Compare the notion of myth as narrative that is "the temporalizing of essence" by the literary critic Kenneth Burke (1970, 201); cited and commented on by Segal 2004, 85. Note also the idea of the anthropologist Paul Radin: "Myths deal with meta-

Myths narrate across these realities of deities, humanity, and the world, but without explaining them, in any modern sense. They narrate the apparent contradictions experienced in human existence, such as violence or trouble in the world, whether in *Enuma Elish*, the Baal Cycle, or the Bible (Gen 1–3), or mortality in Atrahasis and in the Bible (e.g., in Gen 6:1–4). They may relate the divine source of human threat or the divine font of human blessing. And without explaining how, these narratives may claim that the sources of blessings and threat ultimately derive from deities. They do not really tell us *why* these things are but *what* they are and, to some degree, *how*. Different scholars discuss the explanatory (or etiological) function of myth, and surely there are plenty of textual references suggesting the connection between the there and then in the myth and the here and now of the human audience. Yet such a connection is not really explanatory in any modern sense; rather, it indicates that the problems of humanity are bound up with the divine world. In sum, myths narrate realities, by presenting deities and their actions in or affecting the world, and they do so by building relations between these deities with plots that cover and cross over the inexplicable difficulties of human experience. Myths also indicate that in various ways deities are related to humanity in the midst of its hardships. In terms of this discussion, Gen 1 surely shows these hallmarks of ancient Near Eastern myths.

Let us look at the question of Genesis as a myth also in terms of the presentation of deities in earthly settings. In contrast with the Baal Cycle or the Goodly Gods, biblical narrative does not *generally* present deities operating in a bodily manner in the world, or more specifically, on the earthly plane. To be sure, there are biblical snapshots of divine activity: God walking in the garden in Gen 3; or, the "sons of gods" in Gen 6:1–4. To explain this overall difference, one might be tempted to adopt any variety of generalizations to account for the relative rarity of such presentations of gods or God. One might think that avoiding anthropomorphism is key, but this hardly helps us with various prophetic or apocalyptic images of the divine. Or one might be tempted to say that the focus of Israel's narrative in Genesis through Kings is the story of Israel, and God is mediated through this story. Yet even in apocalyptic texts, there is plenty of material that would remind readers of ancient Near Eastern myths, yet even here

---

physical topics of all kinds, such as the ultimate conceptions of reality" (cited from Segal 2004, 37). In other words, myths map reality in the form of narrative sequence.

the divine does not inhabit the earth in quite the same immanent manner. There is divine presence in liturgy (Ps 29) and in prophetic passages (1 Kgs 22 or Isa 6), but descriptions of God in human or "mythic" terms do not form the backbone of biblical narratives. Whatever the presentation of God in other biblical texts, Gen 1 does not present God in this way; indeed, one might argue that it looks decidedly unlike myths in this regard. So is Gen 1 a myth?

Is Genesis 1 a "Creation Myth"?

As we have seen, a long-standing tendency in discussing the Bible and myth has been to generate any number of definitions of myth that could be applied to ancient Near Eastern texts, but not to the Bible. However, commentators in the last quarter century have largely given up this older practice of holding up the uniqueness of the Bible as nonmyth over and against ancient Near Eastern myths.[37] Even in rejecting this approach, one may still wonder why ancient Israel did not preserve longer mythic narratives of the sort seen elsewhere. This may be not a particular function of religious belief as much as a matter of scribal tradition and its particular interests. Behind this tradition, it seems that Israel did transmit a collection of myths or at least constellations of mythic motifs and basic plotlines. The evidence represented by biblical apocalyptic in Dan 7–12 and later in the book of Revelation, with their rich mythic imagery and plots, would seem to support the view that Israel indeed did have a fund of myths from which it could draw. The more appropriate question about the lack of myth would seem to be why Israel's elites in the period generated narratives that look less mythic, as found in the longer collections of Genesis–2 Kings. One should be cautious even here. As has been noted, the Bible is full of the sorts of images associated with myth, even if it does not contain longer mythic narratives apart from apocalyptic and arguably parts of the Primeval History.[38] One could perhaps string together a series of biblical scenes

---

37. See the discussion of Oden 1987, 40–91, esp. 93; and Fishbane 2003, 1–92, with comments on Gen 1 on pp. 34–35.

38. I have discussed this contrast between the relative rarity of myths in the Bible and its many mythic images in an article (1994a). To this degree I am in agreement with Fishbane's emphasis on the mythic in the Bible. See Fishbane 2003, 1–52. Fishbane's discussion does not address sufficiently this difference between what might be regarded as biblical myths and biblical mythic images. In this regard, ancient Israel

that nearly matches scene for scene with the Ugaritic Baal Cycle (or least a great deal of it).

If one asks about what myths are and do textually and compares biblical narratives, then it is evident that myths and some biblical narratives have quite a bit in common. In general, both offer a narrative about a main deity. They also reference natural, social, and religious phenomena. Both show scribal use of older narrative material that includes commemoration, incorporation or use of older texts, modification of older mythic versions,[39] or translation and arguably textual commentary (Gen 1:1–2:3 as commentary on 2:4b–5). Like many ancient Near Eastern texts, Genesis combines myth to materials that are far less mythic looking. Bernard Batto (1992) has argued for Atrahasis in fact as the model for Gen 1–9; both cases link creation and flood. The agglomeration of Gen 1 hardly ends with Gen 1–9 or even the end of Exodus, in chapters 39–40, as noted by many commentators. The trajectory is arguably Sinai as a whole (McBride 2000), with the theme of the Sabbath. Calling Gen 1–11 "primeval history," as many do, has a certain merit, in that these chapters are inextricably linked to Israel's so-called history (or better, its "historiographical narrative") in Genesis through Deuteronomy, and perhaps through the books of Kings. Genealogies in Genesis (in 2:4; 5:1; 6:9; 10:1; 11:10, 27; 25:12, 19; 36:19; and 37:2; see Cross 1973, 301–5; Tengström 1981; Weimar 2008) locate the primordial events of Gen 1–3 in some sort of "historical" time, perhaps analogous to the Sumerian King List's referencing of the flood tradition in

---

perhaps stands closer to the situation in ancient Greece. Here it may be helpful to recall Kirk's observation that I quoted earlier: "The vital fact is that myths in Greek literature exist for the most part only in brief allusions.... The myths were so well known that formal exposition was unnecessary, and in the high classical period, at least, it was felt to be provincial. This changed in the Hellenistic world after the conquests of the Alexander the Great" (see Kirk 1974, 14). In longer biblical narrative, there are little more than allusions to myth, yet the Bible contains many mythic images. Biblical narrative may be a product of a scribal culture accustomed to mythic images yet concerned with matters other than myth, as in pre-Alexandrian Greek literature. Or one might simply wonder if the sample of the Bible is simply too small. Perhaps in the matter of myth, there may be something simply incidental involved. In the end this may be one of the major differences that we scholars need to think about more. There is an abundance of mythic material in the ancient Near East; in comparison, prior to the Hellenistic period, Israel barely has a whole Bible.

39. Sometimes with additional critique of them (see Moran 2002, 45), or perhaps with admiration.

connection with human figures.⁴⁰ Genesis 2:4a labels the contents of Gen 1 as a genealogy of heaven and earth.⁴¹ While this labeling may recall the idea of theogonic myths involving generations of old cosmic pairs including older deities,⁴² in the context of Gen 1 it no longer functioned in this manner. Instead, it serves to express the author's own interpretation of his material as connected to the historiographical material that follows throughout the book of Genesis and beyond. Genesis 1 perhaps looks less like a myth because it stands in the context of a long historical work in Genesis through Kings.⁴³

For all their considerable differences, the parallel between the Sumerian King List and Gen 1–11 is useful for understanding Gen 1 in its larger context and for the related question as to whether it is a myth. The parallel has been noted, mostly for possible traces of shared traditions.⁴⁴ For the purposes of this discussion, it is useful to look briefly at the Sumerian King List for a comparison with Gen 1 in relation to its context in Gen 1–11. Like Gen 1, the King List begins with the heavens ("when kingship was lowered from heaven"). It also relates sequences of time down through the flood and into historical time. Like Gen 1–11, it details preflood and postflood figures. Compared with the reigns of its postflood figures, the Sumerian King List provides much higher dates for the preflood figures. Both Gen 1–11 and the Sumerian King List incorporate various sorts of traditional information. Both are also recognized as composite works. (The preflood material in the Sumerian King List does not appear in all of the twenty-five known exemplars of this text.⁴⁵)

What is the upshot of this comparison for the question of Gen 1 as a myth? No one calls the Sumerian King List a myth, yet within its historio-

---

40. For a convenient translation of the Sumerian King List, see A. Leo Oppenheim's in *ANET*, 265–66. The older critical edition of this text is Jacobsen 1939. For a good discussion of the text, see Michalowski 1983. The discussion of Schmidt 1995 (esp. 2340–41) locates the Sumerian King List within the wider context of Mesopotamian flood traditions. Note also Hallo 1996, 7–15. Hallo's concerns are largely comparative (see below).

41. As noted by commentators, such as Gunkel 1997, 103.

42. For theogonies see the summary discussion of Cross 1998, 73–83.

43. Perhaps the scope in question should be Genesis through Deuteronomy. For a fine consideration of the latter, see McBride 2000.

44. According to Hallo 1996, 10–13, some of the names in Gen 4:17, in particular Lamech, reflect a number of the figures also known in the Sumerian King List.

45. This number is given by Vanstiphout 2003, 12 n. 55.

graphical framework it contains references to "mythic events." Similarly, scholars do not use the label of myth for all of Genesis (much less for Genesis–Deuteronomy or Genesis–Kings), and so Gen 1 in its larger context might not be considered a myth. For all their differences, both the Sumerian King List and Gen 1–11 allude to mythic events, but this does not make either one of them a myth. One might call them mythic, but from a literary perspective they are not myths.

As this comparison suggests, the position of Gen 1 affects the question of whether it is to be viewed as a myth. Genesis 1 stands before any other text. It is given a position above other texts in the Bible, including other creation texts (such as Ps 74:12–17 or Ps 104). To the question raised by this essay, as to whether Gen 1 in its context is a myth, the answer is negative when its position is considered. As the foundational account at the head of Genesis to Deuteronomy and beyond, Gen 1 is not a myth. It is not simply linked to historical time; it is represented as the beginning of historical time.[46]

---

46. Before proceeding to a final consideration of our question as whether Gen 1 is a myth, I would like to briefly consider two general differences between ancient Near Eastern myths and the Bible, one involving an external, formal difference and the second a matter of content. The first is prose versus poetry, and the second is space as represented in ancient Near Eastern myths versus biblical narrative. One textual feature of the longer biblical narratives is their construction primarily in prose, in contrast to the long, poetic versions of myths as generally known in the ancient Near East. As Pardee (2002, 171) remarks, Ugaritic prose is "an extremely rare feature of texts of a mythological nature." With little narrative poetry beyond isolated, single chapters, the longer biblical narrative agglomerations are not constructed primarily as poetry, but as prose. What is one to make of this difference? Are there any leads that might be helpful here? It is true that Gilgamesh tablet XII is thought by commentators to be prose, which was added by an editor to bring the Akkadian closer to the known Sumerian version (see George 2003, 1:47–54). More specifically, the Sumerian text, Gilgamesh, Enkidu, and the Netherworld, was translated into Akkadian as Gilgamesh tablet XII, lines 129–130 (so Foster 2001, 129). Perhaps one key then to the biblical situation is not simply an aversion on the part of Israel's textual elites to depicting the divine. The use of prose itself may be important here.

It has been thought that the prosaic character of most biblical narrative might be at least in part a matter of scribal production overtaking the oral settings that generated Israel's older stories (so Kawashima 2004). It is not clear that this is generally the case. I say this because Kawashima (2004) does not examine or demonstrate the cultural and historical conditions that would support his reconstruction. Instead, he presupposes that this reconstruction was the situation involved and then reads various biblical passages in light of this reconstruction. For example, he assumes the view

So as we reach the end of our exploration of myth, what is the bottom line? Is Gen 1 a myth? The answer is yes and no. From the perspective of its content, it is certainly very mythic. At the same time, the issue is complicated by its position (and perhaps also by its overall lack of anthropomorphism). It is not a self-standing narrative. Its place as the head of Genesis as well as its label as "generations of heaven and earth" (in 2:4a) linked it to historical time. Its textual location also represented an effort or claim to make it first relative to other accounts. In effect, this placement expressed a *priestly* claim for its account of creation in Gen 1 as *the* account of creation, much as readers of the Bible often think of it today. In this manner, we might say that the priestly authors or editors of Gen 1 fundamentally altered the nature of the myth in Gen 1. The priestly tradition in effect effaced the resemblance between the mythic looking content of Gen 1 and what scholars have generally regarded as ancient Near Eastern myths. In short, the priestly tradition made Gen 1 into the beginning of

---

of Frank Cross that ancient Israel enjoyed a long-standing epic tradition until "the death of the rhapsode" (as he expresses the point in his subtitle) and the passing of this oral tradition. The question of epic, and in particular Cross's arguments for it, however, have been highly contested. Dissent from this view from within the tradition of William Foxwell Albright comes from Hillers and McCall 1976 (reference courtesy of Seth Sanders). See also Parker 1997a, 7. Note also the older comments of Talmon 1981, 57. In his discussion of Judg 5, Fritz (2006, 695) emphatically denies epic in ancient Israel: "there was no development of epic verse, as occurred, for example, in ancient Greece." I have noted some reservations about Cross's use of the term (see M. Smith 2007a). What Cross regards at the vestiges and indicators of Israel's epic, I view as something of an "anti-epic" that rejects or displaces Israelite's Canaanite heritage. Despite its use of Cross's notion of epic, Kawashima's book is quite sophisticated and offers a number of important observations.

When we do see poetry in our long narrative texts in the Bible, they display a rather different effect than our ancient Near Eastern myths. In the case of the great poems of Judg 5 and Exod 15, it seems that they function in context to link the older world of the events being described. These poems are written in an older Hebrew relative to their contexts, composed in prose, which are linguistically closer to the world of the human audience of the narrative. As a result, the older poetic pieces evoke that distant past of the purported events, and they are linked to—and interpreted for—the world of the audience's present via the prose accounts. And yet the presence of both poetry and prose also marks their difference in time and context for their scribal composers: these poetic events are ancient for them. So poetry in the longer narratives of the Bible may have a very different function than the long poetic myths of the ancient Near East.

Israel's national and international story. Structurally, Gen 1 ended up no longer looking like ancient Near Eastern myths despite some of its content.

For many religious readers of the Bible, it is impossible to think of Gen 1 as a myth in the first place, in part because of the modern sense of myth as something that is not true. Yet for other readers, the content of Gen 1 reminds them of other creation stories from around the world. For these readers, Gen 1 still looks very much a myth to scholars and laypeople alike. These readers are not uncomfortable with the idea of Gen 1 as one myth among many or as only one of the Bible's ways of looking at creation. We might say that religious readers who view the Bible as God's inerrant word and Gen 1 as historically true follow the view of the priestly tradition itself. For the priestly tradition as for religious readers of the Bible, Gen 1 begins as *the* creation account. In contrast, other readers less concerned with biblical inerrancy may read Gen 1 (or perhaps Gen 1-3) in isolation from its overall position within Genesis-Deuteronomy or Genesis-Kings. In a sense, these two different modern approaches to Genesis echo the ancient situation of Gen 1 with its mythic looking content versus the priestly claim for Gen 1 implied by its position.

To my mind, neither view has the Bible or the biblical view of creation quite right, especially if we consider creation within the Bible's overall scope. On the one hand, Gen 1 is the creation story for the priestly tradition, and it stands at the head of the whole Bible. On the other hand, the biblical tradition did not eliminate other creation texts, for example, the ones we saw in Pss 74 and 104. Instead, the Bible retained both the priestly claim to the primacy of Gen 1 and the witnesses to alternative views in other texts. As the "canonical approach" would remind us, a canonical perspective then is not the same as the priestly view. Instead, the Bible preserves a more complex situation, namely a literarily dominant text in Gen 1 that stands in dialogue with other texts that are less prominent in terms of their placement. A religiously minded person might say that the biblical truth of creation constitutes the range or sum of the truths in all of the various accounts in the Bible.

To put the point in terms of the Bible's own presentation of creation, it might be more accurate to say that the truth of creation in Gen 1 is echoed in other biblical accounts of creation and that their presentations of creation expand on what Gen 1 conveys. In this perspective, Ps 74's emphasis on God's power in creation would stand as a complementary insight into the creation that Gen 1 initially lays out for its readers. Psalm 104 offers a dynamic view of creation and its elements, and an inspiring sense of God's own breath of life infusing the world. This sense of creation adds a dimension missing from Gen 1. Psalm 104's ecologically integrated vision of creation qualifies the human-centered picture presented by Gen 1.[47] Creation is not only good, as Gen 1 reminds its readers; it is also built with divine wisdom, as Ps 104:24 tells its audience. For the Bible as a whole, the other creation accounts magnify the sense of creation and its Creator found initially in Gen 1.[48]

Other creation passages also qualify any sense of absolute truth that might be attached to Gen 1 as the single most important biblical witness to the meaning of creation. The other biblical passages of creation remind readers that the biblical witness to creation is not to be boiled down to some basic truth of Gen 1. (Nor would it be easy to do so.) Other passages potentially serve as foils to Gen 1. If Gen 1 holds up a "good" picture of creation, other passages suggest something of its "downside," as it applies to humanity. The good creation of Gen 1 does not explain human suffering or evil in the world. Other passages remind us of the dark side of God's creation (Isa 45:7; see also Job 3). Finally, yet other creation accounts in the Bible remind readers that Gen 1 is not to be taken as the single account of creation in any historical or scientific sense. To the degree that people take Gen 1 in this way, they fail to understand the full biblical witness to creation. They arguably idealize and idolize Gen 1 and forget the Bible's range of creation accounts. As parts of the Bible, we may say that all of them are "good" in God's sight.

The situation of the different creation accounts in the Bible is more complex precisely because they belong to the Bible. The Bible is not simply its parts or a variety of works that includes creation texts. In this respect, it differed in the long term from creation accounts not only in Mesopotamia and Egypt, but also through most of ancient Israel's history. Creation texts of Mesopotamia and Egypt basically remained separate works offering a range of ideas about creation, a veritable kaleidescope in their perspectives on creation. While Israel's creation texts began as separate works, in time its kaleidoscope of creation became part of a single work that we now know as the Bible. One of the things that ultimately makes Gen 1 different as a creation text is that it belongs to this larger work. In this larger literary context, creation accounts and allusions are no longer sepa-

---

47. Contrast the theological approaches of Alomía 2002 and Habel 2006.
48. There are, to be sure, further complexities beyond these considerations. See Westermann 1984, 175.

rate texts, but passages meant to be read in conjunction with one another. This complex of textual activity, as we see it in later biblical texts and the Dead Sea Scrolls, might be further described as "scripturalizing." By this I mean that texts regarded as holy or inspired were coming to be read and interpreted together; that words or complexes of terms shared by different religious texts not only could be read in tandem but should be read together across the boundaries of their original contexts, beyond the limits of any individual passage or document. It is this process of scriptural reading linking passages across their former textual boundaries that eventually distinguishes works that belong to the Bible.[49] In its placement as the Bible's opening, Gen 1 enjoys a singular place in a singular work where its voice is to be heard not only in the beginning, but also through to its end.

In the end, the question of Gen 1 as myth depends on what we mean by the word *myth* and what we think myths are really about. This issue of the Bible or Gen 1 as myth is as much an issue of our own time as it is about the Bible or its ancient authors. Finally, the question may ultimately depend on what credence readers are prepared to give to either the Bible or to ancient Near Eastern literature in their descriptions of reality.

Works Cited

Alomía, Haroldo. 2002. Sujeción del Planeta en Genesis 1:26–28 y su mensaje ecológico vinculado con el mensaje de la Iglesia Adventista del Séptimo Día. *Theologika* 17, no. 1:42–92.

Averbeck, Richard E. 2003. Myth, Ritual, and Order in "Enki and the World." *JAOS* 123:757–71.

Batto, Bernard. 1992. *Slaying the Dragon: Mythmaking in the Biblical Tradition*. Louisville: Westminster John Knox.

Bordreuil, Pierre, and Dennis Pardee. 1993. Le combat de *Baʻlu* avec *Yammu* d'après les textes ougaritiques. *MARI* 7:63–70.

---

49. I am not claiming or speaking to the matter of intertextual relations among texts in other ancient Near Eastern traditions. It may be the development of such intertextual relations within scribal traditions or canons that underlies Israel's developments of its Bible. I would also place a certain importance on the replacement of a royal-priestly scribal situation in the preexilic context by a priestly scribal situation in the postexilic context, but these large developments lie beyond the scope of this discussion. See van der Toorn 2007.

Burke, Kenneth. 1970. *The Rhetoric of Religion: Studies in Logology.* Berkeley: University of California Press.

Clark, Elizabeth A. 2004. *History, Theory, Text: Historians and the Linguistic Turn.* Cambridge: Harvard University Press.

Coats, George W. 1983. *Genesis; with an Introduction to Narrative Literature.* FOTL 1. Grand Rapids: Eerdmans.

Cross, Frank Moore. 1973. *Canaanite Myth and Hebrew Epic.* Cambridge: Harvard University Press.

———. 1998. *From Epic to Canon: History and Literature in Ancient Israel.* Baltimore: Johns Hopkins University Press.

Dalley, Stephanie, ed. and trans. 2000. *Myths from Mesopotamia: Creation, the Flood, Gilgamesh, and Others.* Rev. ed. Oxford: Oxford University Press.

Dundes, Alan. 1996. Madness in Method Plus a Plea for Projective Inversion in Myth. Pages 147–59 in *Myth and Method.* Edited by Laurie L. Patton and Wendy Doniger. Charlottesville: University Press of Virginia.

Durand, Jean-Marie. 1993. Le mythologeme du combat entre le dieu de l'orage et la mer en Mésopotamie. *MARI* 7:41–61.

Fishbane, Michael. 2003. *Biblical Myth and Rabbinic Mythmaking.* Oxford: Oxford University Press.

Foster, Benjamin R. 1995. *From Distant Days: Myths, Tales, and Poetry of Ancient Mesopotamia.* Bethesda, Md.: CDL.

———. 2001. *The Epic of Gilgamesh: A New Translation, Analogues, Criticism.* New York: Norton.

———. 2005. *Before the Muses: An Anthology of Akkadian Literature.* 3rd edition. Bethesda, Md.: CDL.

Fritz, Volkmar. 2006. The Complex of Traditions in Judges 4 and 5 and the Religion of Pre-state Israel. Pages 689–98 in vol. 2 of *"I Will Speak the Riddle of Ancient Times": Archaeological and Historical Studies in Honor of Amihai Mazar on the Occasion of His Sixtieth Birthday.* Edited by Aren M. Maier and Pierre de Miroschedji. 2 vols. Winona Lake, Ind.: Eisenbrauns.

George, Andrew R. 2003. *The Babylonian Gilgamesh Epic: Introduction, Critical Edition and Cuneiform Texts.* 2 vols. Oxford: Oxford University Press.

Glassner, Jean-Jacques. 1995. The Use of Knowledge in Ancient Mesopotamia. *CANE* 3:1815–23.

Görg, Manfred. 2003. Mensch und Tempel im "Zweiten Schöpfungstext." Pages 191–215 in *Textarbeit: Studien zu Texten und ihrer Rezeption aus dem Alten Testament und der Umwelt Israels*. Festschrift Peter Weimar. Edited by Klaus Kiesow and Thomas Meurer. AOAT 294. Münster: Ugarit-Verlag.

Graf, Fritz. 2004. Myth. Pages 45–58 in *Religions of the Ancient World: A Guide*. Edited by Sarah Iles Johnston. Cambridge: Harvard University Press.

Gunkel, Hermann. 1997. *Genesis*. Translated by Mark E. Biddle. Mercer Library of Biblical Studies. Macon, Ga.: Mercer University Press.

Habel, Norman. 2006. Playing God or Playing Earth? An Ecological Reading of Genesis 1:26–28. Pages 33–41 in *"And God Saw That It Was Good": Essays on Creation and God in Honor of Terence E. Fretheim*. Edited by Frederick J. Gaiser and Mark A. Throntveit. Word & World Supplement 5. St. Paul: Luther Seminary.

Hallo, William W. 1996. *Origins: The Ancient Near Eastern Background of Some Modern Western Institutions*. SHCANE 6. Leiden: Brill.

Harland, P. J. 1996. *The Value of Human Life: A Study of the Story of the Flood (Genesis 6–9)*. VTSup 64. Leiden: Brill.

Harris, Rivkah. 1991. Inanna-Ishtar as Paradox and Coincidence of Opposites. *History of Religions* 30:261–78.

Hassin, Ran R., James S. Uleman, and John A. Bargh, eds. 2005. *The New Unconscious*. Oxford Series in Social Cognition and Social Neuroscience. Oxford: Oxford University Press.

Hillers, Delbert R., and Marsh McCall Jr. 1976. Homeric Dictated Texts: A Reexamination of Some Near Eastern Evidence. *Harvard Studies in Classical Philology* 80:19–23.

Hoffner, Harry A., Jr. 1990. *Hittite Myths*. Edited by Gary M. Beckman. SBLWAW 2. Atlanta: Scholars Press, 1990.

Glassner, Jean-Jacques. 1995. The Use of Knowledge in Ancient Mesopotamia. *CANE* 3:1815–23.

Jacobsen, Thorkild. 1939. *The Sumerian King List*. Assyriological Studies 11. Chicago: University of Chicago Press.

———. 1968. The Battle between Marduk and Tiamat. *JAOS* 88:104–8.

———. 1976. *The Treasures of Darkness: A History of Mesopotamian Religion*. New Haven: Yale University Press.

———. 1987. *The Harps That Once. ... Sumerian Poetry in Translation*. New Haven: Yale University Press.

Kawashima, Robert S. 2004. *Biblical Narrative and the Death of the Rhapsode*. Indiana Studies in Biblical Literature. Bloomington: Indiana University Press.

Kilmer, Anne Draffkorn. 1996. Fugal Features of Atrahasis: The Birth Theme. Pages 127–39 in *Mesopotamian Poetic Language: Sumerian and Akkadian*. Edited by M. E. Vogelzang and H. L. J. Vanstiphout. Cuneiform Monographs 6. Proceedings of the Groningen Group for the Study of Mesopotamian Literature 2. Groningen: Styx.

Kirk, Geoffrey S. 1974. *The Nature of Greek Myths*. London: Penguin.

———. 1984. On Defining Myths. Pages 53–61 in *Sacred Narrative: Readings in the Theory of Myth*. Edited by Alan Dundes. Berkeley: University of California Press.

Lambert, Wilfred G., and Alan R. Millard. 1969. *Atra-ḫasīs: The Babylonian Story of the Flood*. Oxford: Oxford University Press.

Leach, Edmund. 1982. Anthropological Approaches to the Study of the Bible during the Twentieth Century. Pages 73–94 in *Humanizing America's Iconic Book*. Edited by Gene M. Tucker and Douglas A. Knight. SBL Centennial Addresses. Chico, Calif.: Scholars Press.

Lewis, Theodore J. 1997a. The Birth of the Gracious Gods. Pages 205–14 in *Ugaritic Narrative Poetry*. Edited by Simon B. Parker. SBLWAW 9. Atlanta: Scholars Press.

———. 1997b. El's Divine Feast. Pages 193–96 in *Ugaritic Narrative Poetry*. Edited by Simon B. Parker. SBLWAW 9. Atlanta: Scholars Press.

Liddell, Henry George, and Robert Scott. 1996. *A Greek-English Lexicon*. Revised and augmented throughout by Sir Henry Stuart Jones, with the assistance of Roderick McKenzie; with a revised supplement. Oxford: Clarendon.

Machinist, Peter. 2005. Order and Disorder: Some Mesopotamian Reflections. Pages 31–61 in *Genesis and Regeneration*. Edited by Shaul Shaked. Jerusalem: Israel Academy of Sciences and Humanities.

Marcus, David. 1997. The Betrothal of Yarikh and Nikkal-Ib. Pages 215–18 in *Ugaritic Narrative Poetry*. Edited by Simon B. Parker. SBLWAW 9. Atlanta: Scholars Press.

McBride, S. Dean. 2000. Divine Protocol: Genesis 1:1–2:3 as Prologue to the Pentateuch. Pages 3–41 in *God Who Creates: Essays in Honor of W. Sibley Towner*. Edited by William Brown and S. Dean McBride Jr. Grand Rapids: Eerdmans.

Mettinger, Tryggve N. D. 2007. *The Eden Narrative: A Literary and Religio-historical Study of Genesis 2–3*. Winona Lake, Ind.: Eisenbrauns.

Michalowski, Piotr. 1983. History as Charter: Some Observations on the Sumerian King List. *JAOS* 103:237–48.

Moran, William L., and Ronald S. Hendel, eds. 2002. *The Most Magic Word.* CBQMS 35. Washington, D.C.: Catholic Biblical Association of America.

Nagy, Gregory. 2002. Can Myth Be Saved? Pages 240–48 in *Myth: A New Symposium.* Edited by G. Schrempp and W. Hansen. Bloomington: Indiana University Press.

Neumann, Erich. 1954. *The Origins and History of Consciousness.* New York: Pantheon.

Niditch, Susan. 1996. *Oral World and Written Word: Ancient Israelite Literature.* Library of Ancient Israel. Louisville: Westminster John Knox.

Nissinen, Martti. 2003. *Prophets and Prophecy in the Ancient Near East.* SBLWAW 12. Atlanta: SBL.

Oden, Robert A. 1987. *The Bible without Theology: The Theological Tradition and Alternatives to It.* San Francisco: Harper & Row.

Pardee, Dennis. 2002. *Ritual and Cult at Ugarit.* Edited by Theodore J. Lewis. SBLWAW 10. Atlanta: SBL.

———. 2007. A New Ugaritic Song to ʿAttartu (RIH 98/02). Pages 27–39 in *Ugarit at Seventy-Five.* Edited by K. Lawson Younger Jr. Winona Lake, Ind.: Eisenbrauns.

Parker, Simon B. 1997a. *Stories in Scripture and Inscriptions: Comparative Studies on Narratives in Northwest Semitic Inscriptions and the Hebrew Bible.* New York: Oxford University Press.

———, ed. 1997b. *Ugaritic Narrative Poetry.* SBLWAW 9. Atlanta: SBL.

Sasson, Jack M. 1990. Mari Historiography and the Yakhdun-Lim Disc Inscription. Pages 439–49 in *Lingering over Words: Studies in Ancient Near Eastern Literature in Honor of William L. Moran.* Edited by Tzvi Abusch, John Huehnergard, and Piotr Steinkeller. Harvard Semitic Studies 37. Atlanta: Scholars Press.

———. 1994 "The Posting of Letters with Divine Messages. Pages 299–316 in *Florilegium marianum II: Recueil d'études à la mémoire de Maurice Birot, Mémoires de N.A.B.U. 3.* Edited by Dominique Charpin and Jean-Marie Durand. Paris: Sepoa.

Schmidt, Brian B. 1995. Flood Narratives of Ancient Western Asia. *CANE* 4:2337–51.

Segal, Robert A. 2004. *Myth: A Very Short Introduction.* Oxford: Oxford University Press.

Smith, Jonathan Z. 1975. Good News Is No News: Aretalogy and Gospel. Pages 21–38 in *Christianity, Judaism, and Other Greco-Roman Cults:*

Studies for Morton Smith at Sixty. Part One: New Testament. Edited by Jacob Neusner. SJLA 12. 4 parts. Leiden: Brill.

———. 1987. No News Is Good News: The Gospel as Enigma. Pages 66–80 in *Secrecy in Religions.* Edited by Kees W. Bolle. Studies in the History of Religions 49. Leiden: Brill.

———. 1998. Religion, Religions, Religious. Pages 269–84 in *Critical Terms for Religious Studies.* Edited by Mark C. Taylor. Chicago: University of Chicago Press.

Smith, Mark S. 1994a. Myth and Myth-making in Ugaritic and Israelite Literatures. Pages 293–341 in *Ugarit and the Bible: Proceedings of the International Symposium on Ugarit and the Bible, Manchester, September 1992.* Edited by G. J. Brooke, A. H. W. Curtis, and J. F. Healey. Ugaritisch-biblische Literatur 11. Münster: Ugarit-Verlag.

———. 1994b. *Introduction with Text, Translation and Commentary of KTU 1.1–1.2.* Vol. 1 of *The Ugaritic Baal Cycle.* VTSup 55. Leiden: Brill.

———. 1997. The Baal Cycle. Pages 81–179 in *Ugaritic Narrative Poetry.* Edited by Simon B. Parker. SBLWAW 9. Atlanta: Scholars Press.

———. 2002. *The Early History of God: Yahweh and the Other Deities in Ancient Israel.* 2nd ed. Biblical Resource Series. Grand Rapids: Eerdmans.

———. 2006. *The Sacrificial Rituals and Myths of the Goodly Gods, KTU/CAT 1.23. Royal Constructions of Opposition, Intersection, Integration and Domination.* SBLWAW 51. Atlanta: SBL.

———. 2007a. Biblical Narrative between Ugaritic and Akkadian Literature: Part I: Ugarit and the Hebrew Bible: Consideration of Comparative Research. *RB* 114:5–29.

———. 2007b. Biblical Narrative between Ugaritic and Akkadian Literature: Part II: Mesopotamian Impact on Biblical Narrative. *RB* 114:189–207.

Sourvinou-Inwood, C. 1997. Reconstructing Change: Ideology and the Eleusinian Mysteries. Pages 132–64 in *Inventing Ancient Culture: Historicism, Periodization, and the Ancient World.* Edited by Mark Golden and Peter Toohey. London: Routledge.

Stordalen, Terje. 2000. *Echoes of Eden: Genesis 2–3 and Symbolism of the Eden Garden in Biblical Hebrew Literature.* CBET 25. Louvain: Peeters.

Talmon, Shemaryahu. 1981. Did There Exist a Biblical National Epic? Pages 41–61 in *Proceedings of the Seventh World Congress of Jewish Studies: Studies in the Bible and the Ancient Near East.* Jerusalem: World Union of Jewish Studies.

Tengström, Sven. 1981. *Die Toledotformel und die literarische Structur der priestlichen Erweiterungsschicht im Pentateuch*. Coniectanea biblica: Old Testament 17. Lund: Gleerup.

Toorn, Karel van der. 2007. *Scribal Culture and the Making of the Hebrew Bible*. Cambridge: Harvard University Press.

Vanstiphout, Herman L. J. 2003. The Old Babylonian Literary Canon: Structure, Function and Intention. Pages 1–28 in *Cultural Repertoires: Structure, Function and Dynamics*. Edited by Gillis J. Dorleijn and Herman L. J. Vanstiphout. Groningen Studies in Cultural Change 3. Louvain: Peeters.

Von Hendy, Andrew. 2002. *The Modern Construction of Myth*. Bloomington: Indiana University Press.

Wallace, Howard N. 1985. *The Eden Narrative*. HSM 32. Atlanta: Scholars Press.

Walls, Neal. 2001. *Desire, Discord, and Death: Approaches to Ancient Near Eastern Myth*. Boston: American Schools of Oriental Research.

Weimar, Peter. 2008. Die Toledotformel in der priesterschriftlichen Geschichtsdarstellung. Pages 151–84 in *Studien zur Priestschrift*. FAT 1/56. Tübingen: Mohr Siebeck.

Westermann, Claus. 1984. *Genesis 1–11: A Commentary*. Translated by J. J. Scullion. CC. Minneapolis: Augsburg.

Wyatt, Nick. 2005. *The Mythic Mind: Essays on Cosmology and Religion in Ugaritic and Old Testament Literature*. London: Equinox.

Moses' Death

Susan Ackerman

In the opening lines of his article "The Rod of Aaron and the Sin of Moses," William H. C. Propp provocatively quotes the comment of S. D. Luzzato: "Moses our Teacher committed one sin, but the exegetes have loaded upon him thirteen sins and more, since each of them has invented a new sin" (Propp 1988, 19). Luzzato's quote here refers to the many scholarly attempts to interpret Num 20:1–13, the story in which Moses, with Aaron at his side, draws water from a rock to provide drink for the thirsting Israelites, yet brings forth that water in such a way, the text indicates, that he incurs God's wrath. Indeed, so great is the deity's anger that God decrees that as a result of their malfeasance, neither Moses nor Aaron will be permitted to enter into the promised land. But what is it about the means of bringing forth the water that God found so heinous? This is the question that the thirteen and even more possibilities Luzzato finds within the exegetical record seek to address, by arguing, for example, that Moses struck the rock rather than spoke to it, as God commanded,[1] and in fact struck it twice;[2] or that Moses failed, in bringing forth the water, to attribute proper credit and glory to God but rather claimed the miracle for himself and Aaron;[3] or that Moses earlier had callously withdrawn from the Israelite camp to mourn for his sister Miriam, whose death is reported in Num 20:1, rather than attending to the needs of his parched people.[4] These thir-

---

1. For those who put forward this interpretation, see Loewenstamm 1976a, 190–92; Mann 1979, 483; Propp 1988, 21; 1998, 40, 42; see also, for rabbinic interpreters who hold this view, the catalogues in Margaliot 1983, 206 n. 29; and Milgrom 1983, 251 n. 1; Margaliot 1983, 206 n. 30, also catalogues additional proponents of this theory among modern scholars.
2. Rabbinic references in Milgrom 1983, 251 n. 3.
3. A view advanced by Milgrom 1983, 257–58, 264; 1990, 451–52, 456.
4. See the rabbinic references in Milgrom 1983, 251 n. 6.

teen and more explanations often also address a kindred question that is more theological: the perceived disjunction between the punishment—Yahweh's decree that both Moses and Aaron shall not be permitted to enter the promised land—and whatever crime engendered it. This disjunction is even more a problem for the theory that claims the sin originally attributed to Moses (and Aaron) in the tradition has either been lost or deliberately obscured. This "almost unanimous opinion of modern commentators" (Margaliot 1983, 197 n. 4) I take to be a "counsel of despair" on the part of its proponents,[5] an admission that there is no sin that they can locate in the Numbers text as it stands that justifies Yahweh's response.

The reader of Deuteronomy likely feels this problem of disjunction even more acutely. In Deut 1:37; 3:26; and 4:21, as opposed to the Priestly (P) tradition in Numbers (and as opposed to materials elsewhere in Deuteronomy that have been influenced by the P tradition; 32:48–52),[6] Moses is condemned to die outside the promised land not for any misdeed on his part, but because of the *people's* wrongdoing, and especially the people's fearful refusal to invade Canaan from the south after the spies who were sent forth to investigate that possibility reported the Canaanites to be a gigantic people and their cities to be fortified "up to heaven" (1:28). Implied here is a failure on the people's part to trust in Yahweh's abilities as their war leader, and, as a result, Yahweh declared, as quoted by Moses in 1:35 in his review of Israel's wilderness wanderings, "None from this company, from this evil generation, shall see the good land that I swore to give to your ancestors." More important for our purposes, though, are Moses' words about himself as he continues speaking in this retrospective: "Even with me, Yahweh was angry on account of you [בגללכם], saying, 'You also shall not enter there,'" he reports in 1:37. Deuteronomy 3:26 reads similarly, "Yahweh was angry with me on your account [למענכם]," as does 4:21, "Yahweh was angry with me because of you [על־דבריכם]." The result has felt to commentators particularly "tragic" (Coats 1977, 40; similarly,

---

5. See similarly Margaliot 1983, 198; Milgrom 1983, 252; 1990, 448; Propp 1988, 21 n. 18.

6. On the Priestly authorship of Num 20:1–13, see Levine 1993, 483–84; Propp 1988, 21 n. 15, with references; Sakenfeld (1985, 134 and 136) conversely surveys the "classic source analysis of the nineteenth century" (quoted from 134), which took Num 20:1–13 to be the work of two or more authors. Margaliot (1983, 197 and n. 5 on 197–98) likewise surveys (albeit without approval) more modern commentators who hold this view. Deuteronomy 32:48–52 repeats the P text of Num 27:12–14.

Auerbach 1953, 191–92), "heart-rending" (Mann 1979, 481), and "sorrowful" (Mann 1979, 481), as Moses dies in Deut 34 atop Mount Nebo, in sight of, but not within, the boundaries of the land to which he has worked so hard to deliver his people. There, as Propp writes, "an innocent Moses," according to Deuteronomic tradition, "is punished for the people's sin."[7]

In Deuteronomy, moreover, the tragedy and heart-rending sorrow of Moses' death story is further compounded by the fact that, in 3:23–25, Moses plaintively entreats God to let him cross over to the land beyond the Jordan, only to find himself rebuffed and, indeed, summarily dismissed by Yahweh ("Enough of you," the deity tells Moses, in 3:26). It is also the case that, despite Yahweh's refusal to make an exception for Moses in 3:23–26, God elsewhere in Deuteronomy does decree an exception for two members of the otherwise condemned generation of the wilderness wanderers, Caleb and Joshua; and Caleb, Yahweh says, because Caleb has "wholly followed Yahweh" (1:36). It is in addition Moses who is made to report these words that Yahweh spoke regarding Caleb to the people, in his retrospective speech in Deut 1; that is, it is Moses who must report that Yahweh has judged Caleb to have been a man of wholehearted devotion, whereas Moses himself, by implication, is not.

Moses also, in 34:7, is said to die prematurely (but cf. Loewenstamm 1976a, 185 and 212 n. 1), still in the prime of his life, for, although he had reached the veritable age of one hundred and twenty, neither his eyesight nor his "moisture" (meaning vigor?) had abated. He furthermore dies alone atop Nebo, or, more specifically, he dies bereft of human companionship and in the company only of God. And while some commentators have seen God's presence here as "comforting" (Coats 1977, 40), I wonder if we can really be meant to imagine that Moses, who is still so "full of life" and so "hungry to cross the Jordan" (Brown 1999, 47), is able to find comfort in the presence of a deity who has so summarily rebuffed his plaintive request to enter into the promised land. In the composite text of the Pentateuch as it has come down to us, moreover, the tragic quality of these aspects of Moses' death is compounded by comparing the account of Aaron's demise: unlike Moses, Aaron, according to the P account in Num 20:22–29, dies in the company of his family (his brother Moses and his son Eleazar); furthermore, unlike Moses, Aaron dies in the sight of the whole congregation. Unlike Moses as well, we get no indication that Aaron's death, said in

---

7. Propp 1998, 38; see similarly Loewenstamm 1976a, 187; Goldin 1987, 219.

Num 33:38 to have occurred when he was 123 years old, was untimely or premature—although I should be clear that we likewise get no indication that it was not.

To be sure, some exegetes have tried to argue against classifying the Deuteronomy materials regarding Moses' death as tragic, by proposing that because Moses agreed to the plan of sending spies into southern Canaan in the first place, and even endorsed it as "good" according to Deut 1:23, Yahweh rightly condemns Moses in 1:37; 3:26; and 4:21 as a party to the people's failure to put their trust in God (McKenzie 1967, 97b). Propp has also cautioned, regarding the P account in Num 20, against imposing our sense of justice, and the proportionately proper ratio of punishment to crime, on the Hebrew Bible, reminding us, for example, of the account in 2 Kgs 2:23–24 in which forty-two small boys, whose only "crime" was taunting Elijah by calling him "Baldy," were mauled by two she-bears after being cursed by the prophet in the name of Yahweh (Propp 1988, 21 n. 16). Indeed, at least in Num 20, Propp suggests that the "crime" may be deliberately minimized vis-à-vis the punishment; for P, as Propp sees it, was confronted with the challenge of needing to explain a preexisting tradition—that Moses, along with Aaron, was doomed to die outside the promised land—but to explain in such a way that did not assign to Moses and Aaron that which, to P, was unimaginable: the committing of some particularly egregious sin (Propp 1988, 21). Indeed, Propp concludes that P so resists attributing any sin to Aaron that his only fault in Num 20 is that he is present alongside Moses when Moses angers God by improperly executing the miracle of bringing water forth from the rock (Propp 1988, 24, 26; 1998, 42).

But even if we were to accept Propp's analysis here, it—along with similar analyses that see both P and D, or either, as providing a rationale that explains a preexisting tradition locating Moses' and Aaron's deaths in the wilderness—seems to me to beg the question, for unaddressed in such proposals is an etiology of that preexisting tradition. The most obvious etiology of that tradition, moreover—that the Israelites located Aaron's and Moses' deaths in the wilderness because that is where they actually died—is surely to be judged untenable, a relic of a time of historical positivism regarding the exodus and conquest accounts that has long since past, especially in the light of the burgeoning archaeological consensus of the last two to three decades that locates Israel's origins *within* Canaan. But if not a matter of historical fact, then why a seemingly pervasive Israelite storytelling tradition—known to and evoking commentary in both P and D—of

Moses' and Aaron's deaths in Transjordan? Moreover, why do both P and D, and thus presumably the storytelling tradition on which they depend, insist that Moses' death, which is the death I particularly want to focus on here, is premature and in that respect unnatural, not the result, as the biblical writers would claim of other of Israel's legendary figures of death at a "ripe old age," after a life span "full of years" or "days" (e.g., Abraham, Isaac, Gideon, David, Job; see Gen 25:8; 35:29; Judg 8:32; 1 Chr 23:1; 29:28; Job 42:17)? To answer these questions, and others, I will argue in what follows that the traditions regarding Moses' untimely death in Transjordan are perfectly predictable and indeed expected elements within mythological accounts of the lives of religious heroes.

Admittedly, I am hardly the first to think of the story of Moses' death in terms of mythic hero accounts. In 1976 Samuel E. Loewenstamm argued that "it is against [the] background" of Moses as "a superhuman figure" that "the complicated biblical story of Moses' death and burial should be interpreted" (1976b, 219). Shortly thereafter, in 1977, George Coats published an article entitled "Legendary Motifs in the Moses Death Reports," in which he analyzed certain aspects of the Moses death story—Moses' vigor at the end of his life; Moses' spirit of authority, "never to be equaled in the leadership of any other man" (1977, 36); and the intimate relationship "Moses enjoys face to face with God" (37)—in the light of multiple examinations of hero stories from around the word, works such as Jan de Vries's book *Heroic Song and Heroic Legend* (1963); volumes 1 and 3 of H. Munro and N. Kershaw Chadwick's comparative study of traditional literary genres, both oral and written, called *The Growth of Literature* (1932 and 1940); and Joseph Campbell's *Hero with a Thousand Faces* (1949).

In my opinion, though, Coats's evocation of Campbell's work is unfortunate, as Campbell rather imprecisely and uncritically lumps together what the critic H. A. Reinhold (1949, 322) describes as "vague and shadowy parallels" from hero stories across the world to yield what Campbell identifies as a universal "monomyth." The subject of this monomyth, Campbell goes on to argue, is the hero's quest of self-discovery with the goal of self-transcendence, or the awakening of the psychic awareness of the heroic soul to the hero's own identity and, moreover, to the "at-one-ness" or essential unity of all beings and things. But as Mary R. Lefkowitz astutely suggests, this stress on self-discovery in Campbell's analysis, derived as it is from the arguably romanticized and even mystically described theories of Carl G. Jung, is more about our Freudian- and Jungian-influenced worldview than it is about the hero stories of the premodern world that

Campbell ostensibly seeks to explain: "only a hero in the twentieth century," Lefkowitz rather scathingly observes, "would set off on a journey with the goal of discovering himself" (Lefkowitz 1990, 432).[8] Florence Sandler and Darrell Reeck (1981, 7, 8–9) similarly, although somewhat less pointedly, comment, "What appears to be going on in *The Hero with a Thousand Faces* is ... [the] conversion [of hero myths] from one cultural viewpoint to another," from these myths' original context, in which the hero was a "Doer" (e.g., a Heracles required to perform twelve superhuman labors), to a twentieth-century context, in which the hero is a "Knower" (e.g., a Luke Skywalker, who must learn to feel the "Force" flowing through him).

Still, as misguided as Campbell's stress on self-discovery—or what he calls "initiation," a period in which the hero apprehends theretofore unknown mysteries about himself and the larger mysteries of the cosmos—may be, it is interesting that Campbell locates this self-discovery period within the three-part structure of the *rites de passage* as they were originally articulated in 1909 by the French ethnographer and folklorist Arnold van Gennep (ET: 1960). To be sure, van Gennep's original articulation of the tripartite structure of rites of passage—which included (1) separation, in which "a person or group becomes detached from an earlier fixed point in the social structure or from an earlier set of social conditions"; (2) margin or *limen* (from the Latin meaning "threshold), "when the state of the ritual subject is ambiguous; he is no longer in the old state and has not yet reached the new one"; and (3) reaggregation or reincorporation, "when the ritual subject enters a new stable state with its own rights and obligations" (Deflem 1991, 7–8, paraphrasing Turner 1967, 94)—concerned exclusively, as the name "*rites* of passage" implies, matters of ritual (and life-cycle rituals in particular). But many scholars subsequently came to suggest that van Gennep's *ritual* model might apply to elements within religious systems beyond those in which ritual is an overt concern. For example, in *The Myth of the Eternal Return*, the Romanian-born historian of religion Mircea Eliade argued that, because it is "a consecration, an initiation," a movement from "the profane to the sacred," any journey to the "center" is a rite of passage (Eliade 1954, 18), whether that journey be a *ritual* pilgrimage to a sacred place (Mecca, Hardwar, Jerusalem) or a *narrative* account of a heroic expedition in search of some legendary object

---

8. For another trenchant critique of Campbell, see Doniger 1983. Also in critique of Campbell, see Manganaro 1992, 151–85, and esp. the references cited on 165–67; and Segal 1987, esp. 136–40.

(the Golden Fleece, the Golden Apples, the Plant of Life).[9] It is this sense that the rites-of-passage model helps structure stories of heroic adventure that is reflected (although badly mangled, as I have already suggested) in Campbell, who writes, "The standard path of the mythological adventure of the hero is a magnification of the formula represented in the rites of passage" (Campbell 1949, 30).

Perhaps surprisingly, moreover, even van Gennep's most famous follower, Victor Turner, although surely best remembered as a student of *ritual*, also explored the possibility that the rites-of-passage model might be applied to religious *narrative*. In a 1971 article, for example, Turner reflects back on what he describes as the passion of his undergraduate days, the period of the Icelandic Commonwealth (ca. 874–1262 C.E.) and the thirteenth-century sagas that claimed to recount the Commonwealth's history, in order to argue that these sagas might epitomize what he had originally called in his work "social dramas" but that he came to equate, after he read the English translation of van Gennep's *Rites de Passage*, with van Gennep's description of the tripartite structure of a rite of passage. Thus, in Turner's words, the Icelandic sagas are "*nothing but* connected sequences of social dramas" (1971, 353) or, we might say, narratives structured according to a rites-of-passage model. For example, regarding one of these Icelandic stories, "The Story of Burnt Njal" or "Njal's Saga," Turner (369) writes:

> *Njal's Saga* begins with simple breaches of order, minor crises, and informal redress … which cumulate, despite temporary settlement and redress, until finally the "breach" is the killing of a *goði* [a chieftain-priest] who is also a good man, the "crisis" involves a major cleavage of factions consisting of the major lineages and *sibs* [kin groups] in southern and south-eastern Iceland, and the parties seek "redress" at the *Althing* [a general assembly of Icelanders, especially of the Icelandic aristocracy] and Fifth Court [a legal institution created by Njal and convened at the *Althing*].

A decade later Turner presented this same sort of argument about narratives and social drama, but in a more sweeping fashion, in his essay "Social Dramas and Stories about Them." There he explicitly compares the roots he feels both ritual and narrative have in the social drama: "The social

---

9. This discussion of Eliade's brought to my attention by Elliott 1987, 171.

drama, then, I regard as the experiential matrix from which the many genres of cultural performance, beginning with redressive ritual and juridical procedures and eventually including oral and literary narrative, have been generated" (Turner 1980, 158).

This sort of insight has in turn influenced many biblical scholars to locate a rites-of-passage pattern within certain biblical narratives. In the book he coauthored with Edmund Leach, *Structuralist Interpretations of Biblical Myth*, D. Alan Aycock has argued, for example, that the story of Abraham's nephew Lot in Gen 19 should be read as a "metaphoric rite of passage," a journey from an old (and urban) society (Sodom) to a new (and rural) one, a cave in the hills above Zoar (Aycock 1983, 116–17). Ronald S. Hendel similarly comments on the Exod 2 birth story of Moses as a rite of passage, in which Moses is a character "born a slave, the son of Hebrews, who gains a new status as a free person as a result of his passage into and deliverance from the Nile" (Hendel 2001, 617). More notable for our purposes, though, is Hendel's identification of Moses throughout the Moses story as a "mediator" figure (see similarly Cooper and Goldstein 1997, 214; Propp 1998, 38), or, in the terminology of the rites of passage, someone liminal or "betwixt and between." Thus Hendel writes that Moses "experiences and bridges the categories of free man and slave," for example, and also the ethnic categories of Israelite and Egyptian (2001, 617–18). Moses, "as the heir of Pharaoh and agent of Yahweh," mediates as well, as Hendel would have it, between the two "opposed authorities" under whose rule the Israelites live (618); in addition, once the Israelites pass into the domain of Yahweh, "Moses is the link between Yahweh and the elders, who bring the people to the covenant" (618). "Moses' geographic movements," Hendel goes on to argue, "mark him as a mediator in the spatial transition of the people" (from Egypt to Israel), and his role as a theological mediator "between Israel and Yahweh … is basic to his place in biblical memory" (618–19). Finally, Hendel notes that Moses' Levitical tribe occupies a "betwixt-and-between status" within the Israelite community, as it, although fundamentally a part of Israel, is in many respects unlike its fellow tribes, because it alone is landless and because it alone is of priestly lineage (619).

Hendel, moreover, in both his 2001 article and in a 1989 piece, pushes beyond a rites-of-passage analysis that focuses on the story of Moses as an individual in order to see the larger exodus story of the Israelite people, and especially that story's description of the people's transformational journey from Egypt to the land of Canaan, as an exemplar of Turner's rites-of-passage model (Hendel 2001, 617; 1989, 375). This has also been suggested by Alfred Haldar (1950, 5), Shemaryahu Talmon (1966, 50, 54; 1976, 947b), Robert L. Cohn (1981, 7–23), and Propp (1999, 35–36).[10] These scholars disagree, however, on just where to locate the various stages of the rites-of-passage pattern within the story. For example, Hendel had argued that "the liminal stage is represented by the encounter with Yahweh at the holy mountain, Sinai/Horeb," and that the Israelites' subsequent sojourn in the wilderness and entry into Canaan belongs to the "third and final stage of reaggregation" (Hendel 1989, 375). Later, however, Hendel seemed to modify this view somewhat, by suggesting that "the people don't take well" to their transformation into the "people of Yahweh" that Moses effects at Sinai, "as the stories of the 'murmurings' relate," and so "the transformation of the people is not completed until the next generation, which grows to maturity in freedom" (2001, 617). Propp apparently concurs, pointing out that in the typical rite of passage, the participant returns to his starting point: "He, not his home, has changed" (1999, 35). Propp therefore argues, "To fit the initiation pattern as defined by van Gennep and Turner, we should consider Israel's entire absence from Canaan, from Joseph to Joshua, as their liminal period" (1999, 35). In this view, Israel's "betwixt-and-between" identity continues throughout the entire course of the exodus tradition, ending only with the conclusion of the community's forty years of wandering, in Josh 3–5 when the people finally have entered into the promised land.[11] And just prior, Moses has died. Why? Hendel in his discussion of Moses as mediator only devotes one sentence to this issue, but it is an important one: "Moses' death on the threshold of the promised land, after viewing the whole land, leaves him betwixt and between, neither in Egypt nor the Promised Land" (2001, 618). That is, in the language of rites of passage, Moses is left liminal. As I have already noted, this feels to us as readers like a tragic, heartrending, and sorrowful fate. But as André Droogers pointed out in an important article (1980), this is the *typical* fate of religious heroes.[12]

---

10. The Haldar, Talmon, and Cohn references were all brought to my attention by Propp 1999, 35. See in addition, on the rites-of-passage imagery of the Exodus account, my own 2002 article, 64–80.

11. Propp 1999, 35; a similar view of the end of the Exodus narrative's rite-of-passage structuring is found in Talmon 1966, 54; and Cohn 1981, 13.

12. This reference brought to my attention by Elliott 1987, 171.

More specifically, Droogers, who explicitly describes himself as "follow[ing] the path paved by Turner" (1980, 105), catalogues several symbols he defines as marginal or transitional, or what Turner would call liminal, that recur in the biographies of religious heroes he examines: those of Jesus; the medieval merchant-cum-mendicant and lay preacher Waldes; the founder of the Salvation Army, William Booth; a Zaire prophet, Kimbangu; the Buddha; and Muhammad. These symbols include existence within the world of nature (versus culture), traveling and provisional lodging (versus sedentary life), nonviolence (versus violence), absence of distinctions in rank (versus hierarchy), anonymity and humility (versus name and fame), isolation and seclusion (versus life in the heart of society), hardship and ordeal (versus comfort), dirt (versus purity), poverty and begging (versus wealth), and fasting (versus eating) (1980, 105-6).

Droogers furthermore suggests that while some of the liminal or marginal symbols he finds in stories of religious heroes may have their basis in fact, the symbols are often "of an artificial, constructed nature" (1980, 105; see also 118); that is, the biographers of religious heroes often shape their subjects' stories in a way that *deliberately* incorporates and even exploits marginal or liminal imagery. This is not to say, of course, that Droogers wishes to claim that the biographers about whom he writes anticipated by centuries Turner's theoretical insights and thus were seeking to apply some theory of liminality or, worse, some checklist of liminal motifs mechanically and even unimaginatively to their narratives. Instead, Droogers's claim is that certain religious figures rather naturally seem to have their life stories told using what Turner has taught us to describe as liminal motifs and liminal imagery because these figures are understood by their biographers as having lived, at a minimum, unconventionally and even, in more maximal cases, on the extreme margins of society. Hence the language and imagery of unconventionality and even extreme marginality—which is to say, according to Turner's framework, the language and imagery of liminality—are well appropriated into the narratives about these characters. Droogers stresses, moreover, that, typically, this marginality never fully resolves itself: that even the Buddha, for example, although he reengages with Indian society after the decisive moment of his enlightenment, continues during his reengagement to manifest such marginal symbols as traveling and provisional lodging (he wanders around with his disciples, teaching), a preference for the world of nature, versus culture (the Buddha and his adepts often spend the night in gardens, parks, or forests), professions of nonviolence (the Buddhist prohibition of killing is noteworthy here), and an absence of distinctions in rank (here note the Buddhist rejection of the Hindu caste system). Similarly, I would suggest, the story of Moses is one in which marginality never fully resolves itself. Moses dies, to put the matter more simply, on Mount Nebo because his story conforms to the paradigm of the story of the typical religious hero, who is permanently marginal or permanently liminal. As such, Moses cannot be included in the "reincorporated" or "reaggregated" Israel whose liminality ends when the Jordan is crossed.

This I would count as the major conclusion of my paper, but before I close, I would like to speak briefly to another issue, which is the potential significance of blood offerings at crucial points of transition within the exodus story. Obviously, one such crucial point is Josh 3–5 and the three key episodes that mark the people's entry into the promised land in these chapters: (1) the crossing of the Jordan, which is a recapitulation of an earlier crucial point of transition, the crossing of the Reed Sea in Exod 14; (2) the setting up of twelve stones at Gilgal, which is likewise a recapitulation of an earlier point of transition, Moses' setting up twelve pillars in Exod 24 after the covenant-making events at Sinai; and (3) the celebration of Passover, which also is a recapitulation of the Israelites' transition out of their bondage in Egypt as effected by the Passover sacrifice that was made on the night of the tenth plague. In anticipation of the Passover ceremony in Joshua, moreover, there is a mass circumcision of the men who had been born during the years of wilderness wanderings, as it is said they had not yet been circumcised. This is also, obviously, a recapitulation of an earlier moment of transition, of the circumcision—whether actual or symbolic—of Moses and of Gershom in the strange episode of Exod 4:24–26. But the mass circumcision in Joshua is in addition a final spilling of blood in a story where blood has been spilled at almost every critical moment of transition: when Moses returns to Egypt after his sojourn in Midian in Exod 4:24–26; when the Israelites slaughter lambs and smear blood on their doorposts, as they prepare to leave Egypt on the night of the tenth plague in Exod 12; and in 24:3–8, when they enter into the covenant that makes them Yahweh's own people, as Moses dashes the congregation with the blood he has collected from the people's sacrificial offerings.

But what about the rite of the affirmation of the covenant and the related rite of Joshua's investiture that are described in Deut 27:1–31:29: should we not likewise read this as a critical transition point? Yet, quite curiously, no sacrifice is offered in conjunction with this reaffirmation or investiture, and no blood is spilled. Or is it? In my reading, especially if we skip over the secondarily added poems of Deut 32 and 33, the rite of covenant reaffirmation and investiture is sealed by a blood offering, the blood offering of Moses' death.

Indeed, I might be so bold here as to bring my two key proposals together by arguing that, as the original covenant-making ceremony at Sinai marked a point of transition for the Israelites, transforming them from a disparate group of former slaves into the covenant people of Yahweh, so too does the covenant-affirmation ceremony in Deut 27:1–31:29 mark a point of transition, ratifying the Israelites' identity as Yahweh's covenant people and also marking their imminent move out of liminal space and into their rightful (or, we might say, reaggregated) home in the promised land. To mark this transition, the narrative requires, as it has throughout, an offering of blood; what better offering could there be than blood from the figure who symbolizes liminality in their midst and who, moreover, like the typical religious hero but unlike the people, cannot shed his liminal identity? Moses dies on Mount Nebo because his people are moving on, and his blood offering is the one that appropriately marks their transition out of a liminal existence.

Works Cited

Ackerman, Susan. 2002. Why Is Miriam Also among the Prophets? (And Is Zipporah among the Priests?). *JBL* 121:47–80.

Auerbach, Elias. 1953. *Moses*. Amsterdam: Ruys.

Aycock, D. Alan. 1983. The Fate of Lot's Wife: Structural Mediation in Biblical Mythology. Pages 113–119 in *Structuralist Interpretations of Biblical Myth*. Edited by Edmund Leach and D. Alan Aycock. Cambridge: Cambridge University Press and Royal Anthropological Institutes of Great Britain and Ireland.

Brown, Erica S. 1999. In Death as in Life. *BRev* 15, no. 3:40–47, 51.

Campbell, Joseph. 1949. *The Hero with a Thousand Faces*. Bollingen Series 17. Princeton: Princeton University Press.

Chadwick, H. Munro, and N. Kershaw Chadwick. 1932–1940. *The Growth of Literature*. 3 vols. Cambridge: Cambridge University Press.

Coats, George W. 1977. Legendary Motifs in the Moses Death Reports. *CBQ* 39:33–44.

Cohn, Robert L. 1981. *The Shape of Sacred Space: Four Biblical Studies*. AAR Studies in Religion 23. Chico, Calif.: Scholars Press.

Cooper, Alan M., and Bernard R. Goldstein. 1997. At the Entrance to the Tent: More Cultic Resonances in Biblical Narrative. *JBL* 116:201–15.

Deflem, Mathieu. 1991. Ritual, Anti-Structure, and Religion: A Discussion of Victor Turner's Processual Symbolic Analysis. *Journal for the Scientific Study of Religion* 30:1–25.

Doniger, Wendy. 1983. Origins of Myth-Making Man (review of Joseph Campbell, *Historical Atlas of World Mythology*, vol. 1: *The Way of the Animal Powers*). *The New York Times Book Review*, December 18, 3, 24–25. Repr., pages 181–86 in *Paths to the Power of Myth: Joseph Campbell and the Study of Religion*. Edited by Daniel C. Noel. New York: Crossroad, 1990.

Droogers, André. 1980. Symbols of Marginality in the Biographies of Religious and Secular Innovators. *Numen* 27:105–21.

Eliade, Mircea. 1954. *The Myth of the Eternal Return, or Cosmos and History*. Bollingen Series 46. Princeton: Princeton University Press.

Elliott, Alison Goddard. 1987. *Roads to Paradise: Reading the Lives of the Early Saints*. Hanover, N.H.: University Press of New England.

Gennep, Arnold van. 1960. *The Rites of Passage*. Translated by Monika B. Vizedom and Gabrielle L. Caffee. Chicago: University of Chicago Press.

Goldin, Judah. 1987. The Death of Moses: An Exercise in Midrashic Transposition. Pages 219–25 in *Love and Death in the Ancient Near East: Essays in Honor of Marvin H. Pope*. Edited by John H. Marks and Robert M. Good. Guilford, Conn.: Four Quarters.

Haldar, Alfred. 1950. *The Notion of the Desert in Sumero-Accadian and West-Semitic Religions*. Uppsala Universitetsårsskrift 1950: 3. Uppsala: Almqvist & Wiksells.

Hendel, Ronald S. 1989. Sacrifice as a Cultural System: The Ritual Symbolism of Exodus 24, 3–8. *ZAW* 101:366–90.

———. 2001. The Exodus in Biblical Memory. *JBL* 120:601–22.

Lefkowitz, Mary R. 1990. The Myth of Joseph Campbell. *American Scholar* 59:429–34.

Levine, Baruch A. 1993. *Numbers 1–20: A New Translation with Introduction and Commentary*. AB 4A. New York: Doubleday.

Loewenstamm, Samuel E. 1976a. The Death of Moses. Pages 185–217 in *Studies on the Testament of Abraham*. Edited by George W. F. Nickelsburg. Septuagint and Cognate Studies 6. Missoula, Mont.: Scholars Press.

———. 1976b. The Testament of Abraham and the Texts Concerning Moses' Death. Pages 219–25 in *Studies on the Testament of Abraham*. Edited by George W. F. Nickelsburg. Septuagint and Cognate Studies 6. Missoula, Mont.: Scholars Press.

Manganaro, Marc. 1992. *Myth, Rhetoric, and the Voice of Authority*. New Haven: Yale University Press.

Mann, Thomas W. 1979. Theological Reflections on the Denial of Moses. *JBL* 98:481–94.

Margaliot, M. 1983. The Transgression of Moses and Aaron—Num 20:1–13. *JQR* 74:196–228.

McKenzie, John L. 1967. The Historical Prologue of Deuteronomy. Pages 95–101 in vol. 1 of *Papers: Fourth World Congress of Jewish Studies*. Jerusalem: World Union of Jewish Studies.

Milgrom, Jacob. 1983. Magic, Monotheism, and the Sin of Moses. Pages 251–65 in *The Quest for the Kingdom of God: Studies in Honor of George E. Mendenhall*. Edited by Herbert B. Huffmon, Frank A. Spina, and Alberto Ravinell Whitney Green. Winona Lake, Ind.: Eisenbrauns.

———. 1990. *Numbers: The Traditional Hebrew Text with the New JPS Translation*. JPS Torah Commentary. Philadelphia: Jewish Publication Society.

Propp, William H. C. 1988. The Rod of Aaron and the Sin of Moses. *JBL* 107:19–26.

———. 1998. Why Moses Could Not Enter the Promised Land. *BRev* 14, no. 3:36–40, 42–43.

———. 1999. *Exodus 1–18*. AB 2. New York: Doubleday.

Reinhold, H. A. 1949. A Thousand Faces—But Who Cares? (review of Joseph Campbell, *The Hero with a Thousand Faces*). *Commonweal* 50:321–24.

Sakenfeld, Katharine Doob. 1985. Theological and Redactional Problems in Numbers 20:2–13. Pages 133–54 in *Understanding the Word: Essays in Honor of Bernhard W. Anderson*. Edited by James T. Butler, Edgar W. Conrad, and Ben C. Ollenburger. JSOTSup 37. Sheffield: JSOT Press.

Sandler, Florence, and Darrell Reeck. 1981. The Masks of Joseph Campbell. *Religion* 11:1–20.

Segal, Robert A. 1987. *Joseph Campbell: An Introduction*. New York: Garland.

Talmon, Shemaryahu. 1966. The "Desert Motif" in the Bible and in Qumran Literature. Pages 31–63 in *Biblical Motifs: Origins and Transformations*. Edited by Alexander Altmann. Philip W. Lown Institute of Advanced Judaic Studies, Brandeis University, Studies and Texts 3. Cambridge: Harvard University Press.

———. 1976. Wilderness. Pages 946a–49a in *Interpreter's Dictionary of the Bible: Supplementary Volume*. Edited by Keith Crim. Nashville: Abingdon.

Turner, Victor W. 1967. *The Forest of Symbols: Aspects of Ndembu Ritual*. Ithaca, N.Y.: Cornell University Press.

———. 1971. An Anthropological Approach to Icelandic Saga. Pages 349–74 in *The Translation of Culture: Essays to E. E. Evans-Pritchard*. Edited by T. O. Beidelman. London: Tavistock.

———. 1980. Social Dramas and Stories about Them. *Critical Inquiry* 7:141–68.

Vries, Jan de. 1963. *Heroic Song and Heroic Legend*. Translated by B. J. Timmer. London: Oxford University Press.

Myth and Social Realia in Ancient Israel: Early Hebrew Poems as Folkloric Assemblage

Hugh R. Page Jr.

Introduction

In this paper I will assess the strengths, weaknesses, and implications of the use of early Hebrew poems as a control group for the testing of single theories and methodological paradigms aimed at the reconstruction of myth, folklore, and social reality in ancient Israel. Here I build on the work done within the Albright-Cross-Freedman tradition on Gen 49; Exod 15; Num 23–24; Deut 32, 33; Judg 5; 1 Sam 2; 2 Sam 1, 22, 23; and Pss 18, 29, 68, 72, and 78 (see, e.g., Cross and Freedman 1952, 1997; Geller 1979; Cross 1973; Freedman 1980). Holding in abeyance the rather thorny issues of the whether the poems are truly archaic or simply archaizing (for a synopsis of linguistic evidence see Robertson 1972; and Sáenz-Badillos 1993, 56–62), my goal is to offer an experimental reading of the early Hebrew corpus as a poetic *assemblage* containing data that can be used to: (1) delimit the parameters of the divine-human relationship; (2) understand more clearly conceptions of personhood; and (3) determine the extent to which these poems may have been generative of both implicit and explicit *spiritualities* from the eleventh to the fifth century B.C.E. I hope to demonstrate as well that textual *corpora*, even those whose authorship, date, and provenance are contested, can be used to promote creative scholarly conversation about the topography of ancient Israel's intellectual landscape.

Among literary theorists in general, poetry is a contested construct, and its distinguishing features continue to be the subject of great debate (cf., e.g., the works cited in Randall 1971 with the theoretical treatment of Jakobson 1985, and with the definition of Bloom 2005, 1). The same is true of biblical poetry in general and early Hebrew poetry in particular. The study of the latter has become something of an anachronism in twenty-first-century biblical scholarship. In recent years efforts to extend the pioneering work of Cross and Freedman (1952, 1997), Robertson (1972), Geller (1979), and O'Connor (1980) on the corpus have been modest at best. Moreover, the historical reconstruction and cultural analysis of these poems undertaken by Freedman (collected and republished in Freedman 1980) some three decades ago represents perhaps the most significant attempt to utilize this body of poems, in its entirety, as a repository of early Israelite lore and to mine it specifically for the purposes of historical reconstruction and ethnological analysis.

With the reliability of the Hebrew Bible as witness to life in early Israel called increasingly into question (see, e.g., Dever 2012, 368–81), it would appear that passion for this type of research has waned. The studies edited by Wilfred Watson and Johannes de Moor in *Verse in Ancient Near Eastern Prose* (1993) are indicative of a resurgence of interest in the embedding of poetry within prose in ancient Near Eastern literature. Work of this kind promises to help us rethink the process of biblical canon formation and the role that narrative-embedded poems such as Gen 49, Deut 32 and 33, Judg 5, 1 Sam 2, 2 Sam 1, and others have played in that process. The tendency to push positivist research out of the intellectual mainstream is regrettable because there are issues relating to early Hebrew poetry—beyond those focusing on orthography, prosody, and historical veracity—yet to be adequately addressed. One such issue has to do with methodology and its impact on classification and interpretation.

Methodology

When one looks specifically at early Hebrew poetry within the context of a larger inquiry about myth, theories of myth, and the Hebrew Bible, several questions arise as to the nature of their content, their placement in the canon, and scholarly attempts to engage them. Some of the more important are: Do they contain "impressionistic" musings on major events and themes in Israel's early history?[1] Can "reflexes" and "fragments" of myths and other lore be recovered from them? Was their placement within the Jewish canon random? How did those responsible for compiling and

---

1. Many years ago, I recall hearing the late Frank Moore Cross Jr. refer to what one finds at points in the Ugaritic mythological corpus as "impressionistic parallelism." See his definition of this phenomenon in Cross 1997, viii.

editing the Hebrew Bible classify them? What implicit assumptions have scholars from the nineteenth century to the present made about the corpus as a whole? How have these presuppositions influenced their readings? Did early Israelite literati recognize these poems as special? Was this due to their perceived antiquity? Does the delimitation of a body of early Hebrew poems by biblical scholars amount to the imposition of a nonindigenous (i.e., *etic* in anthropological parlance) schema of classification?

These questions point to an implicit tension in research on both biblical myth and ancient Hebrew poetry that centers on two processes. The first process New Testament scholar Vincent Wimbush has labeled *scripturalization*, which he defines as "a social-psychological-political structure establishing its own reality" (2012, 19). In a series of works over the past twelve years, he suggests that this process involves, more broadly, the creation, demarcation, and/or adoption of authoritative texts by individuals and social aggregates (see, e.g., 2000, 2008, and 2011). The second process some social scientists are now designating the *anthropology of collecting*—the cross-cultural historical analysis of behavioral norms that govern the gathering, preservation, and exchange of objects to which members of a society have ascribed significant value and prestige. One can discern in "so-called" biblical myth, early Hebrew verse, and biblical scholarship traces of both processes. For example, as an academic guild we have physical artifacts and literature to study because a community of readers has deemed them of value, collected, and preserved them for posterity. Customs have been established for the preparation of "critical editions" and anthologies that make it possible for us to conduct research on them. In studying these "texts," scholars group them into categories that facilitate certain kinds of analysis and apply interpretive models that make it possible for them both to answer specific questions and to construct explanatory stories about the Bible and its *Weltanschauung*. Neither the primary sources nor the scholarly "interpretations" of them are neutral. They are, in a sense, value-laden lore woven into the texts they describe. The target audiences are not those of the originals. The kinship between the two may be closer than once supposed. This depends, in large part, on how one construes the definition and aims of scholarship and myth.

Theorists fully embracing post-Enlightenment paradigms for biblical engagement would, no doubt, find this assertion troubling at best. Others, such as Claude Lévi-Strauss and Robert Segal, would be perhaps more open to this possibility. For Lévi-Strauss, interpretive writing about myth must be treated as a version of the myths such studies elucidate (see Lévi-Strauss 1963, 216–17). For Segal, myths are stories "about something significant." These stories center on "personalities" that are "either the agents or objects of actions." Moreover, the stories must "be held tenaciously by adherents" (2004, 5–6). Segal's traits could easily be applied to scholarship as well. Therefore, the act of collecting could be understood as associated with, generative of, and perhaps even akin to the creation of myth and scholarship thereon.

Among the many scholarly works that have touched upon both early Hebrew poetry and myth, three illustrate these processes. The first is Robert Lowth's *Lectures on the Sacred Poetry of the Hebrews* (Lowth 1969). Lowth's lectures offer a thorough and erudite treatment of the entire phenomenon of Hebrew poetry. They address issues such as the purpose of poetry; its "species," poetic inspiration, the role of criticism in the theological enterprise, Hebrew meter, Hebrew poetic styles (e.g., parabolic, sententious, and figurative), poetic imagery, allegory, comparison, personification, the sublime and its three forms (expression, sentiment, and passion), the relationship between poetry and prophecy, and the different types of poetry (elegiac, didactic, lyric, dramatic, odes, and hymns). Poetic fragments in the Pentateuch receive special attention as vestiges of the Mosaic age and illustrate for him the sublime nature of poetry and fundamental features of all Hebrew verse. Thus these poems are an important part of the larger body of biblical verse "anthologized" or "collected" by Lowth to accomplish three general goals: (1) to place the poetry of the Hebrew Bible on a par with the great poems of the Western literary tradition; (2) to apply sound principles in the taxonomic classification and interpretation of Hebrew poetry; and (3) to plumb the secrets of the poetic impulse and output in ancient Israel and make such accessible for the purposes of theological speculation and construction (Lowth 1969, xxiii–xlii, 1–97).

The second is James Frazer's *Folk-lore in the Old Testament* (Frazer 1918). For Frazer, the Hebrew Bible contains a disparate "collection" of primitive human survivals. These "traces of savagery and superstition" (1:x) he juxtaposes with a separate body of work within the Hebrew Bible that reflect "a spiritual religion and a pure morality" (1:x)—chiefly found in the Psalter, prophetic literature, and historical writings.

The third is Louis Ginzberg's *Legends of the Jews* (Ginzberg 1998). His magisterial work consists of two collections—the first of harmonized and rearticulated Jewish lore and the second an encyclopedic set of indices to sources used in his mythological reconstructions (1998; see Kugel's introduction, p. xi).

One can see in these studies an impulse toward collection and the definition of boundaries for texts and traditions that have special authority within the academy and the several "publics" served by it. It scarcely needs to be said that one can also see a similar impulse in the Hebrew Bible. That taxonomic classification is at least one of the preoccupations of biblical writers has not gone unnoticed by the recent generation of scholars studying collection as a social process. In the introduction to *The Cultures of Collecting*, John Elsner and Roger Cardinal begin their examination of human classification and collection with an appeal to the stories of Adam and Noah. Noah represents for them the mythological "ur-collector" (1997, ix). The presence of both texts representing an assortment of forms and myriad internal references to archival sources is indicative of the utilization of collections in the compilation of the Hebrew Bible. The care with which attributions are handled in the case of narrative-embedded poetry is another indicator. The several markers within the Psalter (e.g., inscriptions, divine names, doxologies, and items in its lexical inventory) that enable the subclassification of its contents is yet another element pointing to the role that the process of collecting played in canon formation. To date, the treatment given by biblical scholars to the social dimensions of collecting and their impact on canon formation, the selection and placement of key texts, such as early Hebrew poems, and the preservation of myth and epic traditions has not been extensive. However, with the emergence of a new body of research on collection as process, this can begin to be remedied.

Collection

In *On Collecting: An Investigation into Collecting in the European Tradition* (1995), Susan Pearce suggests collection is a conscious act with dimensions related to social praxis, poetics, and politics. Though her focus is on the historical and modern dimensions of collecting in Europe, much of what she has proposed as a heuristic framework can be applied cross-culturally. Her principal suggestion is that collecting "represents one of the fundamental ways in which people use material culture to construct their identities and their social roles" (xiii). She suggests that humans—as collectors—stand at the cross-section of two continuums. One represents the historic tradition of culturally defined customs for collecting. The other represents an individually defined poetics of collection. The latter is an imaginative process that can be further subclassified into three types: souvenir (romantic attribution), fetishistic (object as prime actor), and systematic (intellectual rationale as basis). She also points to a fundamental paradox implicit in collecting. Items collected are, in a sense given a new identity through an act of metaphorical sacrifice. Here she builds on the earlier work of H. Hubert and M. Mauss. She says:

> the sacrifice passes by way of death from life to eternity, a fact of life which is both uplifting and sad. This is the central paradox of all collected pieces. They are wrenched out of their own true contexts and become dead to their living time and space in order that they may be given an immortality within the collection. They cease to be living goods working in the world and become reified thoughts and feelings, carefully kept by conscious preservation. (1995, 24–25)

To her observations, I would add that the collection of artifacts, particularly those that are literary, yields at least five distinct outcomes. First, it commodifies cultural traditions. Second, it creates a hierarchy of textual privilege. Third, it juxtaposes both homogeneous ideas and potentially incongruous ideologies. Fourth, it establishes parameters for meaning potential and intertextual discourse. Fifth, it crystallizes elements that stabilize and destabilize reading communities.

THE EARLY HEBREW POETIC CORPUS AS COLLECTION

Treating the Early Hebrew poetic corpus as a distinctive *assemblage* opens some interesting interpretive possibilities that promise to advance the work done by Cross and Freedman, particularly regarding our understanding of their social and religious function. Freedman has suggested that the poems be subdivided into three historical strata. The first, consisting of Exod 15, Ps 29, and Judg 5, represents a twelfth-century context in which "Mosaic Yahwism" was prevalent. The second, consisting of Gen 49, Num 23–24, and Deut 33, represents an eleventh-century milieu in which a revival of patriarchal religion has taken place. The third, in which the remaining poems can be classed, represents a tenth-century setting in which syncretistic elements from the Canaanite religious sphere have been brought into the Israelite theological matrix (1980, 78–79).

If we draw on the suggestions of Pearce, it seems clear that the poetic employed by biblical compilers does not view early Hebrew poems as souvenirs per se, though the narratives into which those found in the Pentateuch and Deuteronomistic History have been embedded paint a theologically tendentious portrait or Israel's past. Insofar as the attributions these same poems bear call attention to significant personages and events in the national saga, they are clearly texts that have a special authority and, I would add, a *liminalizing power*. As texts that have been "sacrificed," to use the image offered by Pearce, their literary transmutation can be said to have imbued them with a special authority both within and apart from the texts that surround them. To read or hear them "in course" as currently placed is to comply with the redactor's wishes and accept the collection's textual worldview. To read or hear them selectively, randomly, or out of sequence is—perhaps—to reinfuse them with some measure of the vitality they lost as textual artifacts in a larger collection. Thus they might well be considered poetic fetishes with the potential to elicit eschatological convergence through listening, reading, or recitation. The narratives surrounding these poems offer an implicit rationale for their systematic placement, and thereby for their inclusion in the final biblical anthology. Those in the Psalter are more difficult to classify according to these criteria, though each bears an inscription that argues in favor of its inclusion as part of a significant subcollection with this larger anthology.

If these poems are in effect components of an assemblage of early Hebrew poetry, it is a collection of a most unusual nature, given that its individual works are not found in a single location. Here one can only offer a vague guess as to the reason. If Pearce is correct that there is a dialectic at work involving the collector's poetics—and here one has to leave open the possibility that in the case of the Hebrew Bible this was a collective endeavor—and the set of culturally defined parameters within which the process of collecting takes place, then there are two possibilities. The first is that the breaking up of the collection was counterbalanced by the texts' archaic linguistic features and overall appeal to human existential crises. Thus it could be called a *virtual assemblage of poetic lore* embedded within the larger canon. As such, it promotes reflection on the creation of a unified and diverse community, the impact of coalition building, the inscrutability of divine providence, the continuing presence of the ancestors, the folly of war, the religious significance of social margins, and other issues of import for those who were the collection's target audience. The second is that its poems create a safe intellectual place for thinking about these events. Segal follows D. F. Winnicott in suggesting that myth and play create an artificial universe in which belief can be suspended and people can learn to deal with the real world (2004, 138). Could it be that early Hebrew poems acted in a similar manner during the exilic and Persian periods? It is not improbable that such was the case.

More work needs to be done in this area as well as to identify what indigenous customs pertaining to collection were developed in the ancient Near East. Not only will we have to continue looking critically at archaeological assemblages, epigraphic texts, and the Hebrew Bible itself, we will also need to look more closely at work being done by social scientists on collecting in other cultures. Such efforts promise to help us understand the forces driving the creation and collection of stories in the ancient world and our own.

Works Cited

Bloom, Harold. 2005. *The Art of Reading Poetry*. New York: Perennial.

Cross, Frank Moore. 1973. *Canaanite Myth and Hebrew Epic: Essays in the History of the Religion of Israel*. Cambridge: Harvard University Press.

Cross, Frank Moore, and David Noel Freedman. 1952. *Early Hebrew Orthography*. American Oriental Series 36. New Haven: American Oriental Society.

———. 1997. *Studies in Ancient Yahwistic Poetry*. 2nd ed. Biblical Resource Series. Grand Rapids: Eerdmans.

Dever, William G. 2012. *The Lives of Ordinary People in Ancient Israel: Where Archaeology and the Bible Intersect*. Grand Rapids: Eerdmans.

Elsner, John, and Roger Cardinal, eds. 1997. *The Cultures of Collecting*. Repr., London: Reaktion.

Frazer, James G. 1918. *Folk-lore in the Old Testament: Studies in Comparative Religion, Legend and Law*. 3 vols. London: Macmillan.

Freedman, David Noel. 1980. *Pottery, Poetry, and Prophecy: Studies in Early Hebrew Poetry*. Winona Lake, Ind.: Eisenbrauns.

Geller, Stephen A. 1979. *Parallelism in Early Biblical Poetry*. HSM 20. Missoula, Mont.: Scholars Press.

Ginzberg, Louis. 1998. *The Legends of the Jews*. 7 vols. Repr., Baltimore: Johns Hopkins University Press.

Jakobson, Roman. 1985. Poetry of Grammar and Grammar of Poetry. In *Roman Jakobson: Verbal Art, Verbal Sign, Verbal Time*. Edited by Krystyna Pomorska and Stephen Rudy. Oxford: Blackwell.

Lévi-Strauss, Claude. 1963. *Structural Anthropology*. Translated by Claire Jacobson and Brooke G. Schoepf. New York: Basic Books.
Lowth, Robert. 1969. *Lectures on the Sacred Poetry of the Hebrews*. 2nd ed. 2 vols. Anglistica & Americana 43. Repr., Hildesheim: Olms.
Moor, Johannes C. de, and Wilfred G. E. Watson, eds. 1993. *Verse in Ancient Near Eastern Prose*. AOAT 42. Neukirchen-Vluyn: Neukirchener.
O'Connor, M. 1980. *Hebrew Verse Structure*. Winona Lake, Ind.: Eisenbrauns.
Pearce, Susan M. 1995. *On Collecting: An Investigation into Collecting in the European Tradition*. London: Routledge.
Randall, Dudley, ed. 1971. *The Black Poets*. New York: Bantam.
Robertson, David A. 1972. *Linguistic Evidence in Dating Early Hebrew Poetry*. SBLDS 3. Missoula, Mont.: Scholars Press.
Sáenz-Badillos, Angel. 1993. *A History of the Hebrew Language*. Translated by J. Elwolde. Cambridge: Cambridge University Press.
Segal, Robert A. 2004. *Myth: A Very Short Introduction*. Oxford: Oxford University Press.
Wimbush, Vincent. 2000. Introduction: Reading Darkness, Reading Scriptures. In *African Americans and the Bible: Sacred Texts and Social Textures*. Edited by Vincent L. Wimbush. New York: Continuum.
———. 2008. Introduction: TEXTureS, Gestures, Power: Orientation to Radical Excavation. Pages 1–22 in *Theorizing Scriptures: New Critical Orientations to a Cultural Phenomenon*. Edited by Vincent Wimbush. New Brunswick, N.J.: Rutgers University Press.
———. 2011. Interpreters—Enslaving/Enslaved/Runagate. *JBL* 130:5–24.
———. 2012. *White Men's Magic: Scripturalization as Slavery*. New York: Oxford University Press.

Myth and History in Ezekiel's Oracle Concerning Tyre (Ezekiel 26–28)

Marvin A. Sweeney

1. Introduction

Scholars generally recognize the importance of Ezekiel's oracles concerning the downfall of Tyre in 26:1–28:19 among the oracles concerning the nations in Ezek 25–32. Like the oracles concerning Egypt in Ezek 29–32, the oracles concerning Tyre constitute an inordinately large block of material when compared to the smaller oracles concerning Ammon in 25:1–7, Moab in 25:8–11, Edom in 25:12–14, Philistia in 25:15–17, Sidon in 28:20–23, and even Israel/Jacob in 28:24–26. The importance of Ezekiel's Tyrian oracles is generally assessed in relation to Nebuchadnezzar's alleged thirteen-year siege of the city, which ultimately saw the capitulation—but not the destruction—of the city in 572 B.C.E.[1] Most interpreters have focused on diachronic issues in the interpretation of the Tyrian oracles, namely the degree to which Ezekiel's oracles interrelate with the historical event of Nebuchadnezzar's siege of the city and the compositional history of the oracles.[2] In the first instance, uncertainties concerning the course and outcome of the siege complicate efforts at interpreting 26:1–28:19. In the second instance, the formal characteristics and contents of the oracles in 26:1–28:19 indicate that this material is a redactional assemblage of earlier materials.

---

1. For commentaries on the Tyrian oracles, see Allen 1990, 70–100; Block 1998, 28–128; Darr 2001; Greenberg 1997, 528–99; Hals 1989, 186–203; Odell 2005, 333–70; Pohlmann 2001, 374–98; Zimmerli 1983, 21–101.
2. In addition to the commentaries cited above, see Corral 2002; van Dijk 1968. For discussion of historical issues pertaining to Tyre, see esp. Katzenstein 1973, 295–347, esp. 316–37.

Although interpreters are generally correct in their diachronic assessments of Ezekiel's Tyrian oracles in 26:1–28:19, two issues require further study and clarification. The first issue is the role of Ezekiel's mythological allusions in these oracles. Scholars have noted allusions to a variety of mythological motifs known from Mesopotamia, Ugarit, and Israel/Judah, including the combat motifs of the Babylonian *Enuma Elish* and the Ugaritic Baal Cycle; the descent to the netherworld from Inanna's or Ishtar's Descent to the Netherworld; the creation narratives from Gen 1–3; and the narratives concerning the construction of the priestly garments in Exod 28 and 39. Although these motifs have been noted, interpreters have not fully explained their function within Ezekiel's oracles other than to indicate Ezekiel's literary or intellectual breadth in his portrayals of YHWH's actions in relation to Tyre and the world at large. Insofar as Ezekiel's worldview is based upon a mythological paradigm due in large measure to his identity as a Zadokite priest,[3] the issue demands further study, particularly given the predominance of the YHWH recognition formula in this material and its importance for identifying acts of divine revelation.[4] The second issue is the literary relationship between the larger block of material concerning Tyre in 26:1–28:19 and the smaller oracles concerning Sidon in 28:20–23 and the restoration of Israel/Jacob in 28:24–26. Although these oracles were composed for different occasions and literary settings from those of the Tyrian oracles, study of the formal characteristics of the Tyrian, Sidonian, and Israelite oracles demonstrates that the oracles concerning Sidon and Israel/Jacob now clearly form the culmination of the block of materials concerning Tyre in Ezek 26–28.[5]

Further study of the literary form of Ezek 26–28 and the function of the mythological allusions within this block of materials concerning Tyre, Sidon, and Israel indicates an important dimension of Ezekiel's theological worldview: Ezekiel's portrayal of the downfall of Tyre portends the restoration of Israel/Jacob in the book of Ezekiel and thereby points to the restoration of the temple and Israel at the center of creation in the final form of the book of Ezekiel. In order to demonstrate this hypothesis, in this paper I examine several issues, including the literary form and struc-

---

3. For discussion of Ezekiel's identity as a Zadokite priest and its influence on his worldview, see my study in Sweeney 2005a; 2005b, 132–36.

4. For discussion of the YHWH recognition formula, see Zimmerli 1982a, 1982b.

5. For discussion of the literary form of the book of Ezekiel and its bearing on Ezek 26–28, see Sweeney 2005a, 129–42; 2005b, 127–32.

ture of Ezek 26–28 as a whole; the function of mythological motifs known from Mesopotamian, Ugaritic, and Israelite/Judean literature within the constituent subunits of Ezek 26–28; and the place of Ezek 26–28 within the whole book of Ezekiel.

2. The Literary Form of Ezekiel 26–28

Study of the literary form of Ezek 26–28 begins with the observation that an introductory chronological formula appears in 26:1, "And it came to pass in the eleventh year, on the first of the month, that the word of YHWH came to me, saying...."[6] Prior studies of the literary form and structure of the book of Ezekiel indicate that the chronological formulae of Ezekiel introduce the major structural units of the book. In that the next chronological formula does not appear until 29:1, where it introduces the first oracle concerning Egypt in 29:1–16, the chronological formula in 26:1 introduces a major unit of the book in 26:1–28:26. Such an observation indicates that the oracles concerning Sidon and Israel/Jacob in 28:20–26 must be considered structurally together with the Tyrian oracles in Ezek 26–28.

The introductory chronological formula in 26:1 plays an important role in defining the internal structure of Ezek 26–28 as well. The chronological introduction is based on an expanded version of the prophetic word transmission formula as indicated by the appearance of the expression, *hāyâ děbar-yhwh 'ēlay lē'mōr*, "the word of YHWH came to me, saying..." within 26:1.[7] This expression introduces the oracular report concerning Tyre in 26:2–21, and it anticipates the following four examples of the prophetic word formula, *wayěhî děbar-yhwh 'ēlay lē'mōr*, "and the word of YHWH came to me, saying..." in 27:1; 28:1, 11, and 20. Each of these examples of the prophetic word formula introduces four successive oracular reports concerning Tyre in 27:1–36; the prince of Tyre in 28:1–10; the king of Tyre in 28:11–19; and Sidon and Israel/Jacob in 28:20–26. Within the purview of Ezek 26–28, the punishment of Tyre and the restoration of Israel/Jacob are viewed as consequences or results of YHWH's treatment of Tyre and her prince/king in the four oracular reports of 26:1–28:19.

---

6. For methodological discussion, see Sweeney 1999.
7. For discussion of the YHWH word transmission formula, see Meier 1992, 314–19.

Examination of the literary form and structure of each constituent oracular report points to its distinctive concerns and its place within the whole. The first oracular report concerning Tyre 26:1–21 begins with an autobiographical introduction in 26:1, which includes both the above-mentioned chronological formula and the prophetic word formula. YHWH's oracular instruction to Ezekiel then follows in 26:2–21. A statement of the premise of YHWH's oracular instruction in 26:2, which conveys Tyre's celebratory exclamation at Jerusalem's downfall, "Aha! The gateway of the peoples is broken; it is now mine; I shall be filled because it is ruined," then introduces YHWH's oracular statements concerning Tyre's punishment in 26:3–21. It is not clear why Tyre should celebrate the ruin of its key ally in revolt against Babylonia as most commentators maintain; perhaps the oracle conveys Tyre's relief at having escaped destruction and its view that the revolt would end now that Jerusalem had fallen.

The following oracles in 26:3–21 make clear, however, that YHWH will nevertheless bring devastating punishment against Tyre in the form of the Babylonian army. The consequences for Tyre are then laid out in two sets of oracular pairs, each of which is identified by variations of the introductory prophetic messenger formula in 26:3–14 and 26:16–21.[8] The first pair takes up YHWH announcement of punishment against Tyre. The first oracle of the pair in 26:3–6 begins with the formula, *lākēn kōh 'āmar 'ădōnāy yhwh*, "therefore, thus says my lord, YHWH," and announces that YHWH will bring the nations against Tyre to level it to bare rock. The second oracle of the pair in 26:7–14 begins with the syntactically joined formula, *kî kōh 'āmar 'ădōnāy yhwh*, "for thus says my lord, YHWH," and announces that YHWH will bring Nebuchadnezzar against Tyre to destroy the city. The concluding oracular formula in 26:14bβ, *nĕ'um 'ădōnāy yhwh*, "utterance of my lord, YHWH," closes the presentation of the first oracular pair.

Each oracle of this first pair includes elements that tie it into the structure and concerns of the Tyrian block as a whole. The first oracle concludes with an example of the YHWH authorization formula[9] in 26:5aβ, *kî 'ănî dibbartî*, "for I have spoken," and an example of the YHWH self-revelation formula in 26:6b, *wĕyādĕ'û kî 'ănî yhwh*, "and they will know that I am YHWH." The authorization formula certifies the oracle as a statement by

---

8. For discussion of the prophetic messenger formula, see Meier 1992, 273–98.

9. See Hals 1989, 360, who refers to the formula simply as a conclusion formula for a divine speech.

YHWH, and versions of the formula appear again in 26:14b to conclude the first oracular pair and again in 28:10bα to tie the oracle concerning the prince of Tyre into the Tyrian block as a whole. The YHWH self-revelation formula plays a crucial role in identifying events in the human world throughout the book of Ezekiel as revelatory acts of YHWH; in the present case, the Babylonian advance and the projected downfall of Tyre will be recognized not as acts by Babylon or Nebuchadnezzar, but as an act by YHWH, the true sovereign of creation in Ezekiel's view. The formula appears again repeatedly throughout the concluding oracle concerning Sidon and Israel/Jacob in 28:22bα, 23b, 24b, and 26bβ to ensure that the downfall of Tyre and the restoration of Israel/Jacob will be recognized as revelatory acts of YHWH and to tie the concluding oracles concerning Sidon and Israel/Jacob in 28:20–26 into the larger literary framework of the Tyrian oracles in Ezek 26–28.

The two oracles of the second oracular pair in 26:15–21 are again introduced by examples of the prophetic messenger formula, *kōh 'āmar 'ădōnāy yhwh* in 26:15a and *kî kōh 'āmar 'ădōnāy yhwh* in 26:19aα. The first oracle in 26:15–18 emphasizes the mourning of the rulers of the coastlands and rulers of the sea, who intone a brief dirge in reaction to Tyre's downfall.[10] The first oracle thereby points to the worldwide impact of YHWH's previously announced revelatory act. The second oracle in 26:19–21 builds upon the first by emphasizing Tyre's descent into "the Pit" or the netherworld where the *tĕhôm* or "deep" will cover her and where she will join "the people of old," that is, those who have passed on before her. The oracular pair concludes with the formula *ballāhôt 'ittĕnēk wĕ'ênēk ûtbuqšî wĕlō'-timmāṣĕ'î 'ôd lĕ'ôlām*, "Horrors I will make you, and you shall be no more; and you will be sought but you will not be found again forever," conclude the subunit to emphasize the finality of the catastrophe that will overtake Tyre. Insofar as variations of this formula appear in 27:36b (*ballāhôt hāyît wĕ'ênēk 'ad-'ôlām*, "Horrors you have become, and you shall be no more forever") and 28:19b (*ballāhôt hāyîtā wĕ'ênĕkā 'ad-'ôlām*, "Horrors you have become, and you shall be no more forever"), the *ballāhôt* formula plays an important role in tying together 26:1–21; 27:1–36; and 28:1–10/11–19 into a coherent block (cf. Block 1998, 28).

The second major unit of Ezek 26–28 appears in the second oracle report concerning Tyre in 27:1–36. The basic literary structure of this unit

---

10. For discussion of the dirge form, see esp. Jahnow 1923.

is far less complicated than that of the first oracle report in 26:1–21 in that it comprises an autobiographical report of YHWH's instructions to Ezekiel to intone a dirge over Tyre in verse 1 and a presentation of the lengthy dirge per se in verses 2–36. The dirge emphasizes Tyre's boasting that she was perfect in beauty, and it illustrates this beauty by portraying Tyre as a perfect or beautiful ship at sea and as a harbor at which ships from throughout the world were docked. Following a portrayal of the goods brought into Tyre by its extensive trade connections, the dirge then turns to Tyre's downfall by portraying her as a ship that was wrecked at sea with its merchandise and crew sinking into the deep. The dirge concludes with a portrayal of the inhabitants and kings of the coastlands aghast at Tyre's demise and repeating the above-noted formula, "Horrors you have become, and you will be no more forever."

The third major unit of Ezek 26–28 appears in the third oracle report concerning the prince (*nāgîd*) of Tyre in 28:1–10. Again, the unit begins with an autobiographical report in 28:1 of YHWH's instructions to the prophet to speak to the prince of Tyre. The contents of YHWH's instruction appear in verses 2–10, which call for the prophet to announce a prophetic judgment speech against the prince.[11] The grounds for judgment appear in verses 2–5, which charge that the prince has been arrogant by claiming to be a god in the heart of the seas and that the prince's arrogance may be explained by his shrewdness and success in trade. The announcement of judgment in verses 6–10 contends that YHWH will bring ruthless foreigners to strike down the prince and send him to the Pit or netherworld, thereby demonstrating that he is mortal and not a god. The above-mentioned authorization formula in verse 10bα certifies this as a statement by YHWH, and the concluding oracular formula in verse 10bβ closes the unit.

The fourth major unit in Ezek 26–28 appears in the fourth oracle report concerning the king (*melek*) of Tyre in 28:11–19. Since *melek* is frequently employed as a synonym for *nāgîd* in Biblical Hebrew,[12] the oracle in 28:11–19 should be viewed as a development of the oracle in 28:1–10. Again, the unit begins with an autobiographical report of YHWH's instruction to Ezekiel to intone a dirge over the king of Tyre. The dirge is formulated with the language of the prophetic judgment speech, and it

---

11. For discussion of the prophetic judgment speech form, see Sweeney 1996, 23–25, 533–34.

12. *HALOT* 2:667–68.

relates how YHWH created the king of Tyre as the seal of perfection in the garden of Eden; how he was adorned with precious stones like those of the ephod worn by the high priest of the temple; and how YHWH created him as a cherub who resided on G-d's holy mountain. Nevertheless, the dirge charges the king of Tyre with lawlessness, sin, and haughtiness as a result of his commerce among the nations so that the king ultimately desecrated his sanctuaries. As a result, YHWH has destroyed the king of Tyre, and once again kings stare at the horrors that the king of Tyre has become.

The fifth and final major major unit in Ezek 26–28 appears in the fifth oracle report concerning the punishment of Sidon and the restoration of Israel/Jacob in 28:20–26. Although the contents of this oracle report and its formulaic differences from the preceding material indicate that it was composed separately from the Tyrian oracles, 28:20–26 clearly functions as the culmination of Ezek 26–28 in the present form of the book. Again, the unit begins with an autobiographical report of YHWH's instructions to Ezekiel to prophesy judgment against Sidon and the restoration of Israel/Jacob to its land. The judgment against Sidon is expressed sparsely and very generally with threats of punishment that will reveal YHWH's glory and holiness. No particular reason is given for the punishment other than the revelation of YHWH, although the following material concerning the restoration of Israel/Jacob suggests that Israel has been afflicted by neighboring peoples who despise them. The gathering of Israel from the nations to which they have been dispersed and the return of Israel to their own land then serve as the final revelatory acts of the Tyrian oracles that will demonstrate that YHWH is their G-d. In this respect, the downfall of Tyre (and Sidon) entails the restoration of Israel in Ezek 26–28.

3. Mythological Elements in Ezekiel 26–28

Attention may now turn to the identification of the mythological elements that appear throughout this text and the examination of their function within its various units. An important dimension of the use of mythological motifs in Ezekiel is their application to contemporary events. Whereas earlier generations of scholars viewed mythology as stories about the gods as well as the origins of the world and social structures,[13] contemporary scholarship recognizes that mythology relates to social structures and

---

13. See, e.g., Eliade 1959, 68–113; 1974; 1958, esp. 388–436.

realities from the contemporary world in which it is produced.[14] Ezekiel in particular among the prophets and other writings of the Hebrew Bible employs a mythopoeic viewpoint to express his understanding of contemporary events in his world. Such a mythopoeic viewpoint indeed is typical of visionaries in the Bible and the larger ancient Near Eastern world. Ezekiel's visions of the divine throne chariot in his inaugural narrative, his account of the destruction of Jerusalem in Ezek 1–3 and 8–11, and his vision of the restored temple at the center of a restored Israel and creation in Ezek 40–48 constitute primary examples of his use of mythological motifs. These motifs are drawn largely from Israelite/Judean sources, but Ezekiel's visions also display influences from Mesopotamian and Syro-Canaanite mythology. They function as means to express Ezekiel's view of a heavenly reality that stands beyond and informs the earthly reality in which he lives and which he strives to interpret. By interpreting earthly reality in relation to his mythopoeic viewpoint, Ezekiel attempts to demonstrate direct divine involvement in earthly events.

Ezekiel's mythopoeic viewpoint is evident throughout the oracular block concerning Tyre in Ezek 26–28. The use of mythological motifs focuses especially on the sea, since Tyre was an island nation located off the Phoenician coast that gained its wealth, power, and influence in the world through its large navy and its extensive trade connections throughout the Mediterranean. Although small in size, Tyre was easily defended by its control of the sea, which hindered its more land-based opponents from successfully overcoming the sea waters that constituted its first line of defense. The sea is a well-known figure in the mythologies of the ancient Near East (and indeed throughout the world at large). It functions both as a source of life or creation in the world as well as a threat to the life and creation that stems from it. In *Enuma Elish* the sea, personified as the female monster Tiamat, both gives birth to the gods and attempts to destroy them following the murder of her husband Apsu, the god of fresh waters.[15] When Tiamat is killed in battle by Marduk, the city god of Babylon, Marduk cuts her body in two to create heaven and earth and thereby establishes a foundational element in creation. Likewise, Ugaritic mythology portrays the sea, personified as the god Yamm, as the chief opponent

---

14. E.g., Paden 1988, 69–92; for discussion of developments in the study of mythology, see Oden 1992; Bolle and Ricoeur 2005.

15. For a translation of *Enuma Elish*, see *ANET*, 60–72; Heidel 1974; Jacobsen 1976, 165–91.

to Baal, who likewise defeats Yamm in battle and thereby stabilizes the world of creation.[16] Finally, Israelite/Judean mythology posits that YHWH creates world order from the preexisting sea or deep. Although the creation narrative in Gen 1:1-2:3 portrays no battle between YHWH and the sea, other traditions (e.g., Ps 74; Job 38-42; Isa 27:1; 51:9) posit YHWH's defeat of sea monsters such as Leviathan, Behemoth, and Rahab during the course of creation.

Ezekiel's use of the sea motif to portray YHWH's actions against Tyre appears at the outset of the Tyrian block in the first oracular report in Ezek 26:1-21. In the course of announcing an attack against Tyre, YHWH proclaims plans in 26:3-5 to bring nations against Tyre like the crashing of waves against its walls and to reduce the island city to bare rock in the midst of the sea fit only for drying nets. Such an equation of attacking nations with the sea is hardly surprising in mythology. Marduk's establishment of creation following the defeat of Tiamat includes establishing political order in the world—in the form of Babylon's sovereignty over the nations of the world—as well as natural order. Early Ugaritic specialists maintained that Baal's defeat of Yamm played a role in his displacement of the aging creator god El and reflected the establishment of a new political order in Ugarit,[17] but more recent research maintains that El appoints Baal to his position of authority and that such appointment reflects the realities of Ugarit's political and administrative hierarchy.[18] Biblical tradition is also well known for equating threatening nations with the sea, as indicated by YHWH's defeat of Egypt at the Red Sea in Exod 15, Sisera's coalition in Judg 5, and Babylon in Isa 51. Indeed, the motif of the sea continues in Ezek 26 when the oracle portrays the consequences of Tyre's defeat. Not only are Tyre's walls and splendid houses cast into the waters in 26:12, but the coastlands and rulers of the sea mourn and intone dirges over the island nation upon hearing of Tyre's demise in 26:15-18. Such a motif constitutes a reversal of the normal course of events in the sea combat mythologies of the ancient Near Eastern world; normally the protagonist wins the struggle, the victory is celebrated, and temples to the hero god are built. Here quite the opposite takes place as Tyre sinks into the very sea that once formed the basis of its power. At this point, a new mythological motif enters the mix: the descent into the netherworld, well known

---

16. See the Baal Cycle, *ANET*, 129-42; for discussion, see now Smith 1994.
17. See, e.g., Kapelrud 1952, 133; Pope 1955, 83-104.
18. See, e.g., L'Heureux 1979, esp. 3-108; Mullen 1980; see also Handy 1994.

from the mythological patterns of the dying and rising gods, particularly Inanna's or Ishtar's Descent into the Netherworld,[19] the Baal Cycle, and possibly the Legend of Aqhat.[20] In this pattern, the usually male fertility god (Dumuzi, Tammuz, Baal, or Aqhat) dies, leaving the world bereft of water and fertility. A female figure (Innana, Ishtar, Anat, or Paqhat) must descend into the netherworld, risking the possibility that she might never return, to rescue the dead god and restore rain and fertility to the world of creation. Because Israel/Judah lack clear female deities, the motif comes to expression in other ways, particularly through scenarios of national restoration or resurrection that will become important later in this discussion. Because of the finality of death, a compromise generally emerges in which the male figure is allowed to live for half the year but then must return to the netherworld for the second half of the year, thereby explaining the origins of the Near Eastern seasonal cycle of rainy and dry seasons. Again, the usual mythological pattern of overcoming death—at least partially—is absent from Ezek 26. Tyre descends to the Pit to become a horror in the sight of the coastlands and the rulers of the sea, but no hope for Tyre's return from the dead emerges.

The sea motif continues to appear in Ezek 27, the second oracular report of Ezek 26–28, which portrays YHWH's instructions to Ezekiel to intone a dirge over the now dead Tyre. Key to the depiction of Tyre in the dirge is the portrayal of Tyre as a mighty and splendid ship at sea that carries the many goods for which it trades among the nations of the earth. Of course, the ship is wrecked and sinks together with its crew and its merchandise in the midst of the sea while the inhabitants of the coastlands and their kings look on aghast. Such a portrayal builds upon the sea combat motifs examined above, in that YHWH is ultimately the source of Tyre's demise, but the motif also draws upon other mythological patterns known in the ancient Near Eastern world, particularly the Mesopotamian flood traditions and the Adapa legend. The flood traditions posit a human hero figure who, with the help of the gods, builds a ship to save human beings and animals from the floods that inundate creation due to divine

---

19. *ANET*, 52–57, 106–9; see also Jacobsen 1976, 25–73, 135–43, who discusses the ritual and mythological dimensions of the descent to the netherworld by both Inanna and Ishtar.

20. *ANET*, 149–55; see now Wright 2001, who considers the ritual dimensions of Aqhat as a contemporary (for the time of Ugarit's civilization) expression of its mythological expression.

dissatisfaction, irresponsibility, or capriciousness. Examples include Ziusudra from Sumerian tradition, Atrahasis from Mesopotamian tradition, Utnapishtim from the Gilgamesh narratives, and Noah from biblical tradition.[21] But whereas each of the flood heroes builds a ship that saves the lives of its passengers, Ezek 27 reverses the motif by portraying the ship wrecked at sea—it does not save the lives of its passengers but instead serves as the vehicle by which its passengers and even Tyre itself meets their demise. The motif also calls to mind the Adapa legend concerning a sailor who is brought to heaven after he has successfully cursed the winds that threatened to sink his boat.[22] When he refuses the bread and water of life offered to him by Anu, the god of heaven, he and all humankind are then destined to remain mortal and face death. Indeed, the question of mortality appears in the flood myths as well, in that humans are afflicted with mortality as a means to resolve the conflict with the gods in the Atrahasis Epic and Gilgamesh fails to secure the secret of eternal life following his visit to Utnapishtim.

The third oracle report in 28:1–10 shifts from a focus on the sea, in that it is concerned with the prince of Tyre rather than with the city itself, but it continues the earlier interest in depicting the descent to the Pit or the netherworld. The motif is not completely abandoned, however, as the prophetic judgment speech focuses on his haughtiness and claims to be a god enthroned in the heart of the seas. As a result of these claims, he is condemned to the Pit. His wisdom is compared to that of "Daniel" according to the Qere reading, or "Danel" according to the Kethib reading, the major figure of the Ugaritic Aqhat narrative. Likewise, the claim to be a god recalls attempts to challenge the power or rule of the chief god in the Baal Cycle when the god Ashtar sits on Baal's throne while he is in the netherworld, but his feet do not reach the footstool and his head does not reach the top.[23]

The fourth oracle report in 28:11–19 concerning the king of Tyre portrays him as the seal of perfection, who dwells in the garden of Eden, wears precious stones as his adornment, and was created by YHWH as a cherub until his haughtiness caused his downfall once again. The Israelite/Judean garden of Eden narrative from Gen 1–3 looms very large here as the king of Eden, like Adam and Eve, is expelled from the garden to become a

---

21. See *ANET*, 42–44, 104–6, 512–14, 72–99, 503–7; Lambert and Millard 1969.
22. *ANET*, 101–3; Izre'el 2001; Jacobsen 1976, 115–16.
23. *ANET*, 140; see also 129–31; Smith 1994, 210–59.

horror once again in the eyes of those who behold him. His identification as a cherub also recalls the garden of Eden, in that the cherub is intended to guard the garden from unauthorized entry by those who would sin and bring impurity into the garden, but of course the king of Tyre becomes the very agent of sin and impurity himself because of his arrogance. It is important to recall that the garden of Eden is symbolized by the holy of holies of the Jerusalem temple in Judean thought,[24] and the king of Tyre is known in Israelite tradition as one who assisted Solomon in the construction of the temple. In this respect, the role of cherub also comes to mind as the figure that guards the holy of holies in the temple. The listing of precious stones all appear on the ephod of the high priest, who has access to the holy of holies, but only nine of the twelve stones that appear on the priestly ephod are present here. One may only speculate about the reason for the discrepancy. In that Judah, Benjamin, and Levi were left in the south following the destruction of northern Israel, perhaps they represent the lost tribes of the north that came under Tyrian influence following the destruction, but this cannot be known. The identification of the king as the seal of perfection likewise recalls Mesopotamian traditions that the king represents the ideal human being sent from heaven by the gods to rule over the earth.[25]

Finally, the last oracular report in 28:20–26 concerning the punishment of Sidon and the restoration of Israel/Jacob also takes up at least some mythological dimensions. Interpreters have struggled to explain the presence of Sidon here; perhaps the conquest of the Tyrian coastland, including Sidon, played a role in Tyre's ultimate submission to Babylon. No mythological dimension is apparent here, but the restoration of Israel/Jacob to its land does build upon the restoration motifs of fertility and in later times resurrection that are known from Israelite and Judean prophecy.[26] In this case, the restoration of Israel/Jacob to the land emerges as the ultimate consequence of the downfall of Tyre: when the mythological enemy is defeated, the hero god emerges as the ruler of the land. In the present instance, Israel/Jacob is restored in the aftermath of YHWH's victory over Tyre by means of the Babylonians. Note that Babylon is never

---

24. See Levenson 1984; 1985, 111–37.

25. See the discussion of the Assyrian king in relation to the tree of life in Parpola 1993, 165–69; Widengren 1951, 43–58.

26. For the correlation between the restoration of nature and resurrection with national restoration in ancient Israelite/Judean thought, see Levenson 2006.

brought down in the book of Ezekiel; it functions as YHWH's agent of punishment throughout the book.

4. The Composition of Ezekiel 26–28

A wide variety of mythological motifs appear with the Tyrian block of oracle reports in Ezek 26–28, where they give expression to Ezekiel's understanding of divine intent and action in relation to the anticipated fall of Tyre to Nebuchadnezzar and the Babylonian army. No single mythological complex appears to be predominant in these oracles. Key mythologies include the Sea combat myths, the Descent of Ishtar/Inanna to the Netherworld, the flood traditions, the garden of Eden narratives, and the portrayal of the high priest's ephod—all seem to play a role. In the case of the Mesopotamian and Ugaritic traditions, it is striking that Ezekiel tends to reverse the usual outcome of the narrative from deliverance of the protagonist/s to the condemnation and death of Tyre and its king/prince. In the case of the garden of Eden narrative, the demise of the king of Tyre is consistent with the expulsion of Adam and Eve from the garden and their condemnation to mortality. Such a scenario of course reflects Ezekiel's view that YHWH is acting against Tyre ultimately to destroy the city and its monarch.

We have already observed that the mythopoeic viewpoint expressed in the Tyrian block is consistent with Ezekiel's mythopoeic viewpoint as expressed throughout the book. As a Zadokite priest trained for holy service in the Jerusalem temple, Ezekiel's worldview would be defined by its mythopoeic perspective, particularly since the Jerusalemite priesthood would be expected to discern divine intent and action in the world of creation. Since the Jerusalem temple was conceived to be the holy center of creation in Zadokite thought, Ezekiel's knowledge of Israelite/Judean mythological traditions and his assertion of YHWH's presence and actions among the nations and throughout creation at large are to be expected. His use of Mesopotamian and Ugaritic mythological motifs, however, is not. Clearly, Ezekiel's exile to Babylonia would have provided him the opportunity to become familiar with these motifs, although we may only speculate as to how this came about. The Babylonians were known to make use of educated and skilled people who were exiled to Babylonia from their homelands.[27]

---

27. See Schniedewind 2004, 139–64.

As a priest, perhaps Ezekiel was put to work in some sort of Babylonian cultic or administrative context where he would have encountered foreign mythologies as part of his training or professional service. However he may have come about this knowledge, he is clearly able to incorporate it into his mythopoeic worldview concerning YHWH's actions in the world and use of Nebuchadnezzar and Babylonia to achieve divine ends.

Although in the above analysis I have focused primarily on a synchronic reading of the text, even when I draw upon the diachronic dimensions of comparative mythologies, I still need to address several diachronic issues.

First is the question of the historical background of the Tyrian oracles. As noted above, most scholars tend to concentrate on this issue. Although most agree that the background for these oracles must lie in Nebuchadnezzar's thirteen-year siege of Tyre, questions remain.[28] The thirteen-year siege is known only from Josephus (*Ag. Ap.* 1.156–159); contemporary records of Babylon's relationship with Tyre are sparse. It does seem, however, that Nebuchadnezzar began a siege against Tyre in about 586–585 B.C.E. after his conquest and destruction of Jerusalem. Although Ithobaal or Ethbaal III was king of Tyre at the time of the beginning of the siege, by 573–572 B.C.E., Tyre had capitulated to Babylon and Baal II was on the throne. Nevertheless, even this sparse information reveals an important consideration: Tyre was not destroyed in accordance with Ezekiel's prophecies of punishment against Tyre and her king. The same may be said concerning Ezekiel's prophecies of Egypt's downfall and punishment in Ezek 29–32: Nebuchadnezzar never conquered Egypt. The conquest of Egypt was only realized by the Persian monarch Cambyses in 525 B.C.E.

This reconstruction of the historical background of the Tyrian block points to the second diachronic issue in relation to Ezek 26–28: the compositional history of the text. We have already observed that the oracles concerning the downfall of Sidon and the restoration of Israel/Jacob appear to be redactional expansions of an earlier block of material concerned with Tyre in 26:1–28:19. As noted above, the Sidonian and Israelite material in 28:20–26 includes four examples of the YHWH self-revelation formula that highlights the revelatory significance of Ezekiel's oracles. Such a concern is absent elsewhere in the Tyrian block with the exception of 26:5b–6, which includes the only other occurrence of this formula within Ezek

---

28. See esp. Corral 2002, 20–65; Katzenstein 1973, 316–37.

26–28, immediately following the statement that Tyre's daughter towns (i.e., Tyre's vassal cities such as Sidon) will be put to the sword as part of the general destruction. Furthermore, the oracle concerning the downfall of Tyre in 26:2–5a with the YHWH authorization formula and the YHWH oracular formula like those that conclude the parallel oracle 26:7–14 in 26:14b. In that 26:5b–6 disrupts the parallel between 26:2–6 and 26:7–14 and ties the concluding oracles concerning Sidon and Israel to the initial oracles concerning Tyre, it would appear that 26:5b–6 and 28:20–26 are redactional expansions of the text that are designed to reveal YHWH's ultimate intentions to bring down Sidon and restore Israel/Jacob to its land in the aftermath of Tyre's downfall.

The question of the compositional history of the Tyrian block must also consider the following material concerning Egypt in Ezek 29–32. Interpreters have noted the unusual chronological formula in 29:17, which introduces the oracles concerning Egypt in 29:17–30:19. The chronological formula dates the oracles to the first day of the first month of the twenty-seventh year of the exile, that is, 1 Nisan, 571–570 B.C.E., and it alludes to the difficulties that Nebuchadnezzar had in conquering the city of Tyre. Most interpreters maintain that this formula is an update—perhaps by Ezekiel himself—of an earlier reference that would be more in keeping with the years immediately following the fall of Jerusalem.[29] But such an update points to an important dimension of the compositional history of this text: neither Ezekiel's oracles concerning Tyre nor those about Egypt were realized as he envisioned, and the book was updated somewhat to account for this reality. Indeed, we may observe that Ezekiel's vision concerning the restored temple was never realized either, since the structure of the Second Temple does not correspond to the temple envisioned by Ezekiel. It would seem that the book of Ezekiel would have been considered as a book yet to achieve fulfillment in the eyes of its ancient readers, particularly since the Egyptian oracles would have been fulfilled only

---

29. E.g., Greenberg 1997, 616–18. We may also observe that the Egyptian block in Ezek 29–32 disrupts the chronological scheme of the book in other ways as well, i.e., 29:1 begins with a reference to twelfth day of the tenth month of the tenth year, which would predate the first day of the month of the eleventh year assigned to the preceding Tyrian block. The first chronological formula following the Egypt block in 33:21 likewise refers to the fifth day of the tenth month of the twelfth year, which would be prior to the last chronological formula of the oracle concerning the nations in general in 32:17–33:20, which mentions the fifteenth day of the twelfth month of the twelfth year.

in the Persian period with Cambyses's conquest of Egypt and the Tyrian oracles would have been fulfilled only in the early Hellenistic period with Alexander's conquest of Tyre. In the case of the temple, Ezekiel's temple is yet to be built, and subsequent Jewish tradition considers his temple to be the third temple of the days to come.

Such a scenario also points to the addition of the oracle concerning the downfall of Sidon and the restoration of Israel/Jacob at the conclusion of the Tyrian block. We do not know the precise details of the fate of Sidon during Nebuchadnezzar's siege of Tyre, but it apparently submitted to Babylon without much resistance. Cambyses granted Sidon control of the Israelite ports of Dor and Jaffo following his conquest of Egypt in 526 B.C.E.,[30] and Sidon may well have controlled these areas also under Nebuchadnezzar following the siege of Tyre and the decline of its fortunes. Such a scenario would help to explain why the downfall of Sidon is linked to the restoration of Israel. Finally, the restoration of Israel/Judah did not commence until the Persian period as well, first under the rule of Cyrus and later under Darius and Artaxerxes. Even so, the restoration of Israel was never fully completed even in the Persian and Hellenistic periods.

Such considerations aid in positing the compositional history of the Tyrian block; that is, the expansion of the Tyrian block to point to the downfall of Sidon and the restoration of Israel may be placed at any time from the aftermath of Tyre's submission to Babylon, which would have prompted the modification of the chronological formula in 29:17, through the early Persian period when the restoration of Israel appeared to be imminent. Although we cannot be more precise in such a conclusion, it does point to an important dimension of the reading of Ezekiel in the exilic and early Persian period: Ezekiel would have been read as a book yet to be realized. Although Tyre was not destroyed by the Persian period as Ezekiel envisioned, the fulfillment of that punishment—and the concomitant revelation of YHWH's actions in the world—was yet to be realized.

Works Cited

Allen, Leslie C. 1990. *Ezekiel 20–48*. WBC 29. Dallas: Word.

---

30. McClellan 1996. This statement is based on the sarcophagus inscription of King Eshmunazar II of Sidon, whose dates are uncertain, although he is apparently placed early in the Achaemenid period. For the inscription, see *ANET*, 662; for discussion, see Briant 2002, 490.

Block, Daniel I. 1998. *The Book of Ezekiel: Chapters 25–48*. NICOT. Grand Rapids: Eerdmans.
Bolle, Kees W., and Paul Ricoeur. Myth. *ER* 9:6359–80.
Briant, Pierre. 2002. *From Cyrus to Alexander: A History of the Persian Empire*. Translated by Peter T. Daniels. Winona Lake, Ind.: Eisenbrauns.
Corral, Martin Alonso. 2002. *Ezekiel's Oracles against Tyre: Historical Reality and Motivations*. BibOr 46. Rome: Pontifical Biblical Institute.
Darr, Katheryn Pfisterer. 2001. The Book of Ezekiel. Pages 1358–1400 in vol. 6 of *The New Interpreter's Bible*. Edited by Leander E. Keck. 12 vols. Nashville: Abingdon, 1994–2004.
Dijk, H. J. van. 1968. *Ezekiel's Prophecy on Tyre (Ez. 26,1–28,19): A New Approach*. BibOr 20. Rome: Pontifical Biblical Institute.
Eliade, Mircea. 1958. *Patterns in Comparative Religion*. New York: Meridian.
———. 1959. *The Sacred and the Profane: The Nature of Religion*. Translated by Willard R. Trask. New York: Harcourt, Brace, & World.
———. 1974. *The Myth of the Eternal Return: Or, Cosmos and History*. Repr., Princeton: Princeton University Press.
Greenberg, Moshe. 1997. *Ezekiel 21–37*. AB 22A. New York: Doubleday, 1997.
Hals, Ronald M. 1989. *Ezekiel*. FOTL 19. Grand Rapids: Eerdmans.
Handy, Lowell K. 1994. *Among the Host of Heaven: The Syro-Palestinian Pantheon as Bureaucracy*. Winona Lake, Ind.: Eisenbrauns.
Heidel, Alexander. 1974. *The Babylonian Genesis: The Story of Creation*. Repr., Chicago: University of Chicago.
Izre'el, Shlomo. 2001. *Adapa and the South Wind: Language Has the Power of Life and Death*. Mesopotamian Civilizations 10. Winona Lake, Ind.: Eisenbrauns.
Jacobsen, Thorkild. 1976. *The Treasures of Darkness: A History of Mesopotamian Religion*. New Haven: Yale University Press.
Jahnow, Hegwig. 1923. *Das hebräische Leichenlied*. BZAW 36. Giessen: Töpelmann.
Kapelrud, Arvid S. 1952. *Baal in the Ras Shamra Text*. Copenhagen: Gad.
Katzenstein, H. Jacob. 1973. *The History of Tyre: From the Beginning of the Second Millennium B.C.E. until the Fall of the Neo-Babylonian Empire in 538 B.C.E.* Jerusalem: Schocken Institute.
L'Heureux, Conrad E. 1979. *Rank among the Canaanite Gods: El, Baal, and the Repha'im*. HSM 21. Missoula, Mont.: Scholars Press.

Lambert, Wilfred G., and Alan R. Millard. 1969. *Atra-ḫasīs: The Babylonian Story of the Flood.* Oxford: Clarendon.

Levenson, Jon D. 1984. The Temple and the World. *JR* 64:275–98.

———. 1985. *Sinai and Zion: An Entry into the Jewish Bible.* Minneapolis: Winston.

———. 2006. *Resurrection and the Restoration of Israel: The Ultimate Victory of the God of Life.* New Haven: Yale University Press.

McClellan, Harper's Bible Dictionary. Edited by Paul J. Achtemeier. 2nd ed. San Francisco: HarperSanFrancisco.

Meier, Samuel M. 1992. *Speaking of Speaking: Marking Direct Discourse in the Hebrew Bible.* VTSup 46. Leiden: Brill, 1992.

Mullen, E. Theodore, Jr. 1980. *The Assembly of the Gods: The Divine Council in Canaanite and Early Hebrew Literature.* HSM 24. Chico, Calif.: Scholars Press.Odell, Margaret S. 2005. *Ezekiel.* Smyth and Helwys Bible Commentary. Macon, Ga.: Smyth & Helwys.

Oden, Robert. 1992. Myth and Mythology: Mythology. *ABD* 4:946–56.

Paden, William E. 1988. *Religious Worlds: The Comparative Study of Religion.* Boston: Beacon.

Parpola, Simo. 1993. The Assyrian Tree of Life: Tracing the Origins of Jewish Monotheism and Greek Philosophy. *JNES* 53:161–208.

Pohlmann, Karl-Friedrich. 2001. *Der Prophet Hesekiel/Ezechiel, Kapital 20–48.* ATD 22.2. Göttingen: Vandenhoeck & Ruprecht.

Pope, Marvin H. 1955. *El in the Ugaritic Texts.* VTSup 2. Leiden: Brill.

Schniedewind, William. 2004. *How the Bible Became a Book.* Cambridge: Cambridge University Press.

Smith, Mark S. 1994. *The Ugaritic Baal Cycle.* Vol. 1: *Introduction with Text, Translation, and Commentary of KTU 1.1–1.2.* VTSup 55. Leiden: Brill.

Sweeney, Marvin A. 1996. *Isaiah 1–39; with an Introduction to Prophetic Literature.* FOTL 16. Grand Rapids: Eerdmans.

———. 1999. Form Criticism. Pages 58–85 in *To Each Its Own Meaning: An Introduction to Biblical Criticisms and Their Applications.* Edited by Steven L. McKenzie and Stephen R. Haynes. Revised and expanded edition. Louisville: Westminster John Knox.

———. 2005a. Ezekiel: Zadokite Priest and Visionary Prophet of the Exile. Pages 125–43 in *Form and Intertextuality in Prophetic and Apocalyptic Literature.* FAT 45. Tübingen: Mohr Siebeck.

———. 2005b. *The Prophetic Literature.* Interpreting Biblical Texts. Nashville: Abingdon.

Widengren, Geo. 1951. *The King and the Tree of Life in Ancient Eastern Religion.* Uppsala: Almqvist & Wiksells.
Wright, David. 2001. *Ritual in Narrative: The Dynamics of Feasting, Mourning, and Retaliation Rites in the Ugaritic Tale of Aqhat.* Winona Lake, Ind.: Eisenbrauns.
Zimmerli, Walther. 1982a. Knowledge of God according to the Book of Ezekiel. Pages 29–98 in *I Am Yahweh.* Translated by Douglas W. Stott. Atlanta: John Knox.
———. 1982b. The Word of Divine Self-Manifestation (Proof Saying): A Prophetic Genre. Pages 99–110 in *I Am Yahweh.* Translated by Douglas W. Stott. Atlanta: John Knox.
———. 1983. *Ezekiel 2.* Hermeneia. Translated by James D. Martin. Philadelphia: Fortress.

Myth and History in Daniel 8:
The Apocalyptic Negotiation of Power

Amy C. Merrill Willis

> In the conflict between the two, therefore, history has been given, somewhat outrageously, the upper hand.
> —Elie Wiesel

In an essay exploring the often antagonistic relationship that scholars have imposed between myth and history, Elie Wiesel (1980, 20–21) tells the story of his encounter with an old Hasidic rabbi, his former teacher, sometime after the Holocaust.

> "But what are you doing?" he asked. "What were you doing for so many years?"
> "I am writing," I replied. ...
> "What are you writing?"
> I said, "Stories."
> "But what kind of stories?"
> I said, "Stories."
> He said, "True stories?"
> I said, "What do you mean, Rebbe?"
> He said, "Stories of things that happened?"
> And then I caught him. I said, "Rebbe, it's not so simple. Some events happened that are not true. Others are true but did not happen."

For Wiesel, the encounter embodies fundamental problems in the conversation (scholarly or otherwise) about myth and history—the urge to distinguish between true narratives and fictional ones, the simplistic definition of history as stories about "true events," and the lack of clarity that dogs such simple definitions. But it also contains a basic insight that this discussion also depends on, namely, that the literary categories of myth and history, for all their supposed contrasts, share a basic likeness—both are stories, both are narratives of events, and truth can inhabit either regardless of whether the events "happened." Moreover, what is not said, but perhaps implied in the encounter, is that tragedy can render meaningless the formula that says the sum of history equals things that happened and are therefore true. When that happens, one must make use of a different narrative formula to talk about where meaning might be found in human events.

The opposition that biblical scholarship has often created between myth and history comes into clear view in the recent scholarship on early Jewish apocalyptic literature, especially the book of Daniel. In the first section of this study, I sketch the outlines of the supposed opposition and the ways in which it has negatively impacted the study of apocalyptic literature and its use of temporality. By following a recent shift in apocalyptic scholarship toward the rhetorical and ideological function of genres and texts, I argue in the second section that myth and history (or historiography) are not *tensive* worldviews or genres within Jewish apocalyptic literature;[1] indeed, they are not worldviews at all. They are better understood as fundamentally related to each other as different kinds of narrative discourses, each providing their own "equipment for living" for their earliest audiences. I will develop the characteristics of these discourses as they appear in Dan 8 in the third section of this discussion.[2] Moreover, in this essay I assert that these discourses converge in the apocalyptic literature of Daniel

---

1. Indeed, this is to say that myth is not, in my view, a particular worldview or mind-set or mode of perception or psychology—primitive or otherwise. I view it as a literary category, a form of narrative discourse, that nevertheless may have cognitive and psychological functions (though these functions are not unique to myth as such). On myth as an "idiom of expression" rather than a "discrete mode of thought," see Goodman 1993. See also the extensive discussion by Robert A. Segal (1980) on the idea of myth as a mode of perception.

2. This preliminary attempt at a definition assumes the basic definition outlined by Robert Oden (1992a, 949). He notes a general consensus that myths (1) are stories, (2) are traditional (though we will see later in this discussion how traditions may be creatively reshaped in the reuse of myths), (3) "deal with ... characters who are more than merely human," and (4) "treat events in remote antiquity." The definition of myth worked out in this essay also depends, in part, upon the work of Paul Ricoeur (1987), in which he emphasizes the complementarity of myth and history as literary categories, especially in their use of time and temporality. The language of "equipment for living" comes from Kenneth Burke and is used by Stephen O'Leary (1994, 68).

because more traditional forms of Israelite historiography were no longer able to create a meaningful narrative for some Jewish readers in the wake of the tragedy of 167 B.C.E.

Apocalyptic Literature and the Dichotomy between Myth and History

I begin by taking notice of an interchange on myth and history in apocalyptic literature that appeared in *Vetus Testamentum*. It began with a short note written by J. Y. Jindo (2005), which was followed by a response from Lorenzo DiTommaso (2006). These two statements, while quite concise, summarize the impasse in which the scholarly conversation on apocalyptic literature and myth has often found itself during the last several decades. At the heart of the interchange is the notion that the worldview of apocalyptic literature or apocalyptic eschatology, and that of the prophets, or prophetic eschatology, is found precisely in the dichotomization between myth and history.

Jindo argues that the distinction between apocalyptic eschatology and prophetic eschatology can be summarized by the following oppositions: myth versus history; cyclical versus linear views of time; predetermined cosmic frameworks of good and evil versus human agency and freedom in history to choose. According to Jindo, the character of apocalyptic eschatology is informed by the mythical worldview, which "expresses the longing for the eternal, the durative, the perpetual" (Jindo 2005, 412). He contrasts this with the assertion that historical thinking is primarily about "changes and progress" (412). While apocalyptic literature understands time to be cyclical and predetermined, prophetic eschatology is "oriented in history" and holds to a view of time that is linear, open-ended, and dependent upon human choices to seek the good. In keeping with this distinction, Jindo observes that in myth (and thus in apocalyptic literature) there is always only one pattern for events to follow, one involving cosmic chaos and order and struggle, while in historical thinking there are numerous ways for events to develop.

DiTommaso's response to Jindo critiques the latter for his failure to appreciate the historiographical elements of apocalyptic literature. DiTommaso rightly points to the wealth of historical details and concerns that one finds in apocalyptic historical reviews. He goes on to argue that every historical review found in Daniel or other apocalyptic texts become fully intelligible only in a historical sense, that is, in the reflection of what has happened, and in an eschatological sense, that is, in the anticipation of what is still to come. Past, present, and future are inextricably linked together, but the arrow of time is linear, not circular, or spiral. (2006, 415)[3]

For DiTommaso, temporal elements in apocalypses can be understood only in historical terms—time moves only in one direction in apocalypses no less than in historiography. Thus history is still characterized by linear time, but his formulation now aligns apocalypses with history. DiTommaso does not seem to be proposing a new framework for understanding myth and history so much as he is adopting the opposite viewpoint from the old formulation that defined apocalypticism in terms of a cyclical view of time. Cyclical time remains problematic and associated with myth, while apocalypticism now falls under history. While DiTommaso acknowledges that apocalyptic history does make use of mythological language, his statement would minimize to a great degree the contributions of myth, mythic patterns, and mythic narratives.

In fairness to Jindo, he does not claim to originate any of these ideas on myth and history. Indeed, at every turn his discussion recalls and restates arguments that go back thirty or more years to the work of Martin Noth, Mircea Eliade, Paul Hanson, J. J. M. Roberts, and John Collins, among others. What he does wish to do is revise the distinctions by arguing that, despite their opposite characterizations, myth and history do converge in both prophetic and apocalyptic eschatology. This happens in so much as "prophetic eschatology is a history understood mythically, whereas apocalyptic eschatology is a myth understood historically" (Jindo 2005, 412). Although this restatement attempts to revise the old formulation that pits myth and apocalyptic literature against history and the prophets, it also suggests that biblical studies have not really moved beyond that dichotomous framework.

While it is not clear that Jindo consciously subscribes to it, his argument builds upon an old prejudice.[4] This prejudice goes back, rather

---

3. DiTommaso is here referring to the proposal by Flannery-Dailey 1999.

4. Previous discussions have already documented biblical studies' working prejudice against the presence and value of myth in the Hebrew Bible. A fuller discussion of these matters may be found in the following books and articles, inter alia: Rogerson 1974; Oden 1992a; Wyatt 2001.

ironically, to Hermann Gunkel's work more than a hundred years ago (see Gunkel 1994, 10–11 [orig. 1910]; 2006 [orig. 1895]). Even as he denied the presence of myth in the Hebrew Bible, Gunkel did much to show the echoes of ancient Near Eastern myth in the Hebrew Bible, especially in apocalyptic literature's use of the *Chaoskampf* pattern![5]

In more recent decades, however, Gerhard von Rad's *Old Testament Theology* has contributed to the prejudice against myth and also against apocalyptic literature. Although von Rad traced apocalyptic literature's roots to wisdom, rather than to ancient Near Eastern myth, his dismissal of one is related to his criticism of the other. In both cases, his bias against them emerges from his conviction of the unique and central place of historical narrative in Israel's theological witness. Both myth and apocalyptic literature are ahistorical from his perspective (von Rad 1962, 27, 141, 390).[6] Von Rad critiques the visions of Daniel because they "reduced the endlessly varied shapes and forms of history to a number of relatively simple allegorical and symbolical representations" and thereby show "great loss of historical sensitivity" (1965, 305). Moreover, in contrast to the "tension" and contingency at work in the salvation history of the prophets and the Deuteronomistic History, in which human agency seems to determine the course of events, Daniel's visions show history to be predetermined and noncontingent. Instead of moving toward salvation, history in Daniel is moving toward destruction.

Von Rad's conception of history and historiography in the Old Testament, particularly in its opposition to apocalyptic literature, involves a linear and teleological view of human history in which the action is primarily driven by human agency and is moving toward its fulfillment— God's salvation of the people. Nevertheless, this history is open-ended and not determined, in his view, and its details and events cannot be reduced to more generalized images, themes, or schemas in the way that apocalyptic views of history can be. In this brief sketch, one may perhaps see the contradiction at work in von Rad's assessment of the two types of

---

5. Rogerson (1974, 57–65) discusses at length the often contradictory views regarding myth with which Gunkel was working.

6. These references show in brief von Rad's view of mythology as "abstruse" and "opposed to … the enlightened and sober lucidity of the Jahwist's account of Creation" (1962, 141). He also regards it as the work of cultures and nations other than Israel and thus foreign. Von Rad viewed the work of the Hebrew Bible, especially the Pentateuch, as a process of "rigorous demythologizing" (27) of older Canaanite cultic notions.

literature and also note his reductionistic approach to apocalyptic literature and its "ahistorical" qualities. Such reductionism, which overlooks the significant and varying details of apocalyptic historical reviews and distills them down to a few ideas or general "longings," may also be found in Jindo's note.

The next significant milestone in the discussion concerning myth and history in early Jewish apocalyptic literature occurs with F. M. Cross's work in the 1960s and 1970s, which possesses a profound appreciation of myth in the Hebrew Bible generally, and inspired appreciation of Daniel more particularly. Cross's important work *Canaanite Myth and Hebrew Epic* (1973) maintains that the epic form at work in the Primordial History, for example, contains both mythic materials and historical materials. Nevertheless, he maintains the dichotomy between myth and history: "Characteristic of the religion of Israel is a perennial and unrelaxed tension between the mythic and the historical" (viii). The relationship between the two is one in which particular events are shaped by mythic patterns. Human events primarily deal with the horizontal axis—the temporal flow of time in which events unfold in one direction, but which is marked by contingency. But mythic thinking imposes on these events a certain shaping or pattern that is not particular. These mythic patterns seek "static structures of meaning behind or beyond the historical flux" (viii). Moreover, these patterns contribute "a vertical dimension" to Israelite epic events, revealing the cosmos and the impact of divine agency on human events (viii, 343).

According to Cross, mythic materials and their distinctive worldview enjoyed a revival and converged with history and wisdom in the exilic and postexilic periods to give rise to apocalyptic literature (1973, 344). But it was one of Cross's students, Paul Hanson, who took up the task of charting the rise of this new literary form, its worldview, and social movement.[7] For the purposes of this discussion, one notes that Hanson develops further Cross's contrast between myth and history, which he sees as constitutive of an emerging apocalyptic literature. According to Hanson, apocalyptic literature represents a rejection of the contingencies of history that earlier prophecy had once held in tension with visionary or mythic elements. Visionary movements responsible for this literature subscribe

---

7. Hanson's work is to be found in his published dissertation, *The Dawn of Apocalyptic* (first published 1975; rev. ed. 1979), as well as in articles such as, "Jewish Apocalyptic Against Its Near Eastern Environment" (1971); and "Apocalypses and Apocalypticism: The Genre; Introductory Overview" (1992).

to the mythic worldview that characterizes apocalyptic eschatology and refuse to translate events of the cosmic realm in terms of the mundane. Thus apocalyptic literature is escapist literature that retreats from history and withdraws into the cosmos as a result of the political disillusionments of the early postexilic period.

What makes apocalypticism's worldview mythological, in Hanson's argument, is its focus on the cosmic sphere (Hanson 1971, 33, 36, 52; 1979, 18–19, 21–31). The events that take place in the cosmic vision are characterized by transcendence above the contingency of the historical realm. This transcendence calls "into question all mundane institutions and structures, and the realistic element" (1971, 35). Events and structures of the transcendent cosmos perdure and are static (1979, 18). While apocalyptic literature does relate sequences of events taking place in the cosmic realm, these events are unlike history because they are episodic and timeless (1971, 40), by which Hanson seems to mean that they are repeatable and cyclical. Since there is no causal connection between these sets of events, there is no linear and progressive movement of chronological time (1971, 56). Moreover, within this mythic world of the cosmos, divine agency is the primary determiner of action and, since action takes place in episodic and repeatable cycles, events and their outcomes are predetermined. Episodes are closed to other forces that might alter the cycle of events.

In sum, Hanson views myth as having a cyclical, timeless, perduring, cosmic worldview that contrasts with the worldview inherent in Israelite historiography. History he defines as a "historical sequence spanning centuries in an unbroken development" (1971, 38). Historiography follows the unfolding of events from "a distinct beginning point" through the present to a "future unfolding" (40). Not unlike von Rad, Hanson understands this history to be open-ended and driven by human agency and free will. Also like von Rad, Hanson judges apocalyptic eschatology against the norm of the prophetic worldview. The worldview of the prophets, which he terms "prophetic eschatology," reflects this view of history even while wedding it to visionary and cosmic elements. Apocalyptic eschatology, however, divorced the two and discarded the historical altogether.

This reconstruction of apocalypticism's origins vis-à-vis Israelite historiography garnered critical response from different quarters. J. J. M Roberts (1976) critiques Hanson's proposal in some detail because it assumes a cultural dichotomy between Israel and the foreign nations in order to argue for a dichotomy between history and myth. Roberts outlines the nature and extent of these dichotomies in Hanson's thinking and then goes on to argue that the distinction is not as clear as Hanson makes them out to be. But Roberts's primary interest is in Israelite historiography as it compares to Mesopotamian materials; he does not address Hanson's observations of apocalyptic literature. Somewhat ironically, Roberts ends by maintaining that there is a dichotomy between myth and history, even if he disagrees with the particulars of Hanson's distinctions. Roberts does not attempt to construct an alternative distinction, but he does speak briefly of the mythic function of history and the historical function of myth.

At this point, one sees clearly the way in which Jindo's article picks up the exchange between Hanson and Roberts. While postulating Hanson's distinction between apocalyptic and prophetic eschatologies, Jindo rearticulates Roberts's notion of the historical function of myth. But what does "mythicized history" or the "historical function of myth" mean? Are myth and history distinguished by certain functions or certain forms of expression that they nevertheless can somehow share? And if these functions can be used by either kind of genre, what makes them distinctive to that genre?

Critique of Hanson's discussion also came from the scholar of apocalyptic texts, and another student of Cross, John Collins. Collins took issue with Hanson over the substance of the apocalyptic worldview. In particular, Collins upbraids Hanson on his assertion that where prophecy succeeds and apocalyptic literature fails is in translating the cosmic vision into "the terms of real history," which he says sounds like the biblical theology program of demythologization (Collins 1981, 90–93). Instead, Collins asserts that the prophet and the apocalypticist each records what he sees—and for the apocalypticist, the most important action is that which takes place on the cosmic level. Collins also downplays the sharp dichotomy between myth and history, but nevertheless employs ideas that echo Cross and Hanson. Specifically, Collins argues that mythic imagery is constitutive of the apocalyptic genre. Without defining myth or mythology, Collins, like Hanson, asserts that apocalyptic literature "shares the world-view of the ancient cosmic mythologies" (Collins 1997, 84). By this he means that apocalypticists view the most important action as that conflict that takes place between "heavenly mythological beings, in the conflict of God and Belial" (84). Moreover, Collins agrees with Cross that Daniel's various mythic references form identifiable mythic patterns that are repeatable and paradigmatic. These patterns can be identified as deriving ultimately from Canaanite myths, but they are imposed by the apocalypticist onto various historical events to reveal a transcendent reality (Collins 1981, 90–93).

Rather than speaking of myth and history as constituting two opposing realms and worldviews that might be either divorced (Hanson) or in constant tension (Cross) in Daniel, Collins speaks of time and space as the intersecting axes of one universe. The axis of time is the horizontal, again implying linear movement toward the future, while the vertical that intersects with it is the spatial dimension. While Collins connects myth with the spatial axis, especially as it pertains to the "mythological characters" of the heavens, they are not one and the same. As intersecting axes, human history in Daniel opens out onto cosmic space for the visionary. Thus Collins diverges from Hanson by downplaying spatial dualism in apocalyptic literature and worldview and emphasizing instead the homology between the heavenly and the earthly. Indeed, Collins has continued to assert that myth and history cannot be used to distinguish between prophecy and apocalypticism.[8] Moreover, Collins does not use a prophetic worldview as the norm against which to judge apocalyptic literature's use of time and space.

This brief history of the discussion shows that while a strict dichotomy between myth and history has not prevailed in the extreme form articulated by Hanson, nevertheless many of Hanson's fundamental distinctions continue to circulate and find a home. Moreover, Roberts's and Jindo's assertions that the prophets give us "myth understood historically" while apocalypticists give us the opposite sounds remarkably like the language of "mythicized history" and "historicized myth," language first offered by Martin Noth.[9] Such constructions are just further examples of the way in which the obscurities of myth and apocalypticism have proliferated. And, as N. Wyatt (2001, 35) has argued, such language may simply further the old prejudice against myth by trying "to preserve a little bit of 'history' at all costs."

---

8. See Collins 2003; see also the discussion on prophetic eschatology and apocalyptic eschatology in DiTommaso 2007, 387–89.

9. On Noth's use of this term, see Rogerson 1974, 147–48. The notion of "historicized myth" may be found in various studies both within and outside biblical studies. One particularly clear specimen of it within biblical studies is Toombs 1961.

Myth and Apocalyptic Historiography in Daniel 8

Nevertheless, Jindo and DiTommaso's exchange reveals a shifting assessment of apocalyptic literature within recent scholarship. DiTommaso's comments situate him within a growing body of scholarship that has positively reassessed the historiography of apocalyptic historical résumés.[10] Moreover, some of the scholarly work on apocalyptic historiography has demonstrated, rather ironically, that historiography can look and function in ways traditionally attributed to myth. This reality calls into question the traditional oppositions used in defining myth/apocalypticism and history, and this is the territory that this essay must now explore.[11]

Roberts (1976, 13) wisely points out that such explorations are best approached on the level of specific texts first. Thus in the ensuing discussion I propose to test the issues by examining one particular text where apocalyptic historiography meets mythic materials,[12] namely, Dan 8 within the larger context of Daniel's visions.[13] Daniel 8 and its apocalyptic review of history provide an interesting text for examination because it is rich in mythological motifs and patterns but has long suffered neglect because scholars have often deemed it to be a poor copy of Dan 7.[14] Yet this chapter is distinctive from Dan 7 in significant ways, even as it depends on its more famous predecessor.

---

10. This position may also be found in Davies 1978; Newsom 1984; Hall 1991; Addison 1992; Froehlich 1996; and Niskanen 2004.

11. DiTommaso (2007, 388) also challenges "the binary thinking" that has led scholars to make apocalypticism a mythic literature devoid of history.

12. In using the word *mythic*, I refer to distinctive images, plot patterns, characters, or vocabulary that have a demonstrable connection to a particular narrative or body of stories that scholars categorize as myth, even when they disagree on the definition of myth.

13. It might seem more suitable to focus on Dan 7, a text long recognized by scholars to be redolent with myth. Yet Dan 7 has been subjected to so much discussion in the past thirty years that it has become overworked.

14. Susan Niditch (1983, 216) summarizes the negative views of Dan 8 that predominated in earlier scholarship when she comments, "Many scholars feel, in fact, that ch. 8 comes as an aesthetic anticlimax to Daniel 7." See, e.g., Porteous 1965, 119; Montgomery 1927, 325.

The Mythic Pattern of the Rebellious Subordinate

Collins (1977, 106) has argued that Dan 8 employs a mythic pattern and imagery that is also found in Isa 14:4–20, sometimes called the Day Star myth or the myth of the rebellious subordinate.[15] The narrative elements of this mythic pattern include a powerful earthly figure, typically a king or tyrant, whose hubristic imagination leads him to elevate himself up to the heavenly heights, up to the clouds, in an attempt to usurp the divine throne. However, before he can accomplish the overthrow of the divine, God casts him down to the earth in abject humiliation. As Hugh Page (1996, 130) notes, the narrative typically indicates that the ruler's fall "has an impact on the universe."

While some would argue that this mythic pattern may be traced back to a now lost Ugaritic myth, one need not adhere to this reconstruction in order to recognize the importance of this narrative within the Hebrew Bible or its mythic character. Isaiah 14 likens the earthly tyrant to Helel ben Shachar, or Day Star son of Dawn, who is implied to be a member of the divine assembly who revolted against God in a distant, primordial era (Clements 1980, 142–43; Collins 1977, 106–7; Page 1996, 130–31).

In Dan 8 the narrative pattern is applied to Antiochus IV in the aftermath of his desecration of the temple in 167 B.C.E. But Dan 8 adapts the narrative pattern for use in its symbolic vision in two significant ways. The mythic pattern is first subordinated to a broader historiographical schema involving four world kingdoms, within which Antiochus IV appears as the last ruler of the fourth kingdom. Second, it is retold using animal symbolism. While symbolic figures are often associated with myth, and this is indeed the case in Dan 7,[16] Dan 8 uses a symbolic system that is not necessarily tied to mythic narratives or patterns. The use of animals such as the goat and the ram are typical metaphors of mundane leadership in the Hebrew Bible, as are the animal horns. Thus Antiochus IV is the little horn that grows on the he-goat, an offshoot of one of four replacement horns (its identification as a little horn is perhaps a reference to his illegitimate methods of acquiring and exercising power). Nevertheless, the vision report of Dan 8:9–11 retains the spatial language that is important to the

---

15. Niditch (1983, 229–33) also identifies this mythic pattern at work in Dan 8. For extensive discussions of this narrative pattern in Isa 14, see Page 1996, 120–40. Ezek 28 also provides a similar narrative pattern concerning the king of Tyre.

16. On the mythic origin of the animal imagery in Dan 7, see Collins 1993.

mythic pattern. It describes how the little horn grows exceedingly great toward the south, the east, and the west (i.e., the territories that did not originally belong to the Syrian king), and even up to the host of heaven. The little horn breaches the heavenly boundary, confronts the prince of hosts—the archangel Michael—and even succeeds in casting down to the earth some of the heavenly host, or angelic army.[17] He also desecrates or "casts down" the sanctuary—a reference to both the earthly temple and its heavenly counterpart (Gzella 2003, 118–19).

While the symbolic vision form typically provides parallelism between vision report and interpretation, it is significant that some details of this vision report (vv. 3–14) do not match some details provided in the angelic interpretation (vv. 20–25).[18] Notably, the vision report ends with the triumph of the rebellious subordinate and does not record any defeat of the tyrant. Indeed, the vision report elaborates on the success of the tyrant and concludes with the notice that the little horn succeeded in all that he did. It is not until the end of the interpretation that the reader learns of God's defeat of the tyrant. The final three words of verse 25 declare, "but without a hand he will be broken." This is all that is said of the little horn's demise.

Patterns and Meaning in Historiography

The rebellious subordinate narrative unfolds as part of the final, and climactic, segment of the four-kingdoms schema. This historiographical schema, which the author of Dan 8 adapts from Dan 7 (and which Dan

---

17. See further Merrill Willis 2010. The overlap that I discuss there (100 n. 46) between Dan 8 and Isa 14:4–20 include (1) the language and motif of hubristic thinking, (2) self-exaltation to the heavenly host and stars, and (3) the language of casting down to the earth. Notice the following parallels:
   1. Dan 8:25: ובלבבו יגדיל
      Isa 14:13a-b: אתה אמרת בלבבך השמים אעלה
   2. Dan 8:10: ותגדל עד־צבא השמים
      Isa 14:13c-d: ממעל לכוכבי־אל ארם כסאי
   3. Dan 8:10b: ותפל ארצה; Dan 8:12b: תשלך אמת ארצה
      Isa 14:12: נפלת משמים ... נגדעת לארץ

18. On the form of the symbolic vision, see Niditch 1983 (177–241). The parallelism between vision report and interpretation should not be understood as rigid—in Daniel it is not unusual to find slippage, gaps, and other small discrepancies between the two parts of the symbolic vision. Nevertheless, the lack of parallelism in Dan 8 is significant and unusual.

7 borrowed from 2:31–45), recounts the history of foreign rule over the Jews from the Neo-Babylonian Empire down to Greek rule. While Dan 8 makes no mention of Nebuchadnezzar or the Neo-Babylonian period, the text does preserve references to the other three kingdoms—the two horns on the ram symbolize the Median and the Persian empires, while the he-goat is the Greek Empire and its various horns represent Alexander the Great and his successors.[19] The schema, which probably developed in Persia and which is preserved in part by the Greek historian Herodotus as Assyria, Media, and Persia, depicts ancient Near Eastern history as a succession of empires overtaking the same land; but the fourth empire, the Greek, stands out as particularly aggressive and should be resisted. The four-kingdoms schema thus originally functioned as a form of resistance literature (Flusser 1972, 157–59).

Similarly, Dan 8 presents the history of foreign rule as a succession of empires, emphasizing the destructive capacities of the fourth empire. This succession is shaped into a narrative pattern in which one government rises to greatness and then finds itself confronted and broken by the next government. Thus the he-goat shatters the ram horns that represent Media and Persia, but soon after the he-goat's own single horn is shattered and then replaced by more horns. Each successive government grows more aggressive and threatening than the last, culminating in the abusive reign of the little horn, who attacks in every direction and confronts even the heavenly powers.

This presentation of history uses details selectively, conveying only those things that are important for the writer's purpose. The writer is not interested in narrating at any length dates, places, agents, events, and motives that make up a typical history. Nevertheless, these elements are present in the narrative with the explicit identification of Media, Persia, and Greece and the allusive identification of the agents Alexander the Great and some of the Diadochi. Antiochus IV becomes the focus of this narrative and the subject of the text's attention and energy as the narrative recounts his desecration of the Jerusalem temple.

---

19. Of course, Judea never experienced domination by Media. The inclusion of Media clearly reveals the eastern origin of the schema. Jewish scribes apparently learned of it in the eastern diaspora and brought it back to Judea where Babylon and Nebuchadnezzar were substituted for Assyria, but Media remained in the schema. See Swain 1940; Flusser 1972, 148–75.

Carol Newsom (2006) argues that such selective use of details and distinctive narrative patterning may be understood in terms of Paul Ricoeur's concept of historiography. In his discussion of temporality and narrative, Ricoeur argues that historiography is the configuration or emplotment of events in such a way that they may be grasped as a temporal unity. For Ricoeur, emplotted events are not just episodes or listed occurrences, such as one finds in the Sumerian King List. Rather, when the historian emplots events, she takes a string of happenings or "an open series of events" (e.g., a list of four successive kingdoms) and endows them with a narrative structure that comprises a beginning (an original event or initial condition), a middle (events and consequences that involve causes and effects), and an ending that gives definition and meaning to the whole narrative (1984, 1:66–68).

For Ricoeur, such configured narratives of real events form a temporal circle or unity in so much as the beginning can be read in the ending and, once the story is known and repeated, the ending can be read in the beginning. Thus in historiography the configuring and retelling of events allows the arrow of time, as the reader experiences it, to move backward toward the beginning of the story or forward toward its ending (1984, 1:67–68).[20] Ricoeur asserts that the historian does not fabricate or impose

---

20. When I speak of the use of temporality in narratives, I am not simply referring to the presentation of the course of events as happening one after another. I am also referring to the way in which narratives can use and manipulate the perception or experience of time. This has to do with the "aporetics of time" that Ricoeur is grappling with in *Time and Narrative*. These aporetics or contradictions concerning time have to do with the reality that although humans typically speak of time as linear—as something we pass through so that we always find ourselves in the present having come from the past as we head into the future—humans also perceive the past to remain present through memory. The future is present also through anticipation. Ricoeur, enjoining Augustine's observations on this contradiction, notes that *human experience of time*, which is connected to but distinct from the narrativization of human experience into historiography, is not really regulated externally by the sun and the moon and the movement of the heavenly bodies. Our sense of time is, in fact, regulated internally by memory of the past, attentiveness to the present, and anticipation of the future. Although this particular discussion on myth and history is not able to explore this aspect of temporality in apocalyptic texts further, this contradiction is what allows humans to experience the past as contemporaneous with the present. This is what Flannery-Dailey is exploring in her paper on "Non-Linear Time" (1999). She calls it a spiral model of time that allows apocalyptic visionaries to depict the present in terms of past experiences of Eden or Mount Sinai. That is, these past experiences are

this narrative structure on events; rather, she discovers the structure that is prefigured in the experience of the events themselves and re-presents them or configures them.

Historiography as a narrative act does not simply convey data concerning agents, events, and dates. It involves the historian in the *selective* work of identifying the subject, scope, and relevant details from prefigured events to be included in the narrative (Newsom 2006, 218). This work typically seeks thematic coherency as well as temporal coherency. Ricoeur (1984, 1:67) argues that the historian, no less than the novelist, emplots events in such a way that they may "be translated into one 'thought.'" Historical narratives have a center of meaning, a central idea, that ties events together into a temporal unity. So, contrary to von Rad's assumption about the nature of Israelite historiography, historical narrative is never simply a written record of the "endlessly varied shapes and forms of history" (von Rad 1965, 304), but rather preserves a narrative intentionally emplotted around a thematic center.

For Ricoeur and other theorists, the function or purpose of this historical narrative is cognitive in nature—to make historical experience meaningful for its readers, not only in understanding the past but also in making sense of the present by connecting it to a larger narrative. Although von Rad understood history to be fundamentally meaningful because it was the chief means by which Israelite religion saw God at work, Wiesel's interchange with his teacher points out that historical experience is not always "true" or meaningful in and of itself. Present and past experiences may corrode meaning and create dissonance, especially when those experiences involve open-ended tragedy, injustice, and tremendous suffering. Indeed, Ricoeur argues that the experience of temporality in and of itself can be tragic. The ability to discern an ending or anticipate the drawing to a close of events in which one finds oneself stuck in medias res, however, allows one to discern the relevance and weight of such tragic experiences and to see them as limited in both duration and importance. But one can do this only by virtue of being able to construct or project an ending point from which to view those experiences (O'Leary 1994, 40–41).

The foregoing understanding of historiography indicates that the persistent, though oft-challenged, distinction between history as linear,

---

contemporaneous with the present for the apocalypticist. A similar experience of time is also at work in Dan 8, where the present is cast in terms of the exile.

open-ended, contingent events and myth as cyclical and static episodes cannot be maintained. Indeed, Newsom (2006, 215–18) observes that historical narratives in the Hebrew Bible often involve repetition of historical patterns and emplotted themes. One need only look to the Deuteronomistic cycle of history of apostasy, oppression, crying out, and deliverance that one finds in Judges in compacted narratives and in 1–2 Kings as an overarching schema (219). This cycle shapes the telling of particular historical events. In short, history often repeats itself within and between historical narratives in the Hebrew Bible;[21] patterns are not mythic simply because they repeat. Similarly, DiTommaso (2007, 386–87) argues that time and temporality work on different levels within apocalyptic literature and that one of these has to do with "recurrent macrostructural patterns within history."

Indeed, the ability to discern repetition and identifiable patterns within historical events is a chief means by which one makes sense of historical experience and also anticipates or predicts future outcomes (DiTommaso 2007, 387; Newsom 2006, 226). The current financial crisis plaguing America and much of Europe may provide an example of this. When the crisis broke in September of 2008, analysts were quick to look back to the Great Depression and also to Japan's crises that resulted in "the lost decade" of the 1990s. The continuities and discontinuities between the present and these past financial catastrophes have become an important means of prognostication as both Wall Street and Main Street have asked, How long until the economy recovers and the tragedy of lost jobs, houses, and business is ended?[22]

---

21. Not only in the Hebrew Bible, history as repeatable is a concept that J. J. Finkelstein (1963) develops in relation to Mesopotamian historiography as well. Maintaining a close connection between manticism and divination, Mesopotamian sages understood divination to be an effective means of anticipating future events precisely because specific events predictably act as catalysts for specific outcomes. These catalysts were reflected in the particulars of a sheep's entrails, which could be catalogued and used as a guide for other diviners seeking to give advice to the king, such as one finds in the *Šumma Izbu* texts.

22. This is not to imply that apocalyptic literature and apocalyptic historiography always spring out of a definable crisis—Dan 7 reflects no specific catastrophe. However, Dan 8's apocalyptic historiography is directly linked to the crisis of the desecration of the temple by Antiochus IV in 167 B.C.E.

Within Dan 8, the study of history for the purpose of prognostication takes the form of an extended *vaticinium ex eventu*.[23] Using a *vaticinium ex eventu*, the apocalyptist emplots the four-kingdoms schema so that the past, present, and future of foreign domination become a temporal unity with a discernible and imminent ending. Although von Rad charged that Daniel's apocalyptic visions undermine the openness of history by depicting the future as predetermined, it is better to say that the convention of the *vaticinium* allows the apocalyptist to play with the arrow of time. Thus although time appears to move in a straight line from past to future for the reader, the apocalyptist has already traced the flow of time backward to the exile in order to anticipate the future, whether that future is in fact the present time of the writer or the writer's actual future (Newsom 2006, 227). From his study of the past, the apocalyptist discerns that within the course of history foreign powers regularly rise and fall, but the crisis of Seleucid rule brings this schema to a breaking point that necessitates climax and closure of foreign power altogether.

Particular Experiences and Ultimate Realities in Apocalyptic Literature

The crisis of foreign domination is set off by the little horn's aggressive intrigues against other kings, the people, and especially against the divine realm. The writer views Antiochus IV's co-opting of the temple, the abolition of the *tamid* sacrifices, and his prohibition of Torah observances in Jerusalem as going "beyond the usual evil"[24] of imperial aggression against the subjugated people of Judea. These actions represent attacks on the Most High himself that are unprecedented within the historical résumé and within his own reading of Judean history. One might ask how it is that the writer of Dan 8 does not regard Nebuchadnezzar and the Neo-Babylonian Empire, which destroyed the temple, as the start of the crisis. Certainly Dan 8 regards life under the rule of the he-goat and his horns to be an extension of the Babylonian exile. But this exile is divinely initiated through Nebuchadnezzar in Dan 2 and Dan 7. Even Dan 8, which does not mention Babylon or Nebuchadnezzar, seems to understand the com-

---

23. On this understanding of the apocalyptic study of the past in Daniel, see esp. Davies 1978, 19–25; and Newsom 1984, 43–50.

24. To borrow the phrase from J. K. Rowling's description of Voldemort (2005, 502).

munity's experience of foreign domination as part of "the period of wrath" (8:19), a period determined by God. Nevertheless, Dan 8 deems the little horn's actions to be unique because they are not initiated or legitimated by God as punishment upon the Judean community. The actions of Antiochus IV do not fit easily within the assumptions of the traditional Deuteronomistic shaping of exilic history that one finds in 2 Kgs 24–25; nor do they fit the prophetic view of exile found in Jer 28:14 and 27:5–6 (a view adopted in part to speak of Nebuchadnezzar in Dan 2:36). In these views, the foreign king acts as God's servant and instrument for punishment.

The writer of Dan 8 places the political and religious transgressions of Antiochus IV within a much larger scope of vision and agency than one typically sees in other types of biblical historiography. Even a cursory comparison of Daniel's visions with the accounts of Antiochus IV in 1–2 Maccabees illustrates the difference. The propagandistic historiographies of 1 and 2 Maccabees, which were written well after the death of Antiochus IV (and thus not for those stuck in medias res), trains its sight on the earthly. God's actions are not missing from this historiography, but the supernatural comes into play only in terms of earthly events and results, especially those events that support the political legitimacy of the Hasmoneans. The cosmic sphere and its characters are not envisioned and earthly characters and events are not framed in terms of the cosmic. But the writer of Dan 8 narrates Antiochus IV as a character at play in both the earthly and the cosmic spheres—for the imagery of the horn literally takes the reader's eye up the spatial axis and across the boundary between heaven and earth—a boundary that is not typically constructed in the historiography of 1–2 Maccabees or in the Deuteronomistic History. While it would be difficult to assert the writer's intention in doing this, one can argue, as Lenn Goodman (1993, 74–75) does, that the literary *effect* is to situate human experience within both the cosmos and in human time in such a way that the extraordinary, even the ultimate, character of these events may be brought to the fore. This literary feature—the connecting of cosmic or supernatural realities with mundane realities, often through the focus on the cosmos or on remote time—is distinctive to mythic narrative in the Hebrew Bible. Daniel 8 affirms Goodman's insight that myths deal with ultimates—ultimate values and realities and, in the case of apocalyptic literature, ultimate endings.[25] Mythic literature thus "press[es] against

---

25. Some scholars frame myth in terms of the perception of reality's "essential"

the glass of ordinary experience" (Goodman 1993, 76). In their dealings with the ultimate, myths also open up the possibility of extraordinary responses and resolutions to the problems of historical experience.

Thus Dan 8 weaves together both historiography and mythic patterns in order to connect the mundane to the cosmic and the absolute. The symbolic vision shows how the particularity of Seleucid rule and its effects on the righteous community have ultimate significance. The little horn's rule is more than a battle between Hellenistic and Jewish cultures or identities, for Dan 8 it is ultimately an issue of how divine power is and is not manifested through human leadership. The mythic pattern of the rebellious subordinate allows the scribal community, who make up the reading and writing community of Daniel's visions, to explore the ultimate character of the divine relationship to the human king within the particular context of Antiochus IV's rule. It also allows the community to construct a narrative ending to this experience.

It is true that mythic narrative patterns often drive the historical details in Daniel's visions. That is, the mythic patterns can exercise such extensive shaping power over the narrative that the particular details of the historical events can become misshapen and less important than the pattern itself. One can see this in the historical résumé of Dan 11 when Antiochus IV, the last king of the north, is credited with a third, and fictional, campaign into Egypt (Clifford 1975; Newsom 2006, 228). And in Dan 8 the mythic and symbolic characterization of Antiochus IV, as the little horn and rebellious subordinate who breaches the heavenly boundary, eclipses the particular details of his intrigues involving the sale of the high priesthood and the murder of Onias III.

Nevertheless, Dan 8 also shows how historical particularity disrupts the "static structures" of mythic meanings and drives the mythic pattern. This is particularly evident in the vision report, which evokes the specific language of Isa 14 and Ezek 28 to characterize the hubristic attempts by Antiochus IV to usurp the throne of the God. The expected climax to this pattern, the climax used in Isa 14 and Ezek 28, is the dejection of the insubordinate king, who is cast down to the earth and subject to

---

character, which may refer to the same reality as that which I call "ultimate" reality. However, I find myself suspicious of the term *essential* because, as in Jindo's article, it can be used to buttress a reductionistic approach to apocalyptic literature. The language of *ultimate*, however, conceptually moves in a different direction, away from a minimal essence toward a maximal reality.

abjection and horror in his death. But this part of the mythic pattern is rather pointedly absent from Dan 8's vision report, which relates that the rebellious subordinate elevates himself up to the heavenly host and, rather than experiencing dejection, instead casts down the heavenly host, tramples on "the truth"—a reference to Torah observance—and prospers in all that he does.

The vision report of Dan 8, written shortly after the desecration of the temple, lacks the triumphant vision that characterizes the visions of Dan 7 and Dan 10–12.[26] Even though the interpretation of Dan 8 attempts to supply the expected victorious ending by providing the terse statement "but without a hand he will be broken," the supplemented line is anticlimactic in terms of the reader's expectations and the energy of Dan 8's vision. Several aspects of the text's narrative attenuate the significance and triumph of the divine victory over the rebellious subordinate. In the first place, the vision report sets up a pattern of rising and falling empires that initially leads the reader to expect that the power of the little horn too will be confronted and defeated in short order. Thus the horns of Media and Persia rise to such dominance that there was no one to rescue captive countries from their might. But at the height of their power, the horn of Alexander the Great's Greek empire breaks them and attains such dominance for itself that there was no one who could rescue captive countries from its might. But then, at the height of its power, Alexander's horn is broken, and the little horn's power rises to greatness. The repetition of the phrase and the pattern leads the reader to expect the imminent destruction of Antiochus IV's power. Yet the expected defeat does not take place. The lack of parallelism between vision report and interpretation makes the defeat appear to be secondary when it does happen and makes the little horn, not divine power, the focus of this historical summary. Moreover, the lack of elaboration on the divine's defeat of the little horn and lack of a transformed future for the righteous community further undermine the rhetorical power of the victory. Daniel 8 intentionally invokes the mythic pattern of the rebellious subordinate and then narratively and structurally disrupts it.

---

26. Collins (1974, 55) notes this absence in his schema depicting the parallelism of the three visions. He notes that the résumés of chs. 7 and 10–12 divide history into three key sections: (a) events prior to Antiochus IV, (b) the career of Antiochus IV, and (c) the eschatological outcome. While ch. 8 includes sections a and b, it contains no c.

Equipment for Living in the Midst of Tragedy

The skillful interweaving of mythic and historiographical materials in Dan 8 performs a particular kind of work for the earliest reading community of Daniel's visions. Because this material situates readers' particular experiences relative to the ultimate realities of cosmic space and eschatological time, it affords the reader certain tools or "equipment for living" to negotiate the tragic experiences of life under the rule of Antiochus IV.

Recent scholarship on millennial groups and their discourse has highlighted the rhetorical character of apocalyptic discourse in general (O'Leary 1994, 3–19; Brummett 1991). Biblical apocalypses, no less than contemporary millennial groups, utilize apocalyptic language for purposes that are suasive—they use language to frame the world in particular ways intended to be internalized by the reader to make sense of the world and inform certain kinds of actions and dispositions. The language and conventions of this discourse thus constitute the equipment for thinking and acting upon and living within the world.

In particular, apocalyptic language and symbols, historical and mythic patterns work on the symbolic level of language to bring cognitive coherence and meaning when experience and conviction clash (Fishbane 1985, 485–99, 509–11).[27] Since this function may be found in any number of discourses, they are not unique to apocalyptic literature. Indeed, Fredric Jameson, combining rhetorical criticism and ideological criticism with Claude Lévi-Strauss's theory of myth, argues that all kinds of aesthetic productions—mythic or otherwise—can create "imaginary or formal 'solutions' to unresolvable social contradictions" (Jameson 1982, 79). But apocalyptic literature is quite effective at creating symbolic resolutions because of its ability to bring either the cosmos or remote time to bear on the present.

---

27. The reader will recognize here the language of cognitive dissonance, a theory originally developed in relation to millennial groups and their expectations, but with larger applications made to the field of cognitive psychology by Leon Festinger (1962). Robert Carroll (1979) picked up Festinger's theory and applied it to the development of apocalyptic movements. However, more recent articulations of cognitive dissonance in relation to apocalyptic discourse, such as that of O'Leary (1994, 19–20), combine the concept of cognitive dissonance with Lévi-Strauss's notion of myth's function to resolve or mediate contradictions.

In Dan 8 the dissonance that apocalyptic rhetoric attempts to resolve has to do with divine power and presence vis-à-vis the foreign domination of Judea. The ideology of rule that began during the exilic period and prevailed during the Persian period emphasized God's use of the foreign king to rule Judea after the exile. The foreign king was God's messiah (Isa 45:1), the one who delivered the people in accordance with Yahweh's plan. Persian period materials often legitimized the foreign king even as they critiqued local rule.[28] But Dan 7 and Dan 8 indicate the way in which this ideology of rule is shifting under the oppressive weight of Seleucid rule. While Dan 7 provides a vision of God's penultimate validation of kingly rule before ultimately judging all kings,[29] Dan 8 cannot even envision this much. For the author of Dan 8, there is no divine validation of any of the animals or horns. Nevertheless, the author of Dan 8 cannot concede that history somehow unfolds or takes shape outside of God's plan. But in what way does history reveal divine power when the righteous community faces such terrible and overwhelming opposition from the little horn?

The symbolic work of Dan 8 is to construct a different ideology of rule than those that predominated during the exilic and postexilic periods of Judea's history. In place of a Deuteronomistic view of history or a Persian period ideology of kingship, Dan 8 uses myth and history to create an ideology in which God is at work in history to shape its general direction toward the destruction of imperial rule, even though God is not immediately visible within historical events. Daniel 7 had already begun to map this new ideological territory through its reuse of the *Chaoskampf* pattern in an eschatological context. Yet the triumphalist vision of the Ancient of Days and the humanlike one, which dates from before Antiochus's outlawing of Judaism, is not able to make sense of the immediate experience of dejection created by the desecration of the temple. Thus historical experience demands the reworking—but not rejection—of mythic patterns as well as historical patterns, in order to create cognitive coherence concerning the present.

---

28. This dynamic is already apparent during the exile in Jeremiah's language of the signet—used to delegitimize the Davidic king and validate Nebuchadnezzar (Jer 22:24–25). The Chronicler and Ezra–Nehemiah continue this dynamic. See Japhet 1982.

29. The divine council commissions the first three beasts in 7:4–6 by giving the lion a human form and intellect, commanding the bear to arise and devour, and giving dominion to the leopard.

It is the complementary relationship between historical narrative and mythic narrative that provides the equipment for Dan 8 to do this symbolic work. The historical experience that Dan 8 narrates using the four-kingdoms schema is tragic and oppressive, but the narrative of the rebellious subordinate allows the remote time of the future eschaton and the normally invisible realm of the divine to become visible and to invest the present with meaning. At the same time, historical narrative is capable of using the past to anticipate a pattern of increasingly more aggressive yet falling empires. This use of history also expresses and motivates resistance toward the present order as a way of bringing about a future without empire.

Conclusion

In this study of Dan 8 I have demonstrated the persistence of the dichotomy imposed on apocalyptic literature and its relationship to myth and historiography as well as the difficulties inherent in the dichotomy itself. Both myth and historiography are capable of organizing particular events into larger nonparticular schemas. Historiography, understood in terms of narrative configuration and emplotment, often makes use of repeating and identifiable patterns, just as myth can. Its narrative use of temporality involves something more akin to a circle than a straight line moving from past to future. Nevertheless, this is the narrative form that concerns itself with structuring the ongoing experiences of human time and place into meaningful narratives with beginnings, middles, and ends.

The mythic materials apocalyptic literature utilizes in Dan 8, and in Daniel's other visions, are adept at putting human experience into a framework of ultimate realities. Goodman's language here is apt: "in myths, the story is always situated vis-à-vis a known reality." In its relationship to that reality, the content and work of the myth often reveal "an upward and widening spiral, toward the cosmic," by utilizing the remote time of universal origins or endings or by making visible the normally invisible realm of the divine, depicted as spatially "above." Moreover, while myth is often construed in biblical studies as durative, static, and cyclical, in the apocalyptic vision of Dan 8 it shows itself to be adaptable and reworkable in the service of historical particularity. Indeed, the two kinds of narrative must each contribute its own equipment to create meaning, which for the scribal community of Daniel's visions is nothing less than knowledge of God's power and presence in the course of a tragic history.

Works Cited

Addison, Erin. 1992. When History Fails: Apocalypticism in the Ancient Mediterranean World. Ph.D. diss. University of California, Santa Barbara.

Brummett, Barry. 1991. *Contemporary Apocalyptic Rhetoric*. New York: Praeger.

Carroll, Robert. 1979. *When Prophecy Failed: Reactions and Responses to Failure in the Old Testament Prophetic Traditions*. London: SCM.

Clements, Ronald. E. 1980. *Isaiah 1–39*. NCBC. Grand Rapids: Eerdmans.

Clifford, Richard. 1975. History and Myth in Daniel 10–12. *BASOR* 220:23–26.

Collins, John J. 1974. The Son of Man and the Saints of the Most High. *JBL* 93:50–66.

———. 1977. *The Apocalyptic Vision of the Book of Daniel*. HSM 16. Missoula, Mont.: Scholars Press.

———. 1981. Apocalyptic Genre and Mythic Allusions in Daniel. *JSOT* 21:83–100.

———. 1993. Stirring up the Great Sea: The Religio-historical Background of Daniel 7. Pages 121–36 in *The Book of Daniel in the Light of New Findings*. Edited by A. S. van der Woude. Leuven: Peeters.

———. 1997. *Seers, Sibyls, and Sages in Hellenistic-Roman Judaism*. Leiden: Brill.

———. 2003. Prophecy, Apocalypse and Eschatology: Reflections on the Proposals of Lester Grabbe. Pages 44–52 in *Knowing the End from the Beginning: The Prophetic, the Apocalyptic, and Their Relationships*. Edited by Lester L. Grabbe and Robert D. Haak. JSPSup 46. London: T&T Clark.

Cross, Frank M. 1973. *Canaanite Myth and Hebrew Epic: Essays in the History of the Religion of Israel*. Cambridge: Harvard University Press.

Davies, Graham. I. 1978. Apocalyptic and Historiography. *JSOT* 5:15–28.

DiTommaso, Lorenzo. 2006. History and Apocalyptic Eschatology. *VT* 56:413–18.

———. 2007. Apocalypses and Apocalypticism in Antiquity (Part II). *Currents in Biblical Research* 5:367–432.

Festinger, Leon. 1962. *A Theory of Cognitive Dissonance*. Repr., Stanford: Stanford University Press.

Finkelstein, J. J. 1963. Mesopotamian Historiography. *Proceedings of the American Philosophical Society* 107:461–72.

Fishbane, Michael. 1985. *Biblical Interpretation in Ancient Israel*. Oxford: Clarendon.

Flannery-Dailey, Frances. 1999. Non-linear Time in Apocalyptic Texts: The Spiral Model. Pages 231–41 in *Society of Biblical Literature 1999 Seminar Papers*. Atlanta: Society of Biblical Literature.

Flusser, David. 1972. The Four Empires in the Fourth Sibyl and in the Book of Daniel. *IOS* 2:148–75.

Froehlich, Ida. 1996. *Time and Times and Half a Time: Historical Consciousness in the Jewish Literature of the Persian and Hellenistic Eras*. JSPSup 19. Sheffield: Sheffield Academic Press.

Goodman, Lenn E. 1993. Mythic Discourse. Pages 51–112 in *Myths and Fictions*. Edited by Shlomo Biderman and Ben-Ami Scharfstein. Leiden: Brill.

Gunkel, Hermann. 1994. *The Stories of Genesis: A Translation of the Third Edition of the Introduction to Hermann Gunkel's (1910) Commentary on the Book of Genesis*. Translated by John J. Scullion. Vallejo, Calif.: Bibal.

———. 2006. *Creation and Chaos in the Primeval Era and the Eschaton: A Religio-historical Study of Genesis 1 and Revelation 12*. Translated by K. William Whitney Jr. Grand Rapids: Eerdmans.

Gzella, Holger. 2003. *Cosmic Battle and Political Conflict: Studies in Verbal Syntax and Contextual Interpretation of Daniel 8*. BibOr 47. Rome: Pontifical Biblical Institute.

Hall, Robert G. 1991. *Revealed Histories: Techniques for Ancient Jewish and Christian Historiography*. JSPSup 6. Sheffield: JSOT Press.

Hanson, Paul. 1971. Jewish Apocalyptic against Its Near Eastern Environment. *RB* 78:31–58.

———. 1979. *The Dawn of Apocalyptic: The Historical and Sociological Roots of Jewish Apocalyptic Eschatology*. Rev. ed. Philadelphia: Fortress.

———. 1992. Apocalypses and Apocalypticism: The Genre and Introductory Overview. *ABD* 1:279–82.

Jameson, Fredric. 1982. *The Political Unconscious Narrative as a Socially Symbolic Act*. Ithaca, N.Y.: Cornell University Press.

Japhet, Sarah. 1982. Sheshbazzar and Zerubbabel: Against the Background of the Historical and Religious Tendencies of Ezra-Nehemiah. *ZAW* 94:66–98.

Jindo, Job Y. 2005. On Myth and History in Prophetic and Apocalyptic Eschatology. *VT* 55:412–15.

Merrill Willis, Amy C. 2010. *Dissonance and the Drama of Divine Sovereignty in the Book of Daniel*. LHBOTS 520. London: T&T Clark.

Montgomery, James. 1927. *A Critical and Exegetical Commentary on the Book of Daniel*. ICC. New York: Scribner's.

Newsom, Carol A. 1984. The Past as Revelation. *Quarterly Review* 4:40–53.

———. 2006. Rhyme and Reason: The Historical Résumé in Israelite and Early Jewish Thought. Pages 215–33 in *Congress Volume Leiden 2004*. Edited by André Lemaire. VTSup 109. Leiden: Brill.

Niditch, Susan. 1983. *The Symbolic Vision in Biblical Tradition*. HSM 30. Chico, Calif.: Scholars Press.

Niskanen, Paul. 2004. *The Human and the Divine in History: Herodotus and the Book of Daniel*. JSOTSup 396. London: T&T Clark.

Oden, Robert. 1992a. Myth and Mythology: Mythology. *ABD* 4:946–56.

———. 1992b. Myth and Mythology: Myth in the OT. *ABD* 4:956–60.

O'Leary, Stephen. 1994. *Arguing the Apocalypse: A Theory of Millennial Rhetoric*. Oxford: Oxford University Press.

Page, Hugh. 1996. *The Myth of the Cosmic Rebellion: A Study of Its Reflexes in Ugaritic and Biblical Literature*. VTSup 65. New York: Brill.

Porteous, Norman. 1965. *Daniel*. OTL. Philadelphia: Westminster.

Rad, Gerhard von. 1962. *The Theology of Israel's Historical Traditions*. Vol. 1 of *Old Testament Theology*. Translated by D. M. G. Stalker. New York: Harper & Row.

———. 1965. *The Theology of Israel's Prophetic Traditions*. Vol. 2 of *Old Testament Theology*. Translated by D. M. G. Stalker. New York: Harper & Row.

Ricoeur, Paul. 1984. *Time and Narrative*. Translated by Kathleen McLaughlin and David Pellauer. 3 vols. Chicago: University of Chicago Press.

———. 1987. Myth and History. *ER* 10:273–82.

Roberts, J. J. M. 1976. Myth vs. History. *CBQ* 38:1–13.

Rogerson, John. 1974. *Myth in Old Testament Interpretation*. BZAW 134. New York: de Gruyter.

Rowling, J. K. 2005. *Harry Potter and the Half Blood Prince*. New York: Scholastic.

Segal, Robert A. 1980. In Defense of Mythology: The History of Modern Theories of Myth. *Annals of Scholarship* 1:3–49.

Swain, J. W. 1940. The Theory of the Four Monarchies: Opposition History under the Roman Empire. *CP* 35:1–21.

Toombs, Lawrence. 1961. The Formation of Myth Patterns in the Old Testament. *Journal of Bible and Religion* 29:108–12.

Wiesel, Elie. 1980. Myth and History. Pages 20–30 in *Myth, Symbol, and Reality*. Edited by Alan M. Olson. Notre Dame: University of Notre Dame Press.

Wyatt, N. 2001. The Mythic Mind. *SJOT* 15:3–56.

Part 2
Myth in the New Testament and the Greco-Roman World

Recast, Reclaim, Reject: Myth and Validity

Steven J. Kraftchick

What makes today's scholarship so different is that it does not find it necessary to formulate a theology or hermeneutic that deals with myth. (Evans 1993, 36)

Myths are not lies. Nor are they detached stories. They are imaginative patterns, networks of powerful symbols that suggest particular ways of interpreting the world. They shape its meaning. (Midgley 2003, 1)

In a nutshell, the inherent tension between these two quotations defines any conversation about myth and the Bible.[1] Either Midgley is correct and interpreting the Bible is all about myth, or Evans is, and the endeavor is about anything but myth.

These are not the first set of conversations devoted to this tension nor the first convened under the auspices of the AAR/SBL.[2] It is likely not to

---

1. This paper was presented initially for the purpose of outlining some of the issues before the SBL consultation on Bible, Myth, and Myth Theory, which convened in 2006. As a result, my goal was less to solve problems than to state them succinctly and clearly. I do not think that determining the definition of myth or its functions is either simple or direct. It is clear, however, that how one defines the term does dictate the manner in which one considers it to function and subsequently what one considers to be the meaning of myth in truth constructions. See on this relationship of definition and meaning Stout 1982. For a very thorough and fine taxonomy of definitions and the difficulties they pose in myth studies see Doty 1980, 531–62.

2. In 1972–1974 the AAR sponsored sessions on Myth and History (subsequently published in Gibbs and Stevenson 1975), and in more recent times an AAR panel on myth studies "post-Eliade" (1991) culminated in a volume of essays dealing with the topics of myth construction and methods of myth study (Doniger and Patton 1996). One thing that we should consider is how the consultation follows on the work of those symposia and how it differs from them.

be the last either, since the questions surrounding myth—its definition, its forms, how to study it in comparison to other myths and literature—as well as claims for its truth, are genuinely difficult to answer.[3] Moreover, the nature of myth and the fact that one must dwell in some version of it, even while addressing it, mean that finding answers to the above questions that could satisfy even a small majority of us is highly unlikely. That being said, it seems to me that rather than attempt to answer these questions it is better to choose a less direct approach, namely to see how the term *myth* and its definitions shape the answers that some other interpreters have given to these questions. My desire is to investigate how the relationship of our definitions and valuations of myth structure our analyses of it. It will be evident that this paper can be no more than a thought exercise and only a beginning of one at that.

The lexical entry for *mythos* reads, "prim[arily] 'speech, conversation,' also of 'narrative' or 'story' without distinction of fact or fiction, then of fictional narrative (as opposed to λόγος, the truth of history) such as *tale, story, legend, myth*" (BDAG, 660). The entry then cites the appearance of both these meanings throughout Greek literature, both philosophical and religious. The New Testament mentions the term *mythos* five times (2 Pet 1:16; Titus 1:14; 1 Tim 1:4; 4:7; and 2 Tim 4:4), and in all of these instances a pejorative and negative evaluation of myth is suggested. For these writers at least, the notion of myth in relation to the Christian religion is one of contradiction, difference, and exclusion.

However, despite these disavowals of myth, it is clear that the New Testament does employ myths and is itself mythical. I mean this in two senses. First, the New Testament writers (like the Hebrew Bible writers before them) used elements of cultural and religious myths drawn from

---

3. An investigation of myth could take on many forms: e.g., in his history of myth, Andrew Von Hendy (2002) lists the following: the origins of myth, the relationship of myth to truth, myth and literature, myth and consciousness, myth and depth psychology, myth and ideology, myth as an aspect of primitive religion, myth and ritual, myth and folklore, as well as structural, post-structural, and anthropological studies of myth. The array of possibilities is stunning and paralyzing, and I have found helpful Von Hendy's grouping of these different approaches under four rubrics: the romantic, the ideological, the folkloristic, and the constitutive. Defining the different categories takes us far afield, but for purposes of orientation Von Hendy includes Eliade under the first, Nietzsche and Marx under the second, Malinowski and Lévi-Strauss under the third, and the works of poets, such as Yeats, as well as the work of Paul Ricoeur and Leszek Kolokowski as representative of the fourth.

their social and intellectual environment in order to define their own nascent community's beliefs and to distinguish those beliefs from those of competing religious/philosophical groups. Second, the New Testament invokes and assumes a larger enveloping story of the origin of the world, its current conditions, the place of humans in that world, and the relationship of those humans and that world to unseen otherwordly powers and beings. This applies not only to the writers, but also to the people that they write about, such as Jesus, his audiences, his opposition, and his followers. In other words, following Midgely's definition, the New Testament is mythical not simply because it contains stories of miracles and wonders, but because it is a network of stories, symbols, and patterns that interpret the world.

That being said, I am aware that other New Testament interpreters do not accept this position, rejecting the idea that the New Testament is mythical, while others even insist that the New Testament contains no mythic material at all. My reading suggests that the pertinent questions for determining the strength of these two positions revolve around the notions of whether myths create meaning and/or truth. That is, interpreters who take a maximalist position on myth in the New Testament understand its language and stories to be true in the sense that they create meaning for their adherents. In contrast, those who take a minimalist position tend to equate myth with fiction or false claims and therefore discount its ability to create legitimate forms of meaning.[4] With this we move to larger hermeneutical questions, and these too play a role in the evaluation of myth and the Bible.

I think that these questions need answers and, if we wish to make our considerations of the historical and comparative questions about myth most effective, that we should attend to them. However, because of

---

4. In effect, these evaluations relate directly to the two definitions that one finds in the BDAG: the first to the negative use of the term, the second to its more neutral use as story or figurative language. They also inform the question that is behind the dichotomy of myth/logos or myth/history. If one insists on the dichotomy, then history is valued over myth and questions arise over how the NT should be interpreted as history. Alternatively, if one allows that myths do contain truth or truths, the questions then involve the nature of these truths, how are they expressed, and how can they be discerned. In this regard, the question of how myth is true is part of the larger question involved with determining how literature or figurative speech such as metaphor or poetry can be true. For evaluations of the myth/logos dichotomy see the analyses of Lincoln 1999 and Veyne 1983.

the complexity of the questions, attention to them alone would preclude any discussion of the historical and comparative issues. Nevertheless, it appears to me that a preliminary step in this direction could be taken. Thus, in this paper, while I will not answer the hermeneutical questions, I will try to clear the underbrush from the field so that we can start to frame them more acutely and so that they will be part of our historical conversations. To do this I will compare and contrast essays by four authors whose work addresses the role of myth in interpreting biblical texts. Two are from the 1950s and 1960s and two from the 1990s. I have chosen them because they present different understandings of myth and its relationship to the biblical materials and because they are all interested in the questions of how myth creates truth and meaning for its different audiences.

Rudolf Bultmann: Recasting Myth

If any essay on the Bible and myth can serve as a baseline for orientation, Bultmann's (in)famous, "New Testament and Mythology: The Problem of Demythologizing the New Testament Proclamation," is a most likely candidate.[5] Not only does Bultmann describe the issues in precise manners and suggest a program for evaluation of myth in this piece, in one form or fashion all subsequent treatments of the topic are responses, either directly or indirectly, to the polarities found in his discussions.[6]

---

5. Remarkably, this essay was initially addressed to pastors of the German Confessing Church during a conference held in 1941. The essay was originally published as "Neues Testament und Mythologie: Das Problem der Entmythologisierung der neutestamentlichen Verkündigung," in the volume *Offenbarung und Heilsgeschehen* (Bultmann 1941). It is now part of a collection of Bultmann's writings by Schubert Ogden (Bultmann 1984a).

6. From its publication it has created significant responses, both positive and negative, and it remains catalytic. In fact, Schubert Ogden has referred to it "as perhaps the single most discussed and controversial theological writing of the [20th] century" (in Bultmann 1984a, vii). Bultmann is charged with being too radical in the treatment of myth, not radical enough, too conservative in his program of demythologizing, and too far reaching. The various responses, from the left and the right, along with Bultmann's replies can be found in Bartsch 1962–1964 and in the treatments of Bultmann's demythologizing program by John Macquarrie (1955, 1961). Solid and critical analyses of these responses and replies include Ogden 1961; Johnson 1974; and Painter 1987.

Bultmann is not interested in myth study for its own sake, but as it applies to contemporary interpretation of the New Testament. Thus he does not provide a "once for all" definition of myth, but supplies a specific definition pertinent to exploring its role in the New Testament. He states:

> Thus, myth is spoken of here in the sense in which it is understood by research in the history of religions. That mode of representation is mythology in which what is unworldly and divine appears as what is worldly and human or what is transcendent appears as what is immanent, as when, for example, God's transcendence is thought of as spatial distance. Mythology is a mode of representation in consequence of which cult is understood as action in which nonmaterial forces are mediated by material means. "Myth" is not used here, then, in that modern sense in which it means nothing more than ideology. (1984a, 10 n. 5)

Elsewhere he notes that myth is

> the report of an occurrence or an event in which supernatural, superhuman forces of persons are at work (which explains why it is often defined simply as the history of the gods). Mythical thinking is the opposite of scientific thinking. It refers certain phenomena and events to the supernatural, "divine" powers, whether these are thought of dynamistically or animistically or are represented as personal spirits or gods. It thus separates off certain phenomena and events as well as certain domains from the things and occurrences of the world that are familiar and that can be grasped and controlled. (Bultmann 1984b, 95)

Bultmann understands the entire New Testament to be mythological: its world pictured as a three-story universe, its depiction of heavenly and demonic beings, its sense that the human being is under the sway of unseen powers, and so on, up to and including the presentation of the salvation occurrence as a form of blood atonement. Thus expressions like "God sent his Son" "when the time had fully come," terms such as "Lord" and "King," and the idea that the resurrection of Jesus was the beginning of a cosmic catastrophe that would reverse the course of death in the world exemplify the corresponding mythological language of such a world picture.

Inasmuch as such talk is mythological, he argues, it is also "incredible to men and women today because for them the mythical world picture is a thing of the past" (Bultmann 1984a, 2–3). World pictures are situated within historical contexts, and "no one can appropriate a world picture by sheer resolve, since it is already given" (3). Further, although an individual's worldview is not "unalterable," Bultmann points out that "it is impossible to repristinate a past world picture by sheer resolve, especially a *mythological* world picture, now that all our thinking is irrevocably informed by science" (3). Any satisfaction of a demand to adopt this past world picture would require

> a forced *sacrificim intellectus*, and any of us who would make it would be peculiarly split and untruthful. For we would affirm for our faith or religion a world picture that our life otherwise denied. Criticism of the New Testament is simply a given with modern thinking as it has come to us through our history. (1984a, 3–4)

Thus, for Bultmann, the question that confronts contemporary Christianity is whether acknowledgment of this ancient world picture is requisite to faith (3).

It is clear that Bultmann begins with the conviction that the message of the New Testament is true; however, he also holds that the manner in which this message is expressed in the New Testament—specifically its mythic form and worldview—is incomprehensible to the modern mind. Thus demythologizing is not driven so much by historical issues as by interpretive ones. Initially this can be seen from the recognition of the "simple fact that Christ's parousia did not take place immediately as the New Testament expected it to, but that world history continues and—as every competent judge is convinced—will continue" (Bultmann 1984a, 5). More importantly, however, is that the modern person does not conceive of him- or herself as a divided entity susceptible to alien powers that invade our inner beings. Thus appropriating a message that suggests otherwise requires interpretation.

It should be stated that Bultmann is not interested in accommodating the New Testament message to modern constructions of truth. Rather he believes that the biblical message is a fundamental challenge to these constructions and that it should be heard in its own right.[7] His concern,

---

7. In his response to Karl Jaspers, Bultmann makes clear that his intent is not to "salvage faith … in the face of scientific insights" or to make religion acceptable to modern sensibilities, but to "make clearer to modern man what the Christian faith is," and to point out that "the stumbling-block to faith, the *skándalon*, is peculiarly disturbing to man in general, not only to modern man" (Bartsch 1962–1964, 2:182–83).

however, is that the New Testament's mythic forms deflect the modern listener from hearing that challenge and, as a result, it is never recognized or encountered. Thus the primary task for a New Testament interpreter is to produce a reinterpretation of the incidental expressions of these truths so that the message they contain can be experienced by modern listeners (Bultmann 1958, 9). According to Bultmann, if the New Testament is to be heard clearly and correctly, it must undergo a total and radical interpretation of all of its myths and mythic structures, including its presentation of the salvific events themselves. This consistent reinterpretation, which Bultmann calls "demythologizing" (*Entmythologierung*), is, in this regard, thoroughly hermeneutical.[8]

The heart of the issue is that since ancient myth is no longer self-evidently understood as myth, when it depicts the activity of God as this worldly activity, then the transcendence of God is eliminated and the fundamental tenet of God's nature and existence is compromised. As a result, the New Testament message must be demythologized, it must undergo a process of interpretation that

> seeks to bring out the real intention of myth, namely its intention to talk about human existence as grounded in and limited by a transcendent, unworldly power, which is not visible to objectifying thinking. Thus, negatively, demythologizing is criticism of the mythical picture insofar as it conceals the real intention of myth. Positively, demythologizing is an existentialist interpretation, in that it makes clear the intention of myth to talk about human existence. (Bultmann 1984b, 99)

When one asks how this reinterpretation should take place, Bultmann is careful to argue that it is not by means of other myths. Since the fundamental issue with the mythical pictures is their objectification of the transcendent and subsequently their obfuscation of their fundamental intent to reveal the human situation, no form of interpretation that repeats this

---

The point of the interpretation is not to make the gospel message palatable to moderns, but to enable them to be encountered by its message of judgment.

8. "The decisive question, therefore, is whether precisely this salvation event [the proclamation of the decisive act of God in Christ] which is presented in the New Testament as a mythical occurrence, or whether the person of Jesus, which is viewed in the New Testament as a mythical person, is nothing but mythology. Can there be a demythologizing interpretation that discloses the truth of the keryma as kerygma for those who do not think mythologically?" (Bultmann 1984a, 14).

error is allowable. This requires Bultmann to supply a nonmythic form of interpretation that will provide the point of the myths and will be true to their intent. At the same time, while it must avoid this interpretive difficulty, the form of interpretation also must express the fundamental scandal of the myth's intent.[9] This he accomplishes by recourse to an existential analysis of the myths. This is done not because Bultmann insists on adopting existential philosophy in order to interpret the New Testament myths, but because the intent of the myths is consonant with the goals of that philosophy, namely, what it means for the human being to exist properly.[10]

For Bultmann, this is an essential element of interpreting the New Testament because only in this way can the New Testament's claims upon human beings be understood and heard. The scandal of the New Testament "lies in the fact that God's word calls us out of all our anxiety as well as all out self-contrived security to God, and thereby to our own authentic existence, to freedom from the world that we take possession of by the objectifying thinking of science in such a way that we thereby give it power over us" (Bultmann 1984b, 102). Confronted by this message, the hearer is called to the surrender of self-security, which

> can be laid hold of only by a "nevertheless" over against the world; for neither God nor God's act can be visible in a world that constantly seeks its own security and therefore deprives all that it encounters of any existential reference by its objectifying way of viewing things. All mythological talk about God can only serve to conceal this "nevertheless." Demythologizing as existentialist interpretation seeks to make clear the

---

9. "When the revelation is truly understood as God's revelation, it is no longer a communication of teachings, nor of ethical or historical and philosophical truths, but God speaking directly to me, assigning me each time to the place that is allotted me before God, i.e. summoning me in my humanity, which is null without God, and which is open to God only in the recognition of its nullity" (Bartsch 1962–1964, 2:192).

10. As he notes in a reply to his critics, there is no one final philosophy. "The 'right' philosophy is simply one which has worked out an appropriate terminology for the understanding of existence, an understanding involved in human existence itself. Hence it does not pose the problem of existence as an existential question, but asks in existential analysis about the meaning of existence in the abstract: for it is aware that the existential problem can be answered only in existence itself" (Bartsch 1962–1964, 1:193). It is the compatibility of this question with the question that the New Testament poses to its hearers that suggests existential analysis as an appropriate way to recast biblical myths.

character of scripture as personal address and thereby also to clarify the "nevertheless" that essentially belongs to faith. (1984b, 102)

For our purposes it is enough to stop here and assess Bultmann's definition of myth, his understanding of its validity, and his sense of the human condition. Fundamentally myth is a form of narration that depicts the transcendent as imminent, and this Bultmann finds objectionable on theological grounds. Because the mythic story implies that "God" is an actor within nature, this suggests that God is not sovereign over nature. If this is the case, then God is reduced to an actor within the course of the universe, and cannot be its creator. Thus for Bultmann the myths of the New Testament, left uninterpreted, produce a false understanding of God and the God-human relationship. However, if they are rightly interpreted, that is, in terms of the meaning of human existence, then the myths do have validity, primarily because they express the truth of human limit and finitude. When rightly interpreted they challenge the assumption that humans are capable of establishing their own freedom and security. The myths are therefore an affront to the modern mind, but not because of their form and imagery; rather through a radical demythologizing we can recognize that the affront is due to their exposure of human finitude. That is, myth is valid in that it clarifies that human beings are radically dependent for their existence on something beyond their own capacities. Thus myth has a function in a negative sense. It demonstrates that human reason and actions cannot exhaust or fully understand reality. In a positive sense, it places humans in the position of accepting this reality and thus enabling them to see themselves in relationship with something beyond their own limits.

Thus Bultmann recasts myth rather than rejects it. He argues that rightly interpreted it does contain truth, and that truth is a viable form of existence even though it is at odds with contemporary human constructions of truth.

Thomas Altizer: Refashioning Myth

Akin to Bultmann is Thomas Altizer, who also recognizes a dichotomy between ancient religious ideation and modern world constructions. The goal of Altizer's essay "The Religious Meaning of Myth and Symbol" is "to demonstrate that the meaning which is manifest in the religious symbol in our contemporary situation—as expressed in contemporary thought, sensibility, and religious scholarship—is in radical discontinuity with the symbolic meaning which is the product of man's life in the world, of his life in being" (Altizer 1962, 90). Thus, although Altizer shares Bultmann's convictions about the fundamental mythological nature of the biblical material and Bultmann's sense of the incompatibility of the biblical worldviews with those of modern sensibilities, unlike Bultmann, Altizer does not seek to recast the biblical myths, but to reject them as viable modes of understanding.

Altizer conceives of three types of religious myths: those that arise (1) from archaic religions, (2) from mystical religion, and (3) from prophetic-eschatological religions. He argues that the myths of archaic religions are utterly foreign to us because in archaic society (preliterate society) human beings conceived of themselves in fundamental harmony with the cosmos and with the sacred. Myths were expressions of this sense of the harmonious relationships among the self, its surroundings, and the sacred. However, in contrast to the sensibilities of the archaic/preliterate society, modern societies—due to their experience of individual concreteness and historical existence and their goal of autonomous freedom—know nothing of this harmony but only a sense of alienation from their surroundings. Hence the archaic myths are, a priori, incomprehensible to the modern person by the sheer fact that he or she is a "modern person."

In contrast, the modern person's commitment to rational thinking (i.e., nonmystical thinking) also dissolves the openness to romantic and mystical forms of myth (Altizer's second type of religious myth). Situated in the particularities of concreteness and historical existence, rational conceptions of cause and effect and human agency are a necessity, but they also necessarily preclude a seamless harmony between the human, nature, and the sacred. Because the modern person "has chosen the goal of autonomous freedom; and this freedom can only be reached by means of dissolution or negation of the sacred and the transcendent," the harmonious reality between the human, the cosmos, and the sacred to which archaic myth refers can never be experienced as "real" by modern consciousness (Altizer 1962, 91–92).

Altizer notes that in the eighth to the fourth centuries B.C.E., archaic myth was fundamentally altered by "the dawn of philosophy and of a higher aesthetic consciousness in Greece, the prophetic reformations of Palestine and Persia, and the birth of philosophy and a series of religious movements in India and China" (1962, 97). These cultural phenomena share three points in common: (1) an expectation of the immediate end of the world, whether as transformation, reversal, or dissolution; (2) a subordination of mythical visions of "the end" to a radical form of obedience that arises out of a response to "the end"; and (3) they "call their followers out of their lives in history, and into a new interior reality of faith" (105). The upshot is that the "ultimate foundation of both mysticism and eschatology is a radically new participation in the sacred Reality which demands a dissolution or reversal of the reality of the world" (105). But this altered construction of archaic myth is also impossible for the modern human, because its world negation is in fundamental conflict with the goals of the modern "Faustian" human being.

The modern person is committed to concreteness and a sense of historical here and now. This is, in effect, an eclipse of the conception of sacred time and space. That is, the transcendent reality is negated in light of historical existence. Moreover, the quest of the modern man or woman is autonomy in every aspect of life. This self-freedom can be achieved only by negation of the sacred claim of transcendence, and since the myths of the higher religions insist on a negation of the concrete historical world that modern humans inhabit, the two are fundamentally contradictory. Consequently, "myth can in no authentic sense embody what the modern consciousness recognizes as truth," and "modern man is doomed to live in an a-mythical world" (Altizer 1962, 91). It is important to note that the clash here is not one of cognition. It is not simply that the modern person cannot make sense of the ancient mode of myth, but that the modern person's very mode of existing in the world is incompatible with the ancient world-denying perspectives of the versions of the myths such as those found in the Bible. Thus, when Altizer and Bultmann argue that these myths are incomprehensible to the modern person, they are not making this claim on an intellectual level alone—it is an existential difference. For Bultmann the gap is significant, but it can be bridged by means of interpretation. For Altizer it cannot be overcome, so the ancient biblical myths must be reckoned by means of opposition (Altizer 1962, 91–93).

Altizer rejects both the archaic myths and those of the higher religions, albeit for different reasons. In the first instance the gap between how archaic society understood itself in relation to its surrounding realities and how the modern person conceives of his or her relationship to the external world is so broad that it cannot be surmounted. Thus myth cannot function for the modern person the way that it did for the ancients. On the other hand, Altizer's rejection of the myths of higher religion is a matter not so much of function as content. The ultimate goal of those myths (i.e., to demonstrate the continuum of seen and unseen realties to which the human belongs and is subject) is fundamentally antithetical to the modern human's sense of freedom and autonomy in and from this world. Thus the ancient myths are to be rejected in terms of what they state, not simply for how they state it.

However, surprisingly enough, Altizer does not reject myth in and of itself. He grants that even for the modern person myth has a role in the production of meaning. However, unlike with previous constructions and uses of myth, this role is not in producing metaphysical truth or in discerning its presence from beyond, but in coping with the vagaries of present existence. For Altizer the modern person must construct his or her own myths from the profane, from this world and this reality. These myths do not function because they reveal truth or because they have some special mode of meaning. Altizer allows that the biblical myths can provoke thought; they are capable of pointing us to relevant phenomena, but they do not contain truths—they allow us to create them. In this sense, one looks to the biblical materials for inspiration in the creation of new myths suited to the conditions that face and create the modern person. If I have understood him, these myths are a means of producing pragmatic truths; they reflect some deeper metaphysical reality or truth. That is, their value is in provoking our thought, not in reflecting the thoughts or verities of some supernatural being. Thus, for truth the modern human cannot look elsewhere, but must take responsibility upon him- or herself.[11] Thus the message of the New Testament does not so much confront the modern person as prompt him or her to thought.

---

11. In this regard myth, according to Altizer, functions in the same manner that Donald Davidson allows for metaphor. One need only substitute the term *myth* where Davidson uses *metaphor* in the following quotation to grasp his intent. "We must give up the idea that metaphor carries a message, that it has a content of meaning (except, of course, its literal meaning). The various theories we have been considering mistake their goal. Where they think they provide a method for deciphering an encoded content, they actually tell us (or try to tell us) something about the effects metaphors have on us. The common error is to fasten on the contents of the thoughts a metaphor provokes and to read these contents into the metaphor itself. No doubt metaphors often make us notice aspects of things we did not notice before: no doubt they bring surprising analogies and similarities to our attention; they do provide a lens or lattice, … through which we view relevant phenomena. The issues do not lie here but in the question of how the metaphor is related to what it makes us see" (Davidson 1984, 261).

Craig Evans: Rejection of Myth

It is rather apparent where Craig Evans's sympathies lie from the title of his article "Life-of-Jesus Research and the Eclipse of Mythology" (1993).[12] Technically this is not a study of myth and the Bible since Evans is convinced that, at least as far as research into the life of Jesus is concerned, interpreters of the biblical material are in a "post-mythological era" (Evans 1993, 35). Evans distinguishes current "life-of-Jesus" research from previous inquiries, which he considers to have been nothing more "than three consecutive stages in a single and rather coherent era. It was a mythological era, the era whose agenda was all but dictated by the perceived problem of mythology" (35). The first stage was characterized by a search for myth-free history of Jesus, while the second and third stages, dominated as they were by critical work of David Friedrich Strauss and Rudolf Bultmann, were concerned not with the disposal of myth but with its interpretation. "Today however," Evans argues,

> this is no longer the case; myth has ceased to be an item of importance. In my judgment this has taken place primarily because the miracle tradition is no longer the stumbling block that it once was. The scholarly assumption now seems to be that a realistic, relatively myth-free historical picture of Jesus, can, and does, emerge from the Gospels. What makes today's scholarship so different is that it does not find it necessary to formulate a theology or hermeneutic that deals with myth. (1993, 36)

Evans makes his claims based on a "history of interpretation" of life-of-Jesus research. According to Evans, previous Jesus research should be considered as a period of scholarship when dogmatic skepticism punctuated by salvage missions for historical nuggets of history held sway. Evans asserts that the situation changed in the 1970s, when, "[i]n contrast to the systemic skepticism that characterized much of German and North American scholarship, often a concomitant of assumptions about myths in the Gospels, Jesus research in recent years has reflected a greater optimism

---

12. This article is based on Evans's longer treatment of life-of-Jesus research (1989). I have significantly different understandings of the means for research into the life of Jesus and for its theological and epistemological underpinnings. However, those differences are for another occasion. I cite Evans only as a representative of one position with respect to myth and the Bible.

that the Gospels can yield the data necessary for an intelligible reconstruction of the ministry of Jesus" (1993, 14).

Evans next presents five factors that are "involved in the demise of mythology as a relevant issue in life-of-Jesus research" (1993, 14). First, in contrast to the past, the New Testament Gospels are viewed as useful, "if not essentially reliable, historical sources" (14). Second, mainline life-of-Jesus research "is no longer driven by theological-philosophical concerns, at least not overtly" (15–16). It is now characterized solely by a concern for history. Third, miracles are now viewed as part of charismatic Judaism, which means that the stories depicting these miracles were not the result of later Hellenistic influence, but part of the Judaism in which Jesus lived and with which he interacted. Fourth, "the miracle stories are now treated seriously and are widely accepted by Jesus scholars as deriving from Jesus' ministry" (19). Finally, "The fifth and final factor that I think has brought about the eclipse of mythology is the realization that an accurate and helpful picture of the historical Jesus cannot emerge if the miracle tradition is ignored or discarded" (33).

Evans's approach is avowedly nontheological, nonhermeneutical, nonphilosophical, and postmythological.[13] However, when one reads Evans's essay carefully, it is clear that he, and those who share his perspective, cannot avoid philosophical presuppositions about knowledge, truth, and history, or hermeneutics. However one wishes to cast the matter to be "non-" something is still to participate in the issues that form the questions. Thus to be "nontheological" is still to adopt some theological position. In this case, it is to affirm divine characteristics of Jesus' being. Moreover, it is clear that Evans adopts a maximal approach to his understanding of what can be known historically. Thus Evans's real point is not about myth, but about disagreement over the evidence one adduces to do history (his first factor).

Further, the effect of this maximal approach is to move material (particularly reports of miracles) into the category of events available to historical investigation (something Bultmann conceived to be a violation of the miraculous by definition). Since Evans restricts the category of myth to matters of miracle and so does not conceive of it as an overarching nar-

---

13. Whether this is actually the case is a question that more than a few critics have raised, even Gerd Theissen, who considers himself one of the "life-of-Jesus" researchers (as will become evident below). Nevertheless, Evans presents an approach to myth that some biblical interpreters have adopted.

rative that interprets events, the worldview of Jesus or of his contemporaries is not considered mythical. The result of these two perspectives is to reduce myth to minimal incidentals that can be discounted in the "life-of-Jesus" research.

Finally, despite expanding its scope, Evans restricts history to the discovery of events and data. This postpones or ignores the question of the significance of this discovered data. However, if, as Evans claims, life-of-Jesus researchers are interested not just in what Jesus did but what these things "meant to his contemporaries," then the question of interpretation is part of the historian's task. Moreover, a full and accurate account of who Jesus was and what he did cannot be provided without an explanation of what he thought these things represented. Once this is admitted, the claims that the "life-of-Jesus research" is athelogical and aphilosophical are inconsistent, and questions of myth, history, and philosophy must be enjoined at this point. When this occurs, then even life-of-Jesus researchers operate in the realm of theology; to assess the validity of Jesus' claims is to enter into the realm of philosophy, truth, and ultimately the nature of myth with regard to the Christian religion.

Gerd Theissen: Reclaiming Myth

Gerd Theissen, who like Evans identifies himself as a life-of-Jesus researcher, does not agree with Evans's assessment of the role of myth or that research into the life and work of Jesus can be conducted in a "postmythological era." Indeed, he is clearly of the opposite opinion.[14] Not only does myth pervade the biblical materials; Jesus' ministry and self-consciousness were formed by the myths of his religious convictions as a Jew. Theissen insists that primitive Christianity is a combination of myth and history, and one will misunderstand the religion if one insists on dissolving the combination into one of its constituent parts. He further asserts that "everything suggests that neither a myth which was historicized at a secondary stage nor a history which was mythicized at a secondary stage stood at the centre of primitive Christianity. At the beginning stood a unity in tension of both history and myth" (Theissen 1999, 21–22).

Theissen's overall project "seeks to describe in general religious categories the dynamic of primitive Christian belief which governs the whole of

---

14. My comments are based primarily on Theissen 1999; see also 1985.

life. It seeks to make possible a twofold reading of this faith: a view from inside and a view from outside—and above all to mediate between these two perspectives" (1999, 1).

Based on Clifford Geertz's understanding of religion as a cultural system, Theissen posits that "[r]*eligion is a cultural sign language which promises a gain in life corresponding to an ultimate reality*" (1999, 2). As a cultural sign system religion has "three characteristics: religion has a semiotic, a systemic and a cultural character" (2). There are obviously numerous sign systems that human beings use. The religious sign system is a particular "combination of three forms of expression…: myth, rites and ethics" (2–3).

Theissen suggests that there are three dimensions to myth: (1) "Myth is a *text*: a narrative, the action of which is in a decisive time for the world, in which numinous subjects (gods, angels and demons) transform (or will transform) a fragile state of reality into a stable state." (2) Myth is functional; that is, the narrative is a "legitimizing or utopian force which is the basis for a form of social life or puts such a form in question (the latter is the case with some eschatological myths)." (3) "Finally, myth is a *mentality* or a *thought structure*," which provides "another way of ordering the world in forms of perception and interpreting it in categories. To this degree myth is not opposed to the Logos, but a first form of the Logos."[15]

In this last role, myth structures an opposition between the holy and the profane in terms of space and time. Because it serves as an interpretive framework and because it depicts another reality, myth also provides an interpretive context for the religious person's actions, both those of ritual and everyday activity.

When Theissen turns to the specific nature of this mythical narrative, we see a significant difference from Bultmann. Rather than look to existentialist understandings of humans in their world, Theissen turns to the conception of cultural evolution. On the analogy with biological evolution, Theissen posits that humanity ever undergoes transformation. In place of biology's genes, Theissen offers cultural memes; and in place of genetic mutation he suggests the rare appearance of particularly aberrant interpreters. This is how Jesus enters into the world as a radical transformer of his culture. Because of its historicizing activity both the preaching of Jesus and the later proclamation of the early church radically transform

---

15. All quotations from Theissen 1999, 325 n. 5.

the myths of Judaism in which Christianity has its cultural roots and heritage into a new "evolved" form.

In effect, the impulses within the myths of Judaism are intensified in the myths of Christianity. Starting with the two basic axioms of Judaism, monotheism and covenantal nomism, Christianity transforms the mythical expressions of those axioms into its own mythical expression. Thus, for example, Christianity "believes in the one and only God who has bound himself to a single people in his covenant. But with monotheism it combines belief in a redeemer, through which this tie to a single people is extended to all peoples" (Theissen 1999, 290). At a structural level the myth of Judaism is reconfigured. "What is decisive here is that in the depth structure of its convictions, primitive Christianity largely participates in convictions of Judaism. The difference from Judaism lies at this level above all in the christocentric reorganization of the images, motifs, narratives and sign elements which the two religions share" (291).

The dynamic of myth on the structural level means that the truth of the myth is not distilled from its individual sentences by reinterpretation. Rather, it is found in the grammar of the Christian myths that allow particular and new sentences of truth to be constructed. That is, Christianity and its myths create a form of coherent truth. This also allows the mechanism to transcend temporal and notional gaps. The grammatical nature of the myths coupled with Christianity's adaptive evolutionary nature allowed the religion to constantly morph into new formations.

It is just this grammatical capacity that allows the ancient myth to be appropriated into a modern context. One need not reinterpret the myth, but use the grammar of the myth to construct sentences compatible with others that arose from the mythic grammar. Because, according to Theissen, "*It is not so much the content of the statements of religion which create plausibility as the network of basic axioms and basic motifs which form its grammar*" (1999, 292–93). In other words, the viability of the Christian myth is not found in any of its particular axioms, but in the manner by which they are arranged into with respect to one another.

The plausibility of these new expressions is grounded in their correspondence to the world, to people's experiences, and to their relationships with other people. Theissen gives an example with a brief discussion of the Christ hymn found in Philippians. He notes that we have no evidence to substantiate the individual statements of the hymn. "Was there a divine being who descended from his pre-existence in order to be exalted to the name above all names? The first Christians could not verify or falsify such statements any more than we can. They are poetry of the holy. But it is meaningful to ask whether the axiom of change of position contained in the poetry corresponds to reality—and also an ultimate reality" (Theissen 1999, 293). Theissen argues that this axiom and the others of Christianity remain a plausible means for construction and inhabitation of our world. Thus the myths remain true as means for constructing meaning and meaningful existence. However, it is also clear that Theissen has reinterpreted the myth in order to distill its truth. But this time it is a truth discerned at the poetic, interpretive level.

Here one sees a departure from Evans's reading of myth and history and a position closer to Altizer's sense of the dynamic function of myth. However, unlike Altizer, Theissen does not reject the ancient content but retains it. Theissen realizes that he has made a case only for the plausibility of the myths, not for their ultimate truth status. Thus at the end of his book he notes that his theory of primitive Christianity can only make a case for the viability of the Christian myths, it cannot establish them as true. As to the question of their truth, Theissen notes that "any answer has an element of confession—i.e. it is governed by a confession of a theological, an antitheological or an agnostic kind" (1999, 306).

Conclusion

In the end, it is clear that all four of these authors must consider the role of myth in their constructions of religious thought and human understanding. Their means of treating myth is a combination of their respective definitions, their evaluations of the validity of myth as a conveyor of truth, and their conceptions of the human condition in the modern/postmodern social structures we inhabit.

For Evans the topic is diversionary and leads researchers down unfruitful paths. Thus he rejects the investigations into myth. He is convinced that the era of mythological concerns for New Testament researchers, at least those concerned with the life of Jesus, is past. Personally I think that this is unlikely and that Evans's position is due to his limited notion of myth and his sense that theological questions can be answered on historical grounds. Moroever, if, as Theissen and Bultmann argue, Jesus was fully informed by the mythic structures of Jewish thought and belief, then not even life-of-Jesus researchers can ignore this topic. If they do, they will not do justice to the object of their inquiry or to the nature of his teaching and actions.

Altizer also rejects myth as a viable option for the modern person, but not myth per se. Rather he rejects the possibility that the archaic and biblical myths can be meaningful to modern people. This is not because the myths are unrecognizable, but because the integrated worldviews of the ancients are no longer possible for people of modern sensibilities. Further, Altizer also argues that the world-negating myths of the early Christian religion is fundamentally at odds with the world-affirming project of modern humans. Thus the one who wishes to understand these myths is faced with a crisis. To accept them as true is to deny one's present existence and essential commitments. Likewise, to be true to one's social and cognitive-existential makeup the myths of the "higher religions" must be sacrificed. Myth, at least these myths, are an impossibility.

Bultmann also notes the significant clash between the modern-day human being and the myths of the New Testament, and he is in agreement with Altizer that this clash produces a crisis for those who encounter the real content of the New Testament myths. However, it is just this crisis that Bultmann believes is necessary. Then the real crisis that the myths intend to provoke is revealed. The human being who is encountered by the myth recognizes the limits of his or her own finitude and the futility of striving for security. Thus, for Bultmann, incompatibility of thought worlds or the project of humanity is not a reason to reject myth.

Finally, Theissen argues that myth should be reclaimed. He is of the opinion that this is necessary because some forms of truth cannot be expressed without narrative or figurative expression. Hence Bultmann's form of interpretation would be unacceptable to him because it is necessarily derivative and reductionist. At the same time, Theissen is also convinced that the ancient myths of primitive Christian religion should be recast (to use his term, *remythologized*) with other mythic structures, and he proposes the notion of the transition from biological to cultural evolutionary development. Notably Theissen's solutions tend always to be both/ands rather than Bultmann's and Altizer's either/ors. It is not clear to me that Theissen's position is really logically viable or consistent. Despite his claims for compatibility, he simply may be postponing the contrasts that the others see.

My review of these authors raises numerous questions that we might consider as this seminar continues to meet. I suggest four here.

1. In relationship to the Bible, what is the relationship of myth to history, myth to logos, or myth to truth? When one realizes that this question can be addressed on philosophical, literary, and historical grounds, it becomes even more complicated.

2. Are the myths of Judaism and Christianity fundamentally at odds with modern constructions of reality (as Altizer argues), or is there a correlation that can be found (as Theissen suggests)?

3. Whether defined theologically or epistemologically, does myth point to truths that cannot be expressed rationally, or is myth a misleading form of narrative that should be restricted to ornamentation or entertainment? Or should we avoid these categories entirely and consider only how myth functions to provoke thought and imagination?

4. What, if any, are the ethical injunctions that apply to interpreters when myth is studied not simply in its own right but in relationship to the Bible?

I have suggested that a case can be made for these questions on epistemological, historical, and theological grounds. It also seems to me that we should consider them on moral grounds. The above discussion has shown that the matter of myth as truth or falsity plays a role in every deliberation that involves biblical materials. The question of myth and the Bible is not simply restricted to "myths" in the Bible, or the Bible as myth, but also includes how we conceive of the myth of our scholarship, as this epithet from Bruce Lincoln suggests: "If myth is ideology in narrative form, then scholarship is myth with footnotes" (1999, 209).

Although one could consider the term *Bible* simply as a collection of texts contained in particular volume, for large numbers of people the term has a larger connotation. This means that the issue of truth will arise for these readers as much as it does for those who use the term *Bible* descriptively. Thus we have some moral obligation to consider our own understandings of myth and truth as we investigate these ancient texts in relationship to the Bible.

In the epilogue to *Theorizing Myth: Narrative, Ideology, and Scholarship*, Lincoln also notes two seminal moments in the history of myth analysis and construction and sounds one particular note of caution for those who would attempt to interpret myth. The first occurred when, through his contrast between myth and logos, "Plato stigmatized the category [of myth]" as the sphere of the "juvenile and the irrational; the second when [Johan Gottfried] Herder recuperated it, marking it as primordial and authentic" (1999, 209). These two conceptions of myth, the realm of the false and the means of expressing "real truth" that exists beyond the limits of reason, remain in tension with one another and continue to dominate our understandings of myth and how we analyze it, as the entry from BDAG has shown.

Try as we might to avoid them, these two definitions continue to arise and to fight with one another. We are ourselves caught in this fight, and it is in trying to end it, or at least to create some form of détente, that we are most vulnerable to the incursion of bias and self-serving ideologies. Hence attending to how we understand the Bible to be mythic is more than an exercise for the academy—it has consequences for the communities that adhere to and are formed by these myths. There is an obligation for us to consider this in our deliberations, as much, if not more, than our philosophical, theological, and historical concerns. No attempt to construct the fundaments of myth or to interpret them escapes from this reality, and one of the myths that we inhabit (in both senses of the term) is that, as interpreters of myths, we can escape reading without including communal and individual interests. It may just be that attention to these factors of how we determine truths and validity will be that element that will help us explain our relationship of those studies that preceded ours and those that will surely come after.

Works Cited

Altizer, Thomas J. J. 1962. The Religious Meaning of Myth and Symbol. Pages 87–108 in *Truth, Myth, and Symbol*. Edited by Thomas J. J. Altizer, William A. Beardslee, and J. Harvey Young. Englewood Cliffs, N.J.: Prentice-Hall.

Bartsch, Hans Werner, ed. 1962–1964. *Kerygma and Myth: A Theological Debate*. Translated by Reginald H. Fuller. 2nd ed. (only vol. 1). 2 vols. London: SPCK.

Bultmann, Rudolf. 1941. *Offenbarung und Heilsgeschehen*. Beiträge zur evangelischen Theologie 7. Munich: Evangelischer Verlag.

———. 1958. *Jesus Christ and Mythology*. New York: Scribner's.

———. 1984a. New Testament and Mythology: The Problem of Demythologizing the New Testament Proclamation. Pages 1–43 in *New Testament and Mythology and Other Basic Writings*. Selected, edited, and translated by Schubert M. Ogden. Philadelphia: Fortress.

———. 1984b. On the Problem of Demythologizing. Pages 95–130 in *New Testament and Mythology and Other Basic Writings*. Selected, edited, and translated by Schubert M. Ogden. Philadelphia: Fortress.

Davidson, Donald. 1984. *Inquiries into Truth and Interpretation*. Oxford: Clarendon.

Doniger, Wendy, and Laurie Patton, eds. 1996. *Myth and Method*. Charlottesville: University Press of Virginia.

Doty, William G. 1980. Mythophiles' Dyscrasia: A Comprehensive Definition of Myth. *Journal of the American Academy of Religion* 48:531–62.

Evans, Craig. 1989. *Life of Jesus Research: An Annotated Bibliography*. Leiden: Brill.

———. 1993. Life-of-Jesus Research and the Eclipse of Mythology. *Theological Studies* 54:3–36.

Gibbs, Lee W., and W. Taylor Stevenson, eds. 1975. *Myth and the Crisis of Historical Consciousness*. Missoula, Mont.: Scholars Press.

Johnson, Roger A. 1974. *The Origins of Demythologizing: Philosophy and Historiography in the Theology of Rudolph Bultmann*. Leiden: Brill.

Lincoln, Bruce. 1999. *Theorizing Myth: Narrative, Ideology, and Scholarship*. Chicago: University of Chicago Press.

Macquarrie, John. 1955. *An Existentialist Theology: A Comparison of Heidegger and Bultmann*. London: SCM.

———. 1961. *The Scope of Demythologizing: Bultmann and His Critics*. New York: Harper.

Midgley, Mary. 2003. *The Myths We Live By*. London: Routledge.

Ogden, Schubert M. 1961. *Christ without Myth: A Study Based on the Theology of Rudolf Bultmann*. New York: Harper.

Painter, John. 1987. *Theology as Hermeneutics: Rudolf Bultmann's Interpretation of the History of Jesus*. Sheffield: Almond.

Stout, Jeffrey. 1982. What Is the Meaning of a Text? *New Literary History*. 14:1–12.

Theissen, Gerd. 1985. *Biblical Faith: An Evolutionary Approach*. Philadelphia: Fortress.

———. 1999. *The Religion of the Earliest Churches: Creating a Symbolic World*. Translated by John Bowden. Minneapolis: Fortress. [Published in Great Britain as *A Theory of Primitive Christian Religion*. London: SCM.]

Veyne, Paul. 1983. *Did the Greeks Believe in Their Myths? An Essay on the Constitutive Imagination*. Translated by Paula Wissing. Chicago: University of Chicago Press.

Von Hendy, Andrew. 2002. *The Modern Construction of Myth*. Bloomington: Indiana University Press.

"God Was in Christ":
2 Corinthians 5:19 and Mythic Language

Luke Timothy Johnson

Without question, 2 Corinthians is the hardest of Paul's letters to read and understand. This is partly due to the complex character of its composition: even if we do not accept its segmentation into several fragments,[1] the *logos* rhetoric, especially in its arrangement, remains opaque.[2] Paul's extraordinarily dense language intertwines the specific circumstances of Paul and his readers with the work of God in Christ. Readers have always found it difficult to discern precisely where Paul speaks to the very human situation of alienation existing between him and the Corinthian church and the very concrete project of his collection for the saints in Jerusalem, on the one hand, and on the other, where he speaks of God's reconciliation of the world through Christ.

Two recent Emory dissertations have revealed just how intricate are those connections. In *The Character of Jesus: The Linchpin to Paul's Argument in 2 Corinthians* (2003; see now Stegman 2005), Thomas Stegman analyzes the letter from the perspective of *ethos* argumentation, and finds that Paul challenges his readers to display the same character as that shown by Jesus and, Paul is confident, found in himself as well. As Jesus showed obedient faith toward God in his human condition, so are Christians, filled with the power of the Spirit, to demonstrate the same disposition of obedient faith. Similarly, in *Snatched into Paradise (2 Corinthians 12:1–10): Paul's Heavenly Journey in the Context of Early Christian Experience* (2008; see now Wallace 2011), James Buchanan Wallace shows how Paul's account of his ascent to heaven is continuous with the way he speaks

---

1. For representative positions, see Betz 1985; Bates 1965/1966; DeSilva 1993; Furnish 1984, 30–48.
2. See, e.g., Witherington 1994.

elsewhere about both his own religious experience and the experiences of God's power shared by his readers. These recent studies confirm the observation that in this letter Paul stretches the capacity of language by the way in which he confidently merges rather than distinguishes the realms of the human and the divine.

Indeed, the greatest difficulty in reading the Greek of 2 Corinthians is due precisely to such interconnections of divine and human persons and power; in this letter it is impossible to avoid the conclusion that Paul's language about himself and his readers, God and Christ, is mythic. For the purpose of this essay, I define *myth* as first-order statements, often but not necessarily in the form of narrative, that place human and divine persons in situations of mutual agency.[3] Because human agency is involved, such statements can appear to be talking about the empirical world that we all recognize. But because divine agency is also, perhaps primarily, involved, such statements are also impervious to empirical verification.

In this short paper, I begin by affirming the thoroughly mythic character of the statement in 2 Cor 5:19 that sets the theme for the paper. I then place this statement within its immediate literary context of 2 Corinthians, with the specific interest in teasing out the connections among experience, perception, and claim in Paul's argument. Next, I offer by way of analogy some contemporary experience-based claims that both resemble and differ from Paul's mythic language. In the process, I suggest that the truth claims of mythic statements can in fact be tested—at least in part—through assessment of the experience and of the symbolic world within which they make sense. In all this, I write as someone who celebrates rather than deprecates mythic language, who is in fact convinced that without such mythic language, Christians—indeed all religious people—could not express what they consider most true about their lives.[4]

---

[3]. The definition of myth is a classic battleground where several scholarly fields—including classics, history, religion, philosophy, and anthropology—stake out positions. For a sample of discussions, see Sebeok 1955; Murray 1960; Kirk 1970; Schremp and Hansen 2002. Given the variety of definitions abroad, the best bet is to make one's own definition and apply it consistently.

[4]. I have made this argument in a variety of places, including Johnson 1999b; 1996; 1999a.

The Mythic Character of 5:19

My essay cannot give adequate attention to all the exegetical problems that—characteristic for 2 Corinthians—this verse poses. But I can at least indicate what they are.

1. It appears to repeat and expand the verse immediately preceding it: 5:18, *ta de panta ek tou theou tou katallaxantos hēmas heautō dia Christou kai dontos hēmin tēn diakonian tēs katallagēs* ("all things are from God who has reconciled us to himself through Christ and has given us the ministry of reconciliation"); in turn, 5:19, *hōs hoti theos ēn en Christō kosmon katallassōn heautō, mē logizomenos autois ta paraptōmata autōn kai themenos en hēmin ton logon tēs katallagēs*, which I translate as: "that is, God was in Christ reconciling a world to himself, by not reckoning against them their sins, and by placing among us the message of reconciliation." Despite their resemblance and interconnectedness, the clauses are not identical. In 5:18 God reconciled "us," and in 5:19 "a world;" in 5:18 such reconciliation is clearly through the instrumentality of Christ (*dia christou*), whereas in 5:19 the *en Christō* is more ambiguous. The statement concerning the entrusting of reconciliation "to us" is in the first case a *diakonia* and in the second a *logos*. And the clause "by not reckoning against them their sins" in 5:19 expands (and presumably explicates) the process of reconciling "world" or "us."

2. The precise meaning and function of the connective *hōs hoti* in 5:19 is unclear. Most commentators agree that it does not, as in 2 Cor 11:21 or 2 Thess 2:2, suggest something not the case ("as though"),[5] but some think that it may bear some of the sense of those passages by referring to something written or at least traditional, so that Paul in the second clause appeals to what his readers have already been taught (Furnish paraphrases, "as it is said").[6]

3. Most difficult are the participles and prepositional phrases. Should *theos ēn en christō katallassōn* be read as an imperfect, and the preposition as locative ("God was in Christ"), or should the prepositional phrase be read as instrumental, with the imperfect as part of a periphrastic participle: "was reconciling"? In the first instance, God appears to be "in Christ" at

---

5. 2 Cor 11:21 reads, *kata atimian legō, hōs hoti hēmeis ēsthenēkamen*; 2 Thess 2:2 has: *hōs hoti enestēken hē hēmera tou kyriou*.

6. See the discussion in Furnish 1984, 317–18.

least analogously to the way someone is "in Christ" in 5:17;[7] in the second, "in Christ" simply provides a stylistic variation on *dia christou* in 5:18. Also unclear is the precise syntactical function of the other participles that I have translated instrumentally: "by" not counting trespasses and "by" entrusting the message of reconciliation. [8]

The main point I want to make about these interpretive difficulties, however, is that their resolution one way or another does not fundamentally alter the mythic character of both statements. Whether *theos* is "in Christ" in a locative (ontological) sense or achieves reconciliation "through Christ," God is still the subject of a narrative fragment concerning the past, and *kosmos* is an object of such generality as to be intrinsically nonverifiable. The same can be said of the designation "Christ": Paul's statement is set in the past tense (aorist and imperfect) and logically must refer to the historical figure Jesus of Nazareth, but the term *Christos*, like the instrumentality ascribed to him as the agent of God's action, lacks any historical specificity; it is unattached to any specific action, or even any specific character disposition. As for the verbs "reconciling" and "reckoning" and "giving"/"entrusting," they also are too broad and nonspecific to be placed within the realm of empirically verifiable history.

The most specific elements in the statements are the "we" and "they," who presumably stand for "world" and have been reconciled through the nonreckoning of their transgressions, and to whom the ministry or word concerning reconciliation has been entrusted. The statement, "God through Christ was reconciling the world to himself," is just as mythic as "God was in Christ as he reconciled the world to himself"; it is a narrative fragment that speaks of God's agency within the realm of human activity.

Paul's Language in 5:1–21

The character of Paul's statements in the immediate context of 2 Cor 5:19 might help us begin to discern the distinctive combination of elements that constitute Paul's mythic language.

---

7. "If anyone is in Christ, a new creation" (*ei tis en christō, kainē ktisis*).

8. Furnish (1984, 306), for example, translates "not charging their trespasses to them" in flat apposition to "reconciling the world to himself," and makes the second participle into a discrete statement, "and he has established among us the word of reconciliation."

1. Some fourteen statements have humans as their subject and refer entirely to human actions and dispositions at the empirical plane, most of them in the first-person plural: we "are groaning" (5:2), "longing" (5:2), "burdened and groaning" (5:4), "bold" (5:6), "walk by faith" (5:7), "ambitious to be pleasing" (5:9), "persuade" (5:11), "not commending ourselves" (5:12), "we are ecstatic" and "we are sober" (5:13), "we are ambassadors" (5:20), "we make appeal (5:20), "we beg" (5:20). In addition to these "we statements," there is one in the first person, "I hope that" (5:12), and one in the third person, "those who boast in appearance" (5:12). In such statements, agency belongs to Paul, his associates, and his rivals, although Paul asserts that this activity is carried out "before God" (5:13).

2. Five other statements have quite a different character. In these, Paul's "we" is the recipient of action or disposition and God or Christ is the agent. These statements place the empirical "we" in realms that are beyond the empirical. Thus we "have a building from God, a dwelling not made with hands, eternal in heaven" (5:1), "have been given the Spirit as a first installment" (5:5), " must all appear before the judgment seat of Christ" (5:10), are "in Christ a new creation" (5:17), are "reconciled to [God]" (5:18). Unlike the first set of statements, none of the referents here can be located in the arena of ordinary human exchange. They suppose an understanding of reality that includes more than what can be tested by the senses: a dwelling in heaven, a future judgment, a gift of the Spirit.

3. Perhaps most striking in this context is the presence of a set of statements that are explicitly cognitive in character. Again, the "we" that includes Paul and his associates are the subject. Thus, while Paul states in 5:7 that we walk by faith, not by knowledge, his other cognitive statements affirm the importance of a certain form of knowledge: we know that we have been given a heavenly dwelling (5:1), we know that when we are clothed with the body we are away from the Lord (5:6), we know the fear of the Lord (5:11), and we have made the judgment (*krinantas*) that "one died for all; therefore all have died" (5:14). Most elaborate is 5:16, "Consequently, from now on we regard [know] no one according to the flesh; even if we once knew Christ according to the flesh, yet now we know him so no longer." By such statements Paul places human agency within a distinctive understanding of reality that belongs to those included in his "we."

4. The immediate context of 5:19 contains a large number of statements concerning nonempirical persons. The judgment seat before which we will stand is Christ's (5:10); Christ's love constrains us (5:14); in Christ is a new creation (5:17); reconciliation is through Christ (5:18); God is

in Christ (5:19); for the sake of Christ we make appeal and beg (5:20); in him (*en autō*) we are made God's righteousness (5:21). In these statements, Christ is less an active agent and more a means or instrument or identifier. The partial exception is one statement in which Christ is the implied subject: "and he died in behalf of all, so that those who are living might no longer live for themselves but for the one who died and was raised for them" (5:15). In this declaration, which serves to explain the judgment made by Paul and his associates that "one died for all; therefore all have died" (5:14), Christ is the agent of dying, and God is the (implied) agency by which Christ was "raised up."

5. Finally, there are the statements in which agency is ascribed directly to *ho theos*. The heavenly dwelling is from God (*ek theou*, 5:1); God gave us the pledge that is the Holy Spirit (5:5); human actions and dispositions are "before God" (5:11, 13), and humans can be reconciled to God (5:20) and be God's righteousness (5:21); all things are from God (*ek tou theou*, 5:18); God was in Christ (5:19); God made (Christ) sin (5:21).

The Logic of Mythic Language

I think we can all agree that, although Paul's language in 2 Cor 5 is mythical in the way I have defined, it is also unlike the sort of mythic narrative we associate with, say, *Enuma Elish* or Gen 6:1–4. Paul does not speak about figures of the distant past with heroic dimensions, but of his contemporaries and a man who died violently within the lifetime of Paul and his readers. Paul uses mythic language in order to express convictions concerning what is happening in the empirical realm that he shares with his readers.

The question arises, then, as to the logic of such language. On what is it based, and how does it make sense (we assume) to Paul and his readers?

We can approach these questions by means of analogy. There is a class of statements that take the form of an abbreviated narrative escaping any real empirical verification. Such statements are grounded in a historical reality but are not completely defined by it. Take, for example, a widow of one of the men who rushed the pilot's compartment of Flight 93 on 9/11 when the airplane had been taken over by terrorists, and who was killed with all aboard that flight when the plane crashed in a Pennsylvania field. She tells her son who never knew his father, "Your daddy was a great patriot. He died for his country."

There is, we observe, some historical basis for her declaration: her husband actually died in an effort to save lives—those who rushed the cockpit had learned of the terrorists' mission to use the plane as a weapon of destruction. To be sure, it is impossible to verify anything about her spouse's precise motivation or emotions at the critical moment. Perhaps he lingered reluctantly in the back of the group that rushed the cockpit. Perhaps he vomited in fear when the rush began. His widow's statement to her son does not rely, however, on the determination of such things. It is instead based on her experience of and knowledge of her deceased husband: the kind of man she knew him to be.

Her judgment is based on something real beyond the brute fact of the historical event. She does not, however, simply aver that her husband was a good man. Her statement places his action within the symbolic framework of national identity, in which "patriotism" (from the time of Horace on) is most fully expressed by "dying for one's country."[9] This language elevates the sacrificial act of her husband by placing it in a more public and value-laden framework.

Take another example. An Irish-Catholic father reassures his children when his harried wife lashes out in frustration at them while cooking dinner, "Your mother is a saint. You know that she would do anything for you children." In this case, the wife's behavior is negative rather than positive: she shows irritation toward her family. Is the father's interpretation therefore false? Not necessarily. First, he invokes a frame of reference that both he and the children share: saints are those who show heroic love toward others. In the case of their mother, the husband reminds the children, her cooking supper is one among a multitude of ways that her love is in service to them; indeed, he suggests, there is no real limit to that love in practical terms—she would do anything for them. The issue of her momentary anger is subsumed by an appeal to the overall character of the mother demonstrated in repeated actions. The father also bases his statement on his privileged understanding of his wife's true character that he has learned through his constant experience of her.

Such homely examples are, to be sure, only analogies. These statements are not "mythic" in the sense of the definition I have given. There is a great distance between stating that a father dies for his country, and stating that the Messiah died for all humans, so that all have died. Similarly there is a great distance between claiming one's wife is a saint (of sorts) and

---

9. "Dulce et decorum est pro patria mori" (Horace, *Odes* 3.2.13).

claiming that God was in Christ. Nevertheless, the examples provide us a sense of how mythic language concerning the present has a definite logic.

It is based, first, on a speaker's personal experience of the one to whom larger-than-life status is ascribed on the basis of knowledge of actions of that person that define his or her character. Second, it involves a judgment concerning that person's character as revealed by such action. Third, it involves a frame of reference, or symbolic structure, within which such ascription makes sense. In the case of Paul's statement in 2 Cor 5:19, then, an experience commensurate with the judgment that "God was in Christ" would be required, a judgment concerning an action of Christ that reveals his character, and an understanding of the world within which such predication makes sense. The context for this statement in 2 Corinthians contains evidence for all three.

First, the experience: when Paul states in 2 Cor 5:5 that the one who works in him and his associates to prepare them for a heavenly habitation is the God who has given them the pledge that is the Holy Spirit, he echoes a statement that he made earlier in the letter: "God is the one who has secured us together with you into Christ [*eis christon*] and has anointed [*chrisas*] us. And he has sealed us, and has given us the pledge that is the Holy Spirit in our hearts" (1:21–22). For Paul, the experience of the power of the Holy Spirit is the personal experience of God ("in our hearts") in and through Christ, the experience that "anoints" Paul and others, giving them a participation (pledge) in Christ's work (see other passages on the Spirit in 2 Cor 3:3–18; 4:13; 6:6; 11:4; 12:18). They have a "fellowship in the Holy Spirit" (13:13).

This experience of God's powerful Spirit through Christ, in turn, grounds the judgment that Paul shares with his readers concerning Jesus' apparently shameful death by execution—a negative historical fact. Paul and his associates have "reached the judgment" (*krinantas*) concerning Jesus' death: that it was a sacrifice in behalf of all, indeed, an expression of love "for us" (5:14): "He died in behalf of all, so that those who are living might no longer live for themselves but for the sake of the one who died and was raised in their behalf" (5:15). We observe in this statement that not only Jesus' death but also his resurrection were for the sake of Paul and his readers. It is by Jesus' exaltation, Paul tells his readers in 1 Cor 15:45, that the *eschatos Adam* became "life-giving Spirit" (*to pneuma to zōopoioun*). Thus Paul says earlier in 2 Cor 4:14 that "we know that the one raising the Lord Jesus will raise us also together with him and place us with you in his presence."

We note also that Christ's death is interpreted in terms of an exchange: his life for all, so that all might live for him. Participation in the Spirit coming from Christ therefore means participation in the pattern of his existence, as Paul declares in 6:9, "we are as people dying, and behold, we live!" Even when they receive the sentence of death, they put their "trust in the God who raises the dead" (*tō theō tō egeironti tous nekrous*, 1:9). If Christ's death on the cross is experienced by others as life, and if his weakness is experienced by others as power, then the power of God is at work in such a fundamental way that the judgment, "If anyone is in Christ there is a new creation" (5:17), follows, and with it a cognitive reevaluation of everything that appears as empirically real: our real home is in heaven, not on earth (5:1–2); when we are in the body we are away from our home (5:6); when we suffer and groan it is because we long for heaven (5:2); and when God made Christ to be sin (through a death that was cursed by Torah), it was so that we might become "God's righteousness in him" (5:21).

The experience of the resurrection Spirit out of an empirical death demands the use of mythic language as the only possible means of expressing the truth, enables a restructuring of the symbolic world shared by all Jews, and impels a proclamation to the world of a new paradigm of power-in-weakness that is God's message of reconciliation.

Conclusion

My analysis has not made Paul's language any easier to understand. I hope that it has at least pointed to the importance of the resurrection experience—the conviction that the crucified Jesus has become exalted Lord and life-giving Spirit—in generating and making sense of Paul's mythic language. It may be worth asking whether readers who understand the resurrection of Jesus (even when they claim to believe in it) simply as a form of resuscitation, rather than Christ's exaltation to a participation in God's power, can ever adequately grasp Paul's language concerning the implications of that Spirit of life being given to others as a pledge.

For that matter, it is also worth asking whether those of us fundamentally shaped by Enlightenment epistemology can ever really appreciate the truth-telling capacity of myth. Without a phenomenology of Spirit that enables us to understand the capacity of bodies to transcend themselves and inhabit other bodies, we are not able to make sense of Paul's language about our being "in Christ" or of God being "in Christ" without reducing it to a weak form of moral allegiance, or worse, to pious nonsense. But to demythologize Paul's language in 2 Corinthians is to eliminate more than its poetry and power; it is to deny its claim to truth. The passage I have considered challenges contemporary readers to ask whether it is really myth speaking of unseen realities that deceives, or whether it is thought that remains only at the level of appearances that deceives.

Works Cited

Bates, W. H. 1965/1966. The Integrity of II Corinthians. *New Testament Studies* 12:56–69.

Betz, Hans Dieter. 1985. *2 Corinthians 8 and 9: A Commentary on Two Administrative Letters of the Apostle Paul.* Hermeneia. Philadelphia: Fortress.

DeSilva, D. A. 1993. Measuring Penultimate against Ultimate Reality: An Investigation of the Integrity and Argumentation of 2 Corinthians. *Journal for the Study of the New Testament* 52:41–70.

Furnish, Victor Paul. 1984. *II Corinthians.* AB 32A. Garden City, N.Y.: Doubleday.

Johnson, Luke T. 1996. *The Real Jesus: The Misguided Quest for the Historical Jesus and the Truth of the Traditional Gospels.* San Francisco: HarperSanFrancisco.

———. 1999a. *Living Jesus: Learning the Heart of the Gospel.* San Francisco: HarperSanFrancisco.

———. 1999b. *The Writings of the New Testament: An Interpretation.* 2nd ed. Minneapolis: Fortress.

Kirk, G. S. 1970. *Myth: Its Meaning and Functions in Other Cultures.* Cambridge: Cambridge University Press.

Murray, H. A., ed. 1960. *Myth and Mythmaking.* Boston: Beacon.

Schremp, G., and W. Hansen, eds. 2002. *Myth: A New Symposium.* Bloomington: Indiana University Press.

Sebeok, T. A. 1955. *Myth: A Symposium.* Philadelphia: American Folklore Society.

Stegman, T. 2005. *The Character of Jesus: the Linchpin to Paul's Argument in 2 Corinthians.* Rome: Pontifical Biblical Institute.

Wallace, James Buchanan. 2011. *Snatched into Paradise (2 Cor 12:1–10): Paul's Heavenly Journey in the Context of Early Christian Experience.* Beihefte zur Zeitschrift für die neutestamentliche Wissenschaft 179. Berlin: de Gruyter.

Witherington, Ben, III. 1994. *Conflict and Community in Corinth: A Sociorhetorical Commentary on 1 and 2 Corinthians*. Grand Rapids: Eerdmans.

Ancient Greek Demythologizing

James E. Miller

Introduction

Myth is a term and concept that has been used and analyzed in a variety of biblical studies for more than a century. However, the term is often poorly defined, and often this is because it is poorly understood. On the one hand, within modern cultures we may define the term *myth* as we please, and study the concept as defined. On the other hand, we struggle to understand precisely how the term was used in ancient literature, and all too often apply modern definitions to the ancient term.

One method for understanding an ancient term or concept is to explore its boundaries—at what point or under what conditions does myth cease to be myth? The boundaries help us understand the ancient parameters of the term. But when we do this type of analysis on a term that remains in current use, it is also important to analyze modern understandings of the term, so that we are better informed when we import modern understandings into ancient texts. Again, exploring the boundaries of the term will aid our understanding of how the term is used and understood today. In this paper I seek to understand "myth" by studying ancient—and modern—methods and practices of demythologizing. First, the general concept of demythologizing is studied. Following the general study, three examples from biblical studies are given that usually are not studied in reference to myth and demythologizing. Each example offers different insights into ancient and modern demythologizing.

Demythologizing is a modern term that I am using for a set of ancient practices aimed at dealing with undesirable aspects of Greek mythology. Although the term has taken on various specific connotations in biblical studies over the years, I am taking liberties with the term by taking it at its face meaning and using its dictionary definition—demythologizing is the removal of myth from material that is pervaded with myth. *Myth* here is usually understood as supernatural and/or fantastical lore. Of course, varied definitions of myth result in varied methods of demythologizing, as we shall see. In this paper *myth* in turns may be defined as (1) a narrative of deities as personalities interacting with each other socially, sexually, or in conflict, or interacting with primordial monsters, or interacting with humans; (2) any miraculous and/or fantastical narrative; or (3) various combinations of these two concepts. The definition of myth depends on the ancient or modern scholar involved in the demythologizing.

Behind the practice of demythologizing is a devaluation of myth in the culture. Both in ancient times and in modern times this is described as a devaluation of the irrational and a turning toward the rational. Therefore, both in ancient Greek and modern English literature, "myth" (μῦθος) may be used simply to denote any falsehood, with or without divine or miraculous content. However, there are reasons for refusing to accept this understanding. "Myth may sometimes be irrational; it is often symbolic, but irrationality is not a normative feature. Nor is there anything innately irrational about symbolism" (Morgan 2000, 31).[1] The ancient polemic that drove demythologizing should be understood as part of the phenomenon studied, not incorporated into the scholar's presuppositions. One method of demythologizing is commonly called "rationalization," but we should not assume that the mythological source material is any less rational than the products of rationalization.

The problem with disbelief concerning at least some mythology goes back to the Archaic Period and the oldest surviving compendium of Greek myth, the *Theogony* of Hesiod. In the *Theogony* (27–29) the Muses begin their discourse by declaring, "We know how to speak many false things with genuine qualities [ἴδμεν ψεύδεα πολλὰ λέγειν ἐτύμοισιν ὁμοῖα] or, when we want, sing true things." One possible reading of Hesiod's Muses is that even the false things have valuable content (Heiden 2007).[2] However, an almost identical line in *Odyssey* 19.203, possibly the source of Hesiod's line, describes Odysseus's ability to lie convincingly (ἴσκε ψεύδεα πολλὰ λέγων ἐτύμοισιν ὁμοῖα). In any case we should not assume naivete on the part of even our earliest sources of Greek myth.

---

1. For a discussion of myth as symbol, see Des Bouvrie 2002.

2. In Heiden's reading these Archaic Period Muses sound suspiciously like members of the Inklings at Oxford.

One important way of dealing with mythological material is euhemerism, another term for rationalization. These two terms reference a set of closely related practices in ancient historiography by which unacceptable myth is transformed into "rational" history. Another method is allegory, by which the unacceptable elements are resignified into narratives of values. The allegorical methods have already been well studied in various SBL forums and will be passed over here.[3] A third method simply supplies some narrative distance between the story at hand and the myths that lie behind that story. The myth is described, but not promoted as true. This is a method often used by Euripides, especially in *Heracles*.

In this paper I focus on the methods of rationalization, especially euhemerism, in which myth is transformed into history.

Euhemerism and Rationalization

Euhemerism or rationalization was a widespread practice in Hellenic and Hellenistic culture stretching from early historians such as Hecataeus and Herodotus to Plutarch in the Roman period. The term *euhemerism* is derived from Euhemerus, a philosopher-historian who (apparently) created history out of myth by changing the supernatural elements into natural elements, and in particular making divine characters into ancient aristocrats and warriors of exceptional abilities. Other forms of rationalization take mythological monsters and events and find rational explanations for them. The common assumption is that these remarkable tales must have "real," nonmythological stories behind them, and the historian's task is to remove the myth to restore the history

Sometimes the rationalized explanation is based on a name or a pun or a misunderstood statement. A standard example is the Minotaur of Crete, a half-man/half-bull offspring of the queen and a divine bull. In the rationalized version a warrior named Taurus (Bull) has an adulterous affair with the queen of Crete, the wife of King Minos. In Palaephatus (2) it is he who slays the Athenians sent to Crete as tribute. One of Plutarch's sources (*Theseus* 19) claims it is his illegitimate child by the queen who has that role. This "Minotaur," the Taurus of King Minos, is slain by the Athenian hero Theseus. Sometimes other ancient misunderstandings are advanced.

---

3. The phenomenon of allegorizing myth is also well studied in Classical scholarship, e.g., Brisson 2004.

Centaurs are explained as warriors riding horses observed by people who never considered putting horses to such a use. This strange sight of people riding horses led to the mythic twice-told tale of the centaur. Our earliest example of this explanation for centaurs comes from Palaephatus (1). The assumption is that there is a historical kernel in these myths, and one duty of the historian is to find that kernel. The popularity of the method may be seen in its critics. In Plato's *Phaedrus* 229c–d Socrates seems to be criticizing extant portions of Palaephatus, speaking of centaurs, the chimera, the gorgons, and Pegasus and their contrived explanations. This passage assumes widespread familiarity with the methodology of rationalization.

However, Euhemerus may not have been indulging in these practices, or at least not in the manner that we call "euhemerism" (Garstad 2004). What we have from the writings of Euhemerus is third-hand and subject to much interpretation. One important source on Euhemerus is the Christian historian Eusebius, who quoted Diodoros, who in turn quoted and synopsized Euhemerus (*FGrHist* 63 F 2). Another source is the early Latin poet-historian Ennius, who translated the history of Euhemerus into Latin verse (*FGrHist* 63 F 12–26; Warmington 1935, 1:414–31). However, the works of Ennius survive piecemeal in the works of others. His Euhemerus translation is found in the work of Lactantius. These third-hand fragments indicate that Euhemerus treated the gods Ouranos (Uranus), Kronos (Cronus), Zeus, and their brothers, sisters, and wives as human founders of a dynasty with life spans and deaths, in sharp contrast to the deities of the *Theogony*. It is this third-hand Euhemerus that inspired the modern term *euhemerism*.

Euhemerus was also somewhat late, and this historical method of rationalizing myth preceded him by several generations. More important are earlier writers such as Herodotus, whose *Histories* are well known, and his predecessor Hecataeus of Miletos,[4] preserved in fragments as well as secondhand accounts. Another important resource is Palaephatus from whom we have preserved a substantial portion of his *On Unbelievable Things* (Περὶ ἀπίστων). These are examples from Classical Greece. Closer to the New Testament is Plutarch (late first century B.C.E.), who explains his method in his introduction to *Theseus* in the *Parallel Lives*. He states that his task is to clean the myth and have it submit to reason (ἐκκαθαιρόμενον

---

4. Hecataeus of Miletos (ca. 550–490) is not to be confused with Hecataeus of Abdera (ca. 360–290), who was an important influence on Euhemerus.

λόγῳ τὸ μυθῶδες ὑπακοῦσαι) and receive the look of history (καὶ λαβεῖν ἱστορίας ὄψιν). From Hecataeus we have a briefer statement of method. He merely wrote things which he considered true, for "the Greeks have accounts, many and ridiculous [γελοῖοι], or so they seem to me" (*FGrHist* 1 F 1). The phenomenon of rationalizing myth is not confined to Greece's age of reason, but continues as a philosophical and historical discipline into the first century C.E.

Livy (late first century C.E.) used a method that provides a counterpoint. He seems to reference rationalizing historians when he critiques contemporary historians who try to produce a more believable (or reliable, *credunt*) account of ancient events (1.1.2–3). Although he notes that ancient accounts are decorated with *fabulae*, rather than reliable material, he chose to refrain from affirming or denying the veracity of their tales (1.1.6–7).

Scholars who study rationalization or euhemerism share one enduring problem with scholars of ancient pseudepigraphs. There remains the difficult question of how the results should be understood. Did the ancient practitioners actually believe the results of their work? And did the prospective and actual ancient audiences believe the products? Did Herodotus or Plutarch believe that the histories they produced described actual events in the past? This may be paralleled with the question of whether the authors of Jubilees or the Genesis Apocryphon actually believed they were restoring lost first-person accounts (cf. 4 Ezra 14). Did the authors expect their ancient readership to take these accounts at face value, and did their audiences do so? The answers seem mixed. We have evidence of certain documents that were intended and received as fiction (e.g., Mheallaigh 2008), but others are less clear in intent. The few responses that survive speak of both belief and disbelief.

Belief in the results of rationalization implies a will to believe—a desire to find something believable in the classic myth narratives. This is combined with a willingness to ignore and bypass any traditional meaning that the myth had prior to rationalization. Whatever meaning the myth once had, the rationalized myth finds its value in tradition itself.

Modern Euhemerism

Euhemerism is a modern term for the ancient practice, and the existence of the term indicates a modern interest in these practices, an interest sufficient to produce some modern counterparts. It is important to discuss modern movements and methods that have sufficient resemblance to the ancient practices to cause a confusion of concepts. This is especially true in biblical scholarship, where two distinct meanings for the term *demythologize* have become popular in the past century. First we must discuss the Enlightenment thought on the topic.

Euhemerism is an English term dating back to the Enlightenment when practices associated with Euhemerus and other ancient rationalizers were revived. Sometimes nothing more than excision of offending supernatural elements was done. An example is the Bible of Thomas Jefferson, in which he created a scrapbook version of the life and teachings of Jesus by taking the biblical Gospels and removing the miracles. However, other examples show all the ingenuity of the ancient rationalizers.

David Hume is a key player in the Enlightenment rejection of the miraculous. Chapter 10 of *An Enquiry Concerning Human Understanding* (1748) is entitled "Miracles." In this chapter Hume found miracles irreducibly opposed to reason, or perhaps we should say, Reason. Hume defines a miracle as "a violation of the laws of nature," and asserts that "no testimony is sufficient to establish a miracle, unless the testimony be of such a kind, that its falsehood would be more miraculous." Related to euhemerism, Hume's response to eyewitnesses to a miracle is to consider "whether it be more probable, that this person should either deceive or be deceived." Also related to this study, Hume's primary example of things miraculous (which therefore should be rejected) is the idea of resurrection. Hume's philosophical rejection of the miraculous remains basic in the thinking of many today, even among postmodernists.

Demythologizing in New Testament studies is usually associated with the name of Bultmann, who sought to displace literal miracles with the more important proclamation that may be found in the text. Bultmann saw myth as a way of describing powers that were beyond human control. He then juxtaposed two apparently contradictory qualifications on these powers—that they were understood as like worldly power only more so, and that they were transcendent and broke into the mundane (1958, 19–21). Theory aside, Bultmann represented an attempt to preserve the proclamation of the New Testament texts without requiring an engagement with the miraculous. As with enlightenment euhemerism, Bultmann's relationship with myth rarely went beyond an intolerance for miracles.

A distinctly different euhemerism following the Enlightenment model may be found in various treatments of the Gospels exemplified by the popular commentaries of William Barclay. In Barclay we find, for instance, that the feeding of the five thousand (Matt 14:13–21) may be explained as Jesus getting his audience to put away their selfishness and share such food as they have (1975, 103); and his walking on water (Matt 14:22–27) is actually Jesus striding into the shallow water near the shore where the boat with the disciples had been pushed aground by the winds (1975, 105). In the second example Barclay relies on certain ambiguities in the Greek text that may be read as implying no miracle. To be fair to Barclay, the non-miraculous versions are only one option offered for those readers who are miracle intolerant. For readers who do accept miracles, more traditional readings are explored. Barclay's engagement with the proclamation behind the miracle tends to be more earthy than Bultmann's.

The foundations of biblical archaeology are often understood to include Enlightenment euhemerism. More accurately, it is the foundations of Heinrich Schliemann's Homeric archaeology that include the euhemerism of the Enlightenment, and the biblical archaeology movement gained its momentum, and some of its rationale, from Homeric archaeology. Overt euhemerism rarely plays a role in biblical archaeology. Basic arguments in the debates over Homeric or biblical archaeology include the question of whether rejection of miracles therefore requires a rejection of the historicity of persons associated with these miracles—or whether the confirmation of the individuals therefore confirms the associated miracles. Notice that this archaeological method deals only with miracles, and not with larger mythological issues. This is in contrast to scholarship of the Hebrew Bible, the text most often referenced in biblical archaeology, which is interested in a different kind of demythologizing.

The interest in demythologizing among scholars of the Hebrew Scriptures involves an appreciation for the degree to which ancient Israelite and Judahite writers "demythologized" the traditions and myths of surrounding cultures. This appreciation focuses on the full range of ancient mythology and not merely the presence or absence of the miraculous. A few remnants of mythological material remain within the biblical corpus, such as the conflict with the chaos monster Rahab/Lotan (e.g., Pss 74:13–14; 89:9–10; Isa 27:1; 51:9–10). However, one mythological theme, that of divine sexuality, is completely excluded from the biblical corpus, indicating a strong and thorough intolerance for such mythological material by those who formed the texts and canon (Miller 2006, 10–12). The rarity of mythological material in the biblical corpus has long fascinated scholars of these Hebrew texts.

Gerhard von Rad provides an example of the classic understanding of Israelite demythologizing. In his *Old Testament Theology* he sees two broad categories of demythologizing. One is where certain liminal experiences are desacralized (*Entsakralisierung*), and therefore "demythologized" (*Entmythologisierung*). The two most prominent examples are sex and death (1962, 28, 277; 1965, 340, 349; Preuss 1995, 235–36).

The second form of demythologizing bears some resemblance to euhemerism. This is the displacement of myth with history (von Rad 1962, 23–24; 1965, 340–49; Preuss 1995, 208–11). The "history" is not necessarily devoid of miracles, however, but it lacks competing deities, primordial monsters, divine sexuality, and other such mythological entities and motifs. Demythologized narrative means one God in control, either in complete control of other deities (henotheism) or lacking other competing deities (monotheism). This singular God can still interact with the created order by means of miracles and other interventions, some quite spectacular. This tolerance for the miraculous and fabulous distinguishes the Hebrew demythologizing from both Classical and Enlightenment intolerance for the fantastic.

The resulting history, found throughout the biblical text, resembles euhemerized history as it need only have the appearance of history to be understood as demythologized. The focus is on form. The result looks like historical narrative, whether or not the modern scholar believes the events in the narrative happened as described.

There is a sharp contrast in the use of the term *demythologize* in New Testament scholarship and Hebrew Bible scholarship. The New Testament Gospels as they stand, without being "demythologized," are in a form that scholars of the Hebrew Bible are likely to recognize as already "demythologized." The only possible exception is the quasi-mythological role of Satan or demons in some Gospel narratives. In short, we have a distinction in how the term *myth* is understood in the two disciplines, and this results in a distinction in how the term *demythologize* is understood. These modern definitions of *demythologize* cannot be purged from our vocabulary, but rather we are forced to work with multiple definitions of the phenomenon that may take part in any of our discussions. This leaves us a broad field to explore, but requires us to be clear on which parameters define the phenomena we are studying.

In the remainder of this paper I will explore three developments tied in with Classical Greek demythologizing and with biblical studies where the role and consequences of demythologizing are rarely recognized.

Paradise Lost and Found

In *Phaedrus* 229c–d Plato has Socrates ridicule rationalization as intricate and overdone. In this passage Socrates seems to be referencing extant portions of Palaephatus, speaking of centaurs, the chimera, the gorgons, and Pegasus and their contrived explanations. However, Plato is the source of one rationalization that has grabbed the imagination of generations of scholars who today stand on the shoulders of Schliemann and rationalize Plato's rationalization. This is the legend of Atlantis in Plato's *Timaeus* and *Kritias*.

Atlantis is an ancient utopia manufactured from the various Greek mythological traditions of the western paradise. The most obvious defining element of this rationalization is the name Atlantis, which is based on the name of the island's first king, Atlas (*Kritias* 114a). Atlas, of course, was a god, one of the Titans, and making a god into an ancient founding king is a defining characteristic of Classical rationalization, such as associated with Euhemerus. If we ascribe consistency to Plato (which is sometimes risky), the critique in Phaedrus indicates a widespread awareness of rationalization of myth, including its standard methods. We might conclude, based on the obvious euhemerism of Atlas into the first king of Atlantis, that Plato wanted his readers to understand Atlantis as nothing more than a heuristic fiction created from mythological material. In addition, the framing device of receiving the story from an Egyptian source also points to intentional fiction (Gill 1979).

Only a couple of generations removed from Plato the historicity of Atlantis was already being debated, with the defense of historicity seen as a defense of Plato himself (Niehoff 2007, 166–67; Cameron 1983). In this tradition Philo of Alexandria treats Plato's Atlantis as a historical account (*Aet.* 141). If Plato wanted his Atlantis to be a transparent heuristic euhemerism, he did not succeed.

The Titan Atlas is a god associated with the west (Aeschylus, *Prom.* 349–350) and is found in almost every version of the western paradise known as the garden of the Hesperides. The far western sea and the lands associated with this garden are known as ἀτλαντικός ("belonging to Atlas"; Herodotus, *Hist.* 1.203; Euripides, *Hipp.* 3). If nothing else, Atlas is described as close to the Hesperid garden, whether in Hesiod's *Theogony* (517–520) or the labors of Heracles (Euripides, *Heracles* 397–407; *Hipp.* 742–751). Elsewhere Atlas is the father of the Hesperides (Pherekydes, *FGrHist* 3 F 16a, 17) and is otherwise connected to the garden (Appolonius of Rhodes, *Argon.* 4.1399). Also Calypso in the *Odyssey* is described as the daughter of Atlas (1.52–55), and in her island in the far west she offers Odysseus eternal life if he stays with her.

Elysion is another western paradise. In the *Odyssey* and various other sources (*Od.* 4.561–569; Hesiod, *Op.* 167–173; Pindar, *Ol.* 2) the heroes of the Trojan War are offered immortality in Elysion (Elysium) or the Isles of the Blessed, lands associated with the West Wind on the far side of the Oceanus stream. Elysion is also associated with the Titan Kronos, a relative of Atlas. It is interesting that the Latin poet-historian Ennius takes pains to associate his native Italy with Saturn (Latin Kronos) and to emphasize its position west of Greece (Warmington 1935, 13). Euhemerus (according to Ennius) had Saturn/Kronos flee westward (Warmington 1935, 422–23).

From these various elements of the western paradise Plato constructed a western utopia located in the far west beyond the Pillars of Heracles, founded by the king Atlas for whom the island is named. Modern archaeologists have repeatedly attempted to rationalize Plato's rationalized Atlantis, using techniques of which Schliemann would approve. Usually they associate Atlantis with Thera/Santorini, an island with a magnificent Minoan culture buried and preserved when the island exploded in a volcanic eruption. However, Thera is not in the west. Plato is neither the Bible nor Homer, so this identification of Thera with Atlantis is neither Homeric nor biblical archaeology. Atlantis is not mythical, but rather has already been demythologized and presented as a legendary ideal or a utopia. We should be aware of the methods of demythologizing when practicing or critiquing biblical and Homeric archaeology. If we wish to euhemerize what has already been euhemerized, at least we should do so knowingly.

Elysion

Elysion, or the Isles of the Blessed, undergoes an interesting development between the Archaic and Classical periods. The Archaic sources consistently describe Elysion as a place where exceptional people go *instead of* dying. These people tend to be associated with the Trojan War (Homer, *Od.* 4.561–569; Hesiod, *Op.* 156–173). Heroes who die do not go to Elysion. They go to that part of Hades called the Fields of Asphodel (*Od.* 11.539, 573; 24.13), a very different place. In the *Homeric Hymns* (*To Hermes* 221, 344) the Fields of Asphodel are associated with Hermes. The hymn does not directly associate these fields with Hermes's role as conductor of dead souls, however.

Classical sources consistently treat Elysion as a blessed afterlife for the dead (Plato, *Gorg.* 523; Pindar, *Ol.* 2.70-80) as if this place was Homer's Field of Asphodel. It is no longer an alternative to death. This shift from immortality to afterlife has long been recognized by Classical scholars (Rohde 1925, 55-60, 75-76). However, the relationship of this shift to the Classical practice of rationalization has not been explored.

Archaic Elysion is a place—a place located at the ends of the earth, but still a place. It is a physical location where physical humans live in bliss instead of dying. It is associated with Oceanus, a fresh-water stream which encircles the earth, including the salt-water seas. Both the physicality of Elysion and the physical immortality of its inhabitants are at issue. Throughout the Archaic and Classical periods the ancient Greeks were continually discovering new lands and incorporating them into their inventory of known lands. At the same time they had to come to terms with mythological lands that once were outside the edges of the known world, but now seemed to be within reach. Scylla and Charybdis, for instance, became associated with the strait between Sicily and the Italian peninsula, a rationalization of myth based on exploration. It is possible that Elysion would be found—or its existence called into doubt—through continuing exploration. The continual expansion of Greek knowledge of the world probably led to an insecurity about certain mythic locations that should be findable but were not found.

If the pull of rationalization was felt surrounding the Elysion problem, it could have pushed this myth in a new direction. In the Classical period Elysion became a nonphysical place where nonphysical spirits of the dead might go, possibly replacing the fields of Asphodel. As such it need not be found through exploration, and indeed could not be found. This transformation also meant that physical immortality need not be accepted. This transformation of physical Elysion and physical immortality to nonphysical Elysion and a blessed afterlife comes from removing not supernatural elements but physical elements. Because Elysion, the Isles of the Blessed, is commonly cited as a source for the early Christian concept of heaven, the history of this blessed afterlife may be worthy of exploration.

Paul before the Areopagus

In the book of Acts Paul preached before the Areopagus, discoursing on the unknown God, presenting a spiritual henotheism, a divinity that transcends the vulgar mix of polytheistic religions popular with hoi polloi. But suddenly he makes a sharp turn into resurrection, an element of vulgar myth, or worse, sorcery. Of course the respect of these philosophers turned to derision. Resurrection for Paul was a validation of the divine calling of Jesus, but instead among these philosophers it revealed that the philosophical henotheism Paul had been constructing was a mere pretext for one more vulgar myth

The very idea of restoring physical life to the dead may be seen as another casualty of ancient demythologizing. The idea of Heracles wrestling with Hades for Alcestis and returning her alive from the tomb is clearly in the realm of the mythological. In contrast, the idea of Asclepius restoring people at the brink of death, including some who had just died, could have been understood as nonmythological medical skill, similar to modern medical "miracles." But the New Testament emphasis that Jesus was clearly dead, prior to being taken from the cross and interred, places his resurrection within a realm ripe for demythologizing. The spear thrust of the soldier is the most graphic element of this emphasis (John 19:34). This emphasis intentionally runs against the grain of the ancient suspicion of the miraculous. It also lies behind the resurrection of Lazarus in John 11, where several days are placed intentionally between the man's death and resurrection. Martha's insistence that he must be stinking already also draws attention to the graphic physical reality and apparent finality of the death of Lazarus. The emphasis that Lazarus and Jesus were indeed fully and completely dead prior to their resurrections takes precise aim at miracle-intolerant speculations that suppose that resurrected people were not fully dead to begin with.

This emphasis on the real and physical death of Jesus was countered by certain gnostic traditions that denied the reality of that death. We find in the Nag Hammadi *Apocalypse of Peter* that the death of Jesus was merely an illusion, the real Jesus standing aside and having a laugh at his deluded enemies who thought they were indeed crucifying him. This denial underscores the difficulties that some philosophies had with the idea of physical resurrection. In this case the physical death of Jesus is denied, therefore physical resurrection is unnecessary. Of course, this substitutes one "myth" for another. Instead of resurrection there is a divinely mandated mass hallucination. Then again, in some forms of Gnosticism physical reality itself is something akin to a hallucination.

A contrasting movement in formative Gnosticism avoided physical resurrection by restyling resurrection as a nonphysical event, such as in the Nag Hammadi *Treatise on the Resurrection*. Here the term *resurrec-*

tion is affirmed, but redefined as a spiritual maturation and transcendence having nothing to do with revivifying the physical body. The ideological forces that changed physical immortality into an afterlife centuries earlier seem to remain active in early Christianity.

In Greek legend resurrection is as often an act of abominable sorcery as a heroic act. An example of the former is in Heliodoros, *Aeth.* 6.14–15, where the sorcery (μάγγανον) is clearly unholy, obscene, and accursed. Even in heroic instances, such as the *Alkestis* of Euripides, Heracles must deny being a necromancer (ψυχαγωγός, 1128). Positive instances of nonmedical resurrection are rare in this ancient literature.

This is the context in which Paul preached and philosophized before the Areopagus (Acts 17). The negative reaction of the Areopagites is usually explained solely by pointing out how ancient philosophical Greeks found nothing desirable about a return to physical, bodily life in the flesh. However, we should also consider the general intolerance for both mythical and miraculous elements that characterizes fantastic stories popular among the gullible laity, who lack the intellectual rigor and sophistication of the philosophical mind. In other words, Classical rationalized demythologizing, and its intolerance for spectacular miracles, provides a context in which to understand the reaction of these philosophers. Or, if we wish to distance ourselves a bit from the narrative, ancient philosophical rationalization provides a context in which we see an ancient popular portrayal of philosophers personified as Areopagites rejecting the concept of resurrection. On the one hand, physical resurrection adds an element of myth to the story of Jesus. On the other hand, to avoid this particular myth some traditions were willing to substitute another myth of mass hallucination. Demythologizing was not a one-way street within this culture.

Ironically, or perhaps not so ironic, it is the idea of resurrection that provoked this response of the Areopagites in the book of Acts. Resurrection was also the primary object of Hume's rejection of the miraculous. And taking a page from Hume's argument, current evangelical arguments on the resurrection of Jesus focus on how much more unlikely it is that this particular miracle did not occur (Wright 2003, 683–718; Kreeft and Tacelli 1994, 175–98). Somehow the ideological schism between Paul and the Areopagites returned to become a fundamental bone of contention for the Enlightenment, as well as for modernist (e.g., Wright and Borg 2007) and postmodern (e.g., Sheaffer 1991, 127–46) understandings of the Bible and religion in Western culture.

Works Cited

Barclay, William. 1975. *The Gospel of Matthew*. Rev. ed. 2 vols. Daily Study Bible. Louisville: Westminster John Knox.

Brisson, Luc. 2004. *How Philosophers Saved Myths: Allegorical Interpretation and Classical Mythology*. Translated by Catherine Tihanyi. Chicago: University of Chicago Press.

Bultmann, Rudolph. 1958. *Jesus Christ and Mythology*. New York: Scribner's.

Cameron, Alan. 1983. Crantor and Posidonius on Atlantis. *Classical Quarterly* 31:81–91.

Des Bouvrie, Synnøve. 2002. The Definition of Myth: Symbolical Phenomena in Ancient Culture. Pages 11–69 in *Symbolic Phenomena in Ancient Greek Culture*. Vol. 1 of *Myth and Symbol*. Edited by Synnøve Des Bouvrie. Bergen: Norwegian Institute at Athens.

Garstad, Benjamin. 2004. Belus in the *Sacred History* of Euhemerus. *CP* 99:246–57.

Gill, Christopher. 1979. Plato's Atlantis Story and the Birth of Fiction. *Philosophy and Literature* 3:64–78.

Heiden, Bruce. 2007. The Muses' Uncanny Lies: Hesiod, *Theogony* 27 and Its Translators. *AJP* 128:153–75.

Kreeft, Peter, and Ronald K. Tacelli. 1994. *Handbook of Christian Apologetics*. Downers Grove, Ill.: InterVarsity Press.

Mheallaigh, Karen Ni. 2008. Pseudo-Documentarism and the Limits of Ancient Fiction. *AJP* 129:403–31.

Miller, James E. 2006. *Raw Material: Studies in Biblical Sexuality*. Online: http://www.othersheep.org.

Morgan, Kathryn A. 2000. *Myth and Philosophy from the Pre-Socratics to Plato*. New York: Cambridge University Press.

Niehoff, Maren R. 2007. Did the *Timaeus* Create a Textual Community? *Greek, Roman and Byzantine Studies* 47:161–91.

Preuss, Horst Dietrich. 1995. *Old Testament Theology*. Vol. 1 Translated by Leo G. Perdue. OTL. Louisville: Westminster John Knox.

Rad, Gerhard von. 1962. *The Theology of Israel's Historical Traditions*. Vol. 1 of *Old Testament Theology*. Translated by D. M. G. Stalker. New York: Harper & Row.

———. 1965. *The Theology of Israel's Prophetic Traditions*. Vol. 2 of *Old Testament Theology*. Translated by D. M. G. Stalker. New York: Harper & Row.

Rohde, Erwin. 1925. *Psyche: The Cult of Souls and Belief in Immortality among the Greeks.* New York: Harcourt, Brace.
Sheaffer, Robert. 1991. *The Making of the Messiah: Christianity and Resentment.* Buffalo: Prometheus.
Stern, Jacob. 1996 *Palaephatus: On Unbelievable Tales.* Wauconda, Ill.: Bolchazy-Carducci.
Warmington, E. H. 1935. *Remains of Old Latin.* 4 vols. LCL. Cambridge: Harvard University Press.
Wright, Nicholas Thomas. 2003. *The Resurrection of the Son of God.* Christian Origins and the Question of God 3. Minneapolis: Fortress.
Wright, N. T., and Marcus J. Borg. 2007. *The Meaning of Jesus: Two Visions.* San Francisco: HarperSanFrancisco.

Myth, Allegory, and the Derveni Papyrus

John T. Fitzgerald

One of the most notorious aspects of ancient Greek myth was its frequent depiction of the gods as engaging in conduct that is morally problematic. The scandalous manner in which various myths portrayed the gods was doubtless one of the factors that made them popular in many social circles, but these same immoral depictions raised a number of serious intellectual and ethical questions that were debated at length throughout antiquity. The fundamental question was whether these common depictions of the gods were true. If so, the gods were often exemplars of vice rather than of virtue, and human morality was in many instances conspicuously superior to divine morality.[1] In that case, why should humans pray to the gods and give them homage? Furthermore, if the gods were inveterate liars and hypocrites, why should one trust them or give heed to what they said? The basic answer for those who accepted the literal veracity of the myths was that the gods were stronger and more powerful than humans, so it was only prudent for mortals to acknowledge the greater power of the divine. Yet such acknowledgment implied that worship of the gods was essentially concerned with power management, that is, with controlling divine power so as to ensure that humans benefited from that power rather than being harmed by it. One did not have to love Zeus, but it was foolish to ignore him and risk his ire.

---

1. Isocrates, who rejected the poetic attribution of ignoble dispositions and actions to the gods, argued that such depictions made the gods inferior to humans in either morality or power: "According to your own reasoning, the gods are not free from the two most disgraceful faults: for if they do not want their children to be virtuous, they are inferior in character to human beings; but if, on the other hand, they desire it but are at a loss how to effect it, they are more impotent than the sophists!" (*Bus.* 43, LCL).

Although many Greeks continued to believe the traditional image of the gods as given by early authors such as Homer and Hesiod, others began to call these depictions into question. The first to do so were the pre-Socratic philosophers, especially the Ionians. Xenophanes of Colophon (sixth century B.C.E.), for example, lambasted Homer and Hesiod because they "have attributed to the gods all things that are shameful and a reproach: thievery, adultery, and deception of each other" (DK 21 B 11).[2] The same charge is repeated in another fragment of his: "They have spoken as much as possible concerning the wicked deeds of the gods: stealing, committing adultery, deceiving each other" (DK 21 B 12). Such philosophers were not content merely to criticize traditional theology and religion but also offered their own conceptions of the divine as an alternative. These new conceptions were usually rationalistic or naturalistic or both. Xenophanes, for example, mocked traditional anthropomorphic conceptions of the divine (DK 21 B 14-16), arguing that "there is one god, greatest among gods and men, like to men neither in body nor in soul" (DK 21 B 23). This is an early instance of what is today increasingly called "pagan monotheism" (Athanassiadi and Frede 1999), that is, one high god with numerous lesser and subservient deities. Of this highest deity, Xenophanes says, "He sees as a whole, he knows wholly, and hears wholly" (DK 21 B 24). "But without toil he sets all into motion, by the thought in his mind" (DK 21 B 25). "Always he remains in the same place, not moving at all, nor is it appropriate to change his position from one place to another" (DK 21 B 26). As these comments suggest, Xenophanes is "the first thinker systematically to formulate the conception of a cosmic god" (Kahn 1996, 1628). These competing theological claims resulted in an impasse that betrayed human uncertainty about the divine. Xenophanes thus concludes with the concession, "In respect to the truth, no man has there been or will be who knows about the gods and the things which I mention. Even if a man happened to speak the truth, nevertheless he doesn't know it" (DK 21 B 34).

Allegory arises in the broader context of this theological debate and is employed as a tertium quid to address the standoff between traditional theology and new philosophical perspectives on deity. This stalemate was

---

2. On Xenophanes see esp. Lesher 1992. Fragments of the pre-Socratic philosophers are cited from Diels-Krantz 1954 (abbreviated DK). The first number after DK indicates the chapter number, A indicates texts dealing with the individual's life and teaching, B indicates the person's fragments, and the final number is the fragment number. Translations of Xenophanes are those of Rice and Stambaugh 1979, 31–32.

the ancient equivalent of later tensions between faith and reason as well as the modern conflict between religion and science. Allegory, to be sure, probably has a genesis in archaic Greek poetry that is completely separate and apart from this theological debate,[3] but it was quickly employed in that debate as a means of reconciling these conflicts, especially since "it could be used to find deeper meanings in received texts and thereby rescue them from charges of superficiality, error, or blasphemy" (Konstan and Ramelli 2009, 780).

An allegorical interpretation of a passage or myth offered no less than three distinct advantages. First, it rescued the text from the "fundamentalists" of antiquity who were willing to defend its literal meaning, even when that meaning was morally horrific. Second, it defended the authors of authoritative texts from charges of blasphemy or ignorance because of the unethical character traits and immoral actions attributed to the deities in the myths. Allegory thus had an apologetic function. Third, it simultaneously shielded the allegorists from charges of impiety that would have been leveled against them by opponents if they had simply attacked venerable figures such as Homer and/or the religiously authoritative texts they had written.

According to ancient tradition, the first pre-Socratic thinker to employ allegory for this purpose was the grammarian and literary critic Theagenes of Rhegium (fl. 525 B.C.E.), who dealt with the problem of the *Theomachia* in books 20 and 21 of the *Iliad*, where the gods participate in the Trojan War and attack one another. This conspicuous "strife of the gods" (*Il.* 20.66: θεῶν ἔριδι) stood in vivid contrast to the harmonious portrait that Xenophanes endeavored to promote with his idea of one high god who effortlessly sways the entire cosmos by the thoughts of his mind. Instead of attacking Homer as Xenophanes had done, Theagenes defended him by interpreting the divine strife as an allegory of the endless "strife" of the nature of the elements.[4] The much later neoplatonic author Porphyry

---

3. On the history of ancient allegory see esp. McGonagill 2001; and Ramelli and Lucchetta 2004. For a collection of classical allegorical works and fragments, see Ramelli 2007. According to Heraclitus (*All.* 5), "there are plenty of passages" in which the lyric poet Alcaeus (born ca. 620–615 B.C.E.) uses allegory, including frg. 326 (Lobel and Page 1997) (on the ship of state). In that case, allegory has an origin separate from the theological controversy in which it is employed.

4. Later pre-Socratics, such as Heraclitus and Empedocles, were to make "strife" a key concept in their philosophy.

(234–ca. 305 C.E.), who was interested in allegory and wrote an allegorical interpretation of the Cave of the Nymphs that appears in book 13 of the *Odyssey*,[5] credits Theagenes with pioneering this interpretive technique,[6] which is treated as a distinct type of diction (λέξις):

> [1] The general discourse concerning the gods is fixed on what is inappropriate [ἀσυμφόρου], and, similarly, what is unseemly [ἀπρεποῦς], for he [Homer] tells stories [μύθους] about the gods that are not seemly [οὐ πρέποντας]. [2] In regard to such an accusation [κατηγορίαν], some apply a solution from diction, believing that everything about the nature of the elements has been said by allegory [ἀλληγορίαι], as it were in the opposition of the gods. [3] For indeed they say that the dry fights with the wet, the hot with the cold, and the light with the heavy; furthermore, that water extinguishes fire, but fire dries water. [4] Similarly, the opposition accrues to all the elements out of which the universe consists to admit of destruction once in part, but to remain eternally with respect to the whole. [5] [They say] that he arranges battles by naming fire Apollo, Helios, and Hephaestus, the water Poseidon and Scamander, the moon Artemis, the air Hera etc. [6] Similarly, sometimes he even puts names of gods for their dispositions, Athena for wisdom, Ares for stupidity, Aphrodite for desire, Hermes for speech, and they associate [these dispositions] with them. [7] So, this type of defense [ἀπολογίας], being quite old and from Theagenes of Rhegium, who first wrote about Homer, is from diction.[7]

Orpheus and Dionysus

The allegorical method was applied not only to the texts of Homer and Hesiod but also to those attributed to the mythical figure of Orpheus, who was often seen as the worst offender. The orator Isocrates denounces blasphemous poets in general and Orpheus in particular for calumnies

---

5. Porphyry, *De antro nympharum*. For a translation see Lamberton 1983.

6. For the view that allegorical interpretation of Homer begins with Pherecydes of Syros (sixth century B.C.E.), see Tate 1927.

7. Porphyry, *Quaest. hom. Il.* on *Il.* 20.67–75; the translation is that of MacPhail 2011 (slightly modified). For the Greek text see DK 8 A 2. Porphyry emphasizes the problematic nature of the Homeric text by placing "inappropriate" and "not seemly" at the beginning of the first two sentences, respectively, and "unseemly" at the end of the first sentence.

(βλασφημίαι) against the gods, and he gleefully recounts their sufferings as a consequence:

> The poets ... declare that the offspring of the immortals have perpetrated as well as suffered things more atrocious than any perpetrated or suffered by the offspring of the most impious of mortals; aye, the poets have related about the gods themselves tales more outrageous than anyone would dare tell concerning their enemies. For not only have they imputed to them thefts and adulteries, and vassalage among men, but they have fabricated tales of the eating of children, the castrations of fathers, the fetterings of mothers, and many other crimes [ἀνομίας]. For these blasphemies the poets, it is true, did not pay the penalty they deserved, but assuredly they did not escape punishment altogether: some become vagabonds begging for their daily bread; others became blind; another spent all his life in exile from his fatherland and in warring with his kinsmen; and Orpheus, who made a point of rehearsing these tales, died by being torn asunder. Therefore, if we are wise, we shall not imitate their tales, nor while passing laws for the punishment of libels against each other, shall we disregard the unreserved [παρρησίας] vilification of the gods; on the contrary, we shall be on our guard and consider equally guilty of impiety [ἀσεβεῖν] those who recite and those who believe such lies.[8]

The cult of Dionysus[9] was similarly denounced, not only because of various things that initiates did (or were believed to do) that were deemed disgraceful—such as singing hymns to the phallus[10] as well as tearing animals to pieces and eating their flesh raw[11]—but also because Orpheus was

---

8. Isocrates, *Bus.* 38–40 (LCL, modified). Different versions of Orpheus's death circulated in antiquity (see Pausanias, *Descr.* 9.30.5–11; and Graf 1986, 85–86), but the most common tradition was that he died when he was torn into pieces, either by Thracian women or Bacchic maenads. Isocrates gives Orpheus's death a moralizing interpretation, treating it as divine punishment for his slandering the gods. On παρρησία, "frank and unfettered speech," see the studies in Fitzgerald 1996.

9. For a collection of some of the most important sources for the Greek mysteries of Dionysus, see Meyer 1987, 63–109. On Dionysiac cult associations, see esp. Henrichs 1983.

10. Heraclitus of Ephesus charged that "if it were not to Dionysus that they made the procession and sung the hymn to the shameful parts, the deed would be most shameless" (DK 22 B 15; the translation is that of Kirk et al. 1983, 209).

11. Euripides's *Bacchae* is the classic text for the depiction of Dionysus and Dio-

believed to have founded the ancient Greek mysteries of Dionysus,[12] having modeled them on the Egyptian rites for Osiris.[13] Particular opprobrium was reserved for the *Orpheotelestai*, the "initiators of Orpheus," to whom Theophrastus depicts the superstitious man going every month, accompanied by his wife (or if she is too busy, the nurse) and his children, for initiation into the cult (*Char.* 16.12).[14] They appear to have been itinerant initiation priests who hawked their soteriological wares and touted their divinely given power, going "door-to-door" to convince the rich that they had need of their sacred services, which were effective for both the living and the dead. Their wares included a "hubbub of books" (Plato, *Resp.* 364e) that they used in their rituals, which were accompanied by purifications (καθαρμοί) for the living and special rites, called "initiations" (τελεταί) for the deceased, which enabled them to escape the terrors of Hades (*Resp.* 364b–365a). So effective was this religious craftsmanship and the marketing campaign that accompanied it that not only individual laypeople but also entire city-states embraced the worship of Dionysus as well as the Orphic soteriology and eschatology that were central to it (*Resp.* 364e).[15]

The preceding remarks provide the necessary context for appreciating the nature and purpose of an important work on Orphic mythology known as the Derveni papyrus, and it is to the discussion of this papyrus that we now turn.

---

nysian religion from an author who was particularly critical of the attribution of moral shortcomings to the gods.

12. Apollodorus, *Bibl.* 1.3.2. For the link between Orpheus and the Dionysian mysteries, see also Euripides, *Rhes.* 943–944; Aristophanes, *Ran.* 1032; Plato, *Prot.* 316d; Pseudo-Demosthenes, *Or.* 25.11 (= *1 Aristog.* 11); Diodorus Siculus 1.23.1–8; 96.2–6; 3.65.6; 4.25.3; 5.77.3; Pausanias, *Descr.* 2.30.2; 9.30.4; 10.7.2.

13. Diodorus Siculus 1.23.2; 96.4–6; 4.25.3; Plutarch, frg. 212 (Sandbach). Herodotus (*Hist.* 2.81) links Bacchic and Orphic burial rites, derived via Pythagoras from Egypt. Cf. Kern 1922, frg. 237.

14. For bibliography dealing with these itinerant priests, see Diggle 2004, 369–70. The idea of monthly initiations causes some scholars (e.g., Diggle 2004, 369) to interpret τελεσθησόμενος in terms of "to participate in the rites," "to take the sacrament," or "to be consecrated"; but the suggestion of multiple initiations into the same cult is likely to be part of Theophrastus's mockery of the superstitious person.

15. On the *Orpheotelestai* and their religious craftsmanship, see esp. Burkert 1983, 4–6.

The Derveni Papyrus

The Derveni papyrus was discovered in January of 1962 near Derveni, a mountain pass located about 12 kilometers northeast of the city of Thessaloniki in modern Greece. It was found in the debris of a funeral pyre on which it had been burned about 300 B.C.E., with the bones of the person who had been cremated placed in a bronze volute krater inside a tomb near the site of the pyre. When discovered, the tomb had not been plundered, so that a large number of items were found, but none that revealed the name of the deceased, though it is clear that he was a member of the Macedonian elite. The Derveni papyrus had been partly incinerated, and the remaining upper portion of the papyrus was badly charred and in a highly friable condition. To preserve the papyrus, sheets were separated and fragments placed between glass plates.[16] Reconstructing the papyrus, especially its more damaged columns, proved difficult, and the official edition of the papyrus, accompanied by an English translation, introduction, and commentary, was not published until 2006 (Kouremenos et al. 2006). Long before that date, however, investigation of the contents of the papyrus had begun, with numerous studies already published.[17] Now that the official edition has appeared, research on the papyrus will doubtless intensify and new publications will multiply.[18]

The Derveni papyrus is a fourth-century B.C.E. copy of a work that was composed about 400 B.C.E. or perhaps a few decades earlier. The surviving document consists of twenty-six columns of varying breadth and length, with a large number of the columns devoted to the explication of an Orphic cosmogonic and theogonic poem that was written in hexameters and dates from about 500 B.C.E. The Derveni author (as the author of the autograph is usually called) quotes this poem some twenty-four times, then proceeds to indicate the true meaning of the teaching given by Orpheus in the poem.

---

16. On the discovery and preservation of the Derveni papyrus, see Tsantsanoglou in Kouremenos et al. 2006, 1–5; on the contents of the tomb where the deceased was buried, see Barr-Sharrar 2008, 16–18.

17. Some of the most important studies are those of West 1983; Janko 1997, 2001, 2002; Laks and Most 1997; and Betegh 2004.

18. Another edition of the Derveni papyrus text has already appeared in the Teubner series, prepared by Bernabé 2007.

The Derveni author's interpretation of the Orphic mythological poem is remarkable in a number of ways, three of which merit mention. First, he claims that the entire poem is an allegory and is to be interpreted as such. Orpheus, he says, "did not want to tell them unbelievable riddles, but important things in riddles. In fact, he is speaking allegorically from his very first word right through to his last" (7.5–8).[19] This is not the piecemeal application of allegorical interpretation to particular passages that are morally unseemly or problematic in other ways, but rather the use of allegory as a comprehensive method for reading myth.

Second, the author interprets the myth in terms of the science of his day. As is well known, pre-Socratic thinkers were particularly interested in nature and the physical universe, and they gave great attention to the origins of the cosmos, the basic structure of things, and the coherence of things as a whole. Our author cites Heraclitus of Ephesus (fl. 500 B.C.E.) by name (4.8–10), but he is particularly indebted to the physics of Anaxagoras (ca. 500–428 B.C.E.), and his thought has pronounced affinities to that of Diogenes of Apollonia (fl. 440–430 B.C.E.), a thinker who was himself indebted to the thought of Anaxagoras and is generally regarded as the last of the pre-Socratic philosophers. The allegorical method had already been used by Diogenes to interpret Homer. According to Philodemus, "Diogenes praises Homer on the ground that he spoke not mythically but in accord with reality about the divine: for he says that (Homer) believes that Air is Zeus, since (Homer) says that Zeus is omniscient."[20] This kind of interpretation was designed "to reconcile traditional religious belief and practice with the latest scientific progress" (Janko 2001, 5).

The Derveni author does the same thing but appears to go even further than Diogenes in seeking to give a comprehensive "scientific" interpretation of myth. He puts forth the revolutionary thesis that all the Greek deities—Sky, Kronos, Zeus, Earth, Ocean, Air, Mother, Rhea, Aphrodite, Fate, Harmony, Persuasion, and all the other divinities—whether male or female, are simply different names for one and the same God (see esp. 21.5–7; 22.7–11; Janko 2002, 3). Furthermore, he argues that Orpheus "is giving hints about physical reality [περὶ τῶν πραγμάτων] throughout his composition" (13.5–6), so that his poem is really a cosmological allegory about the physical universe. The author then proceeds to show how the

---

19. Translations of the papyrus are chiefly those of Janko 2002 or Tsantsanoglou and Parássoglou in Kouremenos et al. 2006, sometimes modified.

20. Printed in DK 64 A 8; the translation is that of Janko 1997, 80.

philosophical doctrines of Anaxagoras and Diogenes were anticipated and taught by Orpheus.

For example, basic to Anaxagorean and Diogenean physics is the thesis that "nothing comes to be or passes away, but it only appears to do so; rather, things combine and separate. Things are named according to which of the elements dominates [ἐπικρατεῖν] in them" (Janko 1997, 64). Consequently, when the Orphic poem reads:

> Of the firstborn king, the reverend one,[21] and upon him all
> the immortals grew, blessed gods and goddesses,
> and rivers and lovely springs and everything else
> that had been born; and he himself became the sole one (16.3–6),

Orpheus "is indicating that the things which exist [τὰ ὄντα] have always [ἀεί] existed, and those which now are [τὰ νῦν ἐόντα] arise from existent things [ἐκ τῶν ὑπαρχόντων]" (16.7–8). "As for the phrase 'and he himself became the sole one,' by saying this he makes it clear that Mind [νοῦς], being alone, is always worth everything, as if the rest were nothing" (16.9–11).

Next, he proceeds to identify Mind with Air, and subsequently to identify both Air and Fate with Zeus. "Air existed before it was named, and then it was named. For Air existed even before those things which now exist were put together, and it will always exist. For it did not come to be, but existed [οὐ γὰρ ἐγένετο, ἀλλὰ ἦν]" (17.1–3). "Each single thing is named after its dominant element. All things were called 'Zeus' by the same principle, for Air dominates all things so far as it wishes" (19.1–4).

Similarly, "Orpheus called wisdom 'Fate' [*Moira*]" (18.6–7), and "before being called 'Zeus,' Fate was the wisdom of God forever and always. But because (Fate) had been called 'Zeus,' he was [wrongly] thought to have come into existence [γενέσθαι], although he had always existed before but was not named" (18.9–12).

In short, only the names of the deities are new, and the different names serve to mark new stages in the history of the cosmos. Orpheus employed polyonomy in regard to the one high god of the cosmos; this means that Zeus was neither "born" nor came into existence at a particular point in theogonic history but always existed. At a key point in cosmic history, the one high deity became known as "Zeus," and this continues to be his name

---

21. Or, "the penis of the first-born king," as Janko (2002, 33) and others translate it.

at the present time. Furthermore, "this will continue to be his name so long as the things which now exist are put together in the same element in which they had been suspended when they were pre-existent" (17.7–11).

Third, the Derveni author not only uses the poem to articulate his own theology and cosmology but also repeatedly attacks alternative interpretations of the poem. He refers derisively to nonallegorical interpreters of the myths as those who "do not understand" (οὐ γινώσκοντες: 9.2; 12.5; 18.14; 23.5; 26.8; see also 20.2). Inasmuch as such people are identical to those who refuse to learn (οὐ μανθάνουσιν), they are in a state of ignorance (ἀμαθίη: 5.9–10) and thus "quite mistaken" (ἐξαμαρτάνουσι) in their interpretations (12.4–5). Allegorists such as himself, by contrast, are counted among "those who correctly comprehend" (τοῖς ὀρθῶς γινῶσκουσιν: 23.2) because they have deciphered the difficult riddles found in the texts of Orpheus (7.4–5).[22]

Three Aims of the Derveni Author

The ultimate aim of the Derveni author is debated, but at least three purposes seem quite likely.[23] First, he sets out to demonstrate that Orpheus composed a "hymn that tells of wholesome and permissible things" (7.2). His poem is not intended as legislation for the masses but is designed "to teach those who are pure of hearing" (7.10–11). His aim, in short, is apologetic. Orphic myths, which seemed grotesque to many people, are not at all repugnant, but wholesome when they are properly interpreted by those who are morally pure.

Second, he insists "that mere participation in sacred rites cannot be effective unless accompanied by understanding."[24] Column 20 is a blistering attack on "those people who have performed the rites and been initiated in the cities," but who nevertheless "do not comprehend them" (20.1–2). Even worse are those who have paid the initiation fee, been privately instructed,

---

22. The material in this paragraph is borrowed from my brief discussion of the Derveni papyrus in Fitzgerald 2004. Note: Anyone who consults this article will find a number of mistakes (repetitions, etc.) that the copyeditor, without consultation, introduced after I had submitted it. The publisher has promised to correct these should there ever be a corrected edition.

23. See the survey and discussion by Kouremenos in Kouremenos et al. 2006, 45–58. I make no claim that the three listed aims are exhaustive.

24. Kouremenos in Kouremenos et al. 2006, 46.

and yet depart from the initiation ceremony with no more understanding than they had beforehand. Such people have wasted their money (20.3–12), and his interpretation will impart to his readers the knowledge that they should have received when initiated but did not.[25]

Third, the Derveni author offers allegory as an interpretive strategy that prevents the dismissal of Orphic theology by those who think that the literal meaning of the myths is ridiculous. Seen in this way, allegory for him is fundamentally a religious practice (Laks 1997, 138), undertaken for the explicit theological purpose of comprehending the meaning of a *hieros logos*, a sacred utterance or sacred story, such as the poem that he explicates.[26] But it is more than that. It is a *necessary* practice when approaching religious mythology because ignorance is tantamount to lack of faith (5.10), and "to take rituals and sacred texts literally, rather than interpret them allegorically as an explanation of the universe fully in accord with Anaxagorean physics, is to risk losing one's faith" (Janko 2002, 3). Thus he criticizes profane individuals who, overcome by error and pleasure, do not believe in the "terrors of Hades" (5.5–11) that were a standard component of Orphic myth and initiation rites.

As these three aims imply, the Derveni author was neither an opponent of Orphism nor one who was disdainful of religion and religious texts. He is rather, to use the language of Amos Funkenstein (1986),[27] a "secular theologian" committed to both religion and science. "He firmly believes that both Orpheus' revelation and contemporary physics are true," though obviously not in the same way (Most 1997, 122). On the one hand, he is "an up to date believer in divine providence and omnipotence" (Laks 1997, 138), a man for whom "Orpheus is his central spiritual authority" (Most 1997, 122). On the other hand, he is fully convinced of the truth of Anaxagorean physics, and he interprets Orpheus in that scientific light. He is, in short, an ancient example of religious secularization (Laks 1997, 138), "a movement within religion that does not dream of questioning the authority of a sacred text but accepts the challenge of accommodating that text to the most up-to-date doctrines of contemporary secular science" (Most

---

25. On the links between the text and initiation, see esp. Calame 1997, 2005; and Obbink 1997, 2003.

26. On the *hieros logos* (sacred utterance or story) in Greek religion, see Baumgarten 1998.

27. I owe the reference to Funkenstein to both Laks 1997, 138 n. 58; and Most 1997, 122.

1997, 122). His work stems from a period of religious crisis in Greece, which culminated with the execution of Socrates in 399 B.C.E. on charges of impiety. For him, the true impiety was for the profane to dismiss Orphic myth because of a mistaken idea about what it meant. Uncomprehending initiates, on the other hand, deserve pity (20.5, 8) because they sought knowledge but were not given it. Through his allegorical interpretation of the sacred story, he offered enlightenment to all who wished to know the truth of Orphic teaching.

Works Cited

Athanassiadi, Polymnia, and Michael Frede. 1999. *Pagan Monotheism in Late Antiquity*. Oxford: Clarendon.

Barr-Sharrar, Beryl. 2008. *The Derveni Krater: Masterpiece of Classical Greek Metalwork*. Ancient Art and Architecture in Context 1. Princeton: American School of Classical Studies at Athens.

Baumgarten, Roland. 1998. *Heiliges Wort und Heilige Schrift bei den Griechen: Hieroi Logoi und verwandte Erscheinungen*. ScriptOralia 110, series A: Altertumswissenschaftliche Reihe 26. Tübingen: Narr.

Bernabé, Albert, ed. 2007. Papyrus Derveni. Pages 169–269 in *Musaeus, Linus, Epimenides, Papyrus Derveni, Indices*. Part 2, fasc. 3 of *Poetae epici Graeci: Testimonia et fragmenta*. Bibliotheca scriptorum Graecorum et Romanorum Teubneriana. Berlin: de Gruyter.

Betegh, Gábor. 2004. *The Derveni Papyrus: Cosmology, Theology and Interpretation*. Cambridge: Cambridge University Press.

Burkert, Walther. 1983. Craft versus Sect: The Problem of Orphics and Pythagoreans. Pages 1–22 in *Self-Definition in the Greco-Roman World*. Vol. 3 of *Jewish and Christian Self-Definition*. Edited by Ben E. Meyer and E. P. Sanders. Philadelphia: Fortress.

Calame, Claude. 1997. Figures of Sexuality and Initiatory Transition in the Derveni Theogony and Its Commentary. Pages 65–80 in *Studies on the Derveni Papyrus*. Edited by André Laks and Glenn W. Most. Oxford: Clarendon.

———. 2005. Orphic Voices and Initiatory Functions: The Derveni Theogony and Its Commentary. Pages 157–69 in *Masks of Authority: Fiction and Pragmatics in Ancient Greek Poetics*. Myth and Poetics. Ithaca, N.Y.: Cornell University Press.

Diels, Hermann, and Walther Krantz, eds. and trans. 1954. *Die Fragmente*

der Vorsokratiker: Griechisch und Deutsch. 3 vols. 7th ed. Berlin: Weidmann.
Diggle, James, ed. 2004. *Theophrastus: Characters*. Cambridge: Cambridge University Press.
Fitzgerald, John T., ed. 1996. *Friendship, Flattery, and Frankness of Speech: Studies on Friendship in the New Testament World*. Novum Testamentum Supplement 82. Leiden: Brill.
———. 2004. Lexicography Theory and Biblical Interpretation. Pages 49–53 in *Methods of Biblical Interpretation*. Nashville: Abingdon.
Funkenstein, Amos. 1986. *Theology and the Scientific Imagination from the Late Middle Ages to the Seventeenth Century*. Princeton: Princeton University Press.
Graf, Fritz. 1986. Orpheus: A Poet among Men. Pages 80–106 in *Interpretations of Greek Mythology*. Edited by Jan Bremmer. Totowa, N.J.: Barnes & Noble.
Henrichs, Albert. 1983. Changing Dionysiac Identities. Pages 137–70 in *Self-Definition in the Greco-Roman World*. Vol. 3 of *Jewish and Christian Self-Definition*. Edited by Ben E. Meyer and E. P. Sanders. Philadelphia: Fortress.
Janko, Richard. 1997. The Physicist as Hierophant: Aristophanes, Socrates and the Authorship of the Derveni Papyrus. *ZPE* 118:61–94.
———. 2001. The Derveni Papyrus (Diagoras of Melos, *Apopyrgizontes Logoi?*): A New Translation. *CP* 96:1–32.
———. 2002. The Derveni Papyrus: An Interim Text. *ZPE* 141:1–62.
Kahn, Charles H. Xenophanes. 1996. Page 1628 in *The Oxford Classical Dictionary*. Edited by Simon Hornblower and Antony Spawforth. 3rd ed. Oxford: Oxford University Press.
Kern, Otto, ed. 1922. *Orphicorum Fragmenta*. Berlin: Weidmann.
Kirk, G. S., J. E. Raven, and M. Schofield. 1983. *The Presocratic Philosophers: A Critical History with a Selection of Texts*. 2nd ed. Cambridge: Cambridge University Press.
Konstan, David, and Iliara Ramelli. 2009. Allegory: Greco-Roman Antiquity. Columns 780–85 in vol. 1 of *Encyclopedia of the Bible and Its Reception*. Edited by Hans-Josef Klauck et al. Berlin: de Gruyter.
Kouremenos, Theokritos, George M. Parássoglou, and Kyriakos Tsantsanoglou, eds. and trans. 2006. *The Derveni Papyrus*. Studi e testi per il corpus dei papiri filosofici greci e latini 13. Firenze: Olschki.
Laks, André. 1997. Between Religion and Philosophy: The Function of Allegory in the Derveni Papyrus. *Phronesis* 42:121–42.

Laks, André, and Glenn W. Most, eds. 1997. *Studies on the Derveni Papyrus*. Oxford: Clarendon.

Lamberton, Robert, trans. 1983. *On the Cave of the Nymphs*. Barrytown, N.Y.: Station Hill.

Lesher, J. H. 1992. *Xenophanes of Colophon: Fragments. A Text and Translation with a Commentary. Phoenix* Supplementary Series 30. Phoenix Presocratics Series 4. Toronto: University of Toronto Press.

Lobel, Edgar, and Denys Page, eds. 1997. *Poetarum Lesbiorum Fragmenta*. Repr., Oxford: Clarendon.

MacPhail, John A., Jr., trans. 2011. *Porphyry's Homeric Questions on the Iliad: Text, Translation, Commentary*. Texte und Kommentare 36. New York: de Gruyter.

McGonagill, Gary Lance. 2001. A History of Allegorical Interpretation from Homer through Lucretius. Ph.D. diss. Harvard University.

Meyer, Marvin W., ed. 1987. *The Ancient Mysteries: A Sourcebook. Sacred Texts of the Mystery Religions of the Ancient Mediterranean World*. New York: Harper & Row.

Most, Glenn W. 1997. The Fire Next Time: Cosmology, Allegoresis, and Salvation in the Derveni Papyrus. *Journal of Hellenic Studies* 117:117–35.

Obbink, Dirk. 1997. Cosmology as Initiation versus the Critique of Orphic Mysteries. Pages 39–54 in *Studies on the Derveni Papyrus*. Edited by André Laks and Glenn W. Most. Oxford: Clarendon.

———. 2003. Allegory and Exegesis in the Derveni Papyrus: The Origin of Greek Scholarship. Pages 177–88 in *Metaphor, Allegory, and the Classical Tradition: Ancient Thought and Modern Revisions*. Edited by G. R. Boys-Stones. Oxford: Oxford University Press.

Ramelli, Ilaria, ed. 2007. *Allegoristi dell'età classica: Opere e frammenti*. Milan: Bompiani.

Ramelli, Ilaria, and Giulio A. Lucchetta. 2004. *L'età classica*. Vol. 1 of *Allegoria*. Milan: Vita e Pensiero.

Rice, David G., and John E. Stambaugh, eds. 1979. *Sources for the Study of Greek Religion*. SBL Sources for Biblical Study 14. Missoula, Mont.: Scholars Press.

Sandbach, F. H., ed. and trans. 1969. *Plutarch's Moralia*. Vol. 15. LCL. Cambridge: Harvard University Press.

Tate, J. 1927. The Beginnings of Greek Allegory. *Classical Review* 41:214–15.

West, M. L. 1983. *The Orphic Poems*. Oxford: Clarendon.

Part 3
Myth Theorizing and the Bible: A Conversation

THE LIFE OF KING SAUL AS MYTH

Robert A. Segal

The study of hero myths goes back at least to 1871, when the Victorian anthropologist E. B. Tylor argued that many of them follow a uniform plot: the hero is exposed at birth, is saved by other humans or animals, and grows up to become a national hero (see Tylor 1871, 1:254–55).[1] In 1876 the Austrian scholar Johann Georg von Hahn used fourteen cases to argue that all "Aryan" hero tales follow an "exposure and return" formula more comprehensive than Tylor's (see von Hahn 1876, 340). In each case the hero is born illegitimately, out of the fear of the prophecy of his future greatness is abandoned by his father, is saved by animals and raised by a lowly couple, fights wars, returns home triumphant, defeats his persecutors, frees his mother, becomes king, founds a city, and dies young. Similarly, in 1928 the Russian folklorist Vladimir Propp sought to demonstrate that in Russian fairy tales the hero goes off on a successful adventure and upon his return marries and gains the throne (see Propp 1968). Propp's pattern skirts both the birth and the death of the hero.

All three of these scholars limited themselves to finding a pattern and, despite their own theoretical inclinations, did not seek to answer the main theoretical questions: What are the origin, function, and subject matter of hero myths? Of the scholars who have not only delineated patterns but also considered these theoretical questions, the most important have been the Viennese psychoanalyst Otto Rank (1884–1939), the American mythographer Joseph Campbell (1904–1987), and the English folklorist Lord Raglan (1885–1964). Rank later broke irreparably with Sigmund Freud, but when he wrote the first edition of *The Myth of the Birth of the Hero* (*Der Mythus von der Geburt des Helden* [1909]), he was a Freudian apostle (ET 1914).[2]

---

1. On the history of hero patterns, see Dundes 1990 [1977].
2. On the change from the first, Freudian edition of *Myth* to the second, post-

Freud himself wrote the section of the work on the "family romance" (see Rank 2004, 59–62; Freud 1959). While Campbell was never a full-fledged Jungian, he wrote *The Hero with a Thousand Faces* (1949) as a kindred soul of Jung. Raglan wrote *The Hero* (1936 [citations are from Rank et al. 1990]) as a theoretical ally of Frazer. The most influential recent theorist of hero myths has been the French-born literary theorist René Girard. But unlike Rank, Campbell, and Raglan, Girard offers no pattern for hero myths (see especially Girard 1977).

I will outline the theories of Rank and Raglan and then apply them to the life of King Saul.[3] With more space, I would do the same with the theories of Campbell and Girard.

Otto Rank

The Myth of the Birth of the Hero evinces early psychoanalytic theory. Contemporary Freudians, spurred by the development of ego psychology, regard myth far more positively than Freud and the early Rank did. For contemporary psychoanalysts, myths solve problems rather than perpetuate them, are progressive rather than regressive, and abet adjustment to the world rather than flight from it. Myths serve to sublimate and redirect, not merely to vent, bottled-up drives. Myths are as different from dreams as akin to them. And myths serve everyone, not just neurotics.[4] Nevertheless, Rank's monograph remains the classic Freudian analysis of hero myths.

For Rank, following Freud, heroism deals only with what *Jungians* call the first half of life. The first half, from birth through young adulthood, involves the establishment of oneself as an independent person in the external world. The attainment of independence expresses itself concretely in the securing of a job and a mate. The securing of either requires both separation from one's parents and mastery of one's instincts. To depend on one's parents for the satisfaction of instincts and to satisfy instincts in antisocial ways is to be stuck, or fixated, at a childish psychological level.

Freudian one, see my introduction to Rank 2004. Citations to the 1st edition are to Rank et al. 1990.

3. For a full exposition of all four of these theories of hero myths, see my introduction to Segal 2000, 1–38.

4. On the contemporary Freudian approach to myth, see Arlow 1961.

Roughly paralleling von Hahn's pattern, of which he was apparently unaware, Rank's pattern goes from the hero's birth to his attainment of a "career":

> The hero is the child of most distinguished parents, usually the son of a king. His origin is preceded by difficulties, such as continence, or prolonged barrenness, or secret intercourse of the parents due to external prohibition or obstacles. During or before the pregnancy, there is a prophecy, in the form of a dream or oracle, cautioning against his birth, and usually threatening danger to the father (or his representative). As a rule, he is surrendered to the water, in a box. He is then saved by animals, or by lowly people (shepherds), and is suckled by a female animal or by an humble woman. After he has grown up, he finds his distinguished parents, in a highly versatile fashion. He takes his revenge on his father, on the one hand, and is acknowledged, on the other. Finally he achieves rank and honors. (Rank et al. 1990, 57)

Literally, or consciously, the hero, who is always male, is a historical or legendary figure like Oedipus. The hero is heroic because he rises from obscurity to the throne. Literally, he is an innocent victim of either his parents or, ultimately, Fate. While his parents have yearned for a child and abandon him only to save the father, they nevertheless do abandon him. The hero's revenge, if the parricide is even committed knowingly, is then understandable: who would not consider killing one's would-be killer?

Symbolically, or unconsciously, the hero is heroic not because he dares to win a throne but because he dares to kill his father. The killing is definitely intentional, and the cause is not revenge but sexual frustration: "the deepest, generally unconscious root of the dislike of the son for the father, or of two brothers for each other, is related to be competition for the tender devotion and love of the mother" (Rank et al. 1990, 66). Too horrendous to face, the true meaning of the hero myth gets covered up by the concocted story. Rather than the culprit, the hero becomes an innocent victim or at worst a justified avenger: "The fictitious romance [i.e., the myth] is the excuse, as it were, for the hostile feelings which the child harbors against his father, and which in this fiction are projected against the father" (Rank et al. 1990, 63). What the hero seeks gets masked as power, not incest. Most of all, who the hero is becomes some third party, a historical or legendary figure, rather than either the creator of the myth or anyone stirred by it. Identifying himself with the literal hero, the mythmaker or reader vicariously revels in the hero's triumph, which in fact is his own. *He* is the real hero of the myth.

The royal or aristocratic pedigree of the hero bears on the second of the two childhood wishes that hero myths fulfill: the wish for perfect parents. This wish, not to be considered here, is separate from the Oedipal wish.

Literally, the myth culminates in the hero's attainment of a throne. Symbolically, the hero gains a mate as well. One might, then, conclude that the myth fittingly expresses the Freudian goal of the first half of life. In actuality, it expresses the opposite. The wish it fulfills is not for detachment from one's parents and from one's antisocial instincts but, on the contrary, for the most intense possible relationship to one's parents and the most antisocial of urges: parricide and incest, even rape. Taking one's father's job and one's mother's hand does not quite spell independence of them.

The mythmaker or reader is an adult, but the wish vented is that of a child of three to five: "Myths are, therefore, created by adults, by means of retrograde childhood fantasies, the hero being credited with the mythmaker's personal infantile history" (Rank et al. 1990, 71). The fantasy is the fulfillment of the Oedipal wish to kill one's father in order to gain access to one's mother. The myth fulfills a wish never outgrown by the adult who either invents or uses it. That adult is psychologically an eternal child. He is neurotic: "There is a certain class of persons, the so-called psychoneurotics, shown by the teachings of Freud to have remained children, in a sense, although otherwise appearing grown-up" (Rank et al. 1990, 58). Since no mere child can overpower his father, the mythmaker imagines being old enough to do so. In short, the myth expresses not the Freudian goal of the first half of life but the fixated childhood goal that keeps one from accomplishing it.

To be sure, the fullfillment of the Oedipal wish is symbolic rather than literal, disguised rather than overt, unconscious rather than conscious, vicarious rather than direct, and mental rather than physical. By identifying himself with the hero, the creator or reader of the myth acts out in his mind deeds that he would never dare act out in the real world. Still, the myth does provide fulfillment of a kind and, in light of the conflict between the neurotic's impulses and the neurotic's morals, provides the best possible fulfillment.

Rank's theory can be criticized on multiple grounds. One can grant the pattern while denying the Freudian meaning, which, after all, reverses the surface one. Or one can deny the pattern itself. Certainly the pattern fits only those male hero myths that cover heroes in the first half of life.

Excluded, for example, would be the bulk of the myths of Odysseus and Aeneas, who are largely adult heroes. Rank's own examples come from Europe, the Near East, and India and may not fit heroes from elsewhere.

Rank's pattern scarcely fits his own examples, a few of them biblical. Moses, for example, is hardly the son of Pharaoh, does not kill or seek to kill Pharaoh, and does not succeed Pharaoh. Moses is the son of lowly rather than noble parents, is exposed by his parents to save rather than to kill him, and is saved by the daughter of Pharaoh.

Yet far from oblivious to these departures from his scheme, Rank appeals both to nonbiblical versions of the Moses saga that come closer to his pattern and, even more, to aspects of the biblical account that hint at the pattern. Pharaoh's fear of the coming generation of Israelite males and consequent attempt to have them killed at birth, while not directed at Moses specifically, parallel a hero's father's fear and attempted killing of his newborn son. Moses' Israelite father, who is not even named, is secondary to the story, which is about Moses versus Pharaoh. Lacunae at the surface level hint at a disguise. The literal level masks, if also reveals, the symbolic one.

Lord Raglan

Lord Raglan ties hero myths and in fact all myths to rituals. His brand of "myth-ritualism" derives ultimately from the anthropologist J. G. Frazer (1922) by way of the biblicist S. H. Hooke (1933). For both Frazer and Hooke, myth provides the script for ritual. The key ritual involves the king, but Frazer and Hooke conflate two forms of the ritual.[5] In one form the king is a mere human being and simply plays the role of the god. The dramatic enactment of the death and rebirth of the god, who is the god of vegetation, magically causes the rebirth of the presently dead god and in turn of presently dead vegetation. The ritual is performed annually at the end—the would-be end—of winter.

In the other form of the ritual the king is himself divine, with the god of vegetation residing in him, and is actually killed and replaced. The soul of the god is thereby transferred to the new king. The killing of the king does not magically induce the killing of the god but on the contrary pre-

---

5. On the different versions of the ritual presented by both Frazer and Hooke, see my introduction to Segal 1998, 4–6.

serves the health of the god. The king is killed at the first sign of weakness or at the end of a fixed term so short as to minimize the chance of illness or death in office. The state of the king determines the state of the god of vegetation and in turn the state of vegetation itself.

Raglan adopts this second version of the ritual.[6] The killing and replacement of the king *are* the death and rebirth—better, the weakening and reinvigoration—of the god of vegetation and therefore of vegetation itself. The myth describes the life of the figure and the ritual enacts it. The ritual functions to aid the community.

Venturing beyond both Frazer and Hooke, Raglan equates the king with the hero. For Frazer and Hooke, the king may in effect be a hero to his community, but Raglan labels him one. Like Rank, Raglan turns a theory of myth in general into a theory of hero myths in particular. Moreover, Raglan, like Rank, introduces his own detailed hero pattern, which he applies to twenty-one myths, two of them biblical. Unlike Rank's, Raglan's pattern extends from the hero's conception all the way to his death and thus covers both halves of life:

1. The hero's mother is a royal virgin;
2. His father is a king, and
3. Often a near relative of his mother, but
4. The circumstances of his conception are unusual, and
5. He is also reputed to be the son of a god.
6. At birth an attempt is made, usually by his father or his maternal grandfather, to kill him, but
7. He is spirited away, and
8. Reared by foster-parents in a far country.
9. We are told nothing of his childhood, but
10. On reaching manhood he returns or goes to his future kingdom.
11. After a victory over the king and/or a giant, dragon, or wild beast,
12. He marries a princess, often the daughter of his predecessor, and
13. Becomes king.

---

6. For Raglan's own ritualist analysis of the Oedipus myth, see Raglan 1933, especially ch. 26. In addition to *The Hero*, see Raglan 1945; 1949, especially chs. 9–10.

14. For a time he reigns uneventfully, and
15. Prescribes laws, but
16. Later he loses favour with the gods and/or his subjects, and
17. Is driven from the throne and city, after which
18. He meets with a mysterious death,
19. Often at the top of a hill.
20. His children, if any, do not succeed him.
21. His body is not buried, but nevertheless
22. He has one or more holy sepulchres. (Rank et al. 1990, 138)

Clearly, parts 1-13 correspond roughly to Rank's entire scheme, though Raglan himself never read Rank. Six of Raglan's cases duplicate Rank's, and the anti-Freudian Raglan nevertheless also takes the case of Oedipus as his standard.[7] The victory that gives the hero the throne is not, however, Oedipal, for the vanquished is not necessarily his father, and the father is not always the one who had sought his son's death at birth. For Rank, the heart of the hero pattern is gaining kingship—or other title. For Raglan, the heart is losing kingship.

Rank's hero succeeds at the expense of everyone else; Raglan's saves everyone else. In the myth Raglan's hero is driven from the community, and in the accompanying ritual is sacrificed by the community. Like Rank's hero, Raglan's must be male. More narrowly than Rank's hero, Raglan's must be not merely at least aristocratic but outright royal.

For all Raglan's touting of the symbiosis of myth and ritual, his myth and ritual seem incongruously out of sync. In the myth the protagonist is usually human. In the ritual the protagonist is always divine. Raglan nevertheless equates the hero of the myth with the god of the ritual. Many of the events in the life of the hero are supernatural, so that the hero must in fact be divine. Kingship links the hero to the god: heroes are kings, and kings are gods. True, the hero must die, but the hero's death accomplishes a superhuman feat: it ensures the revival of vegetation and thereby the survival of the kingdom. Raglan's heroes have the power to affect the physical world, even if only by dying. And gods, not just humans, die.

Yet where the myth runs from the birth of the protagonist to his mysterious death, the ritual enacts only the portion of the myth that corre-

---

7. For Raglan's own ritualist analysis of the Oedipus myth, see Raglan 1933, especially ch. 26.

sponds to the replacement of the king: the exile of the incumbent. But for Raglan the core of the myth—the toppling of the king—corresponds to the undeniable core of the ritual—the killing of the king once he weakens or completes his term. Strictly, the myth, which describes the life of a past hero, is less the script than the inspiration for the ritual, which involves the killing of the present king. Therefore the myth need not track the ritual. The myth serves to spur the king to submit to the ritual and thereby become the savior of his subjects.

Like Rank's theory, Raglan's can be questioned on various counts. One might grant the mythic pattern but deny a connection to ritual. Or one might grant some connection but deny that, in light of the disparity between the myth and the ritual, it takes Raglan's form. Or one might deny the pattern itself—denying either that it applies worldwide (see Cook 1965) or that it even applies substantially to Raglan's own cases. By Raglan's own tally, none of his examples scores all twenty-two points, and one scores only nine. What of hero myths in which the hero, rather than seeking or becoming king, remains the outsider in conflict with the established king—for example, Achilles's conflict with Agamemnon in the *Iliad* (see Jackson 1982)? Rank can at least assert that hero myths which stray from his scheme are distortions created to keep the true pattern hidden. Raglan has no comparable ploy: nothing in his pattern needs to be kept secret. Why, then, do not any of his hero myths, not to say all hero myths, attain perfect scores?

Rank Applied to the Life of Saul (1 Samuel 8–31)

Taken straightforwardly—that is, without the use of Rank—the life of Saul is purportedly history. It tells the story of the selection of Saul as the first king of Israel and of his career as king. Taken psychoanalytically, the life of Saul is not history but fantasy. The life is not fantasy because the history is unreliable—a charge that has been made more vehemently in the last few decades by "minimalists" than ever before.[8] Rather, the life of Saul, taken psychoanalytically, operates independently of history as a vehicle for the realization of a childhood fantasy: a son killing his father. Whom Saul wishes dead and who wishes Saul dead, we shall see. Where minimal-

---

8. "Minimalists" include the following authors in the bibliography: Exum, Finkelstein, Lemche, J. Miller, and Whitelam.

ists reject the Bible as history, psychoanalysts see the Bible as operating irrespective of history.

Taken straightforwardly, the life of Saul is about a nation. Saul's troubled personality is noteworthy only because of his office. Taken psychoanalytically, the life of Saul is about a family. Taken straightforwardly, the conflicts in Saul's life are with Samuel, David, and God. Taken psychoanalytically, the main conflicts in Saul's life are with his father. Taken straightforwardly, the conflicts are hard to avoid. Taken psychoanalytically, the conflicts are unavoidable.

Looked at psychoanalytically, all of 1 and 2 Samuel is about succession. The focus is less on what judges and kings accomplish *while in office* than on how long they *last in office*. Judgeship, like kingship, is at least tacitly hereditary. Eli's sons do not succeed him only because of their disobedience. Samuel, having been adopted as a surrogate son, replaces Eli. True, Samuel does not kill Eli, but Samuel in effect succeeds Eli even while Eli is still alive. Under Eli, the ark is captured by the Philistines and his sons are killed. Under Samuel, the ark is retrieved. The younger generation outshines the older.

The relationship between Samuel and Saul is overtly antagonistic. In the antimonarchical and anti-Saul narrative, which Julius Wellhausen (1885 [1878]) called the Late Source and which has been argued over ever since, the people demand a king.[9] As with Eli, so here: the judge's sons are unfit to succeed him. But the people also want a king "to govern us like all the [other] nations" (1 Sam 8:4–6). Samuel takes their demand as a rejection of him, even after God, committing the fallacy of the excluded middle, assures him that it is he, God, who has really been rejected (see 8:7).[10] Samuel thus delights in Saul's subsequent failings and in conveying

---

9. On the history of textual scholarship since Wellhausen, see Weiser 1961, 157–70; Eissfeldt 1965, 241–48; Fohrer 1968, 217–27; Birch 1976, ch. 6; Ishida 1977, 27–28; Vannoy 1978, 197–225; Halpern 1981, ch. 6; Eslinger 1983, 61–63; Foresti 1984, 15–24; Baldwin 1988, 20–32; Halpern 1988, ch. 8; Alter 1999, x–xi.

10. The demand for a king is predicted back in Deut 17:14–20, but there the demand is not taken as a repudiation of God, in which case the demand in 1 Sam 8 is "legitimate": see Jobling 1986, 58–63; 1998, 48–49. In Judges (8:22–9:57) Gideon resists the call to be king, whereas his illegitimate son Abimelech makes himself king; see Jobling 1986, 64–89; 1998, 46–50. On Samuel as self-servingly opposing God's decision to grant kingship, see Polzin 1989, 81–88.

to Saul invariably bad news.[11] Samuel dies before Saul and so can hardly kill him. But as with Eli, so with Saul: the news of God's rejection conveyed by Samuel does Saul in. And while Saul dies by his own sword rather than at the hands of someone else, the selection of David in place of him is what drives him to "self-harm."

In the anti-Saul narrative God takes Israel's demand for a king as rejection because till now God has deemed himself the king of Israel: "they [the people] have rejected me from being king over them" (1 Sam 8:7).[12] God thereby makes the king, whoever he is, equal to himself. And surely the elders demand a king in part because of the failure of God so far to defeat Israel's enemies.[13] In his farewell speech Samuel condemns the people's pairing of Saul with God: "And when you [the people] saw that Nahash the king of the Ammonites came against you, you said to me, 'No, but a king shall reign over us,' when the LORD your God was your king" (12:12).

For God, the rejection is like that of a father rejected by his children, as in the case of King Lear—though here by his sons insofar as the elders, who demand a king, are all male. Like a father, God has liberated his children from slavery in Egypt, given them the promised land, and begun to defeat their enemies. Yet they have continually rejected him by above all "serving other gods" (8:8). And who is to replace God now? One of his "sons."

For God to view a human king as his replacement, he must see that king as more than human. Hence even in the anti-Saul narrative Saul, while chosen by lot[14] and while ridiculed for hiding "among the baggage" when Samuel arrives (10:22), is still "taller than any of the people from his shoulders upward" (10:23). In mythology, in contrast to sophisticated theology, the difference between gods and humans is one of degree only: gods are bigger, stronger, or handsomer than humans.[15] (That God is anthropomorphized is exemplified in Samuel's speaking "in the ears of the LORD"

---

11. On Samuel as self-servingly supporting Saul against God's decision to remove him, see Polzin 1989, 104, 146–47.

12. On God as king, see Halpern 1981, 61–85.

13. On the Philistine god as possibly stronger than the Israelite God, see Miller and Roberts 1977, 66–75.

14. On the place of lots here and elsewhere in 1 Samuel, see Lindblom 1962b; Polzin 1989, 103–4.

15. On Gilgamesh as bigger, stronger, and handsomer than his subjects because he is two-thirds divine, see Callender 2000, 99–100.

[8:21].) When, in even the anti-Saul narrative, Samuel declares to the people, "Do you see him whom the LORD has chosen? There is none like him among all the people" (10:24), Saul is again being elevated to divinity.[16] The pro-monarchy and pro-Saul narrative that Wellhausen called the Early Source describes Saul not only as likewise "taller than any of the people" "from his shoulders upward" but also as the "handsomest" man in Israel (9:2)—an additional mark of divinity.[17] Saul need scarcely be godlike in all respects to qualify as a god. Few gods are divine in more than one respect.[18]

The psychoanalytic stake in elevating Saul to a god is to put him on a par with God "the father." There cannot be a conflict between father and son if the father is divine and the son human, even while allowing for cases of crossbreeding such as that of Heracles. Saul's being put on a par with God makes God his human father.

According to the pro-Saul narrative, God appoints Saul to succeed where Israel, even under Samuel's dutiful leadership, has so far failed: to defeat the ever-threatening Philistines. As God himself says to Samuel just before Saul arrives, "Tomorrow about this time I will send to you a man from the land of Benjamin, and you shall anoint him to be prince over my people Israel. He shall save my people from the hand of the Philistines" (9:16). Together with his son Jonathan, Saul does defeat Israel's enemies: "When Saul had taken the kingship over Israel, he fought against all his enemies on every side, ... and delivered Israel out of the hands of those who plundered them" (14:47–48). Yet even so, Saul loses God's favor and thereby his royal line. (By contrast, in the anti-Saul source, God takes credit for saving Israel: see 1:18–19.)

The pro-Saul material gives several reasons for Saul's loss of favor. The first reason is that the desperate Saul, with his army deserting him, offers sacrifices himself rather than waiting any longer for Samuel.[19] This reason

---

16. To be sure, God faults Samuel for assuming that Jesse's son Eliab is God's choice to succeed Saul just because of Eliab's height and looks: see 1 Sam 16:6–12. See Alter 1981, 149–50; Edelman 1991, 115.

17. The folkloristic character of 1 Sam 9:1–10:16 has been recognized since Gressmann 1921, 26ff.

18. On the king as God's son, see von Rad 1962, 41–42.

19. On this sin, see Smith 1899, 96–98; Goldman 1951, 71–72; Hertzberg 1964, 105–6; Ackroyd 1971, 105–6; Gunn 1980, 33–40, 66–67; 1981, 93–94; McCarter 1980, 229–30; Klein 1983, 126–28; Gordon 1986, 133–34; Baldwin 1988, 104–6; Long 1989, 87–90, 132; Polzin 1989, 126–31; Edelman 1991, 77–80; Jobling 1998, 80–82; Alter 1999, 72–73; Nicholson 2002, 41–42; Green 2003, 237–40.

is to be found in neither the main anti-Saul nor the pro-Saul material but in what is conventionally considered a third source, one even more hostile to Saul than the main anti-Saul source. Saul's usurpation of the role of Samuel again pits Saul against Samuel, who then gloatingly informs Saul that had Saul not disobeyed, "the LORD would have established your kingdom forever," but that "now your kingdom shall not continue" and that "the LORD has [already] sought out a man after his own heart; and the LORD has appointed him to be prince over his people" (13:13–14). Samuel, while not quite restored to his premonarchical position, has bested his rival and has set up the conflict between Saul and David.

The pro-Saul narrative makes Saul seem less disobedient than impulsive or careless. Saul commits three sins. First, he halts the priest's consulting the oracle to find out how to proceed when the noise from the Philistines indicates that they are coming and that there is no time to wait for God's answer (see 14:19). Second, Saul fails to ensure that the prohibition against eating on the day that the Philistines attacked reached Jonathan, who eats honey (see 14:24–28). When informed of the prohibition, Jonathan still allows his men to defy it—on the grounds that his father's prohibition has made the men too weak for battle (see 14:28–30).[20] (Someone should have reminded Saul of Napoleon's observation that an army marches on its stomach.) Third, Saul's men, faint from having fought without eating, eat the captured spoils with the blood still in the animals' bodies (see 14:31–33)—in violation of Lev 19:26 and Deut 12:16. Saul's disobedience in the pro-Saul narrative is not nearly so damning as that in the anti-Saul narrative, for Saul proceeds to defeat decisively Israel's enemies (see 14:47–48). In the anti-Saul narrative Saul seems desperate to please both Samuel and God but can never please either.

The anti-Saul narrative gives but one reason for Saul's loss of God's favor: Saul's failure to obey God's commandment to kill all the Amalekites and all their animals (see 1 Sam 15).[21] Again, Saul's disobedience

---

20. On Jonathan's action, see Smith 1899, 113–25; Goldman 1951, 79–80, 83–84; Blenkinsopp 1964; Hertzberg 1964, 114–15, 117–18; Ackroyd 1971, 115; Mauchline 1971, 118–20; Gunn 1980, 65–69; 1981, 95–96; McCarter 1980, 250–52; Klein 1983, 138–43; Gordon 1986, 139–41; Baldwin 1988, 109–10; Polzin 1989, 135–37; Edelman 1991, 88–91; Alter 1999, 80–84; Green 2003, 243–47.

21. On this sin, see Smith 1899, 128–41; Goldman 1951, 89–90; Hertzberg 1964, 124–30; Ackroyd 1971, 122–23, 125–26; Mauchline 1971, 122–26; Gunn 1980, 41–56, 70–75; 1981, 97–99; McCarter 1980, 269–70; Klein 1983, 150–53, 155; Foresti 1984;

is taken as rejection. Saul's excuse—that he was deferring to the people (see 15:24)—pits the people against God and thereby exacerbates the tension between them (see Frisch 1996, esp. 100–101). Pronounces Samuel: "Because you have rejected the word of the LORD, he has also rejected you from being king" (15:23). Samuel spurns Saul's plea for a pardon and refuses to return with him, though Samuel, who normally evinces scant compassion, does "grieve" for Saul (15:35–16:1).

In the main anti-Saul narrative Samuel is scared to go to Bethlehem to anoint David as king, for "if Saul hears it, he will kill me" (16:2). But go he still does, and when he anoints David, "the Spirit of the LORD came mightily upon David from that day forward" (16:13). Simultaneously, according to the pro-Saul narrative, "Now the Spirit of the LORD departed from Saul" (16:14). David succeeds Saul even while Saul remains alive. In the pro-Saul source Saul is unaware of the selection of David as his successor and enlists David to soothe him with his lyre when Saul is afflicted with an evil spirit, also sent by God. Saul comes to "love" David, who becomes his armor-bearer (see 16:21).

The conflict between Saul and David begins with David's slaying of Goliath. Jealous of David's success not only over Goliath but also thereafter—the women sing, "Saul has slain his thousands, and David his tens of thousands" (18:7)—Saul himself nearly kills David; but then, like David in turn toward Bathsheba's husband, Saul instead plots to send him to the front to be killed by the Philistines. Saul is "afraid" of David, recognizing that the spirit of God now resides in David. Saul's attempt to have him killed is a preventive action: he fears being killed himself.

The parallel between Saul and Goliath is blatant. Both are leaders. Both are giants. Both seem invincible. Yet both are defeated by the stripling David. Goliath is really a symbolic double for Saul, and David's killing of him, not merely the public acclaim that follows, rightly terrifies Saul. A boy's fantasy of killing his father, who is always a giant to the boy, is fulfilled.

The love quadrangle among Samuel, Saul, David, and Jonathan evinces the conflict at work. Samuel loves Saul as an adopted son—Samuel does not merely anoint Saul with oil but also kisses him (see 10:1)—and bemoans his downfall (see 15:35). Yet Samuel also fears being killed by

---

Sternberg 1985, ch. 13; Gordon 1986, 142–47; Baldwin 1988, 112–16; Long 1989, ch. 5; Polzin 1989, 139–45; Edelman 1991, 99–111; Frisch 1996; Jobling 1998, 82–83; Alter 1999, 88–94; Nicholson 2002, 42–43; Green 2003, 249–58.

Saul (see 16:2). In turn, Saul feels abandoned by the fatherlike Samuel, who, having parted from him in Gilgal, does not see him again till his death (see 15:34–35).[22] Saul loves David as a son yet fears being killed by him, his own adopted son. David loves Saul as a father yet likewise fears being killed by him. Saul's "adoption" of David as his son parallels the adoption of the king as "son" by God. God feels betrayed, even if not threatened, by Saul. Saul in turn feels abandoned by God as well as by Samuel. So the departing of God's spirit from him repeatedly attests.

Jonathan's love for David—the nature of which is much debated—sets him against his own father, who feels betrayed by him too. Saul even tries to spear Jonathan (see 20:33), just as he twice tries to spear David (see 18:11; 19:10). (Saul needed target practice.) Saul authorizes the execution of Jonathan even before the appearance of David (see 14:46).[23] Saul considers Jonathan a rival in his own right. For Jonathan's military feats the people praise him over Saul (14:45), just as they later do David over Saul (18:7).

God's selection of David rather than Jonathan as Saul's successor also pits Jonathan against David as sibling-like rivals. Jonathan's excessive declaration of his deference to David (see 18:1–4) reveals what it tries to mask. The "love" between Jonathan and David, like that between Saul and David, may be a declaration of loyalty, but it is put in fraternal terms. That Saul (16:21), his servants (18:22), and Israel (18:28) all "loved" (*'āhēb*) David attests to the mix of the emotional with the political.[24]

Saul offers David his eldest daughter, Merab, in marriage—in exchange for David's continuing to fight for him and, so hopes Saul, getting killed in battle (see 18:17). David declines, and she is given to someone else. When Saul learns that his daughter Michal is in love with David, he offers her to David with the same hope (see 18:20). David thus becomes Saul's son-in-law.

When Saul's further plotting to get David killed fails, Saul becomes even more afraid of David and enlists Jonathan to kill David. Jonathan instead warns David, who flees. There ensues attempt after attempt on Saul's part to kill David. Only when, as described in two accounts, David

---

22. On Samuel as Saul's father, see, nonpsychoanalytically, Jobling 1998, 117–24, 253–54.

23. On Saul versus Jonathan, see Gordon 1986, 140.

24. On "love" in 1 Samuel, see Thompson 1974; Brueggemann 1993, 232, 239; Stone 2006, 205–8.

refrains from killing Saul, whom he has at bay, does Saul temporarily acknowledge that David is in fact a loyal servant.[25] Still, Saul's recognition that God has deserted him for David leads to his breakdown and eventual suicide on the battlefield. In conformity with Rank's pattern, David replaces and in effect kills him. Saul is succeeded not by Jonathan but by David. As Rank's pattern dictates, what the king fears comes true.

Seemingly, the fate of Saul is determined by God. It is God who chooses Saul, even if in one version through a lottery, and it is God who abandons Saul for David. Seemingly, the story is about the divinely determined rise and fall of Saul. Seemingly, there is nothing unconscious at work. Saul is all too conscious of his ambivalent feelings toward David.

Looked at psychoanalytically, however, the life of Saul is at heart a fight, one rooted not in divine will but in biology, between a father and a son: at one end between the father Samuel/God and his son Saul, at the other end between the father Saul and his son David. The fight is to the death, and it is fated, not by an external Fate or a character flaw but by human nature.[26]

To begin with, the heart of 1 Samuel is succession. The book is not primarily about war with Israel's enemies. That war is mere backdrop. The main topic is at most who gets to lead Israel against its enemies. There is a seeming succession, but it is continually challenged, and challenged not by a contemporary of the incumbent but by an upstart, by someone from the next generation. At the same time the challenger is, by blood or by nurturing, a member of the incumbent's family, and a beloved member of that family. The challenger is not an outsider, whom the incumbent would only hate or fear. The challenger is an insider, whom the incumbent loves. Consequently, the disconsolate incumbent feels betrayed. And the challenger, for his part, feels as much guilt as hate. Yet the fight cannot be circumvented, and must end in death. The real battlefield is not outward but inward. It is between family members, not nations.

---

25. Still, Saul has real reasons to suspect David of disloyalty: see Malul 1996; Hauer 1969, 160. It was the poet Delmore Schwartz who famously said that even a paranoiac has real enemies.

26. On Saul as the victim of Fate, see Gunn 1980, 1981. On Saul as partly the victim of his own character as well, see Welch 1952, 78–79; Hertzberg 1964, 106; von Rad 1962, 324–25; Humphreys 1978; 1980; 1982; 1985, chs. 2–3; McCarter 1980, 251; Baldwin 1988, 119–20, 172–75; Exum 1992; Brueggemann 1993. See also Nicholson 2002, 36–40. On Saul as responsible for his fall, see Williams 2007.

Even though judgeship is not hereditary, Eli expects his sons, however wayward, to succeed him, thereby turning judgeship into a hereditary and a familial office.[27] But Eli's line is displaced by Samuel. Samuel is the adopted son who, by displacing Eli's biological heirs, has pitted himself against his adopted father. In turn, Samuel expects his equally wayward sons to succeed him and so likewise turns judgeship into a hereditary office. But Samuel's line is itself displaced by Saul. Admittedly, Saul does not come under Samuel's tutelage until God has chosen him as Samuel's successor. But Saul is still the adopted son (see 3:16) who displaces Samuel's biological heirs and thereby is pitted against his adopted father, who had wanted his wayward sons to succeed him.

Because kingship really is a hereditary office, Saul naturally expects his eldest son, Jonathan, to succeed him. In other words, kingship is formally a family affair.[28] But on the one hand Saul is threatened by Jonathan,[29] and on the other hand Saul's line is displaced by David's. In turn, David is continually challenged by his sons. Where does this endless series of filial conflicts begin? With the displacement of God as king by Saul.

Undeniably, nothing is told of Saul's conception, birth, childhood, or young adulthood. By contrast, Samuel's birth to a long barren wife fits Rank's pattern. What the case of Saul does offer is his being raised by lowly parents, at least in the anti-Saul narrative. Says Saul to Samuel: "Am I not a Benjaminite, from the least of the tribes of Israel? And is not my family the humblest of all the families of the tribe of Benjamin?" (9:21)—even though his tribe is not unimportant and even though his father is wealthy (see 9:1–2). Saul's physical distinctiveness among even family members suggests that his real lineage is divine and that he has merely been raised by Kish, who, moreover, plays the absurdly minor role of sending Saul to retrieve his lost asses—and thereby to encounter Samuel (see 9:3–20). Saul's true father is either Samuel or, more likely, God.

---

27. As far back as Judg 8:22–23, the possibility of making judgeship hereditary arises.

28. Alt famously argued that in Israel succession was based on "charisma" and that only in Judah was succession based on lineage; see Alt 1968 [1951]. But the case at hand is in Judah. On Saul's charismatic leadership, see Alt 1968 [1951], 315–17; Noth 1960, 168–69, 175–76; Soggin 1963; Bright 2000, 189–92. Thornton (1963) argues that succession in both kingdoms was based on charisma.

29. Besides siding with David against his father, Jonathan outshines his father in battle and thereby rivals, even defies, him: see Jobling 1976; 1998, 93–99; Whitelam 1979, 78–80. But see also Long 1989, 101–2.

While Saul does become king and in that sense does displace Samuel and God, almost no sooner does he assume office than he is threatened by his successor, David. The relationship between Saul and David parallels that between Saul and Samuel/God. While David's early life, like Saul's, is not given, David more than Saul fits Rank's heroic pattern. On the one hand Saul "loved David greatly" (16:21). The young David comes to live at Saul's court and is treated like a son. On the other hand Saul fears and hates David. Not Saul's love but Saul's ambivalence befits that of a father toward his son.

David is similarly ambivalent toward Saul. David repeatedly asks why Saul seeks to kill him, for he has done nothing to betray Saul and surely loves him.[30] The psychoanalytic answer is that David's existence is the threat. That David twice spares Saul (see 24:3–7; 26:6–11) is beside the point, which is that David *can* kill him. David even addresses Saul as "my father" (24:11). In turn, Saul calls David "my son" (24:16; 26:17, 21, 25). That the terms are meant metaphorically rather than literally misses the point, which is the choice of metaphor.

Read psychoanalytically, the life of Saul is the disguised, symbolic, fantasized fulfillment of a wish: a son's wish to kill his father. The wish is on the part of each new generation of sons: Samuel against Eli; Saul against Samuel and God, who are really both symbols of Saul's real father; and David as well as Jonathan against Saul—followed by Absalom against David. The hero is the son, not the father.[31]

The source of the conflict is not power, which is more an Adlerian than a Freudian motive. The source of the conflict is Oedipal: the father blocks the son from sex with his mother. Is there even a hint of sexuality in the conflict between Saul and David—something akin to Isaac's closeness to his mother and his marrying a mother substitute? The hint is Saul's offer of two of his daughters to David, his adopted son, in marriage (see 18:17–27). Because Saul calculates that David's marriage to either daughter will lead to David's death, marriage within the family is the means by which Saul kills his adopted son. The scheme is a mere twist on the father's killing of his son to *prevent* marriage within the family.[32] A further sexual

---

30. On David's love for Saul, see Wong 1997.

31. Doubtless there is a Freudian analysis of the life of Saul. For a Jungian analysis see Sanford 1985, on which see, briefly and dismissively, Jobling 1986, 21–22; 1998, 87.

32. For a well-meaning but superficial interpretation of the relationships among Saul, Jonathan, David, and Jesse, see Lawton 1993.

aspect of the conflict between David and Saul is that women repeatedly side with David against Saul.[33]

Raglan Applied to Saul

Like Rank's pattern, Raglan's starts with conception and covers birth, infancy, and young adulthood. In both patterns childhood is skirted. Because the life of Saul begins with his selection as king, nothing is said of his early years (points 6 to 8; point 9 thereby fits). Certainly he cannot be the child of either a "royal virgin" or a king (points 1, 2), for kingship begins with him. His mother's kinship ties to his father are unknown (point 3), as is the nature of his conception (point 4). Raglan's hero "is reputed to be the son of a god" (point 5). While this point reinforces the link for Raglan between kingship and divinity, no claim of this kind is made for Saul. Still, Saul's height and good looks make him godlike.

For Raglan, kingship must be earned and cannot be merely inherited. A prospective king must defeat a worthy foe, who, contrary to Rank, need not be either the incumbent or the hero's father (point 11). Heroism for the non-Freudian Raglan is not about the family. In at least the pro-Saul narrative Saul defeats the Ammonites before being crowned, even if after having been selected by God (see 1 Sam 11). Were the victory attained through one-to-one combat, like David's victory over Goliath, Raglan would fit even better. Saul, as the first royal, can hardly marry a princess (point 12). First Samuel deems him so young as likely to be unmarried in one passage (see 1 Sam 10) and married with grown children in another (see 14:49–50).

For Raglan, the accomplishments of the king once on the throne are insignificant: the king for a time "reigns uneventfully" (point 14) and "prescribes laws" (point 15). What counts is that the king "loses favour with the gods and/or his subjects" (point 16) and "is driven from the throne and city" (point 17), after which "he meets with a mysterious death" (point 18), "often at the top of a hill" (point 19).

Fittingly for Raglan, Saul no sooner becomes king than is threatened—by the loss of favor of both God and the people. In the pro-Saul narrative Saul does lead Israel to victory over all of its enemies (see 14:47–48), but even this narrative downplays his accomplishments and plays up the mul-

---

33. On the assisting of David by women, see Jobling 1998, 91.

tiple reasons for his loss of God's favor. Saul, unnerved by the coming of the Philistines, orders the priest to stop casting the oracle (see 14:18–19). Saul fails to ensure that his prohibition against eating reaches Jonathan (see 14:24–30). And Saul fails to keep his people from eating slain animals with their blood (see 14:31–34). God's refusal to answer Saul signifies God's rejection (see 14:37).

In the anti-Saul narrative Saul loses God's favor for one reason: Saul's failure to "utterly destroy" the Amalekites and their possessions (see 1 Sam 15). (The hypothesized third source attributes Saul's loss of God's favor to Saul's usurpation of the priest's role: see 13:7b–18.)

What also fits Raglan is Saul's consequent loss of favor with the people—a loss evinced most painfully in the line sung by Israelite women in greeting Saul: "Saul has slain his thousands, and David his ten thousands" (18:7). The people are practical. They support Saul when he defeats their enemies and turn to David when Saul fails. In the anti-Saul narrative the people abandon Samuel because Samuel fails to deliver. In even the pro-Saul narrative God appoints Saul "to defeat my people from the Philistines" (9:16), which Samuel has failed to do.

For Frazer and Raglan, the cry of the people in the anti-Saul narrative for a "king to govern us like all the [other] nations" (8:5) is natural. The absence of a king is unnatural. (One wonders how Frazer and Raglan make sense of other forms of government.) The people take kingship for granted. For them, the complaint that Samuel is "old" (8:5) is also natural. Leaders, to be successful, must be vigorous. Weak leaders must be replaced.

Religion for Raglan, following Frazer, is the ancient, which is to say "primitive," counterpart to science, both theoretical and applied. There is no morality in science and therefore none in religion. Only later, especially when in modern times science has displaced religion as the way to explain and control the world, does religion add morality. Frazer acknowledges a "higher," ethical side of the Hebrew Bible but considers it secondary and late.[34]

Raglan would consequently reverse the straightforward explanation of Saul's downfall in any of the sources. Read without benefit of Raglan, Saul sins and thereby loses the support of God. He deserves to be abandoned. So too did Eli and his sons, and so too did Samuel's sons.

---

34. See Frazer 1918, 1:x. Frazer focuses on the magic-like, nonethical, primitive side of Israelite religion.

Read à la Raglan and Frazer, sin is an "added-on" explanation. The real reason that Eli and his sons, Samuel and his sons, and Saul and his sons all lose their places is that they have become weak—physically, not morally. Eli is old, Samuel is old, and Saul is unstable. The three are ineffective, failing as they do to defeat Israel's enemies.

But the trio do not fail because God deserts them. They are not weak because of God. On the contrary, God is weak because of them. The strength of God depends on the strength of him in whom God resides. God repeatedly fails to defeat Israel's enemies not because he will not but because he cannot. The fault is not his.

It would clinch the application of Raglan to be able to attribute to Saul the power to control the elements. For Frazer, the king harbors the god of vegetation. Raglan is less rigid. The closest we get is Samuel's asking God to send thunder and rain during the wheat harvest (see 12:16–18)—an event so out of season as to be miraculous. Samuel wants to show Israel the power of God over nature to register his objection to the replacement of God by a king. But then a king would logically be assumed by Israel to have the same power. He would be what lawyers call a rainmaker.

For Raglan, following the second version of Frazer's myth-ritualism, the king is divine. Where Rank demotes God to a human father, Raglan elevates the king to a god. While Raglan would hardly expect to find the king pitted against God as a rival, he would not be surprised to find the king treated by God as an equal and therefore as godlike. And he would note the divine-like attribute of size attributed to Saul in the anti- as well as the pro-Saul narrative.

The issue of divine kingship in Israel has been debated at least since 1943, when Ivan Engnell argued uncompromisingly that the Israelite king was considered fully divine. Hooke, from whom Engnell took his myth-ritualist pattern, as often as not maintained that the Israelite king was merely playing the role of the god—the first of Frazer's two versions of myth-ritualism. Engnell adopted the second, bolder version of Frazer's myth-ritualism: the king is god. Here Engnell is like Raglan.

But whatever the position taken by biblicists, the debate has been on regional grounds. Did other cultures at the time and place conceive of their kings as divine? From which neighbor did Israel adopt the notion of divine kingship? Engnell and Hooke alike distance themselves from Frazer on exactly the ground of origin. Where for Frazer and Raglan, as universal comparativists, divine kingship comes from independent invention, for "controlled comparativists" like Engnell and Hooke it comes from culture contact. Not every culture for Raglan or Frazer has kingship, but every one that does creates it itself.

And for Raglan, following Frazer, every culture that creates kingship creates divine kingship. The divinity of kingship comes, or seemingly comes, not from the replacement of god by a king but from the infusion of a king with god. The king harbors god: the spirit of god resides in the body of the king. In the pro-Saul account Samuel, having anointed Saul with oil, tells him to expect to meet "a band of prophets," at which point "the Spirit of the LORD will come mightily upon you, and you shall prophesy with them and be turned into another man" (10:5–6). So transformed is Saul that it is asked, "What has come over the son of Kish? Is Saul also among the prophets?" (10:11).[35] This infusion of God in Saul (see 10:9–13) even certifies Saul as king. In both the anti- and the pro-Saul material, whenever God is with Saul, the "spirit of God" "comes mightily upon him" (see, e.g., 11:6). God's abandonment of Saul means the departure of God's spirit, or at least of God's "good" spirit, from Saul (see 16:14, 23; 18:10).

Resigned to abandonment by God, Saul meets the Philistines "head on." Wounded by them, he, like Abimelech in Judges, dies by suicide. (In 2 Samuel he beseeches an Amalekite to kill him.[36]) Three of his sons, including Jonathan, are killed by the Philistines and so cannot quite succeed him. His fourth son, Ishbaal, reigns, and in name only, for just two years and is killed by those professedly loyal to David (see 2 Sam 2:8–10; 4:5–12) (point 20). Saul's body is cut up and displayed on the wall of a Philistine city, so that at least initially it is not buried (point 21).

Raglan, following Frazer, would reverse the apparent causal chain leading to Saul's death. For Raglan, the departure of the spirit of God from Saul and entrance into David would be not the cause but the effect of the decision to replace Saul with David, just as the entrance of the spirit of God into Saul would be not the cause but the effect of the decision to replace Samuel with Saul. That God's spirit shifts residence from Saul to David—"Saul was afraid of David, because the LORD was with him but had

---

35. On ecstatic prophecy in 1 Samuel see Lindblom 1962a, ch. 2; 1974; McKane 1963, 122; Eppstein 1969; Sturdy 1970; Ackroyd 1971, 84–86, 91, 160; Mauchline 1971, 99, 143–44; Blenkinsopp 1975, 83–84, 91–93; Parker 1978; Baldwin 1988, 91–92, 133–34; Polzin 1989, 101–8, 183–86; Alter 1999, 55–57, 122; Green 2003, 208–9. On ecstatic prophecy in the Hebrew Bible in general, see Lindblom 1962a, chs. 2–3; Wilson 1979; 1980, esp. 169–84.

36. On this second story as a likely lie, see Alter 1999, 197.

departed from Saul" (18:12)—would be taken by Raglan as the expression of the shift in the people's allegiance.

Undeniably, 1 Samuel taken straightforwardly makes God the cause of the strength or weakness of the ruler. But one might ask why, when even the ruler has not sinned, success for Israel still proves elusive. Why in at least the pro-Saul source cannot the dutiful Samuel, with God always behind him, defeat the Philistines? If God has to appoint Saul to do Samuel's job, then God depends on Saul for success.

To be sure, Raglan himself asserts that the king comes to "lose favour with the gods and/or his subjects" (point 16). Seemingly, then, Raglan is attributing success or failure to the support of God as well as of the people. But Raglan is simply inconsistent. In following Frazer, as he means to do, he cannot account for the ritual of replacing the king—to which for him the heart of the myth corresponds—if God determines the king's strength rather than the king's determining God's strength. The ritual is supposed to be the key event in religion. How key can it be if it merely records rather than causes God's shifting allegiance?

God's residing in a human body is on a par with God's residing in the ark. Only because the Israelites believe that God resides in the ark do they bring it to the front and despair when the Philistines capture it. That the ark can cause havoc to those among whom it is found attests not to God's transcending this physical container but to the power of God from within the container. God is not a disembodied entity but a physical entity who requires a physical residence and is therefore at its mercy. God does not escape from the ark.

For Raglan, Saul dies heroically: facing a stronger foe, he refuses to retreat and gives his life for the sake of his people. He does what kings are supposed to do. Saul has been called a "tragic hero" by many commentators, but they assume that he is tragic because he fails as king and dies. Raglan would maintain that death is the main job specification. Saul is a success, not a failure.[37] The myth of Saul is intended to inspire successors to sacrifice themselves for their subjects.

The Frazerian reading of the life of Saul concentrates not, like the Freudian reading, on Saul's character but on Saul's office. Seen as an exam-

---

37. Preston (1982) also sees Saul's death as heroic, but as tragic heroism. Preston's heroic "pattern" is simply the rise and fall of a leader. He offers no theory to accompany his pattern.

ple of a worldwide myth-and-ritual pattern, the kingship of Saul is hopelessly conventional.

Works Cited

Ackerman, James S. 1991. Who Can Stand before YHWH, This Holy God? A Reading of 1 Samuel 1–15. *Prooftexts* 11:1–24.
Ackroyd, Peter R. 1971. *The First Book of Samuel*. Cambridge Bible Commentary on the New English Bible. Cambridge: Cambridge University Press.
———. 1975. The Verb Love—*'āhēb* in the David-Jonathan Narratives—A Footnote. *VT* 25:213–14.
Alt, Albrecht. 1968 [1951]. The Monarchy in Israel and Judah. Pages 311–35 in *Essays on Old Testament History and Religion*. Translated by R. A. Wilson. Repr., Garden City, N.Y.: Doubleday.
Alter, Robert. 1981. *The Art of Biblical Narrative*. New York: Basic Books.
———. 1999. *The David Story*. New York: Norton.
Arlow, Jacob A. 1961. Ego Psychology and the Study of Mythology. *Journal of the American Psychoanalytic Association* 9:371–93.
Baldwin, Joyce G. 1988. *1 and 2 Samuel*. Tyndale Old Testament Commentaries. Downers Grove, Ill.: InterVarsity Press.
Bergen, Robert D. 1996. *1, 2 Samuel*. Nashville: Broadman & Holman.
Birch, Bruce C. 1971. The Development of the Tradition of the Anointing of Saul in I Sam 9:1–10:16. *JBL* 90:55–68.
———. 1975. The Choosing of Saul at Mizpah. *CBQ* 37:447–57.
———. 1976. *The Rise of the Israelite Monarchy: The Growth and Development of I Samuel 7–15*. SBLDS 27. Missoula, Mont.: Scholars Press.
Blenkinsopp, Joseph. 1964. Jonathan's Sacrilege: I Sam. 14, 1–46: A Study in Literary History. *CBQ* 26:423–49.
———. 1975. The Quest of the Historical Saul. Pages 75–99 in *No Famine in the Land: Studies in Honor of John L. McKenzie*. Edited by James W. Flanagan and Anita Weisbrod Robinson. Missoula, Mont.: Scholars Press.
Bodi, Daniel. 2005. *The Michal Affair: From Zimri-Lim to the Rabbis*. Sheffield: Sheffield Phoenix.
Bright, John. 2000. *A History of Israel*. 4th ed. Louisville: Westminster John Knox.
Brueggemann, Walter. 1990. *First and Second Samuel*. IBC. Louisville: John Knox.

———. 1991. Narrative Coherence and Theological Intentionality in I Samuel 18. *CBQ* 55:225–43.

Caird, George B., and John C. Schroeder. 1953. The First Book of Samuel. Pages 855–1040 in vol. 2 of *The Interpreter's Bible*. Edited by George Arthur Buttrick. New York: Abingdon.

Callender, Dexter E., Jr. 2000. *Adam in Myth and History*. Winona Lake, Ind.: Eisenbrauns.

Campbell, Anthony F. 2003. *1 Samuel*. FOTL 7. Grand Rapids: Eerdmans.

Campbell, Joseph. 1949. *The Hero with a Thousand Faces*. New York: Pantheon,.

Clements, R. E. 1974. The Deuteronomistic Interpretation of the Founding of the Monarchy in I Sam. VIII. *VT* 24:398–410.

Cook, Victor. 1965. Lord Raglan's Hero—A Cross Cultural Critique. *Florida Anthropologist* 18:147–54.

Cooke, Gerald. 1961. The Israelite King as Son of God. *ZAW* 73:202–25.

Dieterich, Walter, and Thomas Naumenn. 2000. The David-Saul Narrative. Translated by Peter T. Daniels. Pages 276–318 in *Reconsidering Israel and Judah*. Edited by Gary N. Knoppers and J. Gordon McConville. Winona Lakes, Ind.: Eisenbrauns.

Driver, G. R. 1968. Old Problems Re-examined. *ZAW* 80:174–83.

Driver, S. R. 1913. *Notes on the Hebrew Text and the Topography of the Books of Samuel*. Oxford: Clarendon.

Dundes, Alan. 1990 [1977]. *The Hero Pattern and the Life of Jesus*. Repr. as pp. 179–223 in Rank et al. 1990.

Edelman, Diana V. 1986. Saul's Battle against Amaleq (1 Sam. 15). *JSOT* 35:71–84.

———. 1991. *King Saul in the Historiography of Judah*. JSOTSup 121. Sheffield: Sheffield Academic Press.

Edenburg, Cynthia. 1985. How (Not) to Murder a King: Variations on a Theme in 1 Sam 24; 26. *SJOT* 12:64–85.

Eissfeldt, Otto. 1965. *The Old Testament: An Introduction*. Translated by Peter R. Ackroyd. Oxford: Blackwell.

Engnell, Ivan. 1943. *Studies in Divine Kingship in the Ancient Near East*. Uppsala: Almqvist & Wiksells.

Eppstein, Victor. 1969. Was Saul also among the Prophets? *ZAW* 81:287–304.

Eslinger, Lyle M. 1983. Viewpoints and Point of View in I Samuel 8–12. *JSOT* 26:61–76.

———. 1985. *Kingship of God in Crisis*. Bible and Literature Series 10. Sheffield: Almond.
Exum, J. Cheryl. 1992. *Tragedy and Biblical Narrative: Arrows of the Almighty*. Cambridge: Cambridge University Press.
Finkelstein, Israel. 1989. The Emergence of the Monarchy in Israel: The Environmental and Socio-Economic Aspects. *JSOT* 44:43–74.
Flanagan, James. 1981. Chiefs in Israel. *JSOT* 20:47–73.
Fohrer, Georg. 1968. *Introduction to the Old Testament*. Translated by David E. Green. Nashville: Abingdon.
———. 1972. *History of Israelite Religion*. Translated by David E. Green. Nashville: Abingdon.
Fokkelman, Jan. 1986. *The Crossing Fates (I Sam. 13–31 and II Sam. 1)*. Vol. 2 of *Narrative Art and Poetry in the Books of Samuel*. Assen: Van Gorcum.
Foresti, Fabrizio 1984. *The Rejection of Saul in the Perspective of the Deuteronomic School*. Rome: Teresianum.
Fox, Everett 1999. *Give Us a King*. New York: Schocken.
Frazer, J. G. 1918. *Folk-lore in the Old Testament*. 3 vols. London: Macmillan.
———. 1922. *The Golden Bough*. Abridged ed. London: Macmillan.
Freud, Sigmund 1959. Family Romances. Pages 235–41 in vol. 9 of *The Standard Edition of the Complete Psychological Works of Sigmund Freud*. Translated by James Strachey et al. London: Hogarth.
Frisch, Amos 1996. "For I Feared the People, and I Yielded to Them" (I Sam 15:24)—Is Saul's Guilt Attenuated or Intensified? *ZAW* 108:98–104.
Girard, René. 1977. *Violence and the Sacred*. Translated by Patrick Gregory. Baltimore: Johns Hopkins University Press.
Goldman, S. 1951. *Samuel*. Soncino Bible. London: Soncino.
Gordon, Robert P. 1980. David's Rise and Saul's Demise: Narrative Analogy in 1 Samuel 24–26. *Tyndale Bulletin* 31:37–64.
———. 1986. *1 and 2 Samuel: A Commentary*. Grand Rapids: Zondervan.
Green, Barbara. 2003. *How Are the Mighty Fallen?* JSOTSup 365. London: Sheffield Academic Press.
Gressmann, Hugo. 1921. *Die älteste Geschichtsschreibung und Prophetie Israels*. Part 2, vol. 1 of *Die Schriften des Alten Testaments*. 2nd ed. Göttingen: Vandenhoeck & Ruprecht.
Grottanelli, Cristiano. 1999. *Kings and Prophets*. Oxford: Oxford University Press.

Gunn, David M. 1980. *The Fate of King Saul.* JSOTSup 14. Sheffield: JSOT Press.

———. 1981. A Man Given over to Trouble: The Story of King David. Pages 89–112 in *Images of God and Man.* Edited by Burke O. Long. Sheffield: Almond.

Halpern, Baruch. 1981. *The Constitution of the Monarchy in Israel.* HSM 25. Chico, Calif.: Scholars Press.

———. 1988. *The First Historians.* University Park: Pennsylvania State University Press.

Hauer, Christian E., Jr. 1967. Does I Samuel 9:1–11:15 Reflect the Extension of Saul's Dominions? *JBL* 86:306–10.

———. 1969. The Shape of Saulide Strategy. *CBQ* 31:153–67.

Hertzberg, Hans Wilhelm 1964. *I and II Samuel.* Translated by J. S. Bowden. OTL. Philadelphia: Westminster.

Hooke, S. H. 1933. The Myth and Ritual Pattern of the Ancient East. Pages 1–14 in *Myth and Ritual.* Edited by S. H. Hooke. London: Oxford University Press.

Humphreys, W. Lee. 1978. The Tragedy of King Saul: A Study of the Structure of 1 Samuel 9–31. *JSOT* 6:18–27.

———. 1980. The Rise and Fall of King Saul: A Study of an Ancient Narrative Stratum in 1 Samuel. *JSOT* 18:74–90.

———.1982. From Tragic Hero to Villain: A Study of the Figure of Saul and the Development of 1 Samuel. *JSOT* 22:95–117.

———.1985. *The Tragic Vision and the Hebrew Tradition.* Philadelphia: Fortress.

Ishida, Tomoo. 1977. *The Royal Dynasties in Ancient Israel.* BZAW 142. Berlin: de Gruyter.

Irwin, W. A. 1941. Samuel and the Rise of the Monarchy. *American Journal of Semitic Languages and Literatures* 58:113–34.

Jackson, W. T. H. 1982. *The Hero and the King.* New York: Columbia University Press.

Jobling, David. 1976. Saul's Fall and Jonathan's Rise: Tradition and Redaction in 1 Sam 14:1–46. *JBL* 95:367–76.

———. 1978. *The Sense of Biblical Narrative: Three Structural Analyses in the Old Testament.* JSOTSup 7. Sheffield: JSOT Press.

———. 1986. *The Sense of Biblical Narrative: Structural Analyses in the Hebrew Bible.* JSOTSup 39. Sheffield: JSOT Press.

———. 1998. *1 Samuel.* Berit Olam. Collegeville, Minn.: Liturgical Press.

Kessler, Martin. 1970. Narrative Technique in 1 Sam 16, 1–13. *CBQ* 32:543–54.
Klein, Ralph W. 1983. *1 Samuel*. WBC 10. Waco, Tex.: Word.
Langamet, F. 1970. Les récits de l'institution de la royauté (I Sam., VII–XII): De Wellhausen aux travaux récents. *RB* 77:161–200.
Lawton, Robert B. 1993. Saul, Jonathan and the "Son of Jesse." *JSOT* 58:35–46.
Lemche, Niels Peter. 1978. David's Rise. *JSOT* 10:2–25.
Lindblom, Johannes. 1962a. *Prophecy in Ancient Israel*. Oxford: Blackwell.
———. 1962b. Lot-Casting in the Old Testament. *VT* 12:164–78.
———. 1974. Saul Inter Prophetas. *Annual of the Swedish Theological Institute* 9:30–41.
Long, V. Phillips. 1989. *The Reign and Rejection of King Saul*. SBLDS 118. Atlanta: Scholars Press.
Luck, G. Coleman. 1966. The First Glimpse of the First King of Israel. *Bibliotheca sacra* 123:60–66.
Lys, Daniel. 1967. Who Is Our President? *Int* 21:401–20.
Malul, Meir. 1996. Was David Involved in the Death of Saul on the Gilboa Mountain? *RB* 103:517–45.
Mauchline, John. 1971. *1 and 2 Samuel*. NCBC. London: Oliphants.
Mayes, A. D. H. 1978. The Rise of the Israelite Monarchy. *ZAW* 90:1–19.
McCarter, P. Kyle, Jr. 1980a. *I Samuel*. AB 8A. Garden City, N.Y.: Doubleday.
———. 1980b. The Apology of David. *JBL* 99:489–504.
McCarthy, Dennis J. 1973. The Inauguration of Monarchy in Israel: A Form-Critical Study of I Samuel 8–12. *Int* 27:401–12.
———. 1978. *Treaty and Covenant: A Study in Form in the Ancient Oriental Documents and in the Old Testament*. New ed. AnBib 21A. Rome: Pontifical Biblical Institute.
McKane, William. 1961. A Note on Esther IX and I Samuel XV. *JTS* 12:260–61.
———. 1963. *I and II Samuel*. Torch Bible Commentaries. London: SCM.
McKenzie, Steven L. 2000. *King David*. Oxford: Oxford University Press.
Miller, J. Maxwell. 1974. Saul's Rise to Power: Some Observations Concerning 1 Sam 9:1–10:16; 10:26–11:15 and 13:2–14:46. *CBQ* 36:157–74.
Miller, Patrick D., Jr., and J. J. M. Roberts. 1977. *The Hand of the Lord: A Reassesment of the "Ark Narrative" of 1 Samuel*. Baltimore: Johns Hopkins University Press.
Miscall, Peter D. 1986. *1 Samuel*. Bloomington: Indiana University Press.

Morgenstern, Julian. 1959. David and Jonathan. *JBL* 78:322–35.

Nicholson, Sarah. 2002. *Three Faces of Saul*. JSOTSup 339. London: Sheffield Academic Press.

Noth, Martin. 1960. *The History of Israel*. Translated and revised by Peter R. Ackroyd. New York: Harper & Row.

Parker, Simon B. 1978. Possession Trance and Prophecy in Pre-Exilic Israel. *VT* 28:271–85.

Pleins, J. David. 1992. Sin-Slayers and Their Sons. *CBQ* 54:29–38.

Polzin, Robert. 1989. *Samuel and the Deuteronomist*. San Francisco: Harper & Row.

Preston, Thomas R. 1982. The Heroism of Saul: Patterns of Meaning in the Narrative of the Early Kingship. *JSOT* 24:27–46.

Propp, Vladimir. 1968. *Morphology of the Folktale*. Translated by Laurence Scott. Repr., Austin: University of Texas Press.

Rad, Gerhard von. 1962. *The Theology of Israel's Historical Traditions*. Vol. 1 of *Old Testament Theology*. Translated by D. M. G. Stalker. New York: Harper & Row.

Raglan, Lord. 1933. *Jocasta's Crime*. London: Methuen.

———. 1936. *The Hero*. London: Methuen. "Part 2: Myth" is reprinted as pp. 89–175 in Rank et al. 1990.

———. 1945. *Death and Rebirth*. London: Watts.

———. 1949. *The Origins of Religion*. London: Watts.

Rank, Otto. 1990 [1913]. *The Myth of the Birth of the Hero*. Translated by F. Robbins and Smith Ely Jelliffe. Repr. as pp. 3–86 in Rank et al. 1990.

———. 2004. *The Myth of the Birth of the Hero*. 2nd ed. Translated by Gregory C. Richter and E. James Lieberman. Introduction by Robert A. Segal. Baltimore: Johns Hopkins University Press.

Rank, Otto, Lord Raglan, and Alan Dundes. 1990. *In Quest of the Hero*. Introduction by Robert A. Segal. Princeton: Princeton University Press.

Robertson, Edward. 1944. Samuel and Saul. *Bulletin of the John Rylands Library* 28:175–206.

Rosenberg, Joel. 1986. *King and Kin*. Bloomington: Indiana University Press.

———. 1987. 1 and 2 Samuel. Pages 122–45 in *The Literary Guide to the Bible*. Edited by Robert Alter and Frank Kermode. Cambridge: Belknap Press of Harvard University Press.

Sanford, John A. 1985. *King Saul, the Tragic Hero: A Study in Individuation*. Mahwah, N.J.: Paulist Press.

Segal, M. H. 1965a. The Composition of the Books of Samuel. *JQR*, NS, 55:318–39.

———. 1965b. The Composition of the Books of Samuel (Continued). *JQR*, NS, 56:32–50.

Segal, Robert A., ed. 1998. *The Myth and Ritual Theory*. Oxford: Blackwell.

———, ed. 2000. *Hero Myths*. Oxford: Blackwell.

Smith, Henry Preserved. 1899. *The Books of Samuel*. ICC. New York: Scribner's.

Soggin, J. Alberto. 1963. Charisma und Institution im Königtum Sauls. *ZAW* 75:54–64.

———. 1974. *Introduction to the Old Testament*. Translated by John Bowden. OTL. Philadelphia: Westminster.

———. 1984. *A History of Ancient Israel*. Translated by John Bowden. Philadelphia: Westminster.

Sternberg, Meir. 1985. *The Poetics of Biblical Narrative*. Bloomington: Indiana University Press.

Stone, Ken. 2006. 1 and 2 Samuel. Pages 195–221 in *The Queer Bible Commentary*, Edited by Dervyn Guest et al. London: SCM.

Sturdy, John. 1970. The Original Meaning of "Is Saul Also among the Prophets?" (I Samuel X 11; 12; XIX 24). *VT* 20:206–13.

Thompson, J. A. 1974. The Significance of the Verb Love in the David-Jonathan Narratives in 1 Samuel. *VT* 24:334–38.

Thornton, T. C. G. 1963. Charismatic Kingship in Israel and Judah. *JTS*, NS, 14:1–11.

———. 1967. Studies in Samuel. *Church Quarterly Review* 168:413–23.

Tsevat, Matitiahu. 1961. Studies in the Book of Samuel, I. *HUCA* 32:191–216.

Tylor, E. B. 1871. *Primitive Culture*. 1st ed. 2 vols. London: Murray.

Vannoy, J. Robert. 1978. *Covenant Renewal at Gilgal*. Cherry Hill, N.J.: Mack.

Von Hahn, Johann Georg. 1876. *Sagwissenschaftliche Studien*. Jena: Mauke.

Weiser, Artur. 1936. I Samuel 15. *ZAW* 54:1–28.

———. 1961. *Introduction to the Old Testament*. 4th ed. Translated by Dorothea M. Barton. London: Darton, Longman & Todd.

Welch, Adam C. 1952. *Kings and Prophets of Israel*. Edited by Norman W. Porteus. London: Lutterworth.

Wellhausen, Julius. 1885 [1878]. *Prolegomena to the History of Israel*. Translated by J. C. Black and Allan Menzies. Edinburgh: Black.

Whitelam, Keith W. 1979. *The Just King: Monarchical Judicial Authority in Ancient Israel*. JSOTSup 12. Sheffield: Department of Biblical Studies, University of Sheffield.

———. 1984. The Defense of David. *JSOT* 29:61–87.

Williams, Peter J. 2007. Is God Moral? On the Saul Narratives as Tragedy. Pages 175–89 in *The God of Israel*. Edited by Robert P. Gordon. Cambridge: Cambridge University Press.

Wilson, Robert R. 1979. Prophecy and Ecstasy: A Reexamination. *JBL* 98:321–37.

———. 1980. *Prophecy and Society in Ancient Israel*. Philadelphia: Fortress.

Wong, G. C. I. 1997. Who Loved Whom? *VT* 47:554–56.

Response to Robert A. Segal, "The Life of King Saul as Myth"

Adela Yarbro Collins

I very much enjoyed reading Professor Segal's paper and learned much from it. It seems odd to me, however, that Segal never defines the term *myth*, although by the end of the paper it is clear that it includes quite a bit more than "stories about the gods." It would have been helpful if he had included some discussion of the nature and range of this category.

If we follow Hooke and define "myth" as the story that a ritual enacts, we then have to decide what counts as "ritual." Do we limit the term *ritual* to gestures that seem to us to be "religious"? Or do we include any human behavior that has a repeated pattern or sequence?

The same problem arises with regard to the term *hero*. Segal provides specific cases of the usage the term, but these differ. For example, for Rank the "hero" is always a male human being, whereas for Lord Raglan, he is divine. Historical and philological questions arise. Is the use of the term in German-, French-, and English-speaking scholarship based on the Greek use? Greek usage of the term varied greatly, but most often it was applied to the powerful dead. If the term *hero* used by the theorists of myth ultimately derived from Greek usage, it is clear that it was adapted to suit its new contexts. An analysis of the origins and history of the term *hero* in scholarship on myth would be interesting and useful.

Some of my colleagues in biblical studies and ancient history have stopped using the term *myth*. One reason is that the category is based on the Greek term μῦθος, and that term means simply "story." In his *Poetics*, Aristotle used it to mean the "plot" of a tragedy. Another reason is that, in American culture at least, "myth" refers to something false. The category of myth, with its negative connotations, is in tension with efforts to use the comparative method to illuminate texts, especially sacred texts like the Bible.

Segal makes a distinction between "universal comparativists" and "controlled comparativists." Another way of putting the issue is to speak about transmission versus independent invention. A case for transmission can be made by providing evidence for cultural contact and the currency of the relevant stories or practices in the milieu of the receiving author.

The notion of independent invention is problematic. According to Bob Scholte, the French anthropologist Claude Lévi-Strauss took as a premise that "both ideas and actions derive from fundamental categories of the human mind (or spirit). The emergence of mind coincides with that of language" (1970, 110). He also assumed that "the structures of the human mind are unconscious and generic, universal and invariable." Thus "the world of mind and language is infinitely diverse with respect to its content, but always limited to its laws" (111). Scholte's focus is on the case of rival paradigms in social anthropological theory in the 1960s and 1970s, the rivalry between the empiricist, largely Anglo-American school, and the rationalist, mainly European school. In his view, only a truly historical perspective on alternative philosophies of social science can resolve the problem of productive communication between rival paradigms (119).

Another issue is the question of origin versus duration. Most theories attribute the duration as well as the creation of myths to a need. The claim that myths originate to meet a need seems intuitively right. The duration of myths, however, may owe more to later "added-on" interpretations or rationalizations than to the persistence of the original need. For example, purity rituals of the Hebrew Bible may have originated in response to fear of the processes of birth, death, and menstruation. Their duration, however, surely owes much to their definition as commandments of God, their status as portions of a sacred text, and the respect accorded to the priests.

In his discussion of Lord Raglan and his theory of hero myths, Segal comments, "For all Raglan's touting of the symbiosis of myth and ritual, his myth and ritual seem incongruously out of sync. In the myth the protagonist is usually human. In the ritual the protagonist is always divine." He finds it odd that "Raglan nevertheless equates the hero of the myth with the god of the ritual." Raglan wrote, "The conclusion suggests itself that the god is the hero as he appears in ritual, and the hero is the god as he appears in myth; in other words, the hero and the god are two different aspects of the same superhuman being" (Raglan 1936, 162). One wonders how a god can lose power, let alone die. Raglan's answer is that it is the hero, not the god, who loses power and then dies—even though the hero and the god are identical!

The same difficulties arise in reconciling the Christian claims that Jesus died on the cross to save humanity and that he is God. Jesus, as the hero, is God as he appears in the narrative Gospels; Jesus as God is the hero as he appears in ritual, that is, the one who has been exalted and given all authority. Because traditional Christian doctrine defines Jesus as fully human and fully divine, he can suffer and die, yet be God. Both the systematic theologian Jürgen Moltmann (1974) and the New Testament scholar Richard Bauckham (1999) have written books with "Crucified God" or "God Crucified" in the title. I wonder whether the lack of full congruence between Raglan's hero myth and hero ritual is due at least in part to the ambiguities and tensions among the Christian affirmations about Jesus.

Segal asks why the patterns of analysts of myth never attain perfect scores. In other words, why don't the hero myths contain all of the elements of these patterns? This question raises acutely the issue of the epistemic status of theories about myths. Must theories in anthropology and religious studies be "inter-subjectively testable," as Karl Popper argued scientific statements must be (2002, 25)? Or is a pattern a scholarly, literary construction, an attempt to define a type of plot that a number of stories have more or less in common?

Segal's psychoanalytic reading of the life of Saul in 1 Samuel is illuminating, as the application of theory to text ought to be. A theoretical problem, however, is whether it is appropriate to take the narrative as a myth and thus, it would seem, to define it as such. Is it enough to define a narrative as myth if God appears as one of the characters? The application of Raglan's theory to the life of Saul is also illuminating. The passages that speak about the spirit of the Lord "rushing upon" Saul do seem to imply at least a temporary "infusion of God in Saul." The statement in 1 Sam 16:14 that "the Spirit of the LORD departed from Saul" does suggest that the spirit had been "infused" into Saul for a long period. An evil spirit, also from the Lord, then fills the vacuum, so to speak, and begins to torment him.[1]

The argument is intriguing that, from the perspective of Raglan's theory, "Saul dies heroically." Although he is flawed, he is supposed to lose the throne and die. "Saul is a success, not a failure." The life of Saul "is

---

1. The return of the spirit of the Lord so that Saul prophesies (1 Sam 19:23) may be, as Kyle McCarter has argued, a late addition to the narrative (1980, 330).

intended to inspire successors to sacrifice themselves for their subjects." That he is a model for later kings fits the narrative better than the idea that the notion of sin and punishment is a warning to all, great and small.

My final comment is that a comparative study of kingship must be made to explain the category of Israelite kingship. The narrative itself uses terms related to the category of "kingship." But is the category of the "hero" equally necessary?

Works Cited

Bauckham, Richard. 1999. *God Crucified: Monotheism and Christology in the New Testament*. Grand Rapids: Eerdmans.

McCarter, P. Kyle, Jr. 1980. *1 Samuel*. AB 8. Garden City, N.Y.: Doubleday.

Moltmann, Jürgen. 1974. *The Crucified God: The Cross of Christ as the Foundation and Criticism of Christian Theology*. Translated by R. A. Wilson and John Bowden. New York: Harper & Row.

Popper, Karl. 2002. *The Logic of Scientific Discovery*. Repr., London: Routledge.

Raglan, Lord. 1936. *The Hero*. London: Methuen. "Part 2: Myth" is reprinted as pp. 89–175 in Rank et al. 1990.

Rank, Otto, Lord Raglan, and Alan Dundes. 1990. *In Quest of the Hero*. 2nd ed. Introduction by Robert A. Segal. Baltimore: Johns Hopkins University Press.

Scholte, Bob. 1970. Epistemic Paradigms: Some Problems in Cross-Cultural Research on Social Anthropological History and Theory. Pages 108–22 in *Claude Lévi-Strauss: The Anthropologist as Hero*. Edited by E. Nelson Hayes and Tanya Hayes. Cambridge: MIT Press.

Theory of Myth and the Minimal Saul

Ivan Strenski

Fans of Robert Segal will find him in classic form here, working the permutations and combinations of both mythical narratives and theorists that he has applied to them. Novel here is Segal's claim that the biblical narrative accounts of the life of King Saul conform to mythical patterns. Closely examined, that is, they show themselves exemplifying classic mythical themes such as the son's desire to kill the father. As interpreted by two major classical theorists, psychoanalyst Otto Rank, and myth-ritualist Lord Raglan, Segal works over the biblical text to show how the perspectives of both Rank and Raglan can be applied to reveal hidden linkages and significance. Appealing to classic Freudian psychoanalytic tropes, Segal says that the "life of Saul is at heart a fight, one rooted not in deed or circumstance, but in biology, between a father and a son" (259). His is a story of struggle. The paper is literally brimming with many such connections, heretofore unseen or suppressed. As such, Segal's excursus into biblical criticism will well serve the interests of those dedicated to fine-grained study of the biblical narrative.

I must confess not doing much of this kind of scholarship. Further, although Segal's mastery of the relations in the text is impressive, I wish he had provided a stronger statement of the thematic payoff of these complex exercises. Until he does, my interest will be drawn more to theoretical questions that surround the text, rather than engaging in its content. It is questions arising from this extratextual perspective, as I shall develop it, then, that I feel pressed to put to Segal.

Segal chooses Rank and Raglan for their prowess as theorists. Yet one oddity in Segal's initial sketch of this paper seems to cast doubt on their qualifying as the theorists of Segal's desire. Segal notes that the first scholars of myth "limited themselves to finding a pattern and, despite their own theoretical inclinations, did not seek to answer the main theoretical questions: What are the origin, function, and subject matter of hero myths?" (245). He then points to Otto Rank and Lord Raglan as "the most important" of those who "considered these theoretical questions" (245). As to the "subject matter" of the Saul myths, Segal exhaustively—at least in some domains—seems to mine this with his relentless digging into the inner relationships of Saul to his various kin and to God. From my point of view, however, I find it difficult to see Rank and Raglan as the paradigm theorists that Segal does.

How can Raglan and Rank hope to answer questions about "origin" and "function" of the Saul stories in the absence of data that could address these? How, for example, can we know how these stories function without considerable historical knowledge of the many different contexts surrounding them? How can we say they speak authoritatively of origin when we know so little of ancient Israel in the time of Saul? We just do not possess data telling us how the Saul stories were understood or "read" in the many different contexts over the past three thousand years in which they were used, much less their "original" contexts. Are these myths to be taken as a kind of literal history of the "days and works" of Saul? Or, alternatively, are they to be read as we read a hero epic like *The Lord of the Rings*, or an episode of *Big Love*? Did the ancient Israelites see in the stories what Segal and his theorists, for example, see in them, and in seeing them so, what did they do in return or in anticipation? Wouldn't we feel that we could adequately, if not exhaustively, speak to such questions of "function" and "origins" if we had the kinds of historical and sociological knowledge to which I refer? Without it, how can we do more than a kind of literary analysis?

Segal thinks that psychoanalytic approaches solve the problem of this lack of historical knowledge. They step in when history leaves us empty, just as my attention to the theorists themselves, as I shall argue, does in absence of the same kind of data. But I have my doubts that psychoanalysis can do what Segal thinks it can. For instance, according to Segal, a psychoanalytic point of view claims that these myths of Saul are "fantasy." Fine. But whose fantasy is it? And how can we be sure? And, as for Raglan, what ritual—as Raglan would inquire—was linked to them—as fantasy or as some other concoction? And how could Raglan know this, if indeed the Saul myths formed a myth-ritual nexus? After all, Raglan's myth-ritual connections are at least putatively real and historical, and not just matters of links at the level of literature.

Now strictly as *literary* analyses, I do not gainsay Segal's readings. Indeed, they bring out how possibly rich and multivalent these biblical stories can be. But they tell us nothing, nor can they, about "origin" and "function" in any social or historical sense—only in some sense described as "psychoanalytic." Again, whose fantasy is embodied in the story of Saul? Now, Rank may be writing as if he were equipped to answer questions of "origin" and "function," and in so doing, to qualify as a "theorist," in Segal's view. But he cannot, as I see it. He must be deemed a "failed" theorist—unless psychoanalysis can save Rank. But can it?

Psychoanalytic theories purportedly address and answer questions of "origin" and "function" by assuming that the patterns of, say, familial strife are rooted in a common, universal human nature. But as a first approximation, given the gap of time and space between the accounts of Saul's life and those familiar to Rank, Raglan, or Segal, can they? Is it plausible that they do, or at least something we should assume, without a good deal more argument? I cite only the work of the great anthropologist Bronislaw Malinowski, who, despite being a great devotee of Freudian ideas, also was one of its greatest critics. Malinowski went right after the universality of Freud's Oedipus complex (Stocking 1986, 13–49, 42)! Freud's ideas had to be adapted, Malinowski felt, to differences between cultures. In the form Freud had articulated the Oedipus complex, Malinowski felt that it wrongly assumed "the existence, at the outset of human development, of a patriarchal family with a tyrannical and ferocious father who repressed all the claims of the younger men" (Malinowski 1992, 56). It was in the struggle between sons and the father that eventually the younger men, denied possession of sexual partners by the father, killed him. But Malinowski's field studies in Melanesia revealed that their families were unlike the patriarchal model prevalent in Victorian Vienna, known as well to Rank. Furthermore, different forms of families generated different psychological roles to family members. In Eastern New Guinea, for example, Malinowski testified:

> the mother and her brother possess ... all the legal *potestas*. The mother's brother is the "ferocious matriarch," the father is the affectionate friend and helper of his children. He has to win for himself the friendship of his sons and daughters, and is frequently their amicable ally against the principle of authority represented by the maternal uncle. In fact, none of the domestic conditions required for the sociological fulfilment of the Oedipus complex, with its repressions, exist in the Melanesian family of Eastern New Guinea. (Malinowski 1992, 56)

Segal falls into line with the Freudian tradition equally well by discounting cultural contexts and differences in the formation of the human psyche and thus in human psychology at large. Having only the texts of the Bible, how are we to claim the applicability of Viennese psychology to the Hebrew life of 1000 B.C.E. or so? While Freud's models may be "applied" with equal ease in both cases, Freudian analysis may not apply, so to speak. Is it likely, given the vast time and space differences between ourselves and the "others," that we should be as similar as Segal wishes?

Perhaps an admission of this lack of fit between "them" and at least the Viennese "us" comes in my failure, in the ancient Israelite case of Saul, to find mention of the promised sexual element, for example, particular to the Freudian Oedipus complex. Where is the paired wheel upon which the Oedipus story rides in the young hero's lust for his mother? Segal's attempt to save this by bringing in Saul's offer of two of his daughters to David does not seem to me to gain much traction as an Oedipal element. We need the lust for the mother, for the king's wife, to complete the Oedipal match. And it just is not there. So maybe Viennese psychoanalytic views do not fit the case of Saul as much as Segal thinks? And, if so, maybe we should be looking more closely at cultural differences than Segal wishes? Not to gainsay homosexuality, either, but only Samuel, David, and God are mentioned besides Saul. Does Segal really wish to reduce the Oedipus complex to a "minimal" version, so that it just names generational "struggle"? Yes, David and Saul were often in conflict with one another. But does that make their conflict best explained in Freudian terms? Why not Foucault? Isn't Freudian struggle a certain *kind* of struggle, not just a garden variety generational struggle that we find in Segal's analysis?

Our inability to answer at least the questions of historical "origin" and "function" is one reason I have argued for moving further out onto the territory *surrounding* both myths and theories of myth into a study of the myth theorists themselves (Strenski 1987). That is why my questions about myth and myth theorists have been *why a theorist would bother* creating such a theory. Why did theorists *think they were right* to say what they said about myth? Given our vast knowledge of the contemporary world, we should have sufficient data to make good hypotheses about such problems—theories that consider salient features of a theorist's time and place in the world. Perhaps I have been wrong to abandon the study of myth as if these stories really did tell us something about people long ago and far away. Perhaps I would be more compelled to work with the ins and outs of the inner relations to be found in myths if I could know more about the various societies in which they have been current.

WORKS CITED

Malinowski, Bronislaw. 1992. Psychoanalysis and Anthropology (1923). Pages 55–57 in *Malinowski and the Work of Myth*. Edited by Ivan Strenski. Princeton: Princeton University Press.

Stocking, George W., Jr. 1986. Anthropology and the Science of the Irrational: Malinowski's Encounter with Freudian Psychoanalysis. Pages 13–49 in *Malinowski, Rivers, Benedict and Others: Essays on Culture and Personality*. Edited by George W. Stocking Jr. Madison: University of Wisconsin Press.

Strenski, Ivan. 1987. *Four Theories of Myth in Twentieth-Century History: Cassirer, Eliade, Lévi-Strauss and Malinowski*. Iowa City: University of Iowa Press.

The Indispensability of Theories of Myth for Biblical Studies: A Response to Robert Segal

David L. Miller

Professor Segal's paper, "The Life of King Saul as Myth," was originally embedded in a longer presentation entitled "The Indispensability of Theories of Myth for Biblical Studies." It was given to a joint session of the American Academy of Religion and the Society of Biblical Literature at their annual meetings in 2009. Professor Segal had attempted to demonstrate his thesis about the indispensability of theories of myth for biblical studies by giving a reading of the Saul narratives in the Hebrew Bible, which was informed by the hero theories of myth in the work of Otto Rank, Lord Raglan, Joseph Campbell, and René Girard. A portion of that demonstration is reproduced in this book, and it is to that portion that I am responding. Segal said clearly in his original presentation that a mythical approach "offers benefits," is "outright indispensable," and that without it one has only "poor history." Segal makes the normative case strongly with his exposition of the Saul narratives, and I am in agreement with this normative judgment. However, his prescriptive argument, that one should utilize myth theory, is in a way anachronistic and beside the point, since theories of myth were in the eighteenth and nineteenth centuries already indispensable for advances and grounding in biblical hermeneutics. There is, therefore, a certain irony in Segal arguing for something that already is the case. It is a matter of *is* rather than *ought*.

I know that Professor Segal knows this. Indeed, he himself wrote in the introduction to *Theories of Myth*: "Many theories of myth from philosophy and especially from religious studies grow out of attempts to decipher the classics and the Bible" (1996, ix). This book features essays by James Barr, C. K. Barrett, Rudolf Bultmann, and John MacKenzie on the relation of theories of myth and biblical hermeneutics. Also, Segal acknowledges the work of J. W. Rogerson on the matter of myth theory in relation to biblical studies in the bibliography of *Myth and Ritual Theory* (Segal 1998, 469).

Concerning the historical facticity of the indispensability of myth theory to biblical hermeneutics, Rogerson's book (1974) is decisive in my view. Rogerson notes that the first attempts in the modern era to use myth as an interpretive tool in biblical studies were between 1775 and 1800. This is confirmed also, prior to Rogerson's publication, by C. Hartlich and W. Sachs in *Der Ursprung des Mythosbegriffes in der modernen Bibelwissenschaft* (1952), and by P. Barthel in *Interprétation du langage mythique et théologie biblique* (1967; see Rogerson 1974, 1 nn. 1–2). I will recount a bit of Rogerson's story.[1]

Robert Lowth, a British literary historian and theorist, lectured in 1753 on Hebrew poetry, focusing on style, not theology. This opened the way to the utilization of literary theory in biblical hermeneutics. By comparing Hebrew poetry with Greek and Latin poetry, Lowth suggested that the Bible could be interpreted on the basis of insights from the study of nonbiblical literature and mythology. These lectures were republished in Göttingen in 1786, and C. G. Heyne developed Lowth's argument for interpretation of Greek myth. It was a student of Heyne, J. G. Eichhorn, who, in an anonymous 1779 article (written in 1775, as he later confessed when he also confessed authorship), first applied his teacher's theories to the interpretation of the opening chapters of Genesis.

Johann Philipp Gabler followed Eichhorn, though they quibbled over a variety of particulars, for example, the mythic or historical status of Gen 2–3. Further, Gabler distinguished Myth, *Fabeln, Märchen,* and Saga. Rogerson argues that Eichorn was the pioneer, especially with regard to New Testament interpretation, but that Gabler was the theoretician.

This mythical school of biblical interpretation was systematized in 1802 by Georg Lorenz Bauer in *Hebräische Mythologie des alten und neuen Testaments mit Parallelen als der Mythologie anderer Völker, vornehmlich der Griechen und Römer.* And, in 1837, J. F. L. George sketched the history of the terms *myth* and *saga* up to the point of their first positive use in biblical studies. George's work was entitled *Mythus und Sage: Versuch einer*

---

1. The historical account that follows in the next paragraphs is taken from Rogerson 1974, 1, 2–3, 5–11, 16–18, 26, 33, 37, 51–64.

wissenschaftlichen Entwicklung dieser Begriffe und ihres Verhältnisses zum christlichen Glauben.

"Myth" had been connected with Greek *mythos* and "saga" with *logos*, the latter imagined to be historical and the former not. But with the rise of historiography, "saga" and "history" were discriminated, and "saga" came to be associated with "myth."[2]

Johann Gottfried Herder's work followed the mythical school, but his writings often provided the antecedent basis for the school's theories, even though he often differed with the works of Gabler and Eichhorn (on Jacob's wrestling as a dream, Balaam's ass, etc.).

The first half of the nineteenth century saw a reaction against the mythological school in two directions: philosophically (J. F. L. George) and historically (Heinrich Ewald), and in both philosophical and historical perspective by W. J. L. de Wette, who anticipated Wellhausen and von Rad on pentateuchal history and Gunkel in the classification of Psalms. Curiously, Ewald, who was opposed to the mythical school, arguing that myths are *Göttersagen* and there are no such in the Hebrew Bible, was influenced in this view precisely and perhaps ironically by Jacob and Wilhelm Grimm. But it is just Jacob Grimm's Indo-European studies (with devastating political implications, as we now know) that gave rise to comparative mythology in the second half of the nineteenth century, which came to England in the work of Max Müller.

There is more to Rogerson's history, but I will only mention it in passing. Heymann Steinthal first directly applied the method of comparative mythology to biblical materials in his examination of the Samson narrative. Steinthal was followed by Ignaz Goldziher. And then there were links from the comparativist school to S. R. Driver, Andrew Lang, E. B. Tylor, W. Robertson Smith, T. H. Gaster, and—of course—the Myth and Ritual school (James G. Frazer, Jane E. Harrison, Gilbert Murray, Stanley Edgar Hyman, S. H. Hooke). So Rogerson strongly and plainly makes the point of the *historical* indispensability of theorizing myth to constituitive aspects of biblical hermeneutics,[3] but he fails to draw the radical conclusions that mention of Jacob and Wilhelm Grimm should have provoked.

---

2. This has been brought up to date more recently by Bruce Lincoln (1999).

3. Ivan Strenski has also argued the connection between biblical criticism and seventeenth- and eighteenth-century critiques of religion, including the impact of comparative studies that juxtapose Christian and Jewish narrative with non-Jewish and non-Christian religious phenomenology (2006, 335, and all of ch. 2).

Franz Bopp, in 1816, published a comparative study of Sanskrit, Greek, Latin, Persian, and Germanic systems of conjugation. This was the beginning of a quickly developed comparative philology of Aryan, Indo-Germanic, or Indo-European thinking (or fantasy), which claimed a continuum from Ireland to India. Some would argue that this Indo-European group was the most productive, most philosophically mature, and culturally sophisticated of all peoples. It was in this tradition that the Grimm brothers, Jacob and Wilhelm, gathered *Märchen* with the belief that they could show in them the broken folkloristic remains of a nuclear Aryan mythology. Even Schopenhauer greeted the discovery in the Occident of the Sanskrit Upanishads as "the most rewarding and elevating reading possible in the world." It would not be long before, in 1839, a French aristocrat, Courtet de l'Isle, would propose a theory of politics on the basis of the new comparativism. His work was called, *La science politique fondée sur la science de l'homme; ou, Étude des races humains*. And there followed Count Arthur de Gobineau's four-volume *Essai sur l'inégalité des races humaines*, and Count Vacher de Lapouge's *L'Aryen et son rôle social*, all of which, along with another work by Houston Stuart Chamberlain in 1890, became the background for Alfred Rosenberg's 1930 work, *Der Mythus des zwanzigsten Jahrhunderts*. And the rest—as one says—is history! But perhaps one should say that the rest is mythology, since we are dealing here with a theoretical underpinning of Fascism.[4]

The point is that if Mircea Eliade, Martin Heidegger, Paul de Man, Kitaro Nishida, Joseph Campbell, and C. G. Jung are to be examined for the possible informing of their interpretations by politics (e.g., see Strenski 1987), then the same logic surely should apply to biblical interpreters. I well realize that what I am pointing to in the history of myth theory is anti-Semitism, but a biblical criticism that comes out of this same theoretical context, though reversed in valence, may ironically be no less ideological, though unconsciously so, to be sure. What I am worrying about in biblical hermeneutics is a logic and an ideologic of unconscious imperialism, Christian triumphalism, evolutionary developmentalism, superiority, essentialism, racism, sexism, and classism, not to mention claims for uniqueness, especially in relation to the thematics of "hero" and "king-

---

4. The account in this paragraph is taken from Joseph Campbell (1976, 8–13), who, ironically, will later be accused of what he here critiques! See Miller 1995.

ship," all of which may well have sources in the checkered history of comparativist theorizing.[5]

The point needs no laboring: theories of myth historically have been indispensable for biblical studies, and if today one does not have knowledge of theories of myth, one's own biblical interpretation may unconsciously be harboring historically haunting hermeneutics that one might have thought better of. Theories of myth have been indispensable to biblical interpretation since the eighteenth century, and one ignores this at one's own peril. Indeed, the normative and prescriptive argument that Segal has made follows from the descriptive and historical facts. The importance of theories of myth for biblical hermeneutics *ought* to be indispensable, because it *has* been indispensable, and perhaps not always as felicitously as Segal's essay implies.

The irony for Segal is that his case was made, at least implicitly, before he ever tried to make it. His amplification of the case in the instance of Saul narratives is useful and important, but the general case for the indispensability of theories of myth for biblical studies does not need to be made. It has already been made.

Works Cited

Campbell, Joseph. 1976. *Primitive Mythology*. Vol. 1 of *The Masks of God*. Repr., New York: Penguin.
Lincoln, Bruce. 1999. *Theorizing Myth*. Chicago: University of Chicago Press.
Miller, David L. 1995. Comparativism in a World of Difference: The Legacy of Joseph Campbell to the Postmodern History of Religions. Pages 168–77 in vol. 1 of *Common Era: Best New Writings on Religion*. Edited by Steven Scholl. Ashland, Ore.: White Cloud.
Rogerson, J. W. 1974. *Myth in Old Testament Interpretation*. BZAW 134. Berlin: de Gruyter.
Segal, Robert, ed. 1996. *Theories of Myth: Philosophy, Religious Studies and Myth*. New York: Garland.
———, ed. 1998. *The Myth and Ritual Theory*. Oxford: Blackwell.
Strenski, Ivan. 1987. *Four Theories of Myth in Twentieth-Century History*. Iowa City: University of Iowa Press.
———. 2006. *Thinking about Religion*. London: Blackwell.

---

5. On "imperialism" in the fields of myth and biblical studies, see Strenski 1987.

Replies to Ivan Strenski, Adela Yarbro Collins, and David Miller

Robert A. Segal

I thank Ivan Strenski, Adela Yarbro Collins, and David Miller for their exceedingly incisive comments on my paper. The version of the paper that I gave at the SBL session in San Diego in 2007 was much longer than the present version. Occasionally, the respondents discuss issues that for lack of space had to be dropped from the published version.

In reply to Strenski, I do not assert that theories, to qualify as theories, must answer all three main questions about myth: those of origin, function, and referent. For me, Bultmann, Jonas, and Camus are still theorists even though they limit themselves to the question of referent. They translate myths into existentialist terms without considering either the origin or the function of myth.

To avoid one confusion, *origin* for theorists means recurrent, not historical, origin. Why myth arose the first time has long been abandoned as an unanswerable question. The issue for theorists is why myth arises—and functions—wherever and whenever it does.

Strenski rightly asks how theorists can know the origin and function of myths in cultures, dead or alive, about which there is inadequate information. He thus contrasts the full knowledge that Malinowski garnered from fieldwork to the sheer speculations of armchair theorists like Rank and Raglan, who were disciples of Freud and Frazer. Above all, how can theorists assume that myths are the same everywhere?

To begin with, theorists do not deny the differences among cultures. They deny the importance of differences. And similarities mean mere similarities, not identities. I have argued against the view that differences are more significant than similarities.

At the same time the origin and function of myth in even a visited, living culture are not directly observable. Rather, they are inferred. Malinowski and, even more rigidly, Radcliffe-Brown insisted on confining the study of myth to what can be seen. But who actually witnesses the origin or even the function of myth? One comes upon the scene with myth already present, and one leaves the scene with myth sometimes not yet even fulfilling its function. Were myth somehow to be serving its function before one's eyes, the function would still be inferred.

Certainly the referent or meaning of myth is not seen either. How to know that myth is to read literally, as for Tylor, Eliade, Malinowski, and Raglan? If, alternatively, myth is to be read symbolically, as for Freud, Rank, Jung, Campbell, Bultmann, Jonas, Camus, and at times Frazer, how to know what myth symbolizes?

Yet the proper conclusion is not that anything goes. The proper conclusion is that research is needed, just as Strenski urges, but the research can be research into theories themselves.

The easiest defense of a theory is that, when assumed, it works. If the theory were false, the application would not work. But theories can be so open-ended as never to fail to work. Still, not all theories fit all myths, so that at least theories that do not fit can be ruled out. But then a theory that does not fit a specific myth or kind of myth can be saved by being narrowed from a theory of myth per se to a theory of, say, hero myths or of creation myths.

Origin and function take one beyond the myth to the mythmakers and users, as Strenski seeks. And there is a way of defending the claims: by venturing beyond myth to the larger domain of the theory. The defense of the origin and function of myth postulated by the theory is a defense of the underlying theory, which can be of the physical world, of culture, of society, or of human nature. To explain the myth of King Saul as the fulfillment of Samuel's, Saul's, Jonathan's, or David's (and in turn the mythmaker's, reader's, or hearer's) Oedipus complex is to presuppose not only the complex but also a whole theory of personality.

If no Oedipus complex exists, then a Freudian interpretation fails, no matter how well the complex, when assumed, makes sense of the myth. It is illogical to use the sense that a theory, when applied, makes as confirmation of the theory itself. Still, theories at the outset often rely on applicability as confirmation of the theory. Hence Freud relied on Rank's evidence of the Oedipus complex in literature as evidence for the complex itself (see Rank 1992 [1912]).

The number of studies undertaken to test Freudian hypotheses is in the thousands, and the tests have been conducted by Freudians, anti-Freudians, and neutral parties. I argue not that Freud's theory has been proved true or even testable but that to whatever extent his theory has proved both testable and true, it can be enlisted to defend its postulated origin and function of myth.

For example, Freudians (and Jungians, too) compare myth with dream. A defense of the Freudian origin and function of dream would support a defense of the Freudian origin and function—and also meaning—of myth. A Freudian theorist of myth need not undertake fieldwork to justify the use of the theory. And for the record, Malinowski's famous use of the case of the Trobriand Islanders to refute the claim of a universal Oedipus complex was refuted by Ernest Jones (1925) and more recently by the anthropologist Melford Spiro (1982).

On the basis of his touted knowledge of the Trobriand Islanders alone, Malinowski never hesitates to make universal pronouncements—about "primitive man," about panhuman needs, and even about the monogamous nuclear family. He asserts that all myths originate and function to fulfill the same mix of individual and social needs, and he reads all myths literally. He is, then, no less of a universalist than Freud.

As for my Freudian interpretation of the life of Saul, I think that the "thematic payoff" is my seeing Saul as a hero rather than as a victim. His enemy is not the Philistines but his father. And the fight is over sex, not power. I am asserting that my interpretation is plausible, no more, but plausible because rooted in an established theory of human nature.

Undeniably, my interpretation, like any other Freudian interpretation, requires liberties with the text. Strenski writes that "we need the lust for [David's] mother, for the king's [i.e., Saul's] wife, to complete the Oedipal match." Instead, all I give, as Strenski notes, is Saul's offer of two of his daughters to David in marriage. Worse, I give no proof of David as the biological son of Saul.

But Freudian evidence is never on the surface. Yet one is not thereby free to say anything. Freud gives a reason, rooted in his overall psychology, that the Oedipus complex is never manifested openly. The expression is disguised even in the case of Oedipus.

Where Strenski focuses on Rank, Adela Collins focuses on Raglan. Before doing so, she raises many sensible issues. To begin with, I was relying on the definitions of myth used by the theorists and thereby sidestepped offering one of my own (which I offer in my *Myth* [Segal 2004, 4–6]). I myself do not limit myths to stories about gods, not least because hero myths, which folklorists prefer to call "legends" exactly because the agents are not gods, would thereby be precluded. As I maintain in my *Myth*, myth may be false, but dismissing myth as merely false, which is a commonplace today, misses the point: that myth, true or false, has a hold that no ordinary belief possesses. The power of myth, to use Campbell's phrase, exceeds its truth value. My own definition does not come from ancient Greeks. I am thus not pitting *mythos* against *logos*. I wish I had more space to elaborate.

All theorists of myth attribute the similarities among myths to independent invention rather than to transmission—a topic that I consider in the unabridged version of my paper. Claude Lévi-Strauss, cited by Collins, is just one more independent "inventionist," controversial only because of the universal source of myth that he proposes. The justification for independent invention presupposed by all theorists is that worldwide similarities cannot convincingly be attributed to cross-cultural contact, which is accepted only in the case of regional similarities. Cultural contact as the source of universal similarities was more popular a century ago than it has been ever since. The favorite example of the arch-independent inventionist Jung is Count Goblet d'Aviella's *The Migration of Symbols* (1894 [1892]). The heretofore Jungian Joseph Campbell shifts from independent invention to transmission in his final opus (Campbell 1983).

Collins is right to tie controlled comparison to transmission. Though S. H. Hooke is in fact indebted to the equally arch-independent inventionist Frazer for his theory of myth, he restricts himself to the ancient Near East and maintains that the myth-ritualist pattern there comes from Mesopotamia. (He also wrongly dismisses Frazer as an intellectualist like Tylor.) Raglan, I might note, is indisputably a Frazerian but at times incorrectly credits Hooke rather than Frazer with the theory of myth that he applies to hero myths.

The need that myth originates to fulfill can change, though theorists, committed as they are to uniform explanations, tend to downplay the malleability of myth. True, Bultmann argues that at least biblical myth once served as an explanation of the world but can no longer do so because of science. But the existentialist interpretation—not really function—of myth that Bultmann offers instead is the meaning that myth has always had. More typical of theorists is Tylor, for whom myth, faced by competition from science, must die out.

Turning to Raglan, I had never thought of Collins's most clever paralleling of Raglan's heroes as once human and divine with the mainstream characterization of Jesus as fully human and fully divine. I was merely following Raglan in paralleling the human hero of ritual with the divine hero of myth—more precisely, of the hero, who is human, with the god. Coincidentally, Raglan, in contrast to Rank, was too timid to name Jesus as an example of his brand of heroism. I doubt that any religiosity on Raglan's part caused what I still consider an inconsistency. By contrast, the arch-atheist Frazer delighted in paralleling Jesus with Mediterranean vegetation gods.

I am pleased by Collins's appreciation of my "Raglanite" take on Saul as a success rather than a failure. Seeing him that way is for me the kind of payoff that a theory can offer. Finally, I retain the category "hero" because Raglan does.

David Miller makes the strong case that theories of myth *have* been indispensable for modern biblical studies, thanks to the influence of folklore, linguistics, and comparative mythology on largely German biblicists in the past two centuries. I second Miller's appreciation of John Rogerson's *Myth in Old Testament Interpretation* (1974). Rogerson, an authority on the influence of German biblical scholarship on English-speaking biblicists, is always meticulous and precise. For instance, he shows how beholden Hermann Gunkel initially was to Herder and the Grimms for his take on biblical mythology. Rogerson contends that, if anything, biblical studies was too susceptible to trendy approaches to myth. Miller himself laments the reactionary politics embedded in some theories.

But has the influence of theories on biblical studies continued? Do most biblicists today invoke theories when they interpret a story? Do they even call a story a myth? Does not the hoary view that the Hebrew Bible tells history and not myth continue to hold sway? In biblical studies, just as in classics, is there not wariness of generalizing?

My argument, which had to be deleted from the present abridgment, is that theories are *logically* indispensable, whatever the history of theorizing. I argue that the concepts used by even the most stalwart particularists—hero, king, god, religion—are generic and that one cannot write a word about Saul as a hero without assuming a generalization about heroism. With the exception of Campbell and perhaps Erich Neumann, though not of Jung himself, no theorist maintains that all cases of heroism are the same. But theorists do maintain that all cases are similar, and they emphasize the similarities over the differences. Even specialists who stress differences must start with similarities and can turn to differences only wherever similarities end. Comparison is inescapable (see Segal 2001).

Theorizing is indispensable not merely for categorizing but even more for analyzing. Most theories give the origin, function, and meaning of all myths. They show not only why there is myth but also how to read myth. These theories provide a comprehensive approach to myth that a focus on a single myth or mythology cannot duplicate. And the claim that in culture X myth arises and functions for economic reasons commits one to making the same claim about myth anywhere else. Otherwise the explanation is insufficient to explain even the case at hand.

Even if, contrary to the history of theorizing in biblical studies that Miller sketches, there were no past theorizing, present theorizing would remain indispensable. A biblicist would simply have to select a theory for the first time.

Works Cited

Campbell, Joseph. 1983. *The Way of the Animal Powers*. Vol. 1 (in 2 parts) of *Historical Atlas of World Mythology*. New York: van der Marck.

D'Aviella, Count Eugene Goblet. 1894 [1892]. *The Migration of Symbols*. Westminster, Eng.: Archibald Constable.

Jones, Ernest. 1925. Mother-Right and the Sexual Ignorance of Savages. *International Journal of Psycho-Analysis* 6:109–30.

Rank, Otto. 1992 [1912]. *The Incest Taboo in Literature and Legend*. Translated by Gregory C. Richter. Baltimore: Johns Hopkins University Press.

Rogerson, J. W. 1974. *Myth in Old Testament Interpretation*. BZAW 134. Berlin: de Gruyter.

Segal, Robert A. 1999. *Theorizing about Myth*. Amherst: University of Massachusetts Press.

———. 2001. In Defense of the Comparative Method. *Numen* 48:339–73.

———. 2004. *Myth: A Very Short Introduction*. Oxford: Oxford University Press.

Spiro, Melford E. 1982. *Oedipus in the Trobriands*. Chicago: University of Chicago Press.

Contributors

Susan Ackerman is the Preston H. Kelsey Professor of Religion at Dartmouth College. She is the author, most recently, of *When Heroes Love: The Ambiguity of Eros in the Stories of Gilgamesh and David* (Columbia University Press, 2005).

Dexter E. Callender Jr. is Associate Professor of Religious Studies at the University of Miami and Extraordinary Associate Professor in the Faculty of Theology at North-West University, Potchefstroom, South Africa. He is the author of *Adam in Myth and History: Ancient Israelite Perspectives on the Primal Human* (Eisenbrauns).

John T. Fitzgerald is Professor of New Testament and Early Christian Literature at the University of Notre Dame and Extraordinary Professor in the Faculty of Theology at North-West University, South Africa. He is co-editor of the recently published collected essays of the late Abraham J. Malherbe, *Light from the Gentiles: Hellenistic Philosophy and Early Christianity* (Brill, 2013).

William Scott Green is Professor of Religious Studies, Senior Vice Provost, and Dean of Undergraduate Education at the University of Miami, where he also is Senior Fellow in the Sue and Leonard Miller Center for Contemporary Judaic Studies. He is co-editor of the forthcoming *A Legacy of Learning: Essays in Honor of Jacob Neusner* (Brill).

Luke Timothy Johnson is the Robert W. Woodruff Professor of New Testament and Christian Origins at Emory University. His most recent publications include *Among the Gentiles: Greco-Roman Religion and Christianity* (Yale University Press, 2009) and *Contested Issues in Christian Origins and the New Testament: Collected Essays* (Brill, 2013).

Robert S. Kawashima is associate professor at the University of Florida in the Department of Religion and the Center for Jewish Studies. He is the author of *Biblical Narrative and the Death of the Rhapsode* (Indiana University Press, 2004), in addition to various articles on the law, language, and literature of the Hebrew Bible.

Steven J. Kraftchick is Professor of the Practice of New Testament Interpretation at Candler School of Theology, Emory University. His recent publications include *II Peter, Jude: Abingdon New Testament Commentary Series* (Abingdon, 2002) and "Reborn to a Living Hope: A Christology of 1 Peter," in *Reading 1–2 Peter and Jude: A Resource for Students* (Society of Biblical Literature, 2014)

David L. Miller is Watson-Ledden Professor Emeritus at Syracuse University. His research and writing are in the areas of religion and literary theory, comparative mythographies, and psychology of religion. He is the author of five books and more than one hundred articles and book chapters, most recently an electronic edition of *Gods and Games: Toward a Theology of Play*. For more information, see http://dlmiller.mysite.syr.edu.

James E. Miller is the author of *Raw Material: Studies in Biblical Sexuality* (2nd ed., 2010), OtherSheep.org, and numerous scholarly articles.

Hugh R. Page Jr. is Vice President, Associate Provost, and Dean of the First Year of Studies; and Associate Professor of Theology and Africana Studies at the University of Notre Dame. His published works include: *Israel's Poetry of Resistance: Africana Perspectives on Early Hebrew Verse* (Fortress, 2013); *The Africana Bible: Reading Israel's Scriptures from Africa and the African Diaspora* (as general editor, Fortress, 2010); *Exodus* (Bible Reading Fellowship-Peoples Bible Commentary Series, 2006); *The Myth of Cosmic Rebellion: A Study of Its Reflexes in Ugaritic and Biblical Literature* (Brill, 1996); and *Exploring New Paradigms in Biblical and Cognate Studies* (editor, Mellen Biblical Press, 1996).

J. W. Rogerson is Emeritus Professor of Biblical Studies, University of Sheffield. His *A Theology of the Old Testament: Cultural Memory, Communication and Being Human* was published in 2010 (Fortress).

CONTRIBUTORS

Robert A. Segal is Sixth Century Chair in Religious Studies, University of Aberdeen, where he has taught since 2006. Previously he taught at Lancaster University, England, and before that, taught in his native United States at Reed College, Stanford, LSU, University of Pittsburgh, and Tulane. His specialty is theories of myth and theories of religion. He has written *The Poimandres as Myth* (Mouton de Gruyter, 1986), *Joseph Campbell: An Introduction* (revised edition Penguin/NAL, 1990 and Penguin/Meridian, 1997), *Theorizing about Myth* (University of Massachusetts Press, 1999), and *Myth: A Very Short Introduction* (Oxford University Press, 2004). He has edited *The Gnostic Jung* (Princeton University Press and Routledge, 1992), *The Allure of Gnosticism* (Open Court, 1995), *The Myth and Ritual Theory* (Blackwell, 1998), *Jung on Mythology* (Princeton University Press and Routledge, 1998), *The Blackwell Companion to the Study of Religion* (Blackwell, 2006), *Myth: Critical Concepts* (Routledge, 2007), and *30-Second Mythology* (Ivy Press, 2012).

Mark S. Smith, Professor of Bible and Ancient Near Eastern Studies at New York University, is the author of fourteen books, most recently *How Human Is God? Seven Questions about God and Humanity in the Bible* (Liturgical Press) and *Poetic Heroes: Warriors and Warrior Culture in the Early Biblical World* (Eerdmans), both to appear in 2014.

Ivan Strenski is Holstein Family and Community Distinguished Professor of Religious Studies at the University of California, Riverside. He holds a BA with First Class Honors (University of Toronto) and a PhD (University of Birmingham, England), studying under the late Ninian Smart. In 2007, he was awarded the degree of Doctor Honoris Causa by the University of Lausanne. From 1979 to 2004 he served as North American Editor-in-Chief of the international journal *Religion*. Strenski is the author of fourteen books and over fifty articles, many of which attempt to locate various efforts in theoretical thinking, such as about myth, gift, or sacrifice, within the larger social, political and religious contexts of modern European life.

Marvin A. Sweeney is Professor of Hebrew Bible at the Claremont School of Theology, Claremont, California, and Professor of Tanak and Chair of the Faculty at the Academy for Jewish Religion California, Los Angeles, California. He is the author of numerous books and studies, such as *Reading Prophetic Books: Form, Intertextuality, and Reception in Prophetic and Post-biblical Literature* (Tübingen: Mohr Siebeck, 2014); *Reading Ezekiel:*

A Literary and Theological Commentary (Smyth and Helwys, 2013); and *Tanak: A Theological and Critical Introduction to the Jewish Bible* (Fortress, 2012). He is Vice-President of the National Association of Professors of Hebrew.

Amy C. Merrill Willis, Ph.D. (Emory University) is Assistant Professor of Religious Studies at Lynchburg College, Lynchburg, VA. She is author of *Dissonance and the Drama of Divine Sovereignty in the Book of Daniel* (T&T Clark, 2010) and "Heavenly Bodies: God and the Body in the Visions of Daniel," in *Bodies, Embodiment, and Theology of the Hebrew Bible* (T&T Clark, 2010).

Adela Yarbro Collins is the Buckingham Professor of New Testament Criticism and Interpretation at the Yale University Divinity School. She served as president of the Society for New Testament Studies from July 2010 until August 2011. Her most recent books are *King and Messiah as Son of God*, co-authored with John J. Collins (2009), and *Mark: A Commentary* in the Hermeneia commentary series, published in 2007.

Index of Primary Sources

Hebrew Bible/Old Testament

Genesis	21, 22, 23, 90–94, 286
1	5, 23, 51, 60, 62, 71–73, 78, 81, 86–96
1–3	88, 90, 94, 130, 139
1–9	23, 24, 90
1–11	22, 90–92
1:1–2:3	90, 137
1:2	19
2	87n
2–3	87, 286
2:4	90, 91
2:10	43
3	22, 87, 88
3:22–24	60
4:17	22, 91n
5:1	90
6–8	23, 85
6–9	71
6:1–4	17–18, 88, 206
6:4	21
6:9	90
9:1–17	62
10:1	90
11:1	21
11:10	90
11:27	90
12:1–3	63
12:2	62
15	63
15:6	65
15:17	64
17:1–14	62
18:19	62
19	110
20:13	62
22	62
25:8	107
25:12	90
25:19	90
35:29	107
36:19	90
37:2	90
49	63, 119–20, 124

Exodus	21, 111n
2	110
3	33
3:14–15	60
4:8	34
4:10	34
4:12	34
4:13	34
4:24–26	113
4:33	34
6:2–3	60
12	113
14	113
15	63, 82, 93n, 119, 124, 137
19:18	64
19:19	34n
20:22	35n
24	113
24:3–8	113
24:4	80n
24:7	65
24:11	64
24:12	80n
28	130

Exodus (cont.)		3:23–26	105
29:46	62	3:26	104, 105, 106
31:12–17	62	4:1–4	40n
31:18	35n, 80n	4:6	37n
32	21	4:9	34
32:9–10	65	4:10	36, 42
32:15–16	35n	4:10–14	33
32:16	80n	4:12	33
34:1	80n	4:13–14	36
34:27	80n	4:21	104, 106
35:1–3	62	4:35	35, 36
39	130	4:35–40	35
39–40	90	4:36	34n, 35n, 42
		4:37–38	35
Leviticus		4:39	35, 36
10	65	4:40	36
19:26	256	5:4	33n
		5:5	34n
Numbers	21, 104	5:22	80n
11:16–17	37n	5:24–25	34n
11:17	40	6	39
11:25	40	6:4–5	36
11:29	37n	6:4–9	36
14:12	65	6:6	36
20	106	6:6–9	36
20:1	103	6:7	36
20:1–13	103, 104n	6:8	31
20:22–29	105	6:9	42
21:4–9	22	6:17	40n
23–24	119, 124	6:20–25	36
27:12–14	104n	6:24	36
27:18–23	37n	8:5–6	42
33:38	106	9:10	35n
		10:1–5	35
Deuteronomy	21, 33, 35–37, 42, 43, 90, 91n, 92, 94, 104–6	11	39
		11:2	42
1	105	11:18–20	36
1:5	33n	11:19	36
1:23	106	12:16	256
1:27	21	17:14–20	253n
1:28	104	17:18	37n
1:35	104	27:1	37n
1:36	105	27:1–31:29	113–14
1:37	104, 106	27:8	37n
3:23–25	105	29:14–15	65

INDEX OF PRIMARY SOURCES

30:19–20	10	10:22	254
31:9	37n	10:23	254
31: 9–13	36n	10:24	2255
31:26	37n	11	262
32	59, 63, 114, 119–20	11:6	265
32:8–9	59	12:12	254
32:48–52	104	12:16	256
33	114, 119–20, 124	12:16–18	264
33:2	63n	13:7b-18	263
33:8–10	37	13:13–14	256
33:9	63n	14:18–19	263
34	105	14:19	256
34:7	105	14:24–28	256
34:9	37n	14:24–30	263
		14:28–30	256
Judges	38, 164, 265	14:31–33	256
5	63, 93n, 119–20, 124, 137	14:31–34	263
5:4–5	63n	14:37	263
8:22–23	260n	14:45	258
8:22–9:57	253n	14:46	258
8:32	107	14:47–48	255, 256, 262
		14:49–50	262
1 Samuel	38, 253, 254n, 258n, 259,	15	256, 263
265n, 266, 277		15:23	257
1:18–19	255	15:24	257
2	119, 120	15:34–35	258
3:16	260	15:35	257
8	253n	15:35–16:1	257
8–31	252	16:2	257, 258
8:4–6	253	16:6–12	255n
8:5	263	16:13	257
8:7	253–54	16:14	257, 265, 277
8:8	254	16:21	257, 258, 261
8:21	255	16:23	265
9:1–2	260	18:1–4	258
9:1–10:16	255n	18:7	257, 258
9:2	255	18:10	265
9:3–20	260	18:11	258
9:16	255, 263	18:12	266
9:21	260	18:17	258
10	262	18:17–27	261
10:1	257	18:20	258
10:5–6	265	18:22	258
10:9–13	265	18:28	258
10:11	265	19:10	258

1 Samuel (cont.)		Job	
19:23	277n	3	95 d
20:33	258	38–42	137
24:3–7	261	42:17	107
24:11	261		
24:16	261	Psalms	287
26:6–11	261	18	119
26:17	261	29	89, 119, 124
26:21	261	37:30–31	37n
26:25	261	45:1–2	81
		46:4–6	43n
2 Samuel	38, 253, 265	68	119
1	119, 120	68:8–9	63n
2:8–10	265	68:18	63n
4:5–12	265	72	119
22	119	74	82, 94, 137, 219
23	119	74:12–14	19
		74:12–17	92
1 Kings	38, 88, 90, 91, 92, 94, 164	74:13–14	219
22	89	78	119
		89	82
2 Kings	38, 88, 89, 90, 91, 92, 94, 164	89:9–10	219
2:23–24	106	104	92, 94–95
24–25	166	104:24	95
		111:10	44
1 Chronicles	38	118	20
23:1	107	118:7–14	18
29:28	107	119	37n, 39–40
		119:34–35	40
2 Chronicles	38	119:43	40
26:22	38	119:98	40n
33:19	39	119:99–100	39
Ezra	170n	Proverbs	
8:16	40n	1:25	42n
8:18	40n	2:6	43n
		8	41, 42
Nehemiah	36, 170n	8:1–10	42n
8:1	36	8:10	42n
8:1–12	36	8:22	41
8:3	37	8:22–31	41
8:8	37, 39	8:25	41
8:17	40	8:27	41
		8:28	41
		8:29	41

INDEX OF PRIMARY SOURCES

8:30	41	26:3–6	132
8:33–34	42	26:3–14	132
8:35–36	43	26:3–21	132
13:13–15	44n	26:5a	132
13:18	42n	26:5b–6	142, 143
15:32	42n	26:6b	132
		26:7–14	132, 143
Isaiah		26:12	137
2:2–3	43	26:14b	132–33, 143
6	89	26:15	133
11:2	37n	26:15–18	133, 137
14	6, 159, 159n, 167	26:15–21	133
14:4–20	159, 160	26:16–21	132
14:12	160n	26:19	133
14:13	160n	26:19–21	133
27:1	137, 219	26	137–38
45:1	170	26–28	129–31, 133–36, 138, 141–43
45:7	95	27	138–39
51	137	27:1	131
51:9	137	27:1–36	131, 133
51:9–10	219	27:36b	133
		28	6, 159n, 167
Jeremiah		28:1	131, 134
22:24–25	170n	28:1–10	131, 133, 134, 139
27:5–6	166	28:2–5	134
28:14	166	28:2–10	134
		28:6–10	134
Ezekiel	130n, 131, 135, 141, 143, 144	28:10b	133, 134
1–3	136	28:11	131
8–11	136	28:11–19	131, 133, 134, 139
25–32	129	28:19b	133
25:1–7	129	28:20	131
25:8–11	129	28:20–23	129–30
25:12–14	129	28:20–26	131, 133, 135, 142, 143
25:15–17	129	28:22b	133
26:1	131, 132, 134	28:23b	133
26:1–21	132, 133, 134, 137	28:24–26	129–30
26:1–28:19	129–31, 142	28:24b	133
26:1–28:26	131	28:26b	133
26:2	132	29–32	129, 142, 143
26:2–5a	143	29:1	131
26:2–6	143	29:1–16	131
26:2–21	131, 132	29:17	143
26:2–36	134	29:17–30:19	143
26:3–5	137	32:17–33:20	143n

Ezekiel (cont.)	
33:21	143n
40–48	136
47:9	43n
47	43

Daniel   150–51, 153–54, 156–57, 160n, 165–67, 169–70

2	165
2:31–45	161
2:36	166
7	19, 158–61, 164n, 165, 168, 170
7–12	77, 89
7:2–3	19
7:4–6	170n
8	6, 149–50, 158–61, 164n, 165–71
8:3–14	160
8:9–11	159
8:10	160n
8:12b	160n
8:20–25	160
8:25	160n
10–12	168
11	167

Joel

3:16	43n

Amos

1:2	43n

Micah

4:1–3	43

Habakkuk

3	63
3:3	63n
3:7	63n

Zechariah

13	43n
13:1	44n
14:8	43n

NEW TESTAMENT

Matthew	
14:13–21	219
14:22–27	219

John	
11	224
19:34	224

Acts	223, 225
17	225

1 Corinthians	
15:45	208

2 Corinthians	7, 201–2, 208, 210
1:9	209
1:21–22	208
3:3–18	208
4:13	208
4:14	208
5	206
5:1	205, 206
5:1–2	209
5:1–21	204
5:2	205, 209
5:4	205
5:5	205, 206, 208
5:6	205, 209
5:7	205
5:9	205
5:10	205
5:11	205, 206
5:12	205
5:13	205, 206
5:14	205, 206, 208
5:15	206, 208
5:16	205
5:17	204, 205, 209
5:18	203, 204, 205, 206
5:19	201–6, 208
5:20	205, 206
5:21	206, 209
6:6	208

INDEX OF PRIMARY SOURCES

6:9	209	Baruch	
11:4	208	3	43n
11:21	203		
12:1–10	201	1 Maccabees	166
12:18	208		
13:13	208	2 Maccabees	166
Philippians	195	4 Ezra	
		14	217
2 Thessalonians			
2:2	203	Jubilees	217

Nag Hammadi

1 Timothy			
1:4	180		
4:7	180	*Apoc. Pet.*	224
2 Timothy		*Treat. Res*	224
4:4	180		
		Genesis Apoc.	217
Titus			
1:14	180		

Other Sources

2 Peter		Aeschylus	
1:16	180	*Prom.* 349–50	221
Revelation	77, 89	Appolodorus	
		Bibl. 1.3.2	234n

Deuterononical Literature, Pseudepigrapha, and Dead Sea Scrolls

		Appolonios	
		Arg. 4.1399	221
Ben Sira/ Sirach	43	Aristophanes	
20:18–20	31	*Ran.* 1032	201n
24	43		
24:2	43	Aristotle	30, 56
24:3	43	*Poet.*	30, 275
24:4	43		
24:6	43	Demosthenes	
24:7	43	*Or.* 25.11	234n
24:8	43		
24:10	43	Derveni Pap.	8, 229, 234, 235, 238n
24:23	43	IV.8–10	236
24:25–27	43	V.5–11	239
24:30–31	43	V.9–10	238
24:32–33	43	V.10	239

Derveni Pap. (cont.)		Rhes. 943–44	234n
VII.2	238		
VII.4–5	238	Eusebius	
VII.5–8	236	FGH F2 302–303	216
VII.10–11	238		
IX.2	238	Ennius	
XII.4–5	238	FGH F12–26	216
XII.5	238	Warmington	216
XIII.5–6	236		
XVI.3–6	237	Hekataeos	
XVI.7–8	237	FGH F1 7–8	217
XVI.9–11	237		
XVII.1–3	237	Heliodoros	
XVII.7–11	238	Aeth. 6.14–15	225
XVIII.6–7	237		
XVIII.9–12	237	Heraclitus	233n, 236
XVIII.14	238	Alleg. Hom. 5	231n
XIX.1–4	237		
XX.1–2	238	Herodotus	28, 161, 215, 138, 185,
XX.2	238	Hist.	216
XX.3–12	239	Hist. 1.203	221
XXI.5–7	236	Hist. 2.81	234n
XXII.7–11	236		
XXIII.2	238	Hesiod	8, 30, 59, 64, 65, 214, 230, 232
XXIII.5	238	Op. 156–73	222
XXVI.8	238	Op. 167–73	222
		Theog. 27–29	214
Diogenes	236–37	Theog. 517–520	221n
Diodorus Siculus		Homer	8, 30, 222, 223, 230–32, 236
1.23.1–8	234n	Il. 20.66	231
1.23.2	234n	Od. 1.52–55	222
96.2–6	234n	Od. 4.561–69	222
96.4–6	234n	Od. 11.539, 573	222
3.65.6	234n	Od. 13	232
4.25.3	234n	Od. 19.203	214
5.77.3	234n	Od. 24.13	222
Euripides		Homeric Hymns	
Alc. 1128	225	1 Herm. 221, 344	222
Bacchae	233n		
Heracl.	215	Isocrates	232
Heracl. 397–407	221	Bus. 38–40	233
Hipp. 3	221	Bus. 43	229n
Hipp. 742–751	221		

INDEX OF PRIMARY SOURCES

Livy		Porphyry	231
1.1.2–3	217	*Quaest. hom. Il.*	232
1.1.6–7	217	*Antr. nypharum.*	232n
Pausanius		Theagenes	231–32
Descr. 9.30.5–11	233n		
Descr. 2.30.2	234n	Theophrastus	
Descr. 9.30.4	234n	*Char.* 16.12	234
Descr. 10.7.2	234n		
		Xenophanes	230
Palaiphatos	216, 221	DK 21 B 11	230
1	216	DK 21 B 12	230
2	215	DK 21 B 14–16	230
		DK 21 B 23	230
Pherekydes		DK 21 B 24	230
FGH 1.16a/17	221	DK 21 B 25	230
		DK 21 B 26	230
Philo		DK 21 B 34	230
*Aet.*141			
221			
Philodemus	236		
Pindar			
Ol 1.27–29	73n		
*Ol.*2	222		
Ol. 2.70–80	223		
Plato			
Gorg. 523	223		
Ion	38		
*Krit.*114a	221		
Phaed.	28		
Phaedr. 229c, d	216, 221		
Prot. 320c	28		
Prot. 316d	234n		
Resp. 364e	234		
Resp. 364b–365a	234		
Tim.	221		
Plutarch	215, 216, 217		
frg. 212	234n		
Thes. 19	215		

Index of Authors

Ackerman, Susan 5, 6, 9n
Albright, William Foxwell 93n, 119
Althusser, Louis 5, 52, 56, 61–62, 63n, 64–65
Altizer, Thomas 7, 187–190, 196, 197–98
Brisson, Luc 28, 29n, 44
Bultmann, Rudolf 7, 182–89, 161, 191, 192, 194, 196–97, 218–19, 285, 291, 292, 294
Callender, Dexter 2n, 4
Campbell, Joseph 76n, 107–09, 245–46, 285, 288, 292, 294, 295
Camus, A. 291, 292
Coats, George 72n, 107
Collins, Adela Yarbro 8, 291, 293–95
Collins, John 6, 152, 156–57, 159, 168n
Cross, Frank Moore 63n, 93n, 119–20, 124, 154, 156
Dalley, Stephanie 76, 81n
DiTommaso, Lorenzo 151–52, 158, 164
Dundes, Alan 75n, 77
Eichhorn, J. G. 286, 287
Eliade, Mircea 52–53, 55, 57, 58, 64, 77, 108, 109n, 152, 179n, 180n, 288, 292
Ennius 216, 222
Euhemerus 215–16, 218, 221, 222
Evans, Craig 7, 179, 191–93, 196
Fishbane, Michael 76, 89n
Freedman, D. N. 40, 41n, 119, 120, 124
Foucault, Michel 5, 53, 55, 282
Frazer, James 17, 122, 246, 249, 263–66, 287, 291–92, 294–95
Freud, Sigmund 245–46, 248, 281–82, 291–93
Funkenstein, Amos 65n, 206

Gabler, J. 286–87
Gennep, Arnold van 6, 108–09, 111
George, J. F. L. 286–87
Girard, René 246, 285
Goodman, Lenn 166, 171
Graf, Fritz 72n, 76
Grimm, Jacob and Wilhelm 287–88, 295
Gunkel, Hermann 19n, 153, 287, 295
Hahn, Johann Georg von 245, 247
Halpern, Baruch 54n, 60
Hanson, Paul 152, 154–57
Hendel, Ronald 110–11
Herder, Johan Gottfried 198, 287, 295
Hooke, S. H. 249–50, 264, 275, 294
Hume, David 218, 225
Isocrates 229n, 232, 233n
Jacobsen, Thorkild 76, 81–82, 84, 85n
Jindo, J. Y. 151–52, 154, 156, 157, 158, 167
Johnson, Aubrey 18–19
Jonas 291, 292
Jung, Carl 75n, 107, 246, 288, 292, 294, 295
Kawashima, Robert 5, 9, 10, 92-93n
Kirk, Geoffrey 76, 78, 90n,
Lacan, Jacques 55–56
Lang, Andrew 87n, 287
Leach, Edmund 77, 110
Lévi-Strauss, Claude 121, 169, 180n, 276, 294
Lincoln, Bruce 45n, 197, 287n
Lowth, Robert 122, 286
Malinowski, Bronislaw 180n, 281, 291–93
Millard, Alan 80, 82n

INDEX OF AUTHORS

Miller, David   8, 291, 295–96
Nagy, Gregory   73, 76
Neumann, Erich   75n, 76n, 295
Newsom, Carol   162, 164
Niditch, Susan   77, 158n, 159n,
Noth, Martin   152, 157
Oden, Robert   27, 150n
Page, Hugh Rowland   6, 159
Pearce, Susan   6, 123, 124–25
Plato   28, 29n, 30, 38, 52, 66, 198, 216, 221–22
Propp, William H. C.   103, 105, 106, 111
Rad, Gerhard von   41–42, 153, 155, 163, 165, 220, 287
Raglan, Lord   8, 245–46, 249–52, 262–266, 275–77, 279–81, 285, 291–92, 293, 294, 295
Rank, Otto   8, 245–49, 250–52, 259, 260–61, 262, 264, 275, 279–81, 285, 291–93, 295
Ricoeur, Paul   44n, 45n, 150n, 162–63, 180n
Roberts, J. J. M.   152, 155–56, 157, 158
Rogerson, John   4, 130n, 286–87, 295
Schliemann, Heinrich   219, 221, 222
Segal, Robert   8, 75, 76n, 121–22, 125, 150n, 275–77, 279–82, 285–86, 289
Smith, Jonathan Z.   5, 52n, 84, 85
Smith, Mark S.   5, 6, 9, 10
Socrates   29–30, 38, 216, 221, 240
Strenski, Ivan   8, 15, 17, 287n, 291–92, 293
Theissen, Gerd   7, 192n, 193–98
Turner, Victor   109, 111–12
Tylor, E. B.   245, 287, 292, 294
Von Hendy, Andrew   73–74, 75n, 76n, 180n
Wellhausen, Julius   253, 255, 287
Wiesel, Elie   149, 163
Wyatt, N.   75n, 157

www.ingramcontent.com/pod-product-compliance
Lightning Source LLC
Chambersburg PA
CBHW031706230426
43668CB00006B/126